THE UNIVERSITY OF
WINCHESTER

Accommodating Poverty

Accommodating Poverty

The Housing and Living Arrangements of the English Poor, c. 1600–1850

Edited by

Joanne McEwan
School of Humanities, University of Western Australia

and

Pamela Sharpe
Professor of History, School of History and Classics, University of Tasmania

First published 2011 by
PALGRAVE MACMILLAN

Palgrave Macmillan in the UK is an imprint of Macmillan Publishers Limited,
registered in England, company number 785998, of Houndmills, Basingstoke,
Hampshire RG21 6XS.

Palgrave Macmillan in the US is a division of St Martin's Press LLC,
175 Fifth Avenue, New York, NY 10010.

Palgrave Macmillan is the global academic imprint of the above companies
and has companies and representatives throughout the world.

Palgrave® and Macmillan® are registered trademarks in the United States,
the United Kingdom, Europe and other countries.

ISBN 978–0–230–54242–6   hardback

This book is printed on paper suitable for recycling and made from fully
managed and sustained forest sources. Logging, pulping and manufacturing
processes are expected to conform to the environmental regulations of the
country of origin.

A catalogue record for this book is available from the British Library.

A catalog record for this book is available from the Library of Congress.

10   9   8   7   6   5   4   3   2   1
20   19   18   17   16   15   14   13   12   11

Printed and bound in Great Britain by
CPI Antony Rowe, Chippenham and Eastbourne

Contents

List of Plates

List of Tables

List of Figures

Preface and Acknowledgements

In 1995 Tim Hitchcock and I wrote letters to each other outlining a plan for a book about poor relief and poverty in England that considered the Old Poor Law period from the middle of the seventeenth century. We noted that Dorothy Marshall's book, *The English Poor in the Eighteenth Century: A Study in Social and Administrative History from 1662 to 1782* (first published in 1926), was still on university reading lists. Marshall's book was republished in 1969. Another new edition was to appear in 2006 by the original publisher, Routledge. I certainly cannot think of another work of social and economic history thought still relevant and worthy of a third edition 80 years after the first edition.

Tim and I planned a substantial, fully contextualised history of poor relief and poverty that set new agendas. The book did not emerge in quite the form we had envisaged. Instead, *Chronicling Poverty: The Voices and Strategies of the Labouring Poor, 1640–1840* appeared, edited by ourselves along with Peter King and also published by Palgrave Macmillan. Those essays were inspired by the seminars about the long eighteenth century in Britain held on a regular basis at the Institute of Historical Research in London. In the event, Tim more than fulfilled his part of the intellectual bargain with his many writings about the world of the London poor, as well as by creating (with Bob Shoemaker) a major new resource for accessing the social and economic history of long eighteenth-century England, through the Old Bailey online project. In the 15 years since Tim and I exchanged those old-fashioned letters, a new agenda for the history of poverty has been set by a number of historians, many of whom appear in this book. The introduction attempts to capture the range of historical approaches that make it possible for us to now have a much clearer picture of the experiences of the poor, while moving the focus towards the world that the poor made for themselves, rather than the legislative framework for poor relief and its administrative implications.

I am certainly conscious that the production of the present book – in many ways conceived as a successor volume to *Chronicling Poverty* – has taken place against the backdrop of many changes in the households and living conditions of those who have contributed. The contributors have worked around their own 'demographic events' and in my own case the book coincided with the birth and raising of Freya Kim

Pennington along with her older sister, as well as the death of both my parents.

Accommodating Poverty has been edited with a former research student, now Dr Joanne McEwan. This volume began as a project of the Australian Research Council group working on 'Beyond the Family: Fragmented Families and Household Dynamics c. 1450–1850', of which I was a Chief Investigator (2003–8) and Joanne McEwan a doctoral student (2004–8). We are thankful to the ARC and to the University of Western Australia for financial support. Philippa Maddern, Susan Broomhall, Stephanie Tarbin, the late Patricia Crawford and students Lisa Mackinney and Kate Riley provided both constructive comments and a great environment for discussion.

All of the authors were present at a 'work in progress' meeting of the contributors hosted by the Cambridge Group for the History of Population and Social Structure in 2006. We are very grateful to Richard Smith and Leigh Shaw-Taylor for helping us to organise this. We also had the privilege of interacting with members of the 'People in Place: Families, Households and Housing in Early Modern London' project (funded by the Arts and Humanities Research Council of Great Britain), both at the Cambridge day and at other stages of the project. In particular we must acknowledge Vanessa Harding for her involvement both in the UK and in Australia.

For comments and feedback at various stages of the book's progress we thank Naomi Tadmor, Keith Snell, Richard Smith, William Baer, Margaret Dorey, Lesley O'Brien and Palgrave Macmillan's anonymous reader. Both Joanne and I appreciate the patience of our contributors, and their willingness to revise their chapters and work towards a more cohesive end result.

Every effort has been made to trace rights holders but if any have been inadvertently overlooked the publishers would be pleased to make the necessary arrangements at the first opportunity.

The cover illustration is 'Weaver's room, Spitalfields' (The Builder, vol. XI, no. 533, p. 257, 1853) reproduced courtesy of the Battye Library, Perth, Western Australia.

Pamela Sharpe
Hobart, Tasmania

Notes on the Contributors

Jeremy Boulton is Professor of Urban History at Newcastle University. He has published extensively on many aspects of the history of early modern London. The chapters on rent, and the elderly (the latter written in collaboration with Leonard Schwarz) both derive from material collected by the ongoing Pauper Biographies Project (http://research. ncl.ac.uk/pauperlives/). He has recently completed a microhistory of Elizabeth Laroon, daughter of the painter Marcellus Laroon the elder (c. 1648?–1702) and is currently working on burial customs and practices in eighteenth-century London.

John Broad taught history at London Metropolitan University. His chapter is based on a current research project examining the rural housing problem from the late medieval period to the late twentieth century for a book. His other research interests lie mainly in the history of English and European rural society from the seventeenth to the nineteenth centuries, and the regional history of the south midlands.

Adrian Green is a Lecturer in History at Durham University. His research focuses on the social and economic history of housing in England between the sixteenth and eighteenth centuries. He has provided an Introduction to *The Durham Hearth Tax*, published in 2006 by the British Records Society, Index Library 119, and co-edited with A. J. Pollard, *Regional Identities in North-East England, 1300–2000* (Boydell, 2007). He is currently completing a book on the relationship between the material form of houses, social relations and the property market, titled *Dwelling in England: Houses, Society and the Market, 1550–1750*.

Steve Hindle is Professor of History at the University of Warwick, where he has taught since 1995. He is author of *The State and Social Change in Early Modern England, c. 1550–1640* (Palgrave Macmillan, 2000), *On the Parish? The Micro-Politics of Poor Relief in Rural England, c. 1550–1750* (Oxford University Press, 2004) and numerous essays and articles on rural social relations in seventeenth-century England. He has co-edited, with Heather Falvey, *This Little Commonwealth: The Layston-with-Buntingford Parish Memorandum Book, c. 1604–1750* (Hertford, 2003), and is the co-editor of *The Economic History Review*. He is currently working on his next monograph, a study of the Warwickshire parish of Chilvers Coton, provisionally titled *The Social Topography of a Rural Community*.

Tim Hitchcock is the author of *Down and Out in Eighteenth-Century London* (Hambledon, 2004), and in collaboration with Robert Shoemaker and Clive Emsley is responsible for the Old Bailey Online, 1674–1913 (www.oldbaileyonline.org). He has also published widely on issues in digital humanities, and on the histories of eighteenth-century masculinity and sexuality. He is Professor of Eighteenth-Century History at the University of Hertfordshire.

Steven King is Professor of Economic History at the University of Leicester and Chair of the Wellcome Trust History and Medical Humanities Grant Panel. His research interests are wide-ranging, spanning women's suffrage in the early twentieth century to the clothing of the poor in the seventeenth and eighteenth centuries. For the next two years he will be completing his Wellcome Trust-funded project on the sick poor in eighteenth- and nineteenth-century England. In addition he will be continuing his work on the clothing of the poor and launching a new project on the economics of the poor law system.

Sarah Lloyd teaches history in the School of Humanities at the University of Hertfordshire and previously worked at the Australian National University. She has published essays and articles on charity, cottages and poverty in the long eighteenth century, and has a monograph on the role of imagination in early modern social policy forthcoming from Manchester University Press.

Joanne McEwan is a Research Associate in the Discipline of History and the Centre for Medieval and Early Modern Studies at the University of Western Australia, where she was recently awarded her doctorate. She has previously published an article in *Parergon*, with Professor Pamela Sharpe, on genteel lodging experiences, and has delivered conference papers on various aspects of gender and crime in the eighteenth century.

Leonard Schwarz has recently retired as Reader in Urban History at the University of Birmingham. He has published extensively on living standards and on eighteenth-century London. He is the author of *London in the Age of Industrialization* (1992) and of the chapter on 'London, 1700–1840' in the *Cambridge Urban History of Britain* (2000). He is engaged with Professor Jeremy Boulton in a major study of the poor in St. Martin-in-the-Fields in the eighteenth and early nineteenth centuries, as well as an analysis of mortality in that parish, and in London in general during the eighteenth century. (http://research.ncl. ac.uk/pauperlives/).

Pamela Sharpe is Professor of History in the School of History and Classics, University of Tasmania in Hobart and a Fellow of the Australian Academy of Humanities. Since completing her doctoral thesis at the Cambridge Group for the history of Population and Social Structure, she has written and edited extensively on aspects of the social and economic history of England since 1600. She now also researches nineteenth- and twentieth-century history in Australia.

Alannah Tomkins is a Senior Lecturer in History at Keele University. She is the author of *The Experience of Urban Poverty, 1732–82* and is one of the editors for the *Narratives of the Poor* collections. She has published articles on medical history and infirmaries and is currently researching aspects of workhouse life drawn from working-class autobiographies.

Samantha Williams is University Lecturer in Local and Regional History at the University of Cambridge. Her research interests encompass poverty and welfare provision under the Old and New Poor Laws, the social history of medicine and the experience of unmarried motherhood in London in the eighteenth and nineteenth centuries. She has published articles in *Agricultural History Review, Rural History, Social History of Medicine* and *Archives*. She has been awarded the T. S. Ashton Prize for her article in *Economic History Review*. She has co-edited (with A. Levene and T. Nutt) *Illegitimacy in Britain, 1700–1920* (Palgrave Macmillan, 2005). Her monograph, *Poverty, Welfare and the Life-course under the English Poor Law*, will be published in 2010.

List of Abbreviations

BL	British Library
Bed.RO	Bedfordshire Record Office
Berk.RO	Berkshire Record Office
CLRO	Corporation of London Archives
CRO	Cumbria Record Office
Dur.RO	Durham Record Office
Derb.RO	Derbyshire Record Office
Dev.RO	Devon and Exeter Record Office
ERO	Essex Record Office
HLRO	House of Lords Record Office
HMC	Historical Manuscripts Commission
LMA	London Metropolitan Archives
Lanc.RO	Lancashire Record Office
Lich.RO	Lichfield Record Office
MCL	Manchester Central Library
Norf.RO	Norfolk Record Office
North.RO	Northampton Record Office
OBP	*Old Bailey Proceedings*, www.oldbaileyonline.org
PP	Parliamentary Papers
TNA	The National Archives
TWA	Tyne and Wear Archives
VCH	Victorian County Histories
WAC	Westminster Archive Centre
WAMR	Westminster Abbey Muniments Room

Introduction: Accommodating Poverty: The Housing and Living Arrangements of the English Poor, c. 1600–1850

Pamela Sharpe & Joanne McEwan

Francis Place's ringing words describing the effect that adjustments to his housing circumstances had on his financial status, providing 'a saving of some importance to us', resound through this book.[1] Our authors aim to trace the symbolic and material value of the housing of the poor in 'long' eighteenth-century England in the first four chapters. The four that follow consider household composition in a situation of high mobility in industrialising England. The third section looks at the way in which parishes and charities provided housing for single people and families in both institutional and individual settings.

Stretching the 'long eighteenth century' back to 1600 might raise some academic eyebrows. However, assimilation of the wealth of recent scholarship about poverty, and placing it in the context of economic and social change, provides ample justification for expanding the boundaries in this way and moving away from the political history division that found post-1750 to be 'modern' and pre-1750 to be 'early modern'. Reaching further back to the beginning of the seventeenth century gives us a long context within which to place the restructuring of the countryside and associated urbanisation and industrialisation.[2] Access to, and provision of, housing is an important and overlooked factor in the changes to society and landscape over this period.

Despite the fact that ongoing debates within social and economic history about the standard of living in industrialising England find rent to account for a large proportion of the expenditure of labouring people, surprisingly little can be said about it with any certainty. In this sense, the essay here by Jeremy Boulton is a pioneering effort. While historians over the last few decades have been interested in material culture and consumption, the accoutrements used by the poor in domestic settings have still received little scholarly attention. Housing

1

remains an area of study that will benefit from an interdisciplinary approach. Archaeological and historical studies still do not often inform each other (though Adrian Green's chapter in this book marries both approaches). Architectural historians have only rarely (and recently) interested themselves in small or multi-occupied dwellings. The history of interiors and exteriors seem to be scarcely studied together. It is a still a rare scholarly endeavour to find art history and economic or social history blended together in pursuit of a common problem. If studies have drawn on a combination of historical, archaeological and architectural records, as for 'The Rocks' area of early Sydney, they remain absent from mainstream history journals.[3]

The spaces inhabited by the poor in the period from the seventeenth to the nineteenth century were small and sometimes of ephemeral construction. As a result they have been overlooked by historians and leave too few traces on the ground for adequate analysis. Green finds one or two room houses in the countryside. In the cities, poor families often inhabited one room and sometimes shared this with fellow lodgers. In workhouses or almshouses, private space was similarly restricted.

The poor must have spent much of their time out of the home: either in the dwellings of others, in workplaces, on the streets or in the fields. In such circumstances the poor were certainly not invisible, and to contemporaries it would have been apparent that, as the Bible reminded them, 'the poor are always with us'. It was the visible presence of a ragged family on a country road that drew the Bristol Quaker Joseph Allen's attention to the plight of George Watts' family in the cold winter of 1747. He wrote to John Frederick Pinney, who was both Lord of the Manor and probably took on the role of parish officer:

> Friend Pinney
> I am one of the People call'd Quakers who in my Journey Pas'd by the cottage of George Watts in the Parish of Broad Windsor & on the road saw some of his Children I think as miserable Objects as Most I Ever Beheld & can't help thinking that the Parish Officers Must Much Neglect their Duty towards them the Man's Wife told me that thee Wast so kind as to order them 16 shillings per month but that the officers Lets them Have but 4. Nothing but Compassion to my fellow Creatures Induces Me to be thus Troublesom to a Person in thy Station to Desire thou wilt be so good as to Remind the Officers to fulfill thy orders
> that the Poor Starving Creatures may have some mannor of cloathing to hide their Nakedness an Sustenance to keep them from Perishing which I think they are as Near too as Most ever I saw

I am Respectfully thy Friend Unknown
Jo Allen – of the city of Bristol.[4]

Several aspects of this letter are interesting. Firstly, relief of the Watts family at a shilling a week apparently fell far short of what was both necessary and had actually been agreed for the family. This case also underlines the danger of the old academic approach to the history of poverty that placed undue reliance on the administrative recording of the Old Poor Law. Overseers accounts, of which many thousands survive, might hoodwink the historian into a false optimism about the generosity of relief. As Lynn Hollen Lees has reminded us,

> Over time the granting of relief became an increasingly formal process, depending more and more upon written records and decisions. Yet it still involved intangibles: deference, paternalism, notions about gender, old age and childhood. 'Appropriate' relief was a protean, changeable concept.[5]

Notably, Joseph Allen makes no mention of the cottage except that the children were on the street in freezing weather. The first priorities for this family were clothing and food, and perhaps the cottage was their only bastion against hardship. Allen spells out that, in his experience, the wretched circumstances of this family are unprecedented. However, the presence of the cottage certainly contributed to his belief that the Watts family was part of the 'settled poor', and therefore had an unequivocal right to relief. This underscores the pivotal role of housing within social arrangements and local economies, which is a point to which we will return.

The picture that has emerged from the scholarship of the last 15 years is that the experience of the poor was extremely diverse. Not only were Poor Laws amended over time, but regional and local differences in both the capability and the desire to apply the law made for a complex pastiche of the availability of poor relief and charity. Local applicability of the Poor Laws meant they were open to manipulation. The capacity of an individual to negotiate for relief varied enormously, as we demonstrated in *Chronicling Poverty* by examining verbal protests, writings and belongings of the poor.[6]

Research has taught us to adopt a wider definition of who the poor actually were than was previously common. For the purposes of this collection, we have adopted the common sense definition of the poor as those who were unable to live unaided, as in the *Oxford English*

Dictionary definition: 'The condition of having little or no wealth or material possessions.' As Alex Shepard found in her study of statements made by deponents before church courts, while 'the labouring poor' were commonly lumped into one group by their contemporaries, there were fine status distinctions within this term that can be teased out with careful analysis.[7] Hoyle and French adopted the term 'poor householders' for the group they were interested in researching. Similarly, when late eighteenth-century metropolitan legal opinion was brought to bear on the long running dispute over the poor pasture in Slaidburn, Lancashire, a differentiation was made between 'poor householders' and the 'indigent poor'.[8]

Paul Slack has suggested a fourfold increase in poverty over the period 1500–1700. By 1700, around 5 per cent of the population was permanently supported by their parish.[9] However, given that poor relief recipients constituted only a fraction of those vulnerable to poverty, Arkell estimated that from 35 per cent to 50 per cent of the population was suffering material hardship in the late seventeenth century.[10] For the time period 1700–1850, Steve King has estimated that perhaps 20 per cent of the population could be seen as 'poverty stricken', yet some 70 per cent of people suffered poverty at some stage of the lifecycle. The implications of these figures are far-reaching. Not only do they render accuracy of statistical analysis of poverty impossible during the early modern period, but they also mean that the housing conditions we describe in this book could have been a life-cycle stage for the lives of a very large number of people prior to 1850.

Dwelling with poverty in rural areas

John Broad's research has opened up our understanding of the housing of the rural poor in southern England. His research suggests that both parishes and charities played a significant part in housing the rural poor in the long eighteenth century. In a microscopic examination of the case of John Butcher, who was refused access in 1660 to housing in Middle Claydon, Buckinghamshire, by Sir Ralph Verney, the sole landowner and Lord of the Manor, Broad found that Butcher's marriage was delayed by three years in an increasingly bitter legal dispute. This demonstrates the importance of access to housing in the marriage decisions of young people who did not have money, property or prospects of either.[11] The local social structure and economy had a decisive effect on these matters. As an improving landlord, Verney had recently enclosed the parish to concentrate on stock raising. The supply of labour then outstripped the demand and Middle Claydon promoted policies to encourage out-migration. The Settlement Law of 1662 'defined residence rights more clearly and sharpened parish and landlord politics'.[12] Migration from these 'close' villages like Middle Claydon was not only to urban areas but also to 'open' villages. In villages that were not actively pursuing plans to reduce their labouring population, Broad identified a move to convert existing larger properties into subdivided tenements. There was also a rise in newly constructed accommodation, often of a temporary type and frequently built on common land. Poor families might also turn to parish and charitable foundations for help. In Broad's contribution to the present volume, he expands on his consideration of parish and charity-built housing in this era. By contrast to the 'close' situation, a small town like Colyton in Devon proved open to any migrants who moved to the parish as work prospects expanded in the late seventeenth century, and cheap housing and doles awaited those who became the settled poor.[13]

Steve Hindle also approaches questions about negotiations, entitlement and allocation of poor relief in early modern rural England, through a series of detailed case studies from different parts of the country.[14] In the seventeenth century and first two decades of the eighteenth century, growth in the provision of rental accommodation for the poor was in part driven by the magistracy, who legitimised housing on wastes or common lands and insisted that overseers provide cottages or tenements for the poor, and maintain existing ones when they fell into disrepair. Yet the provision of housing by no means necessarily guaranteed settled housing for the poor, and supply never met demand. Paupers might be moved to cheaper housing when overseers were paying their rent, transferred into a local almshouse as rooms became available or relocated to parts of the parish where they could be more regularly supervised by parish officers or neighbours. Co-residence, promoting economy, might also be made compulsory, especially in the case of elderly paupers who were expected to care for each other. In a micro-study of the strained relations between Anne Bowman and the poor relief officers of Kirkoswald in Cumbria at the end of the seventeenth century and in the early eighteenth century, Hindle used a source that has been little studied by social historians of the early modern period – petitions to the quarter sessions bench asking for judicial intervention in poor relief matters. The housing situation of the Bowman family reflects the backdrop that Broad has painted so well for us. Kirkoswald was a parish where the better-off inhabitants were concerned about incomers, and about meeting the heavy costs of housing the poor. In turn, the proliferation of housing had attracted poor migrants. Hindle's meticulous dissection of the Bowman case led him to draw several important conclusions. Overall, 'the households of the poor were pieces on the parish chessboard to be moved in accordance with the gambits of the overseers'. Discipline was maintained by withdrawing access to relief.[15] As Hindle asserted, this shows 'the extent to which administration of poor relief not only permeated social and economic relations in the local community but also intersected with the survival strategies of individual paupers and their families'.[16]

Lynn Botelho has also used micro-analytical methods to probe specific questions about the aged poor, who have long been held to represent the 'deserving poor'. In *Old Age and the English Poor Law*, she reconstituted the Suffolk villages of Cratfield and Poslingford and mapped biographies for 337 individuals who lived there in the seventeenth century. In analysing the household economy of those people over the age of 50, she argued that poor relief did not, nor did it intend to, offer complete support to the elderly, and that the individual efforts of the paupers and their kin were as important as parish support. However, the comparative wealth of the parish would determine the generosity of its relief schemes. Cratfield was relatively effective in providing weekly stipends combined with gifts of clothing, food and cash. Relief in Cratfield provided rent so that the aged poor were maintained in independence rather than being forced into subordinate positions or complex housing arrangements with friends, family or other poor. By contrast, the much less magnanimous and abundant circumstances in Poslingford meant that few of the elderly poor could be adequately supported and were forced to survive by their own devices, as the village was 'limited by the very poverty it sought to alleviate'.[17] Terms such as 'deserving' and 'undeserving' poor are perhaps inappropriate Victorian imports?

Any serious future study of the property of the poor must also consider the widely variant lease-holding circumstances in differing areas and parishes. Sub-tenancies leave few traces in records, yet were critical to determining whether those subject to poverty could establish themselves as settled persons under the Settlement Laws that prevailed through most of the period covered in this book.[18] An older scholarship considered that the poor had time-honoured rights to cottages along with commonage, but more recent work has cast doubt on how widely such rights were enjoyed.[19] It is clear that entitlement to housing and the removing of poor dwellings played an important part in shaping the English countryside and rural society.

Transience and overcrowding

Most of the essays in this book are testament to the fact that poor lives were transient lives.[20] Boulton associates the high rates of residential mobility in early modern London with the survival strategies of poor households. Such strategies commonly involved downsizing by leaving a house where the householders had a lease with a non-resident land-lord and were liable for rates, to move into cheaper 'lodgings' with a resident landlord and little or no security of tenure that might be no more than a single room or cellar but enabled the important saving that Francis Place alluded to.[21] While Boulton reminds us of 'Engels' Law', it was nevertheless common to find the less wealthy moving fairly frequently to marginally better or slightly worse houses. Often a move to a more expensive house facilitated combining living space with an area for work, cellarage or a shop. As families grew bigger, it would have been common to add on extra rooms where possible but as children left home, to rent out rooms or subdivide and sublet. Hindle's appren-tices of the 'late' early modern era are found either in alehouses or in the houses of their masters. By implication youths were not generally resident in the parental home contributing to the household economy of his or her parents, and apprenticeship was an extremely common life-cycle stage.[22] Schwarz and Boulton in this book uncover a popula-tion whose acquaintance with the workhouse was so usual that it has to be seen as part of their life strategy.[23] The London lodgers described by McEwan habitually kept their possessions in a moveable box or trunk, and Williams' pregnant but unmarried mothers, often country girls who had found a place in an urban household but were then deserted by the man they planned to marry or seduced by their master, usually found themselves in lodgings if their employers were unsympathetic to their plight. Samantha Williams has found that these women often became wet nurses, putting their own children out to be nursed by still poorer women while waiting for a place at the 'foundling'. The chain of pov-erty was long and finely graduated.

Hitchcock's chapter provides insights into the largely hidden and ambiguous world of the vagrant. In Essex, as in London, the travelling poor met the officials not only with subservience but also sometimes with downright audacity. Chelmsford parish recorded casual pay to the transient poor in 1829 and 1830, when travellers were either offered a one-night stay in the workhouse or given an occasional meal.[24] The price the travelling poor were paid in Chelmsford was based on a careful con-sideration of their characteristics and points of merit (or not) – especially age, origins and idiosyncrasies. Most pitiful were those travelling 'anywhere' such as Robert Anderson and his family: 'Scotch, nailmaker, a distressed looking set'. William Halyard alias Milliard, aged 40, stayed for three weeks 'supposed to be Welch, will not tell where he belongs, sent in ill, Irish no doubt'. His sickness earned him '1 pint of beer per day and extra meat everyday'. Other travellers included a German stonemason with the invented name of David Hunn, a French dyer, Americans, a Portugese, a New Zealander, a 'Black from Baltimore' and the Jewish Mother Took. But those poor who were not foreigners often rejected the accommodation that was offered. Thomas Meredith, aged 25, travelling with George West, 33, were both hatters going from London to Colchester and 'went on, did not approve of the accommodation'. William Fletcher, a corkcutter from Staffordshire with his young wife, was described as being in great distress when shown the apartment. He 'was Impertinent, and said he would not sleep in such a place, went out'; and William Gaywood, aged 21, a blacksmith travelling to Lowestoft, appeared to 'scoff at the place'. The man supervising the casual house seemed to carry no responsibility for making a judgment on whether those who sought accommodation at the expense of the local ratepayers were indeed needy or not, and admitted that some of the travellers were 'a compleat take in'. When the Murphys, a family of Irish labourers, arrived and were asked whether they had any money, 'the woman said she'd devil got a halfpenny, she believed it was two pence she'd got'.

Examining London housing shows a complex use of rooms within buildings and shared use of space.[25] Early modern Aldgate was full of sheds, stables and single rooms inhabited by single people and families.[26] Diarist, author and lawyer James Boswell may not have been in an unusual position when he rented rooms in London where he was allowed use of the parlour 'in the morning only'.[27] If it was the case that those with means shared rooms, the multiple use of space by poorer people must have been extremely common. It would no doubt have confounded those making listings for the purposes of hearth or other taxes, who may have been forced to place some administrative order on the household and the apparent use of space. Overcrowding was certainly not a novel aspect of life by the mid-nineteenth century when it came to be systematically investigated at the same time as the term 'slum' came into regular use.[28]

William Baer has recently surveyed the types of poor housing and living arrangements in London evident from the Certificates and Returns of Divided Houses, which give us a rare insight into ordinary accommodation in the 1630s. The close succession of surveys carried out at this time gives an unusually complete picture of the housing market. Baer outlines the tension between the desire of the authorities to control and limit London's growth and the need for cheap housing. Small time entrepreneurs and speculators defied building prohibitions, 'while scurrying opportunistically to meet the need in unconventional ways'.[29] Baer identifies a 'shadow housing market' of new habitations created from older, usually non-residential buildings aimed at those with low income, and often on the margins of being legal. Grand houses were subdivided into tenements, habitations were created within inns and company halls, and old hospitals were divided into numerous small dwelling houses. Even small houses were divided, and structures such as cow houses, outhouses and stables were turned into homes.

The 'People in Place' project has identified the development of alleyways in former gardens or yards as an important development in the intensification of housing. All but one of the 17 households in Ship Alley, Aldgate were poor in 1630s in the sense of being unable to earn enough to support themselves. Proliferation and subdivision clearly continued, because there were 23 households in the same alley by 1666. There were myriads of such alleys in Aldgate by the second half of the seventeenth century.[30] Early industrial towns expanded in a similar way and urbanisation was rapid from 1810 to around 1830. Development of housing for ordinary people was often hemmed in by privately owned land and this meant that particular urban landscapes developed, as in Nottingham where sprawling urban villages developed rather than suburbs closer to the centre.[31] Maurice Beresford has shown how Leeds' back-to-back houses were a result of the constrained areas of land open to development.[32]

'Improvement' of towns during this era usually created more work opportunities, but sometimes less attractive living conditions, for the poor. When the New Town of Edinburgh was created as a smart middle-class area, across Princes Street in the Old Town, there was 'a grand repository of history; a deep pool of jostling struggling humanity' as two Edinburghs developed, divided by Princes Street. In Old Town, the poor population doubled between 1800 and 1870 and were 'single unconnected phenomena, owning no relation apparently to any other human being ... It is little to say they are scarcely covered'. Youngson described the gross overcrowding of the Old Town:

A wide range of the most sordid and the least productive occupations might be carried on by the inhabitants of a single room, let alone of a single tenement – shebeening, out-of-door apple selling or dram selling, match-making, speech-crying, organ-grinding, thieving, prostitution, or 'subletting' for an hour to vagrant couples not intent upon singing psalms.[33]

'Improvement' might, of course, involve trying to upgrade the housing of the poor or at least trying to situate poverty in aesthetically pleasing surrounds. Orphanages, workhouses, almshouses and estate villages were often rebuilt, sometimes as urban showpieces and perhaps using gothic revival styles in an attempt to beautify poverty.[34] There was really nothing new about this. Guilds, companies and corporations often vigorously tried to meet the accommodation needs of the poor associated with their trade. Bristol's Merchant Venturers, for example, opened new almshouse buildings in the seventeenth century and sometimes met the needs of poor seamen by other means, such as by buying them a boat and thus meeting both their occupational and accommodation needs with one donation.[35] The urban almshouses described by Tomkins in this book operate in a somewhat similar way by removing the poor from areas where they might be a slight on the environment, and providing a visible civic symbol of charitable beneficence. Less decorous institutions of relief have received almost no historical attention. Jeremy Boulton has identified a type of 'nursing home' in late seventeenth and early eighteenth-century London and Elaine Murphy has investigated pauper farms around London in the century that followed.[36]

By the early nineteenth century, busy vestries like St Botolph's in Colchester – an example of what John Black has called a 'casualty parish' – showed an intense preoccupation with the rental of rooms and houses, and there was an expectation that the rental bills of the poor would be met if they were unable to pay them.[37] A warehouseman resident in Shoreditch in 1813 complained that he and his family were about to be evicted. He wrote a vivid narrative of his predicament:

> A Person I dealt with for Bread last winter has served me with an execution on my Goods ... two Men Came into my Place and saw me Ill and my Children almost Naked. Looking Round at my Things says he these things are not worth my Taking I must Gett an[d] Execution an[] take You and it appears to me you will be as comfortable in Jail as in your present Situation.[38]

It was also an expectation of overseers to pay regular relief in advance against debt. Elizabeth Hinds wrote from London in 1820 that she wanted a pound in advance of the quarter money she anticipated to have to 'plage [pledge] all my things'.[39] A letter of 1827 informed the overseers that one of their parishioners who now lived in Cambridge and rented a house from St Peter's College had seven pounds of rent arrears; 'he informs me the overseers of the parish will pay it for him'.[40]

Such 'casualty parishes' were at the generous end of the spectrum in providing housing for the settled poor who were located in situations other than their settlement parish but where there was a shared sense of optimism about their future economic prospects. Yet for many of those who had migrated due to poverty, it is clear that they missed 'home'.

The meanings of home

When looking at the many documents about the poor it is useful to consider historical meanings of 'house' and 'home'. 'House' could mean the portion of a building occupied by one family, whereas 'home' could often mean the village or town rather than the conventional contemporary definition that denotes one's dwelling place.[41] While strategically wise to claim a connection with a home parish, there does seem to be a strong emotional tie of belonging in many migrant writings. If relief was in doubt, it was common to an almost formulaic extent for the poor to write letters threatening to 'come home' to their settlement parish. This is an element in the dogged independence of the people that Steve King describes in his essay in this volume. Both Green and Lloyd consider the emotional space occupied by cottages. Green explores the connection between hearthlessness, heartlessness and unhomeliness. Poverty is a failure to maintain a homely space as a refuge from insecurity: the cottage is a cornerstone of domestic ideology. While nineteenth-century domesticity has largely been seen as a woman's sphere, Tosh has shown the crucial role of the home in formation of male identity. These ideas are generally seen as bourgeois ones but there are many hints in the remnants of the less articulate that these ideas also permeated their home lives and may have done for hundreds of years.[42] The importance of housing in defining status might also be understood through the extent to which it provided individuals and families with privacy. As Amanda Vickery has suggested, 'Life with no vestiges of privacy was understood to be a most sorry degradation which stripped away the defences of the spirit'.[43]

Eighteenth-century observers ran together specific but sometimes divergent meanings of the cottage in debates and discourses about the condition of the poor. A cottage was a philosophical resource to political economists, philanthropists, moral reformers and others. By the nineteenth century, sentiment added an emotional perspective to descriptions of cottages. Lloyd finds they figured in discussions of migrations, manufactures, agricultural profit, the economics of poor relief and the reformation of manners. In particular, the cottage 'provided a new arena for exploring ideas about poverty, crucially one that accommodated both sentiment and attention to individual human behaviour'.[44]

The impact on understanding past households

In his writings from the 1960s to the early 1980s, strongly influenced by Hajnal, Peter Laslett described ordinary households as being a result of the 'Western European marriage pattern'.[45] His analysis was based on consideration of 100 parish 'census type listings', which showed a mean household size of 4.75 people from the sixteenth century to the twentieth century. Western households contained one simple family. Age of marriage was relatively late; there was usually a small age gap between spouses and marriage was the basis for a companionate relationship. The family and the household were largely synonymous. Laslett argued such households were recognisable, 'normal' and anglocentric – the past could therefore be claimed as 'ours'. It was a view that stressed individualism and the primacy of blood relationships. Servants for example were, in his words, 'imported personalities'. The result of units consisting only of parent and children was 'nuclear hardship'. Such small units could not always withstand the ebb and flow of the economic tide and parish poor assistance had to substitute for the assistance of extended family members that would be resorted to in other social arrangements. Laslett was writing in reaction to earlier ideas that families had traditionally been complex and extended and had become simpler with modernisation. He believed such self-sufficient small family units were the ideal form for adapting to changing economic imperatives. Wittingly or not, other historians and journalists appropriated a similar description of the English family as a co-operative team who proved to be the perfect fit for capitalist development.[46] The suggestion proceeding from the singular nuclear family, that kinship was loose and shallow in early modern English society, found ready acceptance.

The influence of Laslett's formulation means that scholars have ascribed less importance to kin in the past than is warranted, and it is probably fair to say that a preoccupation with the nuclear family as the predominant shape of past households has been steadily diluted over the

last few decades. Far from providing a comprehensive safety net of support over a number of centuries, an accumulation of scholarship, in fact
dating from the inception of poor relief in the Elizabethan era, shows
that those who needed parish pension would also need a supplemental
form of support. In many cases kin must have provided this financial
and physical support.[47] Other research has shown that sometimes the
'imported personalities' were actually 'hidden kin' furthering our understanding of blood ties.[48] Brodsky Elliott found that approximately 37
per cent of migrant women in London had kin also living in the capital;
in just over 20 per cent of cases they resided with them.[49] Sam Barrett's
work has contributed significantly to our understanding of the kin links
of the poor.[50] However, as Margaret Pelling has commented,

> the literature does not tell us when or how domestic space began
> to exclude those not members of the family of blood, or how, at
> the level of the household, the domestic servant diverged from the
> apprentice and the employee.[51]

In her examination of life-cycle service, Sheila Cooper has noted that by
the nineteenth century, servants were not considered part of the family and housing arrangements increasingly relegated them to separate
staircases and quarters.[52]

Probably most significant of all for the purposes of this book, Sokoll's
very detailed study, mainly based on the households of the poor in the
two Essex communities of Ardleigh and Braintree in the late eighteenth
and early nineteenth centuries, found that households were neither small
nor simple.[53] Research on the Celtic fringes of England also showed large
and complex households usually living in shared housing situations in
the early modern period.[54] Rather than being adaptable as Laslett claimed,
sheltered and subsidised housing brought about the sort of adaptable
labour force and neighbourhood that landlords, gentry and the better-off
desired. This view is echoed in the chapters found in this book.

Poor housing in wider context

If the new social historians have found households to be less recognisable than the earlier generation of demographic historians, it is the case
that houses and hovels were more ephemeral and less enduring than
we may have imagined. Green has been able to find very few surviving
examples of the housing of the poor. In the colonies in Australia,
described by Lloyd, the few surviving houses of those of ordinary rank

from the 1820s are so tiny and fragile they can have provided little more than shelter. Some houses were known to be built to be portable in England and this was even more common in Australia.[55] Furniture might have also been constructed so as to be easily moved.[56] Gardens may have been scanty or non-existent. Twentieth-century writings by Flora Thompson or Laurie Lee evoke a misleading timeless rusticity to rural homes. When Laurie Lee arrived at the Gloucestershire village of Slad in 1918, he came to a cottage

> that stood in a half-acre of garden on steep bank above a lake, with three floors and a cellar and a treasure in the walls, with a pump and apple trees, syringa and strawberries, rooks in the chimneys, frogs in the cellar, mushrooms in the ceiling, and all for three and sixpence a week.

Such a house for one family would have appeared to be a palace to the poor of three generations earlier.[57]

In the late eighteenth century, Samantha Williams' study of the east Bedfordshire villages of Campton and Shefford found that up to a third of residents in these villages received regular relief at some point in their lives. This number increases when occasional relief is taken into account, and there was a rising dependency of labouring families on the parish in the early nineteenth century. Williams suggests that pensions were received by the elderly for considerable lengths of time, especially older men. By contrast, relief to families was supplementary and limited in duration. In the case of widows and lone women with children, the parish did not make up for the absence of a male wage and these families encountered deeper poverty than that experienced by other families at the time.[58] As Jane Pearson argued in her doctoral thesis about the village of Great Tey in Essex, the implications of the poverty of the early years of the nineteenth century were far-reaching, affecting gender relations and emotional relationships within households. Analysing change over a century from 1730, Pearson wrote that the overseer's job changed from assisting all of the population who fell on hard times to that of providing chiefly for married men and their growing families. She sees this change as 'profound and extraordinary, potentially destabilizing of traditional paternalist attitudes and deeply threatening to the security of all levels in village society. This was a change that brought the stark inequalities of male power into sharp focus'.[59]

Social welfare arrangements, effectively 'public housing' (a forerunner of council houses), were more extensive than hitherto shown. By the early nineteenth century under the Old Poor Law, parishes still demonstrated some willingness to assist in keeping a roof over the heads of their parishioners' heads. Despite rapid population growth, urbanisation and migration to cities and industrial villages, some parishes still maintained and built housing for public use.[60] However, several poor people or families would now share a dwelling that perhaps previously would have housed a single elderly pauper in the seventeenth century, and this type of provision was increasingly threatened and subject to the decisions of parish officials who might be under pressure to put the money to other uses. In fact, by the late eighteenth century Peter King found that poor law officials made inventories of pauper property so they could take control of their possessions in exchange for maintaining them.[61] As the Chapter 1 by Boulton shows, the poor effectively evicted themselves from lodgings in order to match their changing circumstances with their income. Women who were widowed or whose husbands went into the military, families who could not sustain businesses or employment, those with very many dependent children all might have had to downsize, and in some cases family disintegration was the result of the 'saving of some importance to us'.

Following the 1834 Poor Law Amendment, Act arrangements were far less generous and supportive than the out-relief described here. Eviction, while a possibility often mentioned in letters to poor relief officials before 1834 and, as we have argued, a common way of restructuring rural areas, combined with increasing class-based stigma about poor housing. Forced ejection was a very real fear when inability to sustain a household meant either forcing relatives to support poor kin or entering the workhouse.

While the ability to maintain a home had long been a marker of status and independence, its importance rose in combination with a huge expansion in home ownership in the twentieth century. Far from going away, poverty has become more visible in contemporary societies. Experiencing a poor upbringing in a bad neighbourhood and an inadequate house has spawned an entirely new genre of autobiographical writing.[62] Young homeless people are a glaring reminder of the fragility of modern social welfare arrangements. There are few starker social polarities than the extremely high social, political and economic value placed on home ownership in contrast with the minority who cannot access the rental sector and have no choice but to live on the streets. Rented housing – the majority experience within living memory – has become a relatively degraded sector. Council housing, the most significant attempt to house the poor in twentieth-century Britain, largely disappeared in the Thatcher years.

Hopefully this volume makes a contribution to the accommodation experiences of the poor in the same way that recent scholarship has unveiled many more details about the clothing of the poor than we had previously known.[63] The burgeoning of scholarship about poverty has been helpfully accompanied by the publication of many primary sources.[64] As researchers in the history of poverty are well aware, this area of academic endeavour still presents a number of challenges in the archives and those who work in the area need to use ingenuity to advance this area of scholarship. The result of documentary discoveries can still prove to be enlightening and rewarding. As Steve Hindle has aptly put it:

> This is a field in which the scholarship repeatedly bumps up against the limit of what is historically possible. Despite the achievements of the new social history, the doors of the humblest households remain, if not closed altogether, then at least only just ajar.[65]

We are still peering at houses and their inhabitants from the outside in, but at least we are now able to raise a candle to the dark interior and see a glimmer within.

Notes

* Unless otherwise stated, place of publication is London.

1. F. Place, *The Autobiography of Francis Place (1771–1854)*, ed. by M. Thale (Cambridge: Cambridge University Press, 1972), p. 111.
2. In capitalist and commercially orientated areas of England, a permanent poor were apparent by the sixteenth century. For example M. Williams, '"Our Poor People in Tumults Arose": Living in Poverty in Earls Colne, Essex, 1560–1640', *Rural History* 13:2, (2002), 123–43 is able to build on the research of many predecessors regarding social structure in the Essex village of Earls Colne in the century from 1540 to 1640. He excludes life cycle and other types of poverty and concludes that sons and daughters of tenants and husbandmen were reduced to a permanent state of poverty by demographic and market forces. 'They were forced all their lives to depend upon the scattered generosity of the wealthy, or upon their own imaginations and the inability of the wealthy to hold every miscreant to account' (129–30). For a broader picture see J. Whittle, *The Development of Agrarian Capitalism: Land and Labour in Norfolk, 1440–1580* (Oxford: Oxford University Press, 2000).
3. G. Karskens, *The Rocks: Life in Early Sydney* (Melbourne: Melbourne University Press, 1997); G. Karksens, *Inside the Rocks: The Archaeology of a Neighbourhood* (Alexandria: Hale & Iremonger, 1999). P. Guillery, *The Small House in Eighteenth-Century London* (New Haven and London: Yale University Press, 2004) is a significant contribution to the history of houses that are not 'grand'.
4. Bristol University Library, Pinney Papers Box 17.
5. L. Hollen Lees, *The Solidarities of Strangers: The English Poor Laws and the People 1700–1948* (Cambridge: Cambridge University Press, 1998), p. 32.

6. A large range of literature has taken up this point. See S. King, *Poverty and Welfare in England, 1700–1850* (Manchester: Manchester University Press, 2000). See also J. Kent & S. King, 'Changing Patterns of Poor Relief in some English Rural Parishes circas 1650–1750', *Rural History* 14:2, (2003), 119–56 who draw on M. H. D. van Leewen, 'Logic of Charity: Poor Relief in Pre-Industrial Europe', *Journal of Interdisciplinary History* 24, (1994), 589–613; R. Jutte, *Poverty and Deviance in Early Modern Europe* (Cambridge: Cambridge University Press, 1994) and S. R. Ottaway 'Providing for the Elderly in Eighteenth-Century England', *Continuity and Change* 12, (1998), 391–418 and her *The Decline of Life: Old Age in Eighteenth-Century England* (Cambridge: Cambridge University Press, 2004). Also T. Hitchcock, 'A New History from Below', *History Workshop Journal* 57, (2004), 294–8.
7. A. Shepard, 'Poverty, Labour and the Language of Social Description in Early Modern England', *Past and Present* 202, (2008), 51–95.
8. R. W. Hoyle & C. J. Taylor, 'The Slaidburn Poor Pasture: Changing Configurations of Popular Politics in the Eighteenth- and Nineteenth-Century Village, *Social History* 31:2, (2006), 182–205.
9. P. Slack, *Poverty and Policy in Tudor and Stuart England* (Longman, 1988).
10. T. Arkell, 'The Incidence of Poverty in the Later Seventeenth Century', *Social History* 12, (1987), 54–5. For new research on London at the start of our time period see W. C. Baer 'Stuart London's standard of living: re-examining the Settlement of Tithes of 1638 for rents, income and poverty' *Economic History Review*, 63:3 (2010), 612–37.
11. J. Broad, 'Housing the Rural Poor in Southern England, 1650–1850', *Agricultural History Review* 48:2, (2000), 151–70. See also his 'Parish Economies of Welfare 1650–1834', *Historical Journal* 42, (1999), 985–1006.
12. *Ibid.,* p. 153.
13. P. Sharpe, *Population and Society in an East Devon Parish: Reproducing Colyton, 1540–1840* (Exeter: University of Exeter Press, 2002).
14. S. Hindle, *On the Parish? The Micro-Politics of Poor Relief in Rural England, c. 1550–1750* (Oxford: Clarendon Press, 2004).
15. S. Hindle, '"Without the Cry of Any Neighbours": A Cumbrian Family and the Poor Law Authorities c. 1690–1730', in H. Berry & E. Foyster (eds), *The Family in Early Modern England* (Cambridge: Cambridge University Press, 2007), pp. 126–57. For quote see pp. 154–5.
16. *Ibid.,* p. 132.
17. L. A. Botelho, *Old Age and the English Poor Law, 1500–1700* (Woodbridge: The Boydell Press, 2004), p. 154.
18. See, for example, J. H. Bettey, 'Land Tenure and Manorial Custom in Dorset 1570–1670', *Southern History* 4, (1982), 33–54; D. Mackinnon, '"According to the Custom of the Place I now live in": Life and Land in Seventeenth-Century Earls Colne, Essex' (Unpublished University of Melbourne PhD Thesis, 1994), especially the case of John Quilter in the 1670s and 1680s on pp. 260–1; H. French & R. Hoyle, *The Character of English Rural Society, Earls Colne 1550–1750* (Manchester: Manchester University Press, 2007). See also H. S. A. Fox, 'Servants, Cottagers and Tied Cottages during the Later Middle Ages: Towards a Regional Dimension, *Rural History* 6:2, (1995), 125–54.
19. L. Shaw-Taylor, 'Labourers, Cows, Common Rights and Parliamentary Enclosure: The Evidence of Contemporary Comment c. 1760–1810', *Past and Present* 171, (2001), 95–126.

20. P. Fumerton, *Unsettled: The Culture of Mobility and the Working Poor in Early Modern England* (Chicago & London: University of Chicago Press, 2006).
21. J. Boulton, *Neighbourhood and Society: A London Suburb in the Seventeenth Century* (Cambridge: Cambridge University Press, 1987), especially pp. 120–37 and 247–61.
22. As well as his contribution to this volume, see S. Hindle, 'Waste Children? Pauper Apprenticeship under the Elizabethan Poor Laws c. 1598–1697', in P. Lane, N. Raven and K. D. M. Snell (eds), *Women, Work and Wages in England, 1600–1850* (Woodbridge: The Boydell Press, 2004), pp. 15–46. See also A. Levene, 'Honesty, Sobriety and Diligence: Master-Apprentice Relations in Eighteenth and Nineteenth-Century England, *Social History* 33:2, (2008), 183–200; K. Honeyman, *Child Workers in England, 1780–1820: Parish Apprentices and the Making of the Early Industrial Labour Force* (Aldershot: Ashgate, 2007).
23. For further background see J. Boulton, '"It is Extreme Necessity that Makes me do this": Some "Survival Strategies" of Pauper Households in London's West End During the Early Eighteenth Century', *International Review of Social History, Supplement 8*, (2000), 47–69.
24. ERO, D/P 94/18/39 Chelmsford Casual Pay Book 1829–30.
25. See especially the work of the 'People in Place: families, households, and housing in early modern London, 1550–1720' project, as summarised in V. Harding et al., *People in Place: Families, Households and Housing in Early Modern London* (Centre for Metropolitan History pamphlet, 2008).
26. V. Harding, 'Families and Housing in Seventeenth-Century London', *Parergon* 24:2, (2007), 115–38 finds the term 'houseful', coined by historical demographers to be useful when lodging households and singles shared a house with one or more householding families.
27. J. McEwan & P. Sharpe, '"It buys me freedom": Genteel Lodging in Late Seventeenth and Eighteenth-Century London', *Parergon* 24:2, (2007), 139–62; H. Barker & J. Hamlett, 'Living above the Shop: Home, Business, and Family Life in the English "Industrial Revolution"', *Journal of Family History* 35:4, (2010), 311–28.
28. R. Rodger, *Housing in Urban Britain 1780–1914*, 2nd edn (Cambridge: Cambridge University Press, 1995), p. 1. See also J. Burnett, *A Social History of Housing 1815–1985*, 2nd edn (Routledge, 1991).
29. W. C. Baer, 'Housing the Poor and Mechanick Class in Seventeenth-Century London', *London Journal* 25:2, (2000), 13–39; W. C. Baer, 'Housing for the Lesser Sort in Stuart London: Findings from Certificates and Returns of Divided Houses', *London Journal* 33:1, (2008), 61–88, (62). Some different findings were reported by M. J. Power, 'East London Housing in the Seventeenth Century', in P. Clark & P. Slack, *Crisis and Order in English Towns 1580–1700: Essays in Urban History* (Routledge & Kegan Paul, 1972), pp. 237–62.
30. Harding, 'Families and Housing'.
31. S. D. Chapman, 'Working Class Housing in Nottingham during the Industrial Revolution', in S. D. Chapman (ed.), *A History of Working Class Housing: A Symposium* (Newton Abbott: David and Charles, 1971), pp. 133–64.
32. M. W. Beresford, 'The Back-to-Back House in Leeds 1787–1937', in Chapman (ed.), *A History of Working Class Housing*, pp. 93–132.

33. A. J. Youngson, *The Making of Classical Edinburgh 1750–1840* (Edinburgh: Edinburgh University Press, 1966), pp. 255, 267–8, citing J. Heiton, *The Castes of Edinburgh* (Edinburgh, 1860), p. 248. See also E. Sanderson, *Women and Work in Eighteenth-Century Edinburgh* (Basingstoke: Macmillan, 1996), pp. 41–7.

34. A. Tomkins, *The Experience of Urban Poverty, 1723–82: Parish, Charity and Credit* (Manchester: Manchester University Press, 2006) looks in detail at arrangements in York, Oxford and Shrewsbury with a focus on institutional forms of relief examined through record linkage. See also A. Levene, 'Children, Childhood and the Workhouse: St Marylebone 1769–1781', *London Journal* 33:1, (2008), 41–59. For work in progress on the under-researched topic of almshouses see N. Goose & S. Basten, 'Almshouse Residency in Nineteenth-Century England: An Interim Report', *Family and Community History* 12:1, (2009), 65–76 and N. Goose 'The English Almshouse and the Mixed Economy of Welfare: Medieval to Modern', *The Local Historian* 40:1, (2010), 3–19. J. C. Loudon's immense *Encyclopedia of Cottage, Farm and Villa Architecture* (1833, republished 1846), (Shaftesbury: Donhead Publishing, 2000 with a new introduction by E. Mercer) aimed to improve the dwellings of the great mass of society in the countryside and was equally influential in the colonies as in Britain.

35. P. McGrath, *Records Relating to the Society of Merchant Venturers of the City of Bristol in the Seventeenth Century* (Bristol Record Society, 1952).

36. J. Boulton, 'Welfare Systems and the Parish Nurse in Early Modern London, 1650–1725', *Family and Community History* 10:2, (2007), 127–51; E. Murphy, 'The Metropolitan Pauper Farms, 1722–1834', *London Journal* 27:1, (2002), 1–18.

37. Black uses this term for St Clement Danes parish in J. Black, 'Illegitimacy and the Urban Poor in London 1740–1830' (Unpublished University of London PhD Thesis, 1999), pp. 124–5.

38. ERO, D/P 203/18/1, St Botolph's Overseers Letters, 24 April 1813.

39. ERO, D/P 203/12/51, St Botolph's Overseer of the Poor, Vouchers and Bills, 1820.

40. ERO, D/P 203/12/51, St Botolph's Overseeer of the Poor, Vouchers and Bills, 1827.

41. Oxford English Dictionary. L. Baldassar, *Visits Home: Migration Experiences Between Italy and Australia* (Melbourne: Melbourne University Press, 2001) offers perceptive anthropological and sociological insights into meanings of home for migrants.

42. M. Kowaleski & P. J. P. Goldberg (eds), *Medieval Domesticity: Home, Housing and Household in Medieval England* (Cambridge: Cambridge University Press, 2008). See essays by F. Riddy, '"Burgeis" Domesticity in Late Medieval England' and P. J. P. Goldberg, 'The Fashioning of Bourgeois Domesticity in Later Medieval England: A Material Culture Perspective'.

43. A. Vickery '"An Englishman's Home is his Castle?" Thresholds, Boundaries and Privacies in the Eighteenth-Century London House', *Past and Present* 199, (2008), 147–73 (151). See also J. Barrell, *The Spirit of Despotism: Invasions of Privacy in the 1790s* (Oxford: Oxford University Press, 2006), pp. 210–46.

44. S. Lloyd, 'Cottage Conversations: Poverty and Manly Independence in Eighteenth-Century England', *Past and Present* 184, (2004), 69–108 (104).

See also C. Payne, *Rustic Simplicity: Scenes of Cottage Life in Nineteenth-Century British Art* (Aldershot, Lund Humphries, 1998).

45. P. Laslett, *The World We Have Lost – Further Explored*, 3rd edn (Routledge, 1983) is an accessible start to this literature which was very influential from the first edition of this book published in 1965. See also P. Laslett, 'Mean Household Size in England since the Sixteenth Century', in P. Laslett & R. Wall (eds), *Household and Family in Past Time* (Cambridge: Cambridge University Press, 1972), pp. 125–58.

46. F. Mount, *The Subversive Family* (Cape, 1982).

47. I. W. Archer, *The Pursuit of Stability: Social Relations in Elizabethan England* (Cambridge: Cambridge University Press, 1991), p. 195.

48. D. Cooper & M. Donald, 'Households and "Hidden" Kin in Early Nineteenth-Century England: Four Case Studies in Suburban Exeter, 1821–1861', *Continuity and Change* 10, (1995), 257–78; P. Crawford, *Blood, Bodies and Families in Early Modern England* (Longman, 2004) and L. Davidoff, M. Doolittle, J. Fink & K. Holden, *The Family Story: Blood, Contract and Intimacy, 1830–1960* (Longman, 1998) for a later period.

49. V. Brodsky Elliot, 'Widows in Late Elizabethan London: Remarriage, Economic Opportunity and Family Orientations', in L. Bonfield, R. M. Smith & K. Wrightson (eds), *The World We Have Gained: Histories of Population and Social Structure. Essays Presented to Peter Laslett on his Seventieth Birthday* (Oxford: Blackwell, 1986), pp. 122—54; V. Brodsky Elliott, 'Single Women in the London Marriage Market: Age, Status and Mobility, 1598–1619', in R. B. Outhwaite (ed.), *Marriage and Society: Studies in the Social History of Marriage* (Europa, 1981), pp. 81–100.

50. S. Barrett, 'Kinship, Poor Relief and the Welfare Process in Early Modern England', in S. King & A. Tomkins (eds), *The Poor in England, 1700–1850: An Economy of Makeshifts* (Manchester: Manchester University Press, 2003), pp. 199–228.

51. M. Pelling, 'Skirting the City? Disease, Social Change, and the Divided Households of the Seventeenth-Century', in P. Griffiths & M. S. R. Jenner, *Londinopolis: Essays in the Cultural and Social History of Early Modern London* (Manchester: Manchester University Press, 2000), pp. 154–75 (p. 167).

52. S. M. I. Cooper, 'Service to Servitude? The Decline and Demise of Life-Cycle Service in England', *History of the Family* 10:4, (2005), 367–86 and Vickery 'An Englishman's Home'. T. Meldrum, 'Domestic Service, Privacy and the Eighteenth-Century Metropolitan Household', *Urban History* 26:1, (1999), 27–39.

53. T. Sokoll, *Household and Family among the Poor: The Case of Two Essex Communities in the Late Eighteenth and Early Nineteenth Centuries* (Bochum: Brockmeyer, 1993).

54. D. Cullum, 'Society and Economy in West Cornwall c. 1588–1750', (Unpublished University of Exeter PhD thesis, 1994).

55. J. T. Smith, 'Shortlived and Mobile: Houses in Late Seventeenth-Century England', *Vernacular Architecture* 16, (1985), 33–4; J. Gregory, 'Journeying across Colonial Landscapes: Portable Housing in Nineteenth-Century Australia', in A. Mayne (ed.), *Beyond the Black Stump: Histories of Outback Australia* (Adelaide: Wakefield Press, 2008).

56. Campaign beds, which could be taken apart and easily moved were popular in the colonies. M. Ponsonby, *Stories from Home: English Domestic Interiors 1750–1850* (Aldershot: Ashgate, 2007) finds middle class households to be more transient than has perhaps been thought. She mentions that furniture could be hired from cabinetmakers and furniture brokers, pp. 59–60.

57. L. Lee, *Cider with Rosie* (The Hogarth Press, 1959), p. 8; F. Thompson, *Lark Rise* (Oxford: Oxford University Press, 1939). The first chapter of the first book of the trilogy *Lark Rise to Candleford* is 'Poor People's Houses', pp. 17–31.

58. See also J. Humphries, 'Female-Headed Households in Early Industrial Britain: The Vanguard of the Proletariat?' *Labour History Review* 63, (1998), 31–65.

59. J. Pearson, 'The Rural Middle Sort in an Eighteenth-Century Essex Village: Great Tey 1660–1830' (Unpublished University of Essex PhD Thesis 1996), p. 217.

60. See for example N. Alcock, 'Halford Cottages: Mud Construction', *Birmingham and Warwick Archaeological Society* 87, (1975), 133–6.

61. P. King, 'Pauper Inventories and the Material Lives of the Poor in the Eighteenth and Nineteenth Centuries', in T. Hitchcock, P. King & P. Sharpe, *Chronicling Poverty: The Voices and Strategies of the English Poor 1640–1840* (Basingstoke: Macmillan, 1997), pp. 155–191.

62. An early example of this was F. McCourt, *Angela's Ashes* (Harper Collins, 1996), which describes the author's upbringing in a terrible house in a poor part of Limerick.

63. J. Styles, *The Dress of the People: Everyday Fashion in Eighteenth-Century England* (New Haven: Yale University Press, 2007) and a special edition of *Textile History* 33:1, (2002) edited by S. King & C. Payne. More recently, see P. Jones, 'Clothing the Poor in Early Nineteenth Century England', *Textile History* 37:1, (2006), 17–37; V. Richmond, '"Indiscriminate liberality subverts the Morals and depraves the habits of the Poor": A Contribution to the Debate on the Poor Law, Parish Clothing Relief and Clothing Societies in Early Nineteenth-Century England', *Textile History* 40:1, (2009), 51–69; and R. Worth 'Developing a Method for the Study of the Clothing of the "Poor": Some Themes in the Visual Representation of Rural Working Class Dress, 1850–1900', *Textile History* 40:1, (2009), 70–96.

64. For example, the volumes of *Narratives of the Poor in Eighteenth-Century England* (Pickering and Chatto, 2006) under the general editorship of A. Levene; T. Sokoll (ed.), *Essex Pauper Letters, 1731–1837* (Oxford: Oxford University Press, 2001) and more recently the collection of resources on Plebian London Lives, 1690–1800 at www.Londonlives.org. Accessed August 2010.

65. Hindle, '"Without the Cry of any Neighbours"', p. 156.

Part I
The Value of Accommodation

1

'Turned into the Street with My Children Destitute of Every Thing'; The Payment of Rent and the London Poor, 1600–1850

Jeremy Boulton

1.1 Introduction

There has been a great deal of recent work on the family economy of the urban poor. Economic historians, attempting to calculate standard of living indices, have long used real or estimated working-class budgets to assess expenditure patterns and purchasing power. Many others have been interested in the multiple and ingenious ways in which poor households made ends meet. What has been described famously as the economy of 'makeshift and mend' has been analysed minutely to uncover an impressive range of survival strategies. The urban poor have been shown to have had access to (sometimes generous) levels of poor relief and private charity and were able to manipulate local poor relief systems to considerable effect. Survival strategies might also include selective child abandonment, resort to available (and 'able') kin, reliance on credit and pawnbrokers, tactical changes in diet to cheaper foodstuffs, theft, prostitution, begging and the perks available at some (but not all) workplaces. The pauper household economy, moreover, was a cooperative effort, where all who were physically able contributed.[1] Thus far, however, historians have not paid much attention to a vital element in this picture. This chapter is intended as a preliminary foray into that most important, but neglected element of the pauper household economy – namely the payment of rent.

It might be sensible to say, too, what this chapter is *not* about. It is not about the quality and nature of the housing occupied by the poor, something that has, for London, recently been illuminated splendidly by William Baer and, for the eighteenth century, by Dorothy George.[2] Nor does this chapter intend to say much, per se, about the *distribution* of rents paid by *all* London inhabitants, something we also know a great deal about from the work of Craig Spence, Roger Finlay, Malcolm Smuts, Leonard Schwarz and others.[3] What is intended is to make some preliminary remarks on the part that rent played in the lives of the urban poor, on the actual basic costs of accommodation in the metropolis and how rent may have impacted on pauper lives, on their survival strategies and how the basic requirement for shelter and accommodation was treated by poor law and charitable bodies.

The questions that need answering are, therefore, how much did the poor pay for their accommodation? What strategies were employed to meet basic accommodation needs and how did the need to pay rent determine welfare policy and pauper behaviour?

1.2   Rent and the urban poor

The need for shelter is a basic necessity of human life. Since poor people did not, in common with most urban inhabitants, own the freehold of their dwellings, getting access to housing required the payment of rent. Rent is an interesting item of expenditure in the early modern economy because it seems to have almost always been paid in cash. This is significant since, in an economy that was chronically short of specie, most items like food and clothing were purchased on credit. Rent, at least in towns and cities, was different since it required the tenant to pass over hard cash. In this way the payment of rent is akin to the payment of a direct tax.[4] Distraining goods in lieu of available cash was thus commonly employed both by landlords collecting rent arrears and also those collecting the local poor rate (although in the latter case outright sale of such goods was immediate). The fact that urban rents were paid in cash, rather than credit, also meant that rents might have been peculiarly sensitive to times of hardship, as tenants fell quickly into arrears when the local economy hit a downturn.[5] It might also explain why some landlords might discount rent, and provide other services, for respectable tenants who paid regularly.[6] The need to acquire rent money, unsurprisingly, appears with reasonable frequency in the Old Bailey Proceedings as a stated motive for theft. The need to pay rent in cash meant that all urban families, even the very poor, must have had to save money on a regular basis, keeping it hidden away and often locked up. If rent was to be paid quarterly, this could amount to significant sums of money. In 1765, Elizabeth Jones was tried at the Old Bailey for stealing 'a guinea, a nine-shilling piece, and eighteen-pence (three sixpences)' from a 12-year-old girl. The girl claimed 'My mamma gave it to me, to carry home, to put in a drawer to pay a quarter's rent' and further

elaborated that 'her mother gave her that money in order to lock up, to
pay the rent, and not to let her father see it; for he is a coal-heaver, and
a very drunken man'.[7]

1.3   Rent and the parish poor

Payments made by parish overseers to cover the costs of pauper accommodation are not usually made explicit and it is not usual to find many
payments made explicitly to cover rent or housing in any one year
in overseers' accounts. This is partly because parish overseers, at least
in large parishes, rarely recorded detailed reasons for the thousands
of small short-term 'casual' or 'extraordinary' payments made to the
outdoor poor. It is also the case that some temporary accommodation could be recorded as payments to parish nurses. In many London
parishes in the late seventeenth and early eighteenth centuries parish
officers increasingly lodged the sick, destitute and infirm with parish
nurses, whose detailed bills can sometimes be found itemised in overseer's accounts. This provision of accommodation for sick and infirm
paupers could be a very significant item of parish expenditure and itself
indicates the pressing need to provide short-term accommodation for
the parish poor.[8]

It is likely of course, given that workhouses were intended to provide
institutional shelter for the poor, that one would find more payments to
provide pauper accommodation by parishes that lacked workhouses than
in those which had them. In St Martin's in 1724/5, the year *before* the
parish workhouse opened, and discounting the large number of payments made to lodge sick and infirm paupers with those parish nurses
who provided temporary lodgings – in much the same way as did later
workhouses, the overseers made 31 payments (a trivial number compared to the many thousands made in that year) explicitly to cover pauper rent and provide temporary lodgings to parish paupers. Even if the
areas of the parish which became the new parish of St George Hanover
Square are excluded, however, even this tiny number does suggest, as
we shall see, that providing lodgings was more common, as one would
have predicted, before the parish workhouse was available. The parish
workhouse had a much larger capacity than the houses run by parish
nurses.

Nine of these payments were for relatively large sums of money made
to cover large rent arrears or provide long-term accommodation. Four of
these, totalling 49s. 6d., were made to cover a year's rent for the family
of one Grace Bills. Grace might well have been chronically sick, since

she was admitted to the workhouse in December 1726, and after a short stay, sent to Guy's Hospital, where she died in February 1727.[9] Two more of these large sums were made to lodge the 'crazy' Elizabeth Dewberry.[10] The other three substantial payments may also have been made in recognition of either chronic illness or disability, or, possibly, to individuals with a history of service in parish office although this is difficult to establish. The parish paid for the accommodation of William Warburton, workhouse steward, for some years after his dismissal for negligence in 1740.[11] The other payments were all for relatively modest sums of money, and almost all were explicitly made to cover the provision of lodgings, usually at the standard rate of 1s. per week. In only one case was there a (six shilling) payment made to 'Ann Rouson and three children her Goods being seized for Rent'. Another payment referred, uniquely, to the extra services sometimes provided by landlords to poor tenants, when the Overseer of Long Acre Ward paid 1s. 6d. to 'Sarah White's Landlady, she having advanced money to support her in her Illness'.[12]

Payments made to provide short-term accommodation costs are, unsurprisingly, found less commonly after the workhouse was erected in the parish in 1725. Out of 4729 payments listed in the overseer's accounts in 1726–7, only eight explicitly record payments to cover outstanding rent and, in contrast to the year before the erection of the workhouse, just one mentions the provision of temporary lodgings. Two of the large payments were made by the overseers to pay for two quarters rent for Jane Jones and her four children, passed from the neighbouring parish of St Giles in the Fields, at a total cost of £2.[13] Robert Durdant and his family were granted 12s. 6d. to pay the rent, a Mr Hare received 15s. to pay his rent 'and to be no more chargeable to the parish', while Ann Harlow and her four children received 2s. 6d. and her landlord got £1 'for rent' following an order from the local petty sessions. Most of these sums were relatively substantial; there was just one payment of 6d. paid by the overseers to provide a pauper what must have been a few nights lodging in Drury Lane Ward.[14] Those paupers in need of temporary shelter were normally sent to the workhouse after 1725.

Parish overseers in 1726/7 recorded stepping in more frequently than in 1724/5 to redeem goods seized in lieu of rent. Distraining the goods of defaulting tenants was the standard method whereby a landlord could recover rent arrears. There was a body of case law (which awaits its historian) surrounding this practice. It was understood by both landlords and tenants that such distraint had to be done according to prescribed legal forms. Legal changes from 1689 made distraining by landlords much easier, and may have led to greater depredations by landlords and their agents on defaulting tenants. The landlord would 'seize' the goods to force the payment of rent, sometimes locking them into a room to prevent a tenant accessing them. Thus, in 1694, a dispute between a William Hoyle and one Mary Holmes, which led to her death, was

> occasioned by a quarrel that happened between her and the Prisoner about Rent which was but 5*s.* 6*d.* and he would have had 7*s.* of her, because there was three Weeks over the Quarter; for which he Padlockt the Door, and the Deceased would have broke it open for her Clothes.[15]

Only after a period of time could distrained goods actually be sold to recover the rent.[16] It was thus possible for owners to redeem the goods prior to sale. Susan Clark was thus granted 10*s.* 6*d.* to 'Redeem her Good's being Seized for rent' in May 1726, while Elizabeth Curse was given the relatively large sum of 16*s.* 'to redeem her goods being seized for rent' in September 1726. The parish also negotiated directly with aggrieved landlords to recover pauper goods. The overseer of Spur Alley Ward thus recorded a payment of 1*s.* 6*d.* in 1726 being the 'Expences with Mr Farmer returning a poor woman's goods which he Seized for rent'.[17]

The extent to which paupers were evicted, or had their good seized for arrears of rent, or both, is not known in our period. Nor, come to that, is the number of paupers whose rent arrears contributed to their imprisonment for debt. The relief of poor prisoners is also occasionally referred to in overseers' accounts.[18] Landlords are unlikely to have allowed significant rent arrears to build up, although it could be counted a sign of 'mean circumstances' if landlords pressed for rent promptly. Thomas Panting alias Panton of St Mary Woolnoth tried for coining in 1717 'had the Repute of a Man in mean Circumstances' among his neighbours, one sign of which was that 'a Lodger in his House said, that he seemed to be very necessitous, being always very pressing for his Rent as soon as ever Quarter-day was past'.[19] Craig Muldrew found that rent arrears, although commonly found among debtors, rarely amounted to more than a few missed payments although he also found cases of rent arrears going back some years.[20]

Very few paupers, when examined under the settlement laws, referred to landlord attempts to recover rent to explain their current circumstances. Such cases tended to be part of a 'narrative of decline'. Elizabeth Tagg, for example, was examined under the settlement laws two weeks or so after her first admission to the workhouse in January 1744. Her social descent included her landlord distraining her goods for arrears of rent. Elizabeth had nine stays in the workhouse between this first admission in 1744 and her last in 1769. Eight of these were short stays between 1744 and 1752, after which she seems to have succeeded in avoiding destitution. However Elizabeth fell into poverty again in old age, being admitted to the workhouse for the last time in 1769 at the age of 68. She ended her days in the workhouse, dying there at the ascribed age of 70 in 1771.[21] A few other paupers similarly reported losing their goods due to arrears of rent.[22]

Perhaps the most interesting reference to rent arrears is an examination which suggests that absconding at night to avoid paying the rent, the classic 'moonlight flit' or in eighteenth-century parlance 'shooting the moon', was common practice among London's eighteenth-century poor:

> Elizabeth Hill in the workhouse aged about 37 years past from Saint Paul Covent Garden on her oath saith she is the widow of Hercules Hill a Gardiner who died upwards of Six years ago ... took a House in Plumtree Court in Shoe Lane in the parish of St Andrew Holborn of one Mr Greenhill a Quaker who lived in the said Court and that she agreed to pay Eleven pounds by the year Rent and that she continued in the said House about one quarter of a year *when she removed by night for fear her Landlord should seize her Goods having contracted for a year and a Quarters warning* [my italics] that she paid about forty shillings in part of Rent and her Landlord afterwards arrested her on account of the Rent.[23]

Similar cases can be found among the Old Bailey papers, since some absconding lodgers sometimes took the landlord's property with them, commonly linen or furniture, and pawned it.[24] Francis Place records taking part in a case of 'shooting the moon' later in the eighteenth century.[25]

It should be stressed again that payments made explicitly to cover housing costs are infrequent among the thousands of small payments made to the outdoor poor. Nonetheless since most (although not all) paupers paid rent, it must have been a very significant part of a pauper's outgoings, and must have absorbed a very big chunk of the weekly or monthly relief given by overseers. The average pension (which naturally included a range of payments) paid to parish pensioners in St Martin's in 1724/5 was 19.4*d.* per week, equivalent to 7*s.* per month. If, as the above analysis of the costs of lodging paupers suggests, pensioners were paying 4*s.* a month for lodgings, then the money cost of their accommodation would have absorbed at least half of their monthly parish doles. Parish pensions were thus, at least in effect, partly if not wholly rent subsidies.[26] Moreover, casual or 'extraordinary' payments made to the poor, even though they rarely specified rent as the reason, must often have been used to pay rent to landlords in the event of sickness, infirmity and old age. The hidden 'rent component' in parish pensions may also help to explain why pensions paid as out-relief were usually lower after a workhouse had been built than they had been hitherto. The average weekly sum paid to the outdoor 'settled poor' in St Martin's in 1749–51 was just under 15d., quite a bit less than the pension paid to pensioners in 1724.[27] Parishes would not, beyond a certain point, cover pauper accommodation costs outdoors when cheaper shelter could be provided in the local workhouse.[28]

The proportion of parish payments absorbed by accommodation costs must sometimes have been more substantial for many paupers than is estimated here, since rents naturally varied according to location, quality and type of accommodation.[29] Most paupers lodged at the expense of the parish in 1724/5 were single women with or without children occupying short-term lodgings. Such 'lodgings' must often have meant, in practice, sharing both a room and a bed. Married couples seeking to rent a whole room or even part of a house, might well have paid more than a shilling a week for even basic accommodation. Dorothy George thought that the 'standard rent of a London artisan before the great rise in prices after 1795 seems to have been 2s. 6d. a week'.[30] The question of the level of rents paid by the poor, however, obviously needs to be set against their earnings. Before that, however, we should consider what the poor were actually paying for.

1.4 Furnished or unfurnished?

Did the poor usually rent furnished or unfurnished rooms? Common sense would suggest that the poor occupying short-term lodgings, especially the single and unmarried, would mostly have not had much in the way of belongings, and certainly not items of furniture. Such lodgings would have been rented furnished. But what of married couples, or those able to accumulate a little furniture as even the poor were capable of doing? The St Martin's workhouse, as was common practice, stored the property of inmates during their often short stays, and occasionally sold property left by deceased inmates.[31]

The extent to which accommodation was rented furnished or unfurnished is not an easy subject to investigate, and what evidence there is tends, at least on the face of it, to be contradictory. Dorothy George cites evidence from 1772 supplied by the parish of St Botolph Aldersgate, to the effect that there were 555 houses in the parish let at under £10 a year 'chiefly in tenements'. Five hundred tenements in the parish were let 'ready-furnished'. George believed that 'a large proportion of the poorer classes in London lived in ready-furnished rooms, paying a weekly rent'. Although she did find the extent to which they occupied furnished rooms 'surprising', her impression was of 'a floating population living largely as weekly tenants in furnished rooms'.[32] This would certainly explain the frequency with which landlords prosecuted their tenants for theft of furnishings at the Old Bailey, about which a great deal more could be written.

Other sources, however, suggest that unfurnished rooms or apartments were more common. Relatively few paupers in St Martin's described the nature of their rented accommodation on examination. Of the 98 or so who did, however, only one described renting furnished accommodation. He recalled, in 1779,

> living in and renting an Apartment at the House of Mr Beavis near the Guard Room in Scotland Yard in the Parish aforesaid Vizt. two Garrets furnish'd and paid four shillings per week for the same.[33]

Most of the examined poor, however, stated that they currently, or had once, lived in unfurnished dwellings.[34]

Most unfurnished rooms were actually described as 'apartments' by the examined, and all are dated on or after 1775. These were probably often more substantial than the one room lodgings. It is possible that occupying an unfurnished apartment conveyed more respectability and sign of worth to those operating the law of settlement. It would be interesting to know about case law here. Moreover, occupation of many of these unfurnished 'apartments' was recalled as part of a retrospective narrative from the pauper in question seeking to establish his or her settlement. It was often a sign of past (slightly more) elevated social status, rather than current destitution.

Evidence from a survey of 'working class' inhabitants in Westminster in 1840 also suggests that unfurnished dwellings may have been commonplace:

> Lodgers of the working classes, in the two parishes visited, usually rented unfurnished rooms, and they afterwards provided themselves with beds, chairs, and other household furniture. A security for the

punctual payment of the rent was thus afforded to the landlords, in the value of the furniture purchased by the tenants.[35]

A survey taken of working-class families in the fashionable district of St George, Hanover Square, reported that the rents paid were much higher than those in the neighbouring Westminster districts and noted that '4s. 6d. and 5s. were the usual sums paid for an unfurnished room on the second or third floor'. In this Hanover Square district it was common to pawn part of the furniture during habitual unemployment in winter and to redeem it during the summer 'season'.[36] Losing one's property by distraint meant losing the ability to take unfurnished rooms. This, as we shall see, might have had financial consequences, since renting furnished rooms was more expensive.[37]

1.5 Rent as a proportion of total expenditure of the urban poor

Unfortunately, although it is not that difficult to find lists of rents paid by the poor in the early modern period, we have little information about their income. Where we do know something about the income of the poor, moreover, we do not usually know how much those same individuals paid in rent. What little evidence we do have suggests considerable variation, although most estimates lie between 10 and 13 per cent of total expenditure. Ingenious estimates of expenditure and income for poor London widows made by Ian Archer for the early 1580s and mid-1590s estimated that rent might have formed anywhere between 10 per cent and 28 per cent of their total expenditure. Archer properly noted, however, that the rents paid by the poor varied widely from rooms (possibly subsidised by the parish), rented from as low as 4s. to 8s. a year for single rooms to 20s. per year paid by inhabitants of alleys.[38] George calculated that rent took one-eighth of the income (12.5 per cent) of a London artisan, although she thought this might be an overestimate. She also reported the expenses of a journeyman tailor in 1752, which included lodgings at 1s. a week (exactly the same as what St Martin's was paying for pauper lodgings in the 1720s) out of a total weekly spending of 8s. 6d. (11.8 per cent).[39] Estimates derived from published budgets of working-class families suggest that the proportion of expenditure on rent was, nationally, 10 per cent in the late eighteenth century and 13 per cent in the mid-nineteenth century.[40]

More interesting here than the total proportion spent by the poor on rent, however, is the observable fact that rent paid for accommodation did *not* correlate positively with earnings. Housing was a basic necessity of life, like food. In economic terms, therefore, accommodation does not behave as a 'normal' good. Rent paid does not increase in proportion as income rises. Since accommodation is a fixed and unavoidable cost, there is a historical and frequently observed tendency for the *proportion* of income spent on rent to *increase* as earnings *decline*. Those with the lowest earnings thus tend to find that they have to part with a greater proportion of those earnings to pay their rent. In fact there is an observable *negative* correlation between rent paid and weekly earnings among the poor.[41] The best data on rent and income for the London poor is undoubtedly the statistical survey of 'poorer classes' in a district of the East End parish of St George-in-the-East reported to the Statistical Society of London in 1848. These data, which supply both average weekly earnings and average weekly rent paid by various categories of poor, demonstrate the relatively high cost of accommodation among the very poor. Richard Wall, the expert on this survey, has pointed out that the data show that 'widows spent a much greater proportion of their more meagre earnings on rent and economized both on food and clothing'. Widows with children spent no less than 31.1 per cent of their earnings on rent and widows and single women 'without incumbrances' spent 27.6 per cent, compared to married couples and widowers with children who spent only 15.4 per cent of their greater earnings on accommodation. Single men, whose earnings were relatively high, nonetheless spent just 8.5 per cent of their income on rent.[42] It should be noted that those taking the survey were favourably impressed by the degree of crowding and noted that

> this is a population entirely above the wretched system of sub-letting corners of the same room, which occasions such an accumulation of wretchedness, barbarism, and disease, in the few localities to which the rudest and most unsettled of the population resort.[43]

The percentage of average family earnings spent on rent by each occupational group given in the St George-in-the-East data is graphed in Figure 1.1.[44] There was actually a reasonable *negative* correlation[45] between average weekly income and the rent paid. As Richard Wall demonstrated, those at the bottom of the social heap paid proportionately more for their accommodation. This applied to not just single women and widows, but also to low-income occupations such as sailors. It should be noted here that the survey was of the 'poorer classes' so that better-off members of some occupational groups might well have

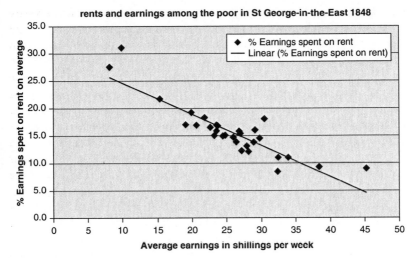

Figure 1.1 Relationship between rent and earnings among the poorer classes of St George in-the-East, 1848

been excluded. These average figures comprised, as the survey details, a much wider spread of values. It should also be noted that life-cycle effects of age and infirmity would have affected earning power and thus the relative burden of rent. Occupations with higher average earnings in the survey, notably engineers, gunsmiths and cigar makers did indeed devote the lowest proportions of their incomes to their accommodation. All in all, the survey demonstrates that the costs of accommodation fell disproportionately heavily on the budgets of the poor.[46]

That rent costs were disproportionately high for the poor is hardly surprising given their relatively low incomes. Rising costs of basic accommodation were part of a life cycle of deprivation that could lead, *in extremis*, to rent arrears, distraint and, in the end, destitution and homelessness.

1.6 The destitute parish poor

Those 'destitute of lodgings' or of 'no habitation' are not frequently encountered in settlement examinations – but neither are they rare. In St Martin's, approximately 767 out of a large sample of some 12,000 examinations, more than one in 20 examinations dated after 1724, were of paupers who claimed to be homeless in some way at the time of their examination, or who in a very few cases recalled earlier periods of homelessness. The original sample consists of paupers who were, at some time, thought to be workhouse inmates. It does not include just under 14,000 examined paupers whose legal settlement was elsewhere or who were never apparently resident in the workhouse. Nor does it include examinations made before the workhouse was erected in 1725. Destitution might have been more common than this sample suggests, since some homeless paupers might not have explicitly reported their homeless state in their examination. Only those explicitly referring to a period of destitution have been included in what follows. The 767 destitute paupers selected for analysis here, moreover, do not include paupers who were removed to St Martin's, or apprehended, under the vagrancy laws or who were confined overnight in the parish Watch house. Some of these latter individuals could as easily have been classed among the local destitute. In practice, there was a significant degree of overlap between those arrested as 'rogues and vagabonds' and parish poor examined under the settlement laws. As will be discussed below, destitute paupers had (mostly) been homeless for only a short time, and most had a demonstrable connection with the parish. Vagrant poor were more likely to be long-distance migrants.[47]

The percentage of examined paupers who reported destitution varied markedly over time. There were relatively few until the mid-1740s, after which, in some years as many as 15 per cent of all those examined reported prior destitution immediately before their testimony.[48] Very few examined paupers reported destitution after 1787, for reasons which are unclear. The proportion of destitute paupers among our sample of examinations seems to have been highest in the 1740s and 1750s. The early 1740s were a period of heightened concern about the level of vagrancy. Nonetheless it should be realised that this information *cannot* be taken as an index of destitution or homelessness in the parish. To begin with, it reflects the extent to which homelessness was mentioned explicitly in this sample of examinations. Moreover, the incidence of destitution must reflect the effectiveness and vigour of local policing and detection as much as the incidence of homelessness among the examined poor. This last is a truism that could apply to most data generated by early modern regulative activity. It might also be that some of the parish homeless might have been removed via the eighteenth-century vagrancy laws rather than dealt with under the law of settlement.[49] Fluctuations in numbers of the destitute might reflect changes in local regulative policy rather than reflect real changes in levels of homelessness and destitution.

Who were these destitute paupers, the 'down and outs' among the parish poor? As the quote at the start of this chapter suggests, becoming homeless was the natural result of the disproportionate burden of rent costs on the poor. The exact reasons for their current homelessness was rarely specified by examinants. Some of those who became destitute did so after the deaths or desertion of male breadwinners, although many widows clearly spent months and very often years providing for themselves before total destitution struck. A case from 1734 was that of

> Sarah Newlove aged thirty three years having sat up these two nights past in the Strand in this parish Saith she is the wife of James Newlove who hath been gone from her these ten years to whom she was marryed at Saint Bride's London seventeen years ago That he was bound an apprentice to Mr Edmund Purser in Harthsorn Lane in the parish of seven years and that she married to him in the month of August next after the expiration of his said Apprenticeship she this examinant knowing him whilst an apprentice and then living with her mother in Harthsorn Lane aforesaid And further Saith that since the Expiration of his apprenticeship he never kept house rented ten pounds by the year or was a yearly hired Servant and that She hath One Daughter now an Apprentice in the parish of St Giles in the Fields.[50]

We can add a little context to this case of destitution. Sarah had actually been examined before by the parish in July 1725, less than a year after her husband left her. At this time she was said to have been

> [l]odging with her Mother in Hartshorn Lane, Saith she is the Wife of James Newlove who hath been from her ever since October last [i.e. In October 1724] and where he now is or by what means to find him out knoweth not.[51]

Her desertion by her husband prompted parish support, one means by which she made ends meet after the desertion of her husband, in addition to living with her mother. Sarah's daughter was being maintained as a parish orphan between 1728 and 1733.[52] Sarah's destitution in 1734 prompted the first of four stays in the parish workhouse, where she died at the age of 39 in May 1740.[53] Other types of family breakdown could also cause homelessness and destitution. Stepchildren, of which there were many in the capital, might have been in an exceptionally precarious position.[54] Thus on 11 March 1748 the 16-year-old Mary Carroll told the examining officials that she was destitute of lodging having been 'turned out of doors this Day by her father-in-law George Heath who refuses to provide for her'. Ejecting Mary was presumably a desperate economic measure. Mary was the eldest of six surviving children by her late father. Mary's problems presumably dated from the remarriage of her mother to George, 'he was married to her present mother Abigail Heath at May Fair Chapel about a year and a half ago as she has heard her mother say'.[55] Mary was admitted to the workhouse for six weeks the day after this examination. Her stepfather would have known that the workhouse would provide her with at least temporary accommodation.[56] The availability of workhouse accommodation might therefore have enabled family heads, and employers, to eject dependents with a clearer conscience. Many paupers, often female domestic servants, found themselves on the streets following the deaths or departures of their employers.[57]

The gender balance, as measured by the sex ratio, of the destitute was very similar to that of the examined poor, with both populations showing a heavy surplus of women (the sex ratio was 29 men per 100 women for the destitute, 33 per 100 for all those in our sample of examinations).[58] Few young children became destitute, but homelessness became a significant risk for the examined poor once reaching teenage years. The percentage of paupers claiming destitution thereafter remained at roughly similar levels until old age. Elderly paupers (those claiming to be aged 60 and above) were less likely to report destitution and homelessness than other ages. Of 515 examined paupers claiming to be 70 or above, only 11 reported destitution. This may well reflect the greater level of parochial and familial support directed at the elderly, and a greater willingness to house them at parish expense.[59]

Most of the parish homeless described themselves formulaically as 'destitute of lodging' or in a few cases destitute. Occasionally they resorted to more informative or evocative descriptions. Some of the parish homeless had 'no habitation' or reported lodging, or lying, in the streets. Twenty-one of the examined had 'sat up' in the street for a night or two,[60] such as the pauper who 'saith she Sat up last night in Castle Street near the mewse' or the woman who 'sat up last night in St Martins Churchyard'.[61] The parish church of St Martin's seems to have been a place of resort for the homeless, as it is today.[62] Mary Lloyd, for example, a 40-year-old single woman reported that 'she lodged last in Shorts Gardens in the Parish of St Giles in the Feilds and that for these four nights last past she hath sat up in the Porch of this Parish Church' while Elizabeth Noble 'sat up last night under the Portico of the Church of this parish' in 1733.[63] Other paupers, such as the widow Mary Baldwin, had 'no habitation but has layn in the streets for these three Weeks last past and lay for 3 nights last past upon the steps of St Martin's Church'.[64] One presumes that such individuals were hoping to evoke the traditional Christian duty of charity by locating themselves in or near the church. This did not always work.[65] A handful of paupers exploited the existence of the empty dwellings in the parish, essentially becoming short-term squatters. Nine out of 11 of these cases dated between 1741 and 1745, a period of marked stagnation and depression in the London building trade.[66] Four paupers lodged in empty houses in Hartshorne Lane. Two paupers did not even enter the empty dwellings. One woman, 'lay last night at the door of an empty house in Drury Lane near Russell Street' and another 'laid last night on the steps of an empty house in St Martin's Lane'.[67] Only a few examined paupers specified finding shelter in Barns or Stables.[68]

The impression from the examinations is that few of the parish destitute spent long on the streets.[69] The time they spent homeless would have depended, at least to some extent, on the relative efficiency of local policing by ward beadles and constables, and the extent to which such homeless paupers travelled from parish to parish to avoid detection. In the minority of cases where any time was specified, it tended to be only 'last night' or a few nights. Only a handful of examined paupers admitted to more than a few weeks on the streets, such as Mary Baldwin discussed above, Sarah Pembrook, 'lodging last in a Barn at North End which she left three Weeks ago and hath lain about in the Streets of this Parish ever since'[70] or Elizabeth Hatley, a 32-year-old widow

> lodging last at Mrs Tench's in Castle Street by Dirty Lane where she lodged 2 nights and before that in Holborn where she lodged a Quarter of a year that she quitted her lodging in Dirty Lane about two months ago and hath lain in the streets all the time since.[71]

1.7   The poor paying no rent

Some, a small minority, of the poor lived rent free. Apart from those who absconded without paying rent or who lived on the streets, some paupers were given temporary shelter as an act of charity.[72] Another way to live rent free was to occupy property whose ownership was in dispute. This enabled 72 pauper families to live rent free in the low-rent district of Palmer's Village in St Margaret's Westminster in 1840.[73] Another group of paupers living rent free, and probably the most numerous, were those occupying almshouses. Many London parishes had a collection of almshouses, usually built up from charitable endowments, and run by the churchwardens and overseers.[74] St Martin-in-the-Fields maintained almshouses that housed anything between 55 and 80 aged females in the eighteenth century. The inmates received a respectable weekly pension, as well as free accommodation. Some, nonetheless, were not averse to letting out their rooms and living elsewhere, presumably to avoid the irksome restrictions of institutional life.[75] Another source of free accommodation was London's extra parochial endowed almshouses and 'hospitals'. It would require a separate chapter to discuss these institutions in full, but in the mid-eighteenth century, London had at least 98 endowed almshouses (excluding hospitals that delivered medical care), ranging from the mighty and highly atypical 'hospital' of Charterhouse which housed 80 men and 44 boys to humble institutions such as the almshouse in 'Tothill side, Westminster, consisting of two Rooms ... founded by Judith Kifford, Anno 1705, for the Reception of so many decayed Gentlewomen, who have an Allowance of five pounds per annum each'.[76] A count of the capacity of those listed in the second edition of Maitland's *History of London* suggests that these extra parochial institutions would have housed at least 1357 individuals – not that many in the context of a city of more than half-a-million people but significant to those most in need of accommodation, particularly since most accommodation came with a pension as well. Many were very small. More than a half of all London almshouses listed by Maitland contained ten or fewer residents. Many of these almshouses, moreover, and some of the parochial ones, seem, like Kifford's and Charterhouse, to have drawn their intake from the respectable poor and often from the gentry and middling sort down on their luck, rather than from the really destitute, and often highly disreputable, parish poor.[77]

1.8   Conclusion: Rent and the 'micro-economies' of the urban poor

What can be concluded from this preliminary survey? It is probable that many of the urban poor found rent a bigger financial burden than did their better-off neighbours. How they reacted to the need to pay for shelter must have varied considerably across the life cycle. What emerges from settlement examinations is the relatively wide residential experience that many poor people had. At the bottom of the heap were the destitute; the next up were those staying for short periods as temporary lodgers, probably sharing rooms and beds. The next step up the residential ladder would be to take a furnished room or rooms. Those able to accumulate furniture would be able to take relatively cheaper unfurnished rooms, and this may have been seen as preferable. Occasionally, pauper narratives suggest periods of relative prosperity in substantial rented properties. It would require a close and detailed analysis of settlement examinations to establish a typology of all the residential cycles that paupers claimed to have experienced. To establish the extent of social mobility among the poor remains, as yet, an unfulfilled objective.

For most of the paupers studied here, however, their examinations under the settlement laws are ultimately records of financial, residential and social decline if not unremitting hardship. Most of the poor in our sample, after all, were or became workhouse inmates. It is, in fact, a striking testimony to the precariousness of social position in the eighteenth century that some workhouse inmates must have had memories of occupying often quite substantial housing, far removed from the shared beds and segregated wards of the parish workhouse. Thus, to take one admittedly atypical example, Sarah Hatchett, the 47-year-old widow of a former overseer of the poor, examined in 1781

> in the workhouse of and in the Parish of St Martin in the Fields upon her oath saith that she is the Widow of George Hatchett deceased ... that her said husband was a Linnen Draper and lived in and Rented an House the Corner of St Martin's Court in Castle Street in the said Parish of St Martin in the Fields for the space of Sixteen or Seventeen years at the yearly Rent of Ninety Pounds besides taxes, and then Died which is about three years ago, that she this Examinant hath not kept House rented a tenement of ten Pounds by the year nor paid any Parish taxes since.

Sarah remained in the workhouse for the remainder of her life, dying there, aged 51, of 'consumption' in 1785.[78]

We need to know more about the extent of social mobility, as well as the impact of the life cycle, before we achieve a rounded picture of the accommodation experienced by the poor during their lives. This chapter suggests that other topics, too, would be worth further investigation. The nature and functional value of landlord–tenant relations would be one. The ways in which rent was collected, accumulated and transmitted would be another.

We need further research, too, on what might be termed the 'micro economies' of the poor. Thus, although the relatively high levels of intra urban mobility among the urban poor are now well established, the meaning of this movement is worth further consideration.[79] Since, even at this most humble level, rent could vary considerably depending on locality, number of rooms, furnished or unfurnished and so on, making residential moves could have a significant impact on the family economies of the urban poor. This is not normally something remarked on by contemporaries in our period, but we do at least have one case. Francis Place, in his autobiography, recording his early married life in the early 1790s, recalled the early lodgings that he and his young family occupied. These were usually one-room lodgings.[80] His wife was brought to bed of their first child in a large and 'commodious' room in Little Shire Lane. This room was, Place says later, rented for 4s. a week, at a time when he was fully employed and earning about 26s. a week – about 15 per cent of his total income. His subsequent move to cheaper, unfurnished, accommodation thus represented a significant weekly saving:

> I worked incessantly, and soon saved money enough to buy some good cloaths and a bedstead, a table three or four chairs and some bedding, with these and a few utensils we took an unfurnished back room up two pairs of stairs at a chandlers shop in Wych Street, and began to congratulate ourselves on the improvement of our circumstances and the prospect before us. We paid four shillings a week for the room we quitted and two shillings for that we removed to. This was a savings of some importance to us.[81]

This move halved Place's outgoings on rent. The ability to accumulate furniture and furnishings opened up the prospect of taking a cheaper unfurnished room, and thus decreasing one's weekly outgoings. Making frequent residential moves, at least for some poor families, was another survival strategy practised by the urban poor.[82]

Notes

The quotation is found in the following passage: 'thinking that quarter day was on Thursday I promised my landlord his money & as I now owe him two quarters Rent he has just now put an Execution in & will not be prevaild on to wait any longer & unless I can pay him on Friday I shall be turned into the street with My Children Destitude of every thing', Mary Godfry resident in St Pancras, Middlesex, London, writing to the overseer of the poor, Braintree, Essex, 25 September 1833, T. Sokoll (ed.), *Essex Pauper Letters, 1731–1837* (Oxford: Oxford University Press, 2001), pp. 145–6. The author would like to thank the ESRC and latterly the Wellcome Trust for funding the 'Pauper Biographies Project' since 2004, and Drs John Black, Peter Jones and Rhiannon Thompson who have all, at various times, worked tirelessly on the project. For the latest news on the Project, directed by Dr Leonard Schwarz and this author, see, http://research.ncl.ac.uk/pauperlives/. 27 August 2010.

1. For an introduction to what is now a large literature on this subject, see S. King and A. Tomkins (eds), *The Poor in England 1700–1850: An Economy*

of Makeshifts (Manchester: Manchester University Press, 2003). See also,
J. Boulton, '"It is Extreme Necessity that makes me do this": Some "Survival
Strategies" of Pauper Households in London's West End during the Early
Eighteenth Century', *International Review of Social History, Supplement* 8
(2000), 47–70. For living standards, see, L. D. Schwarz, *London in the Age of
Industrialisation: Entrepreneurs, Labour Force and Living Conditions, 1700–1850*
(Cambridge: Cambridge University Press, 1992), pp. 157–78; J. Boulton, 'Food
Prices and the Standard of Living in London in the "Century of Revolution",
1580–1700', *Economic History Review*, 2nd ser., 53:3 (2000), 455–92.
2. W. C. Baer, 'Housing the Poor and Mechanick Class in Seventeenth-Century
London', *London Journal* 25:2 (2000), 13–39; M. D. George, *London Life in the
Eighteenth Century* (Kegan Paul, 1976 edn), pp. 73–115. For some examples of
poor quality housing, see T. Hitchcock, *Down and Out in Eighteenth-Century
London* (Hambledon, 2004), pp. 29–32.
3. For recent work on London rents, see C. Spence, *London in the 1690s.
A Social Atlas* (Centre for Metropolitan History, Institute of Historical
Research, University of London, 2000), esp. pp. 66–75, 106–114; R. Finlay,
Population and Metropolis: The Demography of London 1580–1650 (Cambridge:
Cambridge University Press, 1981), pp. 70–82; R. M. Smuts, 'The Court and
Its Neighborhood: Royal Policy and Urban Growth in the Early Stuart West
End', *Journal of British Studies* 30:2 (1991), 117–49; Schwarz, *London in the
Age of Industrialisation*, pp. 52, 175–7. William C. Baer is currently doing
fascinating work on the 1638 London Tithe Survey which will include impor-
tant data on the relationship between rents and incomes. Peter Earle has
made a useful brief survey of the range of rents paid by Londoners: P. Earle,
A City Full of People: Men and Women of London, 1650–1750 (Methuen, 1994),
pp. 168–71.
4. C. Muldrew, *The Economy of Obligation: The Culture and Credit and Social
Relations in Early Modern England* (Basingstoke: Macmillan, 1998), p. 107.
5. Rental income from property in London fell dramatically during the English
Civil War, as a result of the decay of trade and population contraction,
B. Coates, *The Impact of the English Civil War on the Economy of London,
1642–50* (Aldershot: Ashgate, 2004), pp. 224–5. Proclamations banning gentry residence in London, enforced sporadically between 1596 and 1640, also
affected the fashionable property market, J. F. Merritt, *The Social World of Early
Modern Westminster: Abbey, Court and Community, 1525–1640* (Manchester:
Manchester University Press, 2005), pp. 152–3.
6. Boswell's landlord reduced his rent in order to retain Boswell as a lodger in
1762. Boswell lodged in comfortable furnished lodgings in Downing Street.
His landlord 'was in such circumstances that he was not obliged to let lodgings
for bread', F. A. Pottle (ed.), *Boswell's London Journal 1762–1763* (Heinemann,
1950), pp. 58–9. Boswell fell out with his landlord and left Downing Street in
1763.
7. OBP (www.oldbaileyonline.org, 28 November 2008), 17 April 1765, trial of
Elizabeth Jones (t17650417-33). Jones was acquitted, since doubt was cast on
both the girl's testimony and that of her mother. For theft of a substantial
amount of rent money, kept in a leather bag in a (unlocked) box in a drawer
in 1848, see *OBP*, 27 November 1848, trial of Sarah Huxford, Henry Goodson
(t18481127-13).

8. J. Boulton, 'The Parish Nurse in Early Modern London', *Family and Community History* 10:2 (2007), 127–52.
9. WAC, F4002/2; F462/347, 348, 353, 356, 357, 359, 360; F459A/398, 392, 384, 377.
10. WAC, F459A/259, 265. Elizabeth Dewberry entered the workhouse in the late 1730s, dying there in 1741 at the age of 49, WAC, F4073.
11. Warburton was chosen as Steward on 7th January 1734/35, WAC, F2006/426. He was suspended in 21/2/1740, and his dismissal was confirmed on 7 April 1740, F2007/2v, 4v. Payments to cover Warburton's lodgings and periods of sickness can be found in the overseer's accounts up to 1751. See, for example, F511/193; F519/347; F526; F529/82, 26th August 1751 'To Warburton while he lay sick 3s'.
12. WAC, F459A/419, 385. For such services see P. Earle, *The Making of the English Middle Class: Business, Society and Family Life in London, 1660–1730* (Methuen, 1989), p. 173; I. K. Ben-Amos, 'Gifts and Favors: Informal Support in Early Modern England', *Journal of Modern History* 72:2 (2000), 312–3; P. Clark, 'Migrants in the City: The Process of Social Adaptation in English Towns 1500–1800', in P. Clark & D. Souden (eds), *Migration and Society in Early Modern England* (Hutchinson, 1987), p. 284.
13. WAC, F462/160, 167.
14. WAC, F462/242, 264, 265 292.
15. *OBP*, 11 July 1694, trial of William Hoyle (t16940711-24).
16. For a brief summary of the nineteenth-century law covering distraint, see D. Englander, *Landlord and Tenant in Urban Britain 1838–1918* (Oxford: Clarendon, 1983), pp. 22–7. Peter King notes the inventories of goods taken by landlords to cover arrears of rent in eighteenth- and early nineteenth-century Essex, which sometimes included a 'legal statement from the landlord that "if you do not pay the ... arrears or replevy the said goods and chattels within five days ... I shall cause the said goods and chattels to be appraised and sold"', P. King, 'Pauper Inventories and the Material Lives of the Poor in the Eighteenth and Early Nineteenth Centuries', in T. Hitchcock, P. King & P. Sharpe (eds), *Chronicling Poverty: The Voices and Strategies of the English Poor, 1640–1840* (Basingstoke: Macmillan, 1997), p. 158. For a contemporary account of the law covering accommodation, see the comprehensively titled R. Sutton, *A Complete Guide to Landlords, Tenants, and Lodgers; Being a Methodical Arrangement of the Whole Law as it now Stands, Respecting the Taking or Letting Lands, Houses, or Apartments* [1800]. Sutton's work went into many later editions. The law of distraint as it stood in 1799 is given on pp. 53–73.
17. WAC, F462/175, 208, 236.
18. For the law covering debt 'a system of legalized bullying', see, J. Innes, 'The King's Bench Prison in the Later Eighteenth Century: Law, Authority and Order in a London Debtors' Prison', in J. Brewer & J. Styles (eds), *An Ungovernable People: The English and their Law in the Seventeenth and Eighteenth Centuries* (New Brunswick: Rutgers University Press, 1983 edn), pp. 250–98, especially pp. 251–61.
19. OBP, 11 September 1717, trial of Thomas Panting (t17170911-5).
20. Muldrew, *The Economy of Obligation*, p. 107.
21. For her workhouse admissions, see WAC, F4074; F4005/83, 113, 239, 287; F4007/251, 259, 485. For her settlement examination, see F5035/405.

Elizabeth was buried as a workhouse pauper at parish expense on 14 February 1771.

22. See the examination of Margaret Wright, who left her house on St Martin's Lane following the landlord distraining her goods for rent, WAC, F5022/291. For another case, see F5033/84.

23. WAC, F5026/49.

24. George, *London Life*, p. 100.

25. F. Place, *The Autobiography of Francis Place (1771–1854)*, ed. by M. Thale (Cambridge: Cambridge University Press, 1972), pp. 79–80.

26. Ian Archer's pauper budgets similarly suggest that rent would have absorbed a huge proportion of a standard parish pension in the late sixteenth century. Rent costs were estimated at 10s. or 20s. a year, between 39 per cent and 77 per cent of a standard pension of 26s. a year, I. W. Archer, *The Pursuit of Stability: Social Relations in Elizabethan London* (Cambridge: Cambridge University Press, 1991), p. 194.

27. See the lists of pensioners and settled poor listed in WAC, F459A/209-231; F2223/1-35; F526/1-71; F529/20-133. No pensions were paid at all for a decade or so after the workhouse opened, and far fewer parishioners received them. See Hitchcock, *Down and Out*, p. 138.

28. For the 'capping' of parish pensions in this way, see Chapter 9 in this volume by Boulton and Schwarz.

29. Earle, *A City Full of People*, p. 169.

30. George, *London Life*, p. 100.

31. King points out that many paupers disposed of much of their property before entering a workhouse, so that such sales do not necessarily reflect the property that paupers had before their admission, see King, 'Pauper Inventories', pp. 155–91, and especially p. 158. The parish of St Martin's had been appropriating the goods of the poor since the mid-seventeenth century, see J. Boulton, 'Going on the Parish: The Parish Pension and its Meaning in the London Suburbs, 1640–1724', in Hitchcock, King & Sharpe (eds), *Chronicling Poverty*, pp. 35–6. The rules of the neighbouring parish workhouse of St Giles, included a regulation that 'the Nurses, at the Death of any Person in their respective Wards, shall deliver up to the Matron, all the Cloaths, Money and Goods belonging to such Person', *Regulations which were Agreed upon and Established The Twelfth Day of July 1726, by the Gentlemen of the Vestry then Present, for the better Government and Management of the Work-House Belonging to the parish of St Giles's in the Fields, Humbly offered to the Consideration of the House of Commons of Ireland* (Dublin: A. Rhames, 1727), p. 10.

32. George, *London Life*, pp. 100–2.

33. WAC, F5066/165.

34. See for example, WAC, F5065/114.

35. 'Report of a Committee of the Statistical Society of London, on the State of the Working Classes in the parishes of St. Margaret Westminster and St John Westminster', *Journal of the Statistical Society of London* 3:1 (April 1840), 14. Legal opinion agreed that 'a distress for the rent, in all probability, will recover the possession, as well as the rent' in the case of apartments let unfurnished, Sutton, *A Complete Guide to Landlords, Tenants and Lodgers*, p. 21.

36. C. R. Weld, 'On the Condition of the Working Classes in the Inner Ward of St. George's Parish, Hanover Square', *Journal of the Statistical Society of London* 6:1 (1843), 17–18.
37. Unfurnished accommodation 'was obviously much cheaper', Earle, *A City Full of People*, p. 169. He cites the case of a bookkeeper whose rent for a furnished room was halved when he decided to furnish the room himself. Of course, the quality of furnishings might vary greatly. 'Well' furnished rooms were found to be in the minority in St George-in-the-East, 'Report of an Investigation into the State of the Poorer Classes in St Georges in the East', *Quarterly Journal of the Statistical Society of London*, August 1848, p. 210 reprinted in R. Wall (ed), *Slum Conditions in London and Dublin* (Farnborough: Gregg International Publishers,1974), pp. 213–15.
38. Archer, *The Pursuit of Stability*, pp. 192–4. Archer's budgets use rents of between 10s. and 20s. per year for working and non-working widows, with and without dependants.
39. George, *London Life*, pp. 104, 170.
40. C. H. Feinstein, 'Pessimism Perpetuated: Real Wages and the Standard of Living in Britain during and after the Industrial Revolution', *The Journal of Economic History* 58:3 (1998), 634–5.
41. This same phenomenon has long been observed for expenditure on basic foodstuffs and has its own 'law', 'Engels Law'. Engel's Law states that as incomes increase, the proportion spent on food falls. The lower a family's income, the greater the proportion of it spent on food. It was devised by the statistician Ernst Engel (1821–96), see http://faculty.washington.edu/krumme/resources/engel.html. 27 August 2010.
42. See the important and wide-ranging article by Richard Wall, which contains some analysis of this survey, 'Some Implications of the Earnings, Income and Expenditure Patterns of Married Women in Populations in the Past', in J. Henderson & R. Wall (eds), *Poor Women and Children in the European Past* (Routledge, 1994), pp. 313–14.
43. 'Report of an Investigation into the State of the Poorer Classes in St George's in the East', *Quarterly Journal of the Statistical Society of London* (August 1848), 210, reprinted in R. Wall (ed.), *Slum Conditions in London and Dublin* (Farnborough: Gregg International, 1974).
44. Data from 'The State of the Poorer Classes of St George's in the East', Table VII, pp. 208–9, reprinted in Wall, *Slum Conditions*.
45. The correlation coefficient is -0.88337.
46. Data on working-class households in four early twentieth-century towns demonstrates equally clearly that those on the lowest incomes devoted proportionally far more of their earnings to the payment of rent, see, A. L. Bowley and A. R. Burnett-Hurst, *Livelihood and Poverty: A Study in the Economic Conditions of Working-Class Households in Northampton, Warrington, Stanley and Reading* (Routledge, 1915), pp. 23–4.
47. Over 300 paupers were passed to the parish under the vagrancy laws. According to their examinations, 76 or so were apprehended as 'rogues and vagabonds' under the vagrancy statutes. The best article on London vagrancy in this period is the classic piece by Nicholas Rogers: see his wide ranging, 'Policing the Poor in Eighteenth-Century London: the Vagrancy Laws and Their Administration', *Histoire Sociale* XXIV 47 (1991), 127–47.

Rogers notes that there was 'relatively little difference' between examined paupers and those classed (and punished) as vagrants 'save that the majority of the vagrants were drawn from outside the metropolitan area', p. 138. For a recent splendid treatment of the 'down and outs' of London, see Hitchcock, *Down and Out* and also Chapter 5 in this volume.

48. Readers should note that relatively few examinations in the sample date from the 1730s, as a consequence of the sampling technique adopted. Only examinations of paupers found in the workhouse have been collected and, unfortunately, there is a gap in the workhouse admission register in the 1730s.

49. For the vagrancy statutes of 1713, 1740 and 1744, see Rogers, 'Policing the Poor', p. 131 and P. Slack, *The English Poor Law 1531–1782* (Basingstoke: Macmillan, 1990), pp. 39, 63. Slack identifies 'a temporary panic about the disorders of the poor in the early 1740s' (p. 39). Hitchcock reports a crackdown on beggars by London's Lord Mayor between 1738 and 1742, Hitchcock, *Down and Out*, p. 6. Efforts to enforce vagrancy laws locally are recorded in 1729 and 1738, WAC, F2006/322, 481, 483. The St Martin's vestry minutes also mention a campaign to rid the streets of beggars and vagrants in February 1740, following a request from the Speaker of the House of Commons, WAC, F2007/2r. There were also sporadic efforts to clear beggars out of 'the passage leading from Spring Gardens into St James's Park' in 1731, 1742 and 1777, *ibid.*, F2007/10v, 587.

50. WAC, F5027/97. The IGI confirms that the marriage of James Newlove and Sarah Barker did indeed take place on 4 August 1717 at St Brides, Fleet Street.

51. WAC, F5018/ 493.

52. WAC, F468/140, F472/128, F476/159, F478/199, F482/171, F485/172c, orphan pension for Sarah Newlove. Sarah, the daughter, was in the workhouse in 1736, when she was examined herself, see, F5028/247.

53. WAC, F4003/8; F4073. The workhouse registers record these latter two stays as her third and fourth. There is a gap in the workhouse admission register in the 1730s.

54. For the 'precarious' London family see in particular, V. Brodsky, 'Widows in late Elizabethan London: Remarriage, Economic Opportunity and Family Orientations', in L. Bonfield, R. M. Smith & K. Wrightson (eds), *The World We Have Gained: Histories of Population and Social Structure. Essays presented to Peter Laslett on his Seventieth Birthday* (Oxford: Blackwell, 1986), pp. 134–40.

55. An IGI record confirms that George Heath married one AIGAIL [*sic*] CARROLL at Saint George Mayfair, Westminster on 28 June 1746. The examination places Abigail's first marriage in the Fleet. The IGI also shows that a Miles Carrell married Abigail Bell in the Fleet on 21 June 1730. For Mary's examination see WAC, F5039/9.

56. WAC, F4005/265.

57. For the length of tenure of domestic servants, see T. Meldrum, *Domestic Service and Gender 1660–1750: Life and Work in the London Household* (Harlow: Longman, 2000), pp. 23–5; Earle, *A City Full of People*, pp. 128–9. For an example of the abandonment of a pregnant servant girl, see WAC, F5061/178 and her admission to the workhouse, F4077/148.

58. Hitchcock notes, similarly, that 'It is certain that most of London's beggars were women', even though their male counterparts had a higher literary profile, Hitchcock, *Down and Out*, pp. 4–5.
59. For treatment of the elderly in St Martin's, see Chapter 9 in this volume by Boulton and Schwarz.
60. Very occasionally this 'sitting up' occurred in what seem to have been rooms or cellars used as basic shelters. For 'sleeping rough' in eighteenth-century London, readers should consult Hitchcock, *Down and Out*, pp. 23–48.
61. WAC, F5022/199; F5029/300. For another case of sitting up in the church-yard, see F5026/318.
62. http://www.connection-at-stmartins.org.uk/about-us/history.asp. 27 August 2010.
63. WAC, F5026/16, 341.
64. WAC, F5035/124. For other cases of paupers lying on the steps of the church see, F5036/216, F5037/187, F5060/438, F5067/219.
65. For two females arrested as vagrants 'on the steps at the Parish Church of St Martin in the Fields' in 1742, see WAC, F5034/325, 327.
66. Schwarz, *London in the Age of Industrialisation*, pp. 79–84.
67. WAC, F5035/61; F5036/342. Empty dwellings were relatively common in the capital, for a definitive discussion, see Spence, *London in the 1690s*, pp. 57–60.
68. For four cases see, for example, WAC, F5019/109; F5020/184; F5029/137; F5033/289.
69. This is at variance with many of those appearing in Tim Hitchcock's *Down and Out*, many of whom seem to have spent long periods of time sleeping rough. This was probably because Hitchcock's down and outs were often long term, even 'professional' rogues and vagabonds, some of whom begged for a living.
70. WAC, F5027/217.
71. WAC, F5031/312.
72. For the example of Jane Austin, a failed applicant to the St Martin's work-house in 1765, see Hitchcock, *Down and Out*, p. 29.
73. 'State of the Working Classes in the parishes of St. Margaret Westminster and St John Westminster', pp. 16–17, 21.
74. For a poor Westminster sailor's wife, living in a 'parish house' 'shee troubling the parish for nothing more than her rent', see Earle, *A City Full of People*, p. 170.
75. For this, see Chapter 9 in this volume. Almsmen in Westminster are known to have let out their apartments in 1779: see WAMR, 66002. I owe this reference to the kindness of Tim Hitchcock.
76. W. Maitland, *The History of London from its Foundation by the Romans, to the Present Time*, 2nd edn (1756), II, Book VI, pp. 1291–2, 1311. I have excluded here the atypical French Hospital (1717), which contained 220 inmates, some of whom were privately supported (p. 1303). I only included those resident in Charterhouse. For some background to the latter, see S. Porter, 'Order and Disorder in the Early Modern Almshouse: The Charterhouse Example', *London Journal* 23 (1998), 1–14.
77. Maitland, *History of London*, II, pp. 764–1325. For an excellent recent study of almshouse accommodation, see, A. Tomkins, 'Almshouse versus Workhouse: Residential Welfare in 18th-century Oxford', *Family & Community History* 7:1 (2004), 45–58.

78. Her examination is at WAC, F5067/161. For her workhouse admission and discharge, see, F4078/500. Sarah clearly retained some vestiges of her previously relatively elevated social position. Although 'discharged' at her death on 03/02/1785, Sarah, widow of a former overseer, was described in the Sexton's Books as 'of Charing Cross' at her burial rather than being recorded as buried from the workhouse. Unlike most workhouse inmates who were buried at parish expense, Sarah's burial fee was a substantial £2 1s. 4d. WAC, 239, Sexton's Notebook, 8 February 1785. George Augustus Hatchett died in office in 1778, see the 1778 Overseer's account, F573. For the even more spectacular fall of one Elizabeth Dodd, see WAC, F5068/289. For her workhouse career, see F4079/87, 96.
79. For the residential mobility of early modern Londoners, see Finlay, *Population and Metropolis*, pp. 43–7; J. Boulton, *Neighbourhood and Society: A London Suburb in the Seventeenth Century* (Cambridge: Cambridge University Press, 1987), pp. 206–7; R. B. Shoemaker, 'Gendered Spaces: Patterns of Mobility and Perceptions of London's Geography, 1660–1750', in J. F. Merritt (ed.), *Imagining Early Modern London: Perceptions and Portrayals of the City from Stow to Strype, 1598–1720* (Cambridge: Cambridge University Press, 2001), pp. 144–65.
80. Many poor people lived only in one 'room', but it was, of course, entirely possible to erect rudimentary room dividers, for an example of this ('an Iron rod close to the cieling, on which ran a couple of curtains'), see Thale (ed.), *Autobiography of Francis Place*, p. 124.
81. *Ibid.*, p. 111.
82. For an illuminating recent study, see J. Kok, K. Mandemakers and H. Wals, 'City Nomads: Changing Residence as a Coping Strategy, Amsterdam, 1890–1940', *Social Science History* 29:1 (2005), 15–43.

2
The Lodging Exchange: Space, Authority and Knowledge in Eighteenth-Century London

Joanne McEwan

A large proportion of London's eighteenth-century populace lived in lodgings of some description, ranging from cramped spaces shared with strangers to spacious 'rooms' within someone else's house. The prevalence of lodging in the metropolis has been widely acknowledged by historians, but specific studies of such arrangements remain limited. Further discussion is important, not only to inform our understanding of lodging as a particular residential arrangement but also to advance historical knowledge about urban living and household compositions more broadly. Among the wealthier ranks of Londoners, reasons for lodging might include factors such as companionship, networking or convenience.[1] For the remaining two thirds of the population – the working and labouring poor – motives can be attributed more readily to financial necessity and spatial restriction. As Jeremy Boulton has suggested,[2] we know that monetary concerns influenced the residential situations of poor eighteenth-century Londoners from contemporary statements such as the oft-quoted passage from Francis Place's autobiography:

> We paid four shillings a week for the room we quitted and two shillings for that we removed to. This was a saving of some importance to us.[3]

Much less is known about the spatial aspects of lodging arrangements.

This chapter examines negotiations and expectations regarding space, authority and knowledge in households containing lodgers. Using a methodology similar to that adopted by Naomi Tadmor in her analysis of the 'household-family',[4] it utilises legal narratives in which eighteenth-century people identified themselves or others as specific members of a household. These sources, especially depositions and courtroom testimony, were often generated at points of conflict or tension. The descriptive details they contain offer a particularly valuable, although admittedly partial, insight into domestic social dynamics. A better understanding of the interactions that took place within the household space promises to contribute towards answering the questions Susan Wright posed over a decade ago regarding the relationships between lodgers and householders.[5]

Many of the problems historians encounter when studying lodgers stem from their obscurity in historical records. They are, for example, often difficult to identify with certainty in demographic sources, where identification of individuals *as lodgers* relied upon subjective interpretations by others, both past and present, of the space and status they occupied within a household. When taxation lists were compiled, the labelling of certain people as lodgers was dependent upon the attitude and vigilance of both the enumerators and the household heads they questioned to acknowledge their presence within the house, and also to describe them as subsidiary members of the primary household rather than as a separate one. A similar discrepancy arises concerning the physical partitioning of buildings.[6] If the parish official responsible for recording a return viewed lodgers as a separate, discrete household unit (as opposed to lodgers attached to the primary household), the fact that they occupied the same dwelling would be obscured in the record. The frequent subdivision and partitioning of physical buildings in eighteenth-century London might also have contributed to this confusion by making boundaries ambiguous and difficult to pinpoint.[7] This was perhaps especially likely when lodgers had a separate door to the street.

The identification of lodgers in historical records is further complicated by their somewhat transient nature as a demographic unit. While some of the population remained lodgers (if not always in the same lodgings) for long periods of time, others took on the status of lodger intermittently. Servants who were out of place temporarily became lodgers until they could find another place of employment.[8] This was also common when they fell ill. Elizabeth Cotton, for example, quit her place as a servant to Diana Dormer because she had smallpox and could not work. She told the church courts that she lodged with Mrs Wells in Piccadilly for approximately 17 weeks, then with Mrs Holt, a widow in Piccadilly, until she was well and found another place.[9] The indeterminacy of lodgers as a succinct group is also heightened by the use of variable terminology. Labels such as 'boarder', 'lodger', 'sojourner' and 'inmate' were often used interchangeably, making the perceived contemporary difference between them difficult to grasp. In other situations, specialised terms were replaced with more general ones when circumstances changed. Elizabeth Melvin acted as a character witness for her lodger, Thomas Andrews, when he was charged with burglary in 1732.[10] Andrews had been quartered at her house, she explained, and had behaved so well that when his 'quarters were out' she had allowed him to stay on as her lodger. Andrews' new status reflects greater choice and control on Melvin's part, in that she now chose to house him and could stipulate terms, but it is unclear whether any practical changes in Thomas Andrews' living conditions had occurred.

2.1   The practicalities of lodging

Some historians have suggested that lodging was a life-cycle stage situated between leaving the parental household and forming one's own marital household.[11] What is noticeable in London, however, is the large number of people who did not move on and attain the status of householder. Rather, a proportion of the poor population seem to have lived in lodgings, both as singletons and with their families, for most of their adult lives. Although many of the individuals examined by justices of the peace as to their legal settlement in this period referred only to whether they had rented a house of £10 or more (upon which condition settlement could be obtained), the inclusion of essentially irrelevant details about houses of lesser rent in some cases perhaps suggests, as Peter Earle has argued, that the distinction in status between householder and lodger was important to contemporaries, and that declaring one had possessed such a status was common in depositions as a source of pride.[12] By extension, this might increase the likelihood that people who did not mention being a householder at some point had never been one. In other cases, perpetual lodging is described more explicitly. Rachel Miles, for example, told the St Clement Danes justices in 1736/7 that since his apprenticeship, she and her late husband had only ever lived in furnished lodgings.[13]

The plethora of lodging options available in London ranged from temporary respite at an inn or the house of friends, to paying for accommodation in a common lodging house, to renting space in a private house. Specialised lodgings were also common in areas that were densely populated with specific occupational groups, such as those provided specifically for sailors by the many women Peter Earle has documented in London's East End in the early eighteenth century.[14] However, these lodging options all generally required a steady, if meagre, income or a patient and charitable landlord. As Tim Hitchcock has noted, the vast expanse of the city also incorporated a large number of stables, barns, outhouses, bog-houses and kitchens that provided free or low-rent shelter for the needy.[15] In especially dire circumstances, doorways and the overhanging shop counters could provide some semblance of protection, but the harsh London weather and threat of being 'taken up' by the authorities meant that those who could sought out enclosed spaces.

A number of common lodging houses in London sought to make money by providing cheap temporary lodging without any concessions to space, or even the sole occupancy of a bed. The cost of lodgings was dependent upon their location. Especially in the more unsavoury parts of the metropolis – places such as St Giles, Black Boy Alley, Chick Lane, Rosemary Lane and Rag Fair – lodging houses of dubious reputation offered respite for two or three pence a night. This was half to a third of the price that would generally be paid for lodgings in a respectable alehouse.[16] The number of these 'low' lodging houses increased between 1730 and 1760 as a result of economic stagnation,[17] and their proliferation aroused concern among justices, who associated them with prostitution, intoxication, the fencing of stolen goods and the harbouring of organised gangs.[18] Saunders Welch, a Middlesex justice of the peace, lamented:

> I assisted My Henry Fielding in taking from under one roof upwards of seventy lodgers of both sexes. Suppose the number of these houses to be only two hundred; and compute only twenty persons to a house, the number is 4000; and, much I fear, not one fourth could obtain a just character of honesty and industry: the rest consisting of rotten whores, pickpockets, pilferers, and others of more desperate denominations.[19]

Irrespective of whether Welch exaggerated to suit his reformist agenda or not, two contemporary assumptions about lodging houses are evident in his quote. The first is that they were crowded and occupied by a large number of people at any one time; the second that authorities clearly feared the close and stifling atmosphere of living conditions within them, and assumed that it bred crime and immorality.

For those who could afford to avoid lodging houses, renting space in a private house was a more respectable option. The heavy demand for living space, caused by steady population increase that was not met by a similar increase in housing stock, meant that the taking in of lodgers was a widespread practice.[20] Generally, the number of lodgers per house was inversely proportional to the wealth of the householder, making them more numerous among poorer households.[21] There were at least ten people living in Ann Nash's house in James Street, St George Hanover Square, when it caught fire on 16 April 1764. Nine of the inhabitants were lodgers, occupying four rooms between them. The six people who lodged on the second floor, and who died in the fire, included a mother and her two children who lived in one room, and a couple with their daughter in the other.[22] This supports the findings of other historians, who have concluded that among the poor entire families frequently occupied a single room, resulting in large numbers of inhabitants per dwelling.[23]

Within private houses, first floor – or 'one pair of stairs' – front rooms were the most favourable, and most costly, lodging quarters within a house. They were followed by first floor back rooms, second floor front and back rooms respectively and then ground floor rooms if they contained sleeping quarters.[24] Garrets, or attic rooms, when not occupied by servants or apprentices, were also let out as mean lodgings. So too were cellar apartments, which had become frequent places of habitation despite their unfavourable conditions – including low light, dampness and cramped space – because of restrictions placed on new building during the seventeenth century.[25] The predilection for first floor rooms is also perhaps explained in part by the Building Acts that governed post-fire building within the City. According to the stipulations set out for new building, first floor rooms were to have higher ceilings than other floors.[26] This would have allowed more light and more air to circulate, making them seem roomier. They were also slightly removed from the unpleasant stench of privies that plagued ground floor rooms, but closer to the ground than the higher rooms in case of fire or collapse.

Lodging served as a beneficial arrangement for both sides of the lodging exchange. For householders, taking in lodgers contributed to the household economy and functioned as an expedient in the 'economy of makeshifts'.[27] Women, especially widows, were particularly likely to take in lodgers for this reason. The rent they received supplemented (or in some cases solely provided) the income of the householders, and in return they shared their living space with others. The poorer someone was, the more space they were willing to sacrifice. Jane Sharp, for example, told the Old Bailey in 1761 that she had shared a bed with her lodger Sarah Pettit.[28] For lodgers, the ability to rent rooms 'ready furnished' negated their need to purchase expensive household items, such as bedding. Lodgers were also exempt from assessed taxes based on the income of household heads, or on the physical features of houses, such as window or hearth taxes. Moreover, lodging offered flexibility in what was already a very fluid and mobile city. As Jeremy Boulton has suggested, moving to cheaper accommodation when circumstances changed was a common strategy employed by the eighteenth-century poor, and could facilitate considerable savings in rent.[29] Not being tied to a particular house allowed people to downgrade or move to cheaper or smaller lodgings relatively easily as children and spouses left, or worse, died.

2.2   Negotiating lodging terms

Despite the prevalence of lodging in eighteenth-century London, there were few legal regulations governing the negotiation of lodging agreements. Clerks' manuals contained templates of contracts that could be drawn up between landlords and lodgers, which typically stipulated the number of rooms to be let, the furniture or goods contained within them, the commencement date and term of the lease and the value of the rent to be paid. More specifically, an agreement cited in *The Young Clerk's Magazine* for 1739 also instructed that upon cessation of the agreement or a default in payment, the room and its goods were to be 'peacefully relinquished' to the landlord 'in good and sufficient plight and condition'.[30] While contracts such as these could function to clearly outline the agreed terms and itemise any items belonging to the landlord included in the arrangement, there is little evidence to suggest that they were routinely drawn up among the poor and working classes. Rather, many lodging arrangements came about through word of mouth, charity or ad-hoc negotiation. The frequent movement of Londoners between lodgings suggests that they were not tied to their previous residences by legally binding contracts. Additionally, many of the incidental details that emerge about lodging arrangements in sources such as court testimony imply that short-term lodging was common. In cases where landlords experienced a high turnover of short-term lodgers, it is unlikely that they outlaid either the time or the expense of drawing up a legal contract for each fleeting tenant.

Lodging agreements, where they can be identified, rarely made concessions for the protection of the lodger. As Jennifer Melville has suggested, lodgers often had no more legal recourse than servants if they were turned out of doors, because (unlike apprentices) they had no statutory premise from which to argue about what they were owed.[31] In fact, apart from the passage of an Act that made theft from ready-furnished lodgings a felony,[32] there were no statutory regulations specifically governing the relationship between private lodgers and landlords until an 'Act to Amend the Law Relating to the Public Health' established minimum sanitary requirements for lodgings in 1866.[33] The individualised case-by-case nature of lodging agreements, as John Paul explained in an eighteenth-century manual about tenant-landlord agreements, actually precluded them from the specific conditions outlined in more general legislation regarding leases:

> The case of *lodgings* depends on the *particular contract* upon which they are taken, and is an exception to the general rule.[34]

This placed both lodgers and landlords in a precarious position when conflicts arose. Lodgers were vulnerable to eviction and occasionally seem to have endured uninhabitable living conditions without any assurance that their landlord would rectify the situation. John Eliott told the Old Bailey in 1761 that he had rented two rooms in Mrs Adams house, but that the back room was so infested with bugs that he was unable to use it.[35] Lodgers also complained of thefts from their lodgings by other members of the household. This was a particularly tenuous situation given the 'Distress for Rent' Act that was passed in 1737.[36] According to this statute, a tenant's goods could be seized and held for arrears in rent. It also gave permission for houses, rooms or any locks securing the goods to be broken open in order to seize them. While the Act did outline specific preconditions for its use, it is plausible that in the absence of written contracts or well-informed legal knowledge, contestations over goods could boil down to allegations of theft versus the perceived lawful seizure of goods for rent. On the other hand, housekeepers were also faced with the reciprocal threat of desertion and theft.

From descriptions of their lodging rooms by eighteenth-century Londoners, it is clear that many rooms were let as ready-furnished lodgings. In 1794, magistrate Patrick Colquhoun observed that it was customary for the poor to live 'in a miserable half-furnished lodging from week to week'; suggesting that even the meanest of lodgings contained some basic furnishings.[37] The extent and value of these furnishings tended to be proportional to the rent being charged for the room.[38] This presumably fostered an understanding and a certain level of expectation among eighteenth-century lodgers as to how particular rooms would be furnished and what amenities they would provide.

2.3   Authority and knowledge

On 17 September 1735, a boy arrived at a house in St Paul Covent Garden carrying a coffin. The householder's wife, Sarah Edwards, told him that he had the wrong house, for there was no dead body in hers. After further discussion, it appeared that Margaret Hambleton, Edwards' lodger, had ordered the coffin for 'a maid who was out of place and had died suddenly'. Still sceptical, Sarah Edwards forced open the door to Hambleton's room, and discovered the body of a young woman lying on the floor.[39] This case highlights a number of critical issues *vis-à-vis* the expectations of authority and knowledge between lodgers and householders. Upon breaking open the door and finding a dead body in her lodger's room, Sarah Edwards gathered her neighbours, who then notified the parish. She also sent for her husband who was on duty as a Guard at St James'. That Edwards perceived the situation pressing enough to summon her husband from work suggests that, although she did not have unrestricted access to the room in which the body had been discovered (she had forced the door using strong twine and a stick), she felt an obligation as the landlady to intervene in the matter. Her lodgers, Margaret Hambleton and her daughter, thought otherwise; they insisted that it was none of Sarah Edwards' business, and argued that it was impudent of her to enter their room without permission.[40] Two related issues are evident in this altercation. First, a disparity clearly exists between Sarah Edwards and her lodgers regarding the extent to which 'shared' domestic space was accompanied by an expectation of shared knowledge. She believed, as did her husband, that if there was a dead body in her house she should have been acquainted with the fact. Her lodgers, on the other hand, saw no reason to inform her about events that took place within their room. Second, there is also a disagreement over the landlady's authority to access the lodging space.

While relationships between lodgers and household members inevitably varied depending on individual personalities and arrangements, the presence of both within a domestic space forged reciprocal expectations premised on insider knowledge. Living in close proximity to other inhabitants made lodgers privy to information and events that occurred within the 'privileged' space of the household.[41] With this knowledge came certain expectations regarding action and responsibility. For instance, when Esther Mascall died in her lodgings in 1748, the other lodgers in the house all heard the violent alteration between Esther and her husband begin, and also heard her calling out to the landlord for help.[42] John Palmer, the landlord, had previously interfered in their disputes, but on this occasion he had refused. Therefore, while all of the household inhabitants were aware of the reason for the disturbance, they held a shared expectation that, when required, intervention should be the remit of the householder. Similarly, when knowledge of the dead body in her house had reached Sarah Edwards, she had a similar idea about her responsibility to act.

In the ensuing confrontation between Sarah Edwards and Margaret Hambleton, a disagreement is clearly evident regarding the authority of the landlady over the space she let out. When Edwards was informed that there was a corpse in her house, she claimed authority to breach the boundary between the general household space and the more circumscribed space of Hambleton's lodging room. That she felt entitled to force open the door suggests a belief on her part that she retained a right to access the room in the interest of controlling activities that took place within her house. The dispute, therefore, centred on Hambleton and Edwards' differing expectations regarding access and control. As Jennifer Melville has argued, certain spaces within a house were often considered off limits to particular household members. The authority to restrict access rested largely with the master and mistress of the household, which can be understood, according to Melville, as 'an expression of their monopoly of control over spaces'.[43] This is most clearly illustrated in the measures taken to restrict and allow access to houses by locking street doors and entrusting certain people with the task of monitoring access. For Elizabeth Whitaker of the Great Almery, this extended to locking her lodger, Ann Roach, *into* her room in May 1774.[44] However, the monopoly on control over space was compromised in many cases by the location and accessibility of the keys to the locks through which householders had exerted control. Householders often put them in readily identifiable places within the household space – on hooks, in drawers – or left them in the possession of other household members when they went out.[45] Henry Robinson told the Old Bailey that on 15 March 1744, the day his house in Leicester Street was robbed, he had left the key with his lodger, Isaac Adams, and had instructed him to 'take care of the house'.[46] Adams, in turn, left the key with a neighbour when he went out. Thus, on 15 March, at least two other people had complete access to Robinson's house when they were entrusted with his keys.

The multiple uses and occupancies of domestic space, especially when dwellings contained shops or operated as public houses, suggest that houses were relatively open to the street. As a result, spaces within houses were frequently equipped with locks to control access. This allowed lodgers to restrict the access of the householder to their room, as Margaret Hambleton did. Similarly, when Thomas Bridge told his landlord in 1739 that he needed to get into his room urgently (because his wife had died) but could not find his key, not only was there no spare, there was also

[a]n Iron bar, which runs across the back of the door, and when the door is shut, and that bar not taken off, (which falls into a hook) no one can get in, but through the window.[47]

Limited access had significant repercussions for the householder, especially when the room was let as a furnished lodging, because they were unable to monitor the state and continued presence of the goods they had supplied with the room. This provided ample opportunities for theft. In many cases, lodgers were able to conceal the removal of goods for long enough periods of time to fence them on by failing to return the key when they vacated their lodgings. When Sarah Crispe left her lodging in Richard Elby's house sometime prior to October 1747, she took the key with her. After hearing that Crispe had taken a new lodging near Red-Lion Square, Elby's wife sent someone to retrieve the key. When she finally regained access to Crispe's room, Mrs Elby discovered that a bed-quilt, blankets, bed-curtains, sheets, a looking glass, a copper saucepan, a pair of bellows and pillowbears were missing. Richard Elby admitted that Crispe could have taken these goods from his house throughout the twelve-month period that she had lodged there. However, he was totally unaware they were missing until the lodging arrangement ceased and the key to the room was returned. As in other cases, it was his wife who noticed that the goods were missing and who provided a description of them in court.[48] This perhaps suggests that women were often more involved in the material business of letting rooms and negotiating arrangements than their husbands.

Theft from lodgings was a recurring offence tried at the Old Bailey during the eighteenth-century. Its frequency is difficult to gauge, because it is impossible to know how many cases were settled informally or rejected by the grand jury owing to unsubstantiated claims or insufficient evidence. In her detailed analysis of theft cases tried at the Old Bailey in the 1780s, Lynn Mackay has suggested that on average nine women and four men a year admitted to committing this crime.[49] Cases that did proceed to trial give us descriptions of the goods that had allegedly been stolen from lodging rooms. As such, they provide some indication of how lodging rooms were furnished.[50] Although lodging rooms were by no means uniform, when similar items were reported as stolen in a number of cases, it can be assumed that they were commonly present in ready-furnished lodgings. Bed sheets are the most common example. In a comparison of items stolen from furnished lodging rooms in the 1750s and the 1790s, John Styles has calculated that sheets comprised 78 per cent and 79 per cent of complaints respectively.[51] Other items that repeatedly disappeared were pots, pans, kettles, blankets, pillows, spoons, cups, rugs, curtains and bolsters. When rooms were shared, charges over the disappearance of money and clothing were also common. In February 1731, Thomas Bennet charged his 'lodger and bed-fellow', John Hall, with the theft of £15 because he had placed the money in a closet next to the bedside when he went to bed and discovered it missing the next morning.[52] In some cases, opportunity and proximity may indeed have proved too tempting for lodgers to resist. Regardless, these factors made lodgers, with the possible exception of servants, the most obvious suspects when thefts occurred within the household.

Theft from lodgings was a difficult offence to prosecute in practice, because in letting the room as 'ready-furnished', the landlord had essentially granted the lodger possession of the goods contained within it for the duration of their tenancy. Prior to the passage of 'An Act to take away Clergy from some Offenders and to bring others to Punishment' in 1692, it was necessary to prove that a defendant had entered into a lodging agreement with the primary intention of stealing goods rather than lodging in the room. However, from 1692, the removal of any goods or furniture from lodging rooms with the intent to steal them, whether premeditated or not, was indictable as a capital offence.[53] Legal commentators categorised the theft of goods from lodgings as an offence involving a breach of trust.[54] This notion of 'trust' implies a relationship between landlords and their lodgers that extends beyond the basic exchange of money for living space. It predicates some degree of personal interaction and conscionable respect for each other's belongings. The issue was further complicated by the ambiguity surrounding the concept of 'appropriate use', which made theft difficult to prove while the lodging agreement was ongoing. When Collibery Ford was accused of theft by her landlady in October 1730, she confessed that she had taken the shirt she was charged with stealing, and had pawned it. However, she also said that she had intended to return it.[55] Ford was acquitted, most likely because she insisted that she had intended to bring the shirt back. This attests to the fluidity in the way many eighteenth-century Londoners conceived of the legitimate use and temporary appropriation of material goods. Again, this hinged on contested ideas regarding authority and control: if goods were leased out as part of an agreement, and returned at the end, did it in fact matter how they were used in the interim? Lodgers seem to have pawned what was at their disposal when in need, but the legal owners of these goods viewed their right to do so differently. Similarly, historians investigating women's crime have argued that accusations of theft from lodgings were commonly a by-product of a large informal network of female borrowing, where the line between ownership and authority was blurred.[56]

The prevalence of lodging generally, and the tendency for lodgings to be let as furnished rooms, led much of the mobile London population to store their personal possessions within locked boxes and chests.[57] In theory at least, the presence of the landlord's goods within the room and the lodger's goods within the house should have formed a reciprocal relationship whereby expectations about access to and appropriate use of each other's possessions were respected. Storing goods in boxes and trunks had the added benefit of making them portable. In this way people could secure their goods and transport them when they moved to different accommodation. However, this was not always the case and conflicts erupted over the authority to open such boxes, especially when they occupied ambiguous household space. When John Eliott prosecuted Nicholas Adams and William Woodley for theft in 1761, he accused them of stealing his chest and breaking it open.[58] He had been Adams' lodger, and left the chest in her house when he moved to a different lodging nearby. Mary Banks moved into John Eliott's second floor lodging room on the same day he moved out, testifying to the heavy demand for furnished lodgings in London. What is interesting about this case is that John Eliott's chest was still in the room when Mary Banks took possession of it as 'ready-furnished', implying that she would have use of the goods contained within it for the period of her tenancy. This type of negotiation becomes somewhat more ambiguous when articles of furniture that did not belong to the landlady were present in room. In 1764, the story of a trunk brought into John Nutting's house in Long Ditch, St Margaret Westminster, and passed between lodgers as a favour – to its owner in the first instance and then to its various other minders – was pieced together during a coroner's inquest in Westminster. The trunk moved from room to room within the house for years until Richard Cradock, the last lodger who had agreed to store it, died and his widow broke the lock. Inside the trunk was a coffin containing a dead baby.[59] The relatively easy movement of this trunk from one lodger to the next suggests that it was quite customary to leave locked chests in storage under good faith arrangements with friends and fellow lodgers, and that people were willing to accommodate such requests until they became burdensome. When Mary Bland, who had first agreed to store the chest, wanted it removed from her room, its owner John Williams re-appeared and negotiated to have it moved to Richard Cradock's garret lodging in the same house. He told Cradock that the chest contained important papers, an explanation Cradock seems to have been happy to take at face value.

Unfortunately, some of the best evidence we can garner as to how responsibility over space was perceived by lodgers is recorded as a result of catastrophes such as house collapses. When two adjoining houses collapsed in Silver Court on 5 December 1763, William Hunter, Mary Anderson and another lodger named Sophia were killed. Merryman Smith, who lodged in one of the cellars, told the coroner that while he was cooking dinner that day, bricks had fallen down his chimney. He had notified Mr Spence, the *owner* of the house, who came and put props against the chimney and the back wall. That night, the house where Smith lodged and the one adjoining the back wall collapsed. When Matthew Told, the *landlord* of the house, heard noises coming from his closet in the middle of the night, he assumed the house was falling down. It is unclear whether he had been notified about the earlier episode and the resulting props.[60] Smith's assumptions regarding authority and responsibility over the household space in this case are revealing. He described himself as a tenant of Matthew Told. However, when he perceived a structural problem with the building in which his lodgings were located, Smith sought out the non-resident owner directly. This perhaps suggests that while householders were regarded as the arbiters of household space and its boundaries, their responsibilities did not extend to maintenance of the physical framework.

More knowledge about the spaces and tasks that were shared between householders and lodgers, as Susan Wright has argued, is needed to further historical understanding of the relationships that developed between them.[61] The extent of interaction between lodgers and other household members would undoubtedly have varied, but the use of shared spaces such as common staircases and passages meant that some exchange had to take place. Where rooms were not equipped with fireplaces, lodgers often interacted with the householder's family and other lodgers around a common fire. The sharing of food and drink is often mentioned as a sign of voluntary social interaction. In 1761 Sarah Ewers told the Old Bailey that Mrs Adams and John Eliott had lived on very good terms, and implied that she knew this because they often ate and drank together.[62] While amicable relations with lodgers were desirable, however, there were limits to the degree of social interaction that was considered acceptable. For female landladies especially, there was a danger in appearing too friendly with their male lodgers. When Elizabeth Sayer prosecuted John Warwick in September 1736 for housebreaking and theft, she found herself being questioned as to the nature of her relationship with Warwick, who had taken lodgings in her coffeehouse in St Clement's Church Yard to store goods. She was repeatedly asked if she and the prisoner had lived together as man and wife, and whether they had shared money.[63] The sharing of money between lodgers and their landlords or landladies often aroused suspicion and invited speculation regarding the relationship between the two parties.[64] This is likely because it suggested more complicated interactions than the straightforward and businesslike exchange of money for space. In the case of Elizabeth Sayer, further suspicion was aroused when she told the court that Warwick had a wife living in Sheer Lane. She was interrogated as to why a married man was lodging in her house without his wife. The veiled assumption that there was something suspicious about their arrangement, and that Sayer was not only privy to the details but was also complicit, reveals an eighteenth-century anxiety regarding the possibility for immoral behaviour to be hidden and protected if committed within the domestic space.

Even when the relationship between landlords and lodgers began indifferently, tensions within the shared domestic space could quickly lead to conflict. In January 1731, Jane Corklin was tried at the Old Bailey for attempting to extort money from her landlady, Mary Lamb, using the threat of violence. Corklin was accused of sending Lamb a threatening letter that said she would be 'burnt in her bed' unless a sum of two guineas was left in a particular location.[65] Lamb alleged that Corklin was responsible for the letter because she had picked it up and passed it on without checking the intended recipient. Thus, according to Lamb, the knowledge that the letter was addressed to her and not another occupant of the house was sufficient to arouse suspicion. Irrespective of whether Corklin was actually involved in the production of the letter, the suspicion that it came from within the household would have made the threat seem all the more immediate to Mary Lamb. Those who shared Lamb's domestic space, by their close physical proximity, were afforded opportunities to harm her. The domestic space can arguably be read as a vulnerable space because it was expected that its inhabitants were protected from outside threat by physical walls, locked doors and controlled access. Threats from within were often overlooked.

Jane Corklin denied any knowledge of the threatening letter and instead insinuated that Lamb had maliciously accused her because of a disagreement between them. Witnesses testified to animosity between Lamb and Corklin after a gentleman who also lodged in the house left. Lamb was unwilling to lose the man as her lodger, and seems to have blamed Corklin for his decision to leave. Perhaps this was a quarrel over competing attempts to attract the attention of an eligible bachelor, or perhaps more overt interference by one or the other women in an ongoing relationship. Regardless, it is obvious that the disruption of this domestic arrangement created a household tension that made threats of violence seem plausible.

2.4　Conclusion

In conjunction with the more widely recognised financial motive, the premium for living space in the metropolis contributed to the prevalence of lodging among the eighteenth-century working poor. Many of them formed what Dorothy George has described as a 'floating population living largely as weekly tenants in furnished rooms'.[66] Undoubtedly, lodging arrangements varied enormously and it would be unwise to draw definitive conclusions about the relationships between all lodgers and householders based on a few case studies. However, it is clearly not sufficient to assume that the diversity of such arrangements precludes any attempts to better understand the common *negotiations* that took place between lodgers and the households in which they resided. The close sharing of physical space carried some general implications for both lodgers and householders that could not be avoided. These centred largely around expectations concerning the delineation of domestic space, the boundaries of authority within it and the extent to which knowledge within that space was to be shared. Whether or not a written contract was signed, lodging arrangements in which space would be shared implicitly entailed more than a simple exchange of money for space. People sharing household space, as a result of living in close proximity to one another, became privy to information about each other's lives that was not amenable to outsiders. Additionally, they became entangled in an implicit relationship of trust whereby they were expected to respect each other's goods and space (where non-communal locked spaces were involved) and not violate the agreement through spontaneous desertion or eviction. Ambiguity surrounding the issues of authority and control meant that expectations regarding lodging arrangements often varied. When this happened, the direct and immediate effect such tensions had on people's lives caused conflicts to erupt.

Notes

The author would like to thank Pamela Sharpe, Stephanie Tarbin, Susan Broomhall, Philippa Maddern, Patricia Crawford, Vanessa Harding, Kate Riley, Margaret Dorey and Andrew Broertjes their suggestions on draft versions of this paper.

1. See J. McEwan & P. Sharpe, '"It Buys Me Freedom": Genteel Lodging in Late Seventeenth and Eighteenth-Century London', *Parergon* 24.2, (2007), 139–61.
2. See Chapter 1 in this volume.
3. F. Place, *The Autobiography of Francis Place (1771–1854)*, ed. by M. Thale (Cambridge: Cambridge University Press, 1972), p. 111.
4. See N. Tadmor, *Family and Friends in Eighteenth-Century England: Household, Kinship, and Patronage* (Cambridge: Cambridge University Press, 2001), esp. pp. 9–11.
5. S. J. Wright, 'Sojourners and Lodgers in a Provincial Town: The Evidence from Eighteenth-Century Ludlow', *Urban History Yearbook* 17, (1990), 27.
6. Thank you to Jeremy Boulton for this suggestion.
7. On subdivision and ad-hoc building, see M. J. Daunton, 'Housing', in F. M. L. Thompson (ed.), *The Cambridge Social History of Britain, 1750–1950* (Cambridge: Cambridge University Press, 1990), II, p. 202.
8. On pregnant servants who moved into lodgings when they were dismissed or left their place of employment, see Chapter 8 in this volume by Samantha Williams.
9. 'Evidence of Elizabeth Cotton', quoted in P. Earle, *A City Full of People: Men and Women of London 1650–1750* (Methuen, 1994), p. 190.
10. *OBP*, 23 February 1732, trial of Thomas Andrews, (t17320223-40).
11. See for example Wright, 'Sojourners and Lodgers in a Provincial Town', p. 23.
12. Earle, *A City Full of People*, p. 167.
13. T. Hitchcock & J. Black (eds), *Chelsea Settlement and Bastardy Examinations, 1733–1766* (London Record Society, 1999), I, no.46, p. 14.
14. Earle, *A City Full of People*, p. 81.
15. T. Hitchcock, *Down and Out in Eighteenth-Century London* (Hambledon, 2004), p. 25. Peter Earle has argued that although there is evidence of people 'sleeping rough' in London, the infrequency suggests that 'the great majority of Londoners had a roof over their heads and lived in a house or part of a house'. Earle, *A City Full of People*, p. 166.
16. Hitchcock, *Down and Out*, p. 25.
17. P. Guillery, *The Small House in Eighteenth-Century London: A Social and Architectural History* (New Haven: Yale University Press in association with English Heritage, 2004), p. 32.
18. See M. D. George, *London Life in the Eighteenth Century* (Kegan Paul, Trench, Trubner & Co., 1925), p. 88; H. Shore, 'Crime, Criminal Networks and the Survival Strategies of the Poor in Early Eighteenth-Century London', in S. King & A. Tomkins (eds), *The Poor in England 1700–1850: An Economy of Makeshifts* (Manchester: Manchester University Press, 2003), pp. 137–65.
19. S. Welch, *A Proposal to Render Effectual a Plan, to Remove the Nuisance of Common Prostitutes from the Streets of This Metropolis* (1758), p. 53.
20. J. Boulton, *Neighbourhood and Society: A London Suburb in the Seventeenth Century* (Cambridge: Cambridge University Press, 1987), p. 85. Richard Wall has suggested that houses in the capital in c.1700 contained an average of 1.7 lodgers. R. Wall, 'Regional and Temporal Variations in English Household Structure from 1650', in J. Hobcraft & P. H. Rees (eds), *Regional Demographic Development* (Croom Helm, 1979), p. 103. Based on Poll Tax returns from 1692, Craig Spence has also estimated that 47 per cent of houses in London

at this time contained subsidiary lodgers. See C. Spence, *London in the 1690s: A Social Atlas* (Centre for Metropolitan History Institute of Historical Research University of London, 2000), pp. 89–99, esp. p. 90.

21. T. Sokoll, *Household and Family among the Poor: The Case of Two Essex Communities* (Bochum: Brockmeyer, 1993), pp. 82–3.

22. WAMR, Westminster Coroner's Inquests, 16 April 1764: 'Inquisition on the several bodies of Diana Towers, Charles Towers, Sarah Towers, John Nichols, Mary Nichols & Mary Nichols lying dead in the parish of St George Hanover Square'.

23. See Guillery, *The Small House in Eighteenth-Century London*, p. 30; George, *London Life*, p. 93.

24. See for examples F. Grose, *The Olio: Being a Collection of Essays, Dialogues, Letters, Epitaphs, &C* (1793), p. 75; J. B. Bird, *The Laws Respecting Landlords, Tenants, and Lodgers, Laid down in a Plain, Easy, and Familiar Manner* (1794), p. 81. See also A. Vickery, 'An Englishman's Home is his Castle? Thresholds, Boundaries and Privacies in the Eighteenth-Century London House', *Past and Present* 199, (2008), 160.

25. In accordance with post-fire Building Acts, new buildings in the City were divided into four categories and a maximum height restriction was placed on each. This prevented London from building upwards to accommodate its burgeoning population. See 18 & 19 Cha. II c. 8, (1666); 22 Cha. II c. 11, (1670).

26. 18 & 19 Cha. II c. 8, (1666).

27. On the 'economy of makeshift', see O. Hufton, *The Poor of Eighteenth-Century France, 1750–1789* (Oxford: Clarendon Press, 1974), Chapter 3.

28. *OBP*, 16 January 1761, trial of Sarah Pettit, (t17610116-25).

29. J. Boulton, "It is extreme necessity that makes me do this': Some "survival strategies" of Pauper Households in London's West End During the Early Eighteenth Century', in *International Review of Social History, Supplement* 8 (2000), 47–70 (56).

30. *The Young Clerk's Magazine: Or, English Law-Repository. Containing a Variety of the Most Useful Precedents* (1739), p. 14; *The New Pocket Conveyancer; or, Gentleman, Tradesman, Lawyer and Attorney's Magazine of Law. Being a Collection of Choice Approved Precedents* (Dublin, 1765), I, p. 25.

31. J. D. Melville, 'The Use and Organisation of Domestic Space in Late Seventeenth-Century London' (unpublished University of Cambridge PhD, 1999), p. 176. Reasonable efforts have been made to contact Dr Melville for permission to cite her unpublished work. For their assistance, the author thanks Keith Wrightson, Amanda Flather and staff at Jesus College, the Cambridge University Library and the Cambridge University Alumni Association.

32. 3 & 4 William and Mary c. 9 s.5, (1692).

33. 29 & 30 Vict. C. 90, (1866). Laws governing the prosecution of disorderly housekeepers and the regulation of common lodging houses were passed in 1752 (25 Geo. II, c. 36), 1851 (14 & 15 Vict. c. 28) and 1852 (16 & 17 Vict. c. 41).

34. J. Paul, *The Laws Relating to Landlords and Tenants* (1791), p. 73.

35. *OBP*, 16 September 1761, trial of Nicholas, wife of William Adams, otherwise Lawrance, otherwise Law, William Woodley (t17610916–16).

36. 11 Geo. II, c. 19 (1737–8). This statute was preceded by the 'Landlord and Tenant Act, 1730', 4 Geo II, c. 28. For a discussion of further legislation in the Victorian period, see D. Englander, *Landlord and Tenant in Urban Britain, 1838–1919* (Oxford: Clarendon Press, 1983), Chapter 2.

37. P. Colquhoun, *Observations and Facts Relative to Public Houses* (1794), p. 26. Also quoted in George, *London Life*, p. 93.

38. J. Styles, 'Lodging at the Old Bailey: Lodgings and their Furnishing in Eighteenth-Century London', in J. Styles and A. Vickery (eds), *Gender, Taste and Material Culture in Britain and North America, 1700–1830* (Yale University Press, 2006), p. 61.

39. *OBP*, 15 October 1735, trial of Margaret Hambleton, Rebecca Hambleton, Margaret Hambleton, (t17351015 5).

40. *Ibid.*

41. Prescriptive literature from the seventeenth century promoted the idea of the household as a miniature commonwealth, over which the household head was responsible for maintaining good order. In theory, this rendered the household as a space of minimal outside interference. See S. D. Amussen, *An Ordered Society: Gender and Class in Early Modern England* (Oxford: B. Blackwell, 1988). For arguments that neighbours frequently did intervene in household affairs, see, for example, A. Flather, *Gender and Space in Early Modern England* (Suffolk: Royal Historical Society: Boydell Press, 2007), p. 42.

42. *OBP*, 15 January 1748, trial of John Mascall (t17480115–30).

43. Melville, 'The Use and Organisation of Domestic Space', p. 171.

44. Ann Roach was intoxicated and presumably a nuisance to the rest of the household. She fell out of the window and died after being locked into her room by her landlady. WAMR, Westminster Coroner's Inquests, 23 May 1774: 'Inquisition on the Body of Ann Roach lying dead in the Parish of St Margaret Westminster'.

45. For a detailed discussion of control over locked spaces and keys as emblems of authority and trust, see Vickery, 'An Englishman's Home is his Castle?', pp. 159–62, 168–70 .

46. *OBP*, 4 April 1744, trial of Susanna Read, otherwise Jefferies (t17440404-10).

47. *OBP*, 18 July 1739, trial of Thomas Bridge (t17390718-16).

48. *OBP*, 9 December 1767, trial of Sarah Crispe, otherwise Ridge (t17471209-2).

49. L. Mackay, 'Why They Stole: Women in the Old Bailey, 1779–1789', *Journal of Social History* 32:3, (1999), 631.

50. Thank you to Vanessa Harding for this suggestion.

51. Styles, 'Lodging at the Old Bailey', pp. 72–3.

52. *OBP*, 2 June 1731, John Hall (t17310602-4).

53. 3 & 4 William and Mary c. 9 s.5, (1692).

54. See W. Hawkins, *A Treatise of the Pleas of the Crown; or a System of the Principal Matters Relating to That Subject. Edited by Thomas Leach*, 7th edn, (1795).

55. *OBP*, 14 October 1730, trial of Collibery Ford (t17301014-8).

56. For arguments that thefts from lodgings were related to informal female borrowing networks, see Mackay, 'Why They Stole'; Styles, 'Lodging at the Old Bailey', p. 77; S. Howard, 'Investigating Responses to Theft in Early Modern Wales: Communities, Thieves and the Courts', *Continuity and Change* 19:3, (2004), 409–30.

57. See Melville, 'The Use and Organisation of Domestic Space', pp. 157–8; Vickery, 'An Englishman's Home is his Castle?', p. 164.
58. *OBP*, 16 September 1761, Nicholas, wife of William Adams, otherwise Lawrance, otherwise Law, William Woodley (t17610916-16).
59. WAMR, Westminster Coroner's Inquests, 5 October 1764:' Inquisition on Body of a female child lying dead in the parish of St Margaret'.
60. WAMR, Westminster Coroner's Inquests, 5 December 1763: 'Inquisition on the Body of a woman unknown lying dead in the parish of St George Hanover Square'.
61. Wright, 'Sojourners and Lodgers in a Provincial Town', p. 27.
62. *OBP*, 16 September 1761, Nicholas, trial of wife of William Adams, otherwise Lawrance, otherwise Law, William Woodley (t17610916-16).
63. *OBP*, 8 September 1736, trial of John Warwick (t17360908-37).
64. See for another example *OBP*, 9 July 1740, trial of John Foster (t17400709-32).
65. *OBP*, 15 January 1731, trial of Jane Corklin alias Cockland (t17310115-64).
66. George, *London Life*, p. 94.

3
Heartless and Unhomely? Dwellings of the Poor in East Anglia and North-East England

Adrian Green

'Home is where the heart is.' Nineteenth-century ideals of homeliness left a large proportion of society occupying dwellings that, by virtue of their poverty, were seen as heartless and unhomely. Historians' acceptance, however, that homeliness was the preserve of the middle classes may risk perpetuating assumptions of the desensitising force of material deprivation. It would be unfeeling to underestimate hardship and distress, but it requires an equal lack of empathy to assume that poorer people were unable to find consolation in their own home. In the absence of detailed investigation into the material reality of poor households, historians have emphasised the testimony of reformers that housing conditions were both bad and squalid. While accounts of squalor and cramped conditions reflect, in part, a real deterioration in housing conditions in the late eighteenth and early nineteenth centuries, these emotive descriptions are problematic because they also reflect a new set of concerns over the home. Alternative sources for the materiality of poorer households do not quite accord with remorseless misery, and archaeologists have recently found that the excavated evidence for nineteenth-century cities contradicts 'slum' conditions.[1] Rather than accepting the notion that poverty prevented people from living in anything but squalor, we should recognise that poorer households generally endeavoured to maintain a homely space. Not everyone succeeded, and the anguish that losing a home created is clearly conveyed in pauper letters. But true squalor – living in filth through the absence of care – did not simply reflect degrees of poverty, or even differences in attitudes to hygiene so much as the psychological problems which arose from a failure to maintain homely space as a refuge from insecurity.

In the seventeenth century the household was upheld in law, as a 'man's house is his castle, and each man's home is his safest refuge'.[2]

But this exaltation referred to orderly households, and the poor were separated in conceptions of society that assumed householders were masters in control of subservient members. The domestic life of the poor was irrelevant when concern over household order was focused on the exercise of authority. This marginalisation is reflected in the cursory references to poorer dwellings in documentary sources. Witness Nicholas and Thomas Flemming who had 'lately erected two poor cottages or sheddes to shelter themselves upon the lord's waste' in Auckland manor, or the cottagers on Whickham manor 'called the smalls', in the Durham parliamentary surveys of 1647.[3] A generation later, Gregory King categorised all 'cottagers and paupers' as decreasing the wealth of the kingdom in 1688. But a century later, the early-modern patriarchal household had been succeeded by a conception of the home as a family domain, and concern over the family as the basis of social and economic stability now extended to direct scrutiny of impoverished living conditions.[4] Nathaniel Kent's *Hints to Gentlemen of Landed Property* (1775) included 'Reflections on the great importance of cottages' –

> The shattered hovels which half the poor of this kingdom are obliged to put up with, [are] truly affecting to a heart fraught with humanity. Those who condescend to visit these miserable tenements, can testify, that neither health nor decency can be preserved within them.

This moral concern was given political urgency in the 1790s, when the Board of Agriculture set out to reform the housing of the labouring poor as a means to avoid revolutionary unrest. Optimists in the debate meanwhile emphasised the progress enjoyed by modern Britons, and a paper 'On the Comforts enjoyed by the Cottagers compared to those of the ancient Britons' appeared in the *Annals of Agriculture* in 1797. It was in this context of family independence that the cottage became idealised as a comfortable, homely space, centred on a cheerful hearth.[5]

An intensification of interest in the home was related to the later eighteenth-century shift in attitudes summarised as the 'rise in sentiment'. This alteration in sensitivities involved a new recognition of poverty as 'misery'. The Norfolk parish of Watton's overseers' book for 1769–1802 has 'Alias the Chronicle of Misery' on its title page. While sympathies varied, direct interest in domestic lives contrasts markedly with the apparent lack of polite attention earlier in the eighteenth century.[6] Consequently, we lack equivalent evidence for the state of poorer housing between the mid-seventeenth and mid-eighteenth centuries to compare with the abundance of commentary and pictorial representations produced thereafter. Moreover, the notions of homely comfort versus unhomely squalor which emerged in the second half of our period have remained normative assumptions about impoverished domesticity. The evidence presented in this essay suggests that these assumptions should be questioned. In going beyond outsider perspectives on misery, hovels and slums, we need to ask what the material and emotional reality for poor households was like, and query whether poorer folk lived in fundamentally different ways from their more prosperous neighbours. The following explores the qualities of comfort versus insecurity in poorer households between the mid-seventeenth and early-nineteenth centuries, in the two contrasting regions of East Anglia and North-East England, particularly Norfolk and Durham.

The proportion of households in poverty in the later seventeenth century can be gauged from hearth tax records.[7] The hearth tax was collected from 1662 to 1688 and includes lists of those exempted from paying two shillings per hearth. Table 3.1 indicates that a third of recorded Norfolk households (in line with much of southern England) and approaching one half in Durham (like most of the North) were exempt from paying.[8] The county averages conceal significant variations. Only 37 Norfolk parishes (mainly in the north-east of the county) have reliable exemption returns for 1664, varying between 10 and 55 per cent of households exempt, whereas Durham had few places in 1666 with fewer than 15 per cent and many with over 55 per cent exempt. Both counties contained concentrations of poverty in particular rural communities (often associated with enclosure), but the very highest proportions in Durham were in the industrial districts along the Tyne (with over 70 per cent of households exempt), and maritime communities around the coast from South Shields to Sunderland and Hartlepool (where over

Table 3.1 Exempt households in the hearth tax

	Norfolk 1664	Durham 1674	Norwich 1671	Newcastle 1665
% exempt	33	44	58	43
No. recorded	1738	5870	3008	1038

Source: *Norfolk Genealogy* XV, 1983; *An Historical Atlas of Norfolk*, p. 109; *Durham Hearth Tax* (British Record Society, 2006); *Norfolk Hearth Tax Exemption Certificates* (British Record Society, 2001); R. Welford, 'Newcastle Householders in 1665', *Archaeologia Aeliana* (3) VII (1911), 49–76.
Note: Norwich's exemption rate is an extrapolation from several records (1673 alone gives 33%).

50 per cent were commonly exempt). In Norfolk, exemption levels were generally lower, with higher levels particularly apparent for market towns such as Thetford (37 per cent) and North Walsham (45 per cent) in 1664, and the larger coastal boroughs of Great Yarmouth (32 per cent) and King's Lynn (34 per cent) in 1674. The majority of exempt households had one hearth, but the coastal communities of Great Yarmouth and Hartlepool stand out for the number of two-hearth houses exempt, reflecting fragile maritime-household economies.[9] The largest towns had a different order of poverty. In both Norwich and Newcastle there were dramatic differences between districts, with the most extreme poverty being the 80 per cent of hearths exempt in St. Peter Southgate, Norwich and the 79 per cent of households exempt in Sandgate, Newcastle.[10]

Hearth tax exemption generally only captures the stable sections of the population as the more marginal and transitory (including large numbers of lodgers, vagrants and squatters) were not usually recorded. Although the recorded exempt were not usually destitute, not paying the hearth tax certainly reflected a measure of poverty. Local officials responsible for administering the tax frequently described the exempt as 'paupers'. The lists of non-chargeable (who were technically exempt because they occupied dwellings or land worth less than £1 in yearly rent) which were sent with the main Exchequer Return for Norfolk Michaelmas 1664 refer to 'noe poor retorned' for Taverham Hundred and 'Burrough of King's Lynn Noe poore retorned'. John Pound has demonstrated for Norwich that although most local officials described the exempt as poor, these householders were not usually in receipt of poor relief and actual paupers were not often recorded among the exempt at all. Margaret Spufford concludes that the Norwich exempt represent 'a *stratum* of people, including some on relief, who mainly were more prosperous than that, but not prosperous enough to pay the 2/- a year for the Hearth Tax'. In the Durham records some households oscillated over the years between qualifying as payers and being exempt, with many of the recorded exempt being the better off of the seventeenth-century poor and the poorest in many places, especially areas with considerable turnover in employment, were not listed at all.[11]

Since those in relative poverty were described as poor by officials, it is likely that these 'non-solvent' households felt themselves to be poor – a feeling that would be reinforced wherever exemption had a discernible relationship to the material appearance or internal furnishing of dwellings.[12] The absence of a chimney stack may itself have been taken to signify poverty, and many exempt cottages would have had a wattle-and-daub smokehood rather than a projecting stone or brick chimney. For those who paid the tax there was considerable variation in the accommodation of single-hearth households. In Durham, Christopher Dodds, thatcher, died with movable goods worth £7 accommodated in two rooms, whereas John Bunting, yeoman, also paying on one hearth, lived in a one-and-a-half storey farmhouse with six rooms. Bunting was probably in an older house, while his neighbours in newly built houses had heated parlours, a separate kitchen and even heated bed-chambers. By contrast, there appears to have been greater uniformity in the single-hearth accommodation of those who did not pay the tax. In both Durham and Norfolk smaller single-hearth dwellings usually consisted of one main room and a secondary space for sleeping and storage. This basic form of housing was common to the larger towns and the countryside, and did not alter considerably over the eighteenth century.[13]

The form and age of accommodation was largely determined by the historic housing stock, which itself turned on the economic trajectories of the two regions. Whereas Norfolk had been prosperous and populous in the fifteenth and sixteenth centuries, Durham's population enjoyed more modest levels of wealth before 1600. In the North-East, industrialisation in the seventeenth century prompted a commercial agriculture that was geared to feeding the increasing wage-labour population, while in rural East Anglia there was a relative decline in the cloth industry and no spectacular population increase. In both regions, migrants were drawn to employment in the major towns, with Norwich's population rising from 20,000 in the 1620s to 30,000 by 1700 and Newcastle's from 10,000 in 1600 to 16,000 in 1700.[14] Employment and population patterns thus intersected differently with the pre-existing housing stock. In East Anglia generally there were many older houses, originally built in the fifteenth and sixteenth centuries, for the poor to inhabit, often in sub-divided form. This tradition of sub-division, encouraged by the flexibility of timber-framed construction, continued into the eighteenth century when farmhouses might be built of slight timbers with the expectation that they would soon be converted into cottages.[15] Norfolk manor courts record sub-division and additions to established holdings, as at Holt in 1734 when a custody grant for Benjamin Leake involved

one parcell of Ground containing in Length forty ffeet and in Breadth twelve ffeet with a Cottage built lying in wast at the north end of a free house of Ethelbred Authy Widow.[16]

In the North-East, less prosperity before 1600 and increases in population in the following two centuries meant that the older housing stock was inadequate and alternative accommodation had to be found.[17]

For those taking up industrial employment in Durham the lack of available housing meant temporary to permanent shelters on commons and wastes. In the Pennine uplands, where lead mining was expanding, the great expanse of Raily Fell was allowed for squatting by lead miners.[18] Around the pits of the Tyne and Wear coalfield, wooden 'huts' were erected with brick chimneys for burning coal.[19] These likely resembled the colonial wooden cabins constructed in North America (see Plate 3.1). Accommodation and fuel were usually provided by employers, and this form of colliers' housing was only intended to stand as long

Plate 3.1   Reconstructed wooden cabin at Salem, Massachusetts, 1630. A close parallel for the wooden huts with chimneys erected for coal workers in Durham. (Samuel Chamberlain (1937), *Open House in New England* (Battleboro, Vermont: Stephen Daye Press), p. 37)

as the pit was open. Employers' strategies for accommodating colliers nevertheless generated frictions with established residents. At Chester le Street, coal owners encroached upon the waste to build cottages and 'unlawfully erected therein certaine new cottages and placed therein certain ill disposed persons aliens and forinners'.[20] The development of more permanent pits led to the formation of pit villages, located away from the established villages where middling households and farm labourers predominated. Housing the industrial workforce required a reconfiguration of Durham's settlement pattern, and many apparently nineteenth-century pit villages originated in the seventeenth and eighteenth centuries. Philadelphia Row emerged in the eighteenth century as just such a colliers' settlement, at the bottom of the bank from the somewhat genteel hilltop settlement of Newfield.[21] More securely employed industrial workers, in salt panning and metal manufacture, might have stone cottages, such as the two-storied dwellings dated 1691 for German swordmakers at Shotley Bridge.[22]

Representing the origins of the working class terrace, labourers' cottages were frequently built in rows from the later seventeenth century. The salt pan industry at South Shields was described in 1636 by Sir William Brereton as being 'carried on by a few poor dwellers near the coast', but by the end of the seventeenth century salt pan workers were regularly housed in rows of purpose built cottages. Such workers' terraces provided a rentier income for their genteel, often female, owners. Mrs Johnson of Durham advertised 'Six Salt-Pans at South Shields, with a Mansion House, and other Houses' in 1723, while Widow Crisp sold 'ONE Salt Pann, with the Salter's Houses, and several other Dwelling houses' in North Shields in 1728, and 'A Row or Onset of Houses, at the East End of South Shields' was advertised for sale in the *Newcastle Courant* in 1729.[23] The gentry Salvins of Croxdale Hall near Durham similarly derived an income from house rents and lodgings at South Shields.[24] Terraced housing was initially intended for those with relatively secure wages, and the relationship of Georgian houses along Sunderland's High Street (usually of timber-frame construction with a brick skin and sashed-windows), to the terraced cottages on the lanes nearer to the River Wear is well illustrated on the Eye Plan of 1785–90 (see Plate 3.2).[25] But such 'working class' housing might fall into poverty; as when payments for 'house rent' were made by the parish of Pittington to the inhabitants of 'Pitt Houses' in 1695 and 1696, presumably for widows and males too old, or ill, to work.[26]

In Durham the settled poor of the community, such as underemployed labourers and those who experienced life-cycle poverty in widowhood or old age, were more likely to dwell within village

76

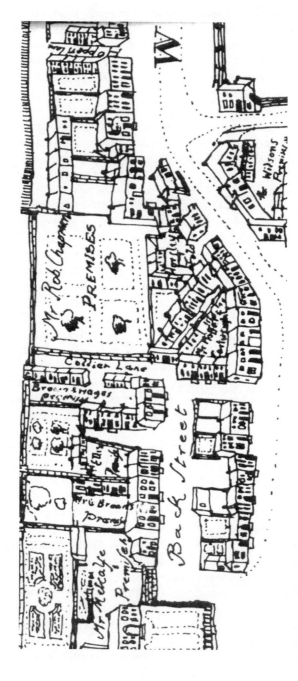

Plate 3.2 Single-storey cottages in Sunderland. (Reproduced and edited by Michael Clay, Geoffrey Milburn and Stuart Miller (1984), *An Eye Plan of Sunderland and Bishopwearmouth 1785–90*, by *John Rain* (Newcastle-upon-Tyne: Frank Graham), p. 24. © Sunderland Antiquarian Society)

settlements. Even those immediately disadvantaged by enclosure might receive parish support, though this was usually short-lived and the disadvantaged were ultimately expected to find alternative employment.[27] Impoverished but established members of the community might expect to receive assistance from parish officers for the rent and repair of their houses. Rent payments – both occasional and regular – are well documented in churchwarden accounts, and seem to have been directed at the deserving poor, particularly the elderly and those in ill health.[28] Extreme misfortune might be quickly remedied, as when John Hutton and John Hudson were sent 'five shillings each on account of damages done in their respective houses by two great floods' at Dinsdale on Tees in December 1763. In January 1767 Hudson 'who still continues so weak as to be unable to work' received five shillings more, and in May 1769 was given a further five shillings 'towards ye education of his children the last quarter, and five shillings towards ye payment of his house rent the last half yeare'. Records of Hudson's relief continue through to 1775, and his son was apprenticed to a flax-dresser in Sedgefield in 1779 at a fee of two guineas to the parish.[29] Parish accounts also record thatching repairs in both Norfolk and Durham villages throughout the eighteenth century.[30] As with fuel payments, house repairs were intended to protect inhabitants' health and were an effort to avoid the appearance of physical and social dereliction within the community. The condition of housing was a vested interest for parishes that derived an income from house rents, and occupants were well aware of the monetary value of parish upkeep. Thomas Baker in 1718 paid 50 shillings yearly rent 'for the house I now dwell in late yeares and the Hempland I occupye with it', but 'if the said churchwardens or the townshipp of Disse putt the same into good repayre I will pay them 3*l*. per. Anno'.[31] Manor courts were similarly involved in the provision of housing, and had social and legal obligations to provide well-maintained housing. Charitable endowments also provided for the poor, as in 1695 when a new house was built for four poor inhabitants at New Buckenham, or the conveying of rents from a cottage 'to the use of the poor inhabitants of Paston' in 1691.[32] In both regions, throughout the eighteenth century, parish records reveal a high level of attention to the housing needs of the settled poor.[33]

In both East Anglia and the North-East the very poor were often on commons; a practice that helped consolidate residential and social segregation, and which the established residents generally tolerated.[34] In the 1680s, Bishop Crewe gave permission 'to ye inhabitants wardons and overseers of ye poor ye manor of Stockton to erect build and sett up [...] houses for dwellings for poor and impotent persons in any wast or Comons'. At Staindrop the poor were granted their own land, with Raby manor court ordering in October 1690 'that none shall make a way through the poores land', while at Bishop Wearmouth complaints were made of a great influx of poor 'principally occasioned and incoraged by ye inhabitants thereof in respect of their building and structing diverse small cottage Houses in wch ye sd p people inhabit wch they Leet and farme'.[35] There were further conflicts between communities over the use of waste and moor by the poor, as when the inhabitants of Ketton in Durham refused to contribute towards the building of huts upon the moor for the poor of Brasserton.[36] But this was a conflict between parishes over paying for housing, and there seems to have been general agreement that the waste was the best place for the poor. The accretion of squatter settlement on common land could lead to the formation of permanent settlements, as at Spennymoor (originally an area of moor between medieval settlements) in the Wear Valley.[37] More piecemeal occupation of the commons was the norm in Norfolk, particularly in socially mixed 'open' villages where single-estate landlords were not dominant. In 1710 the Seething manor court admitted Robert Adams and his wife Sarah, with the consent of the rector and inhabitants of Kirstead, to a piece of waste, part of the common pasture of Kirstead, with a cottage built on it. While at Tasburgh in 1747 the quarter sessions authorised the building of a cottage on wasteland; the churchwardens and overseers

> shewing that whereas there are many poor familys and aged and impotent persons belonging to the said parish who are not able to provide Habitations for themselves and praysing that leave might be given to erect a cottage upon some convenient place on the waste, if the Lord of the Manor consenteth thereto.[38]

Quarter session, manor court and parish records all indicate that the settlement of the poor on waste ground was highly regulated in the seventeenth and eighteenth centuries. Severe restrictions were thus placed on situations where people could provide themselves with shelter without paying rent.

Those on the margins of communities were often in short-lived structures, and cottages on commons might lack proper foundations. Earth-fast construction involved posts rammed into the earth; a technique transferred to settler cabins in America.[39] Such structures, like encroachment within villages, could be upgraded by succeeding occupants and examples of seventeenth- and eighteenth-century cottages on such sites still stand. At North Lopham in south Norfolk, a one-and-a-half storied timber-framed eighteenth-century cottage still stands on North Lopham common, while a timber-framed cottage built around 1600 remains at the end of the village street, clad in wattle-and-daub plaster and thatched. Cobbler's Cottage was 'a single-celled, single-storeyed building without a fireplace, open to the roof inside' until the mid-eighteenth century, when a floor was inserted and a chimney built into a new north gable. Later in the eighteenth century a further room was added against the gable and a full stair provided, creating the house-space occupied to this day (see Plate 3.3).[40] While Cobbler's Cottage illustrates the upgrading of an 'open-hall' house in the mid-eighteenth century, two tiny seventeenth-century cottages survive unaltered at Stiffkey in north Norfolk; Apple and Pip Cottage both consist of a single ground floor room, with bread ovens built into the fireplace of both, and a small storage space against the chimney stack in the slightly larger Apple Cottage (see Plate 3.4).[41]

Plate 3.3 Cobbler's Cottage, North Lopham, Norfolk. Originally a single-hearth one room cottage (built c. 1600); ceiling and chimney inserted c. 1750; extended to the right of the new chimney-gable before 1800; pantiled outshut added later. (National Monuments Record, English Heritage. © Mrs. C. Cole)

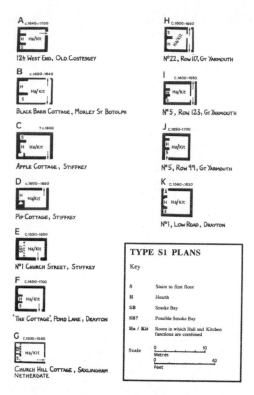

Plate 3.4   Norfolk houses built before 1700 with one room on the ground floor. (A. Longcroft, 'Plan-forms in smaller post-medieval houses: a case-study from Norfolk', *Vernacular Architecture*, 33, (2002), p. 40, fig. 5 [Type S1 refers to RCHME classification] © Vernacular Architecture Group)

Pauper inventories indicate that such cottages in Norfolk villages could be well furnished, even though these very lists document household goods in parish ownership.[42] 'Town Goods in ye Possession of Francis Semmons (on ye Common)' were listed by the Redenhall overseer in January 1740. 'In ye Low Room' were 'One Porridge pot, 3 Glass Bottles, 3 Trenchers, one Ovel Table, one Square Table, one Looking-Glass, a Cubbard, a Keep, a small Trunk, one Spinning-wheel, a Real, 3 old Chairs, some Tea Earthen-ware, a Hake, a Hook, a Hatchett, a Sithe, an old Spade' while 'Above Stairs' were 'One Bed, Bedstead, Bolster, a Rugg one Blankett and Curtains, 3 pair of Sheets'.[43] Semmons' tools indicate a labouring life, while his wife generated income from her spinning wheel. The Semmons' cottage was relatively well furnished, though cupboards, chests, tables and chairs were routinely described by parish appraisors as small and old. Pauper inventories were ephemeral documents and have only survived when copied, pasted or pinned in to parish account books; some 200 pauper inventories have been identified for Norfolk but only a mere handful have been located for Durham.[44] The Redenhall with Harleston and Wortewell records contain one of the largest Norfolk collections, with 45 inventories from 1731 to 1743 written in reverse at the rear of the overseer's book.[45] Most parishes have only a few surviving inventories. The Ashwellthorpe Book contains eight inventories entered between 1695 and 1742, though the last was very poorly written: '30th September 1742: The Goods of Edward Rushbrook: The Bebb and Furinenez, 2*l*.; Boyler, fryan pan and warman paine, 7*s*.; A Table, 9*d*., & His Lumber of all sortes 1*l*. 10*s*.', prompted the professional scribe who wrote the accounts for 1750 to remark in his own perfect script: 'Query: whether ye above was not don by a Jobbernol viz a Blunderbuss'.[46]

The majority of pauper inventories survive from the clay-lands of south and central Norfolk, where a wood-pasture economy supported a variegated social structure. The few places with inventories north of Norwich can similarly be located on heath, marsh or loamy soils. Along with some of the smaller market towns, it was in Norfolk's 'open' villages that household goods were circulated as an aspect of parish relief, and the homes of the poor in estate-dominated villages remain closed to us. Inventory survival reflects differences in parish record keeping, and customs governing the taking of goods into parish ownership, for sale, or loan to other paupers, could be highly localised. The Shelton records were unusually explicit about the context in which inventories were taken. Parish practice was to receive goods on the death of a pensioner to cover the costs of burial, as when the overseer 'received for ye goods of An Butcher deceased 5*s*. 6*d*.' in 1670. Or 'The Widow Lords goods [...]3*l*. 16*s*. 4*d*. that the Town took after her decease' in 1676. The value of Widow Lord's goods slightly exceeded the 3*l*. 4*s*. 1*d*. that the parish had spent on wood to fuel her fire, as well as cash payments for rent and a carer's allowance in the year before her death. Pauper goods in parish ownership were either sold or recycled in the community. This circulation of goods between paupers is again clear at Shelton. In 1685 ten shillings was 'due from Rob't Jermyn and Thomas Jermyn ye town for takeing Prudence Bookman' into their care. A year later, the 'goods remaining to ye use of ye poor yt were Amy Bookeman widow to ye value of 5*s*. 8*d*.' were recorded. Then, on 1 April 1689

Mem. yt ye Officers and Inhabitants did then lend to Anne Roberts Widow one bed, one bolster, and one coverlet bought by ye town for fourtine shillings when Edm: Roberts ye late husband of ye said Anne lay sick of ye small pox.[47]

Pauper inventories, like probate inventories, cannot be taken as a comprehensive record of a household's contents, especially if prized items were dispersed to real or fictive kin. In some instances goods 'gone' or 'taken away' were recorded, but many gifts or sales were silently omitted. In most cases goods were given up to the parish to defray the costs of care in old age. Only a minority of middle-aged householders had their goods seized for debt, distrained for non-payment of rent or taken to cover the costs of discharge from gaol, and in one case failure to comply with jury service.[48] A schedule of the 'whole estate' of Anthony Balls, husbandman, of Diss, was taken on his discharge from Norwich gaol in *circa* 1700. His extensive debts included 2s. 5d. owed to William Eastall of North Lopham 'upon a Contract for Cattle about 9 yeares since', and 15 shillings 'To Mr James Harling of Eye Green a debt for Grocery Wares above 2 yrs'. His 'goods household stuffe and personall estate' comprised bedding, furniture, hearth tools – 'a payre of dogg irons; one fire pann one payre of tongues and a paire of bellowes' – and 'ffoure old wooll wheeles for his wife and children to spinn att. As to house and lands or any other reale estate he hath none'. Balls' family experienced extreme distress owing to his debts, and the majority of inventories were taken to offset the costs of more routine parish relief. At Gissing in January 1735, for instance, Robert Lawrence bought Samuel Beck's goods worth 12s. 9d. in lieu of 'a quarter's Rent due at Christmas last and one pair of new shoes'.[49]

The few pauper inventories that give room names (see Table 3.2) indicate that most pauper households consisted of a multi-purpose living room, commonly called the kitchen in eighteenth-century Norfolk, and a chamber. Very few had outhouses; Widow Little at Hingham in 1724 had tubbs, pails, mustard quorns, an ale stool, two vessels and two hog troughs in hers, though how recently these had been used is obscure. In some instances paupers occupied lodgings, such as the 'apartment' in John Pidgeon's 'declaration concerning parish goods in the use of Sarah Brown, widow, 1757', which refers to 'all the Goods and Chattels now in the lower Room and one chamber being part of the House wherein I now dwell'. Some of the entries in Table 3.2, particularly those referring to 'low room' and 'chamber', will also refer to lodgings rather than free-standing households. Pauper inventories seldom document households with the range of rooms normally encountered in probate inventories for middling households. Even the modestly extensive set

Table 3.2 Norfolk pauper inventories with room names

Year	Room names mentioned	Name	Other information	Value	Place
1693	Hall / Parlour / Buttery / Chamber / Chamber	Jonathan Coote	Turner	28-13-2	Diss
1700	ye Fire room and closet by it / ye other room / ye chamber	Francis Karrington	Relief of himself and family	9-19-0	Shelton
1701	Hall / Bed chamber / ye chamber within	Henry and Susen Barret	Husband and wife on relief	6-13-0	Moulton
1718	Kitchen / Chamber / Seller	John Spall	For charge to parish	5-3-6	Surlingham
1720	Low Rooms / Chamber	John Dorman	Collectioner	4-9-6	Shipdham
1724	Kitchen / Buttery / Chamber / Outhouse	Widow Little	On relief		Hingham
1726	Kitchen	John Gooch	Collectioner; cooper's tools		Gissing
1726	Kitchen / Parlour / Chamber	Gilbert Band	Collectioner		Gissing
1727	Lodging Room / ye Room they Sleep in	William Carr	Relief of himself and family	2-7-0	Bressingham
1734	Kitchen / Chamber	Godphrey Goodrum			Wortwell
1738	Kitchen / Chamber	James Keely			Redenhall
1739	Kitchen / Parlour	Widow Searls	Widow		Redenhall
1739	Lower Room / Chambers	Samuel Harman	In house of Crashfield Revitt		Redenhall
1741	Low Room / Above Stairs	Francis Semmons	On ye Common		Redenhall
1741	Low Room / Above Stairs	Richard Hammond			Redenhall
1749	Kitchen / Chamber	Widow Fuller	Widow, deceased		Trowse
1751	Kitchen	Sarah Brown	Widow		Shelton
1757	Low Room / Chamber	Thomas Taylor	Distrained for rent		Shelton

(continued)

Table 3.2 Continued

Year	Room names mentioned	Name	Other information	Value	Place
1766	Chamber / Cellar	Thomas Trip			Holme
1769	Kitchen / Bed Room / Kitchen Chamber / Scullery	Widow Elvey	Widow		Shelton
1770	Parlour	John Bell	Sold to parish	1-12-6	Moulton
1773	Kitchen / Chamber	William Adkins	Of Brydon, deceased		Bressingham
1773	Low Room / Buttery / Chamber	Mary Bravenett			Bressingham
1773	Low Room / Chamber	Henry Fisher			Bressingham
1774	Kitchen / Pantry / Bed Room / First Chamber / Second Chamber / ye Shop	William Buck	On relief	3-12	Stratton St. Mary
1781	Kitchen / Chamber	William Long	Goods bought of for parish	4-12	Newton Flotman
1784	Kitchen / Chamber	Thomas Cullams	Sold for rent and collection		Forcett St. Peter
1786	Kitchen	William Rice	For use of mayor money	3-1-0	Trowse
1796	Kitchen	William Read Senior	Pauper		Hapton
1804	Kitchen / Pantry / Chamber	Jonathan Minter	Pauper		Brockdish

Source: Norf.RO, PD 100/140; 358/41; 489/29; 611/37; 337/158; 575/128; 50/71; 111/170; 295/102; 216/90; 629/50; 122/54; 83/15; 421/133; 236/51; 477/43.

May 21 1737: Ralph Cary and Robert Eaton Churchwardens and Thomas Gilbert and Elizabeth Kemp Overseers of ye Poor of ye parish of Gissing in ye County of Norfolk. Bought of John Goss of Diss in ye County aforesaid 'Two Feather Beds and Bedsteads 2 Bolsters 2 pillows 2 Coverlids 3 sheets 2 Blankets 3 Bed Mats 2 Bed lines a Iron poridge pott 1 Hake 1 Frying pan 1 pair of Tongs 5 Chairs a peel 1 pail 2 kellers 6 Trenchers 1 dish 1 platter 3 spoons and a small Kettle five Wimbles 1 Ax 3 Chizzles 1 Gonge 1 Mallett a Gimblett 1 hammer handsaw and shovel at 3*l*. 1*s*.' Their received of ye aforesaid officers Three Pounds one shilling being ye full Contents of this Bill I say received p. me. John Goss. Test. Saml Alexander.

May ye 21st 1737 Borrowed and Received of ye above said Officers all ye above-mentioned goods bought by them of ye above said John Goss on purpose and in order to lend me for the necessary use of myself and family. As witness my hand

More the Best Bed and bedstead, 1 Boulster, 1 pillow two blankets and Curtens and Curtens Rods one beedwill (in all they stand) the sum of 2*l*. 5*s*.
One warmeing pan 1 pair of Cobb irons one Hoak one speet one Dresser one pair of tongs one Table. Value together 14*s*.   Judah Goss   Her *** mark

Borrowed and Received these of the above said Officers all the abovementioned goods, bought by them, and lent to me for the Necessary use of My Self, and Family, wch I promise to deliver upon demand to the abovesd Officers or their Successors. As Witness my hand *Henry Goss*

Source: Norf.RO, PD 50/71.

Figure 3.1   Example of a Norfolk pauper inventory

of rooms in which William Bucks' goods lay in 1774 – kitchen, pantry, bed room, first chamber, second chamber and 'ye shop' – includes no parlour nor anywhere to eat separate from the kitchen.[50] And those lists with more than a couple of rooms invariably relate to middle-aged debtors rather than elderly paupers.

Pauper inventories can reveal very basic household goods. An inventory from Hingham in 1724 records 'ye Goods of John Hansard p[ensione]r. Seized by the churchwardens, overseers and 'constibell': 'Two Little Kittles, one frying Pann (5*s*.) one turnep how, one Speet, one Gridg-Iron, and a payre of Andirons a payre Tongs (3*s*.) two chairs (1*s*.) and two hakes (1*s*.). Sum is 10*s*.' The household stuff and tools to support a poor family is well illustrated from the 1737 Gissing inventory (see Figure 3.1), where the overseers used parish funds to purchase goods from John Goss of Diss for the use of Henry Goss and family of Gissing. The more basic inventories often relate to the wid-owed elderly, especially those lodging in a single room. 'Of the Goods in the Possession of Widw. Goldspink, taken by Mr. John Edwards overseer' on 26 June 1731 there were just 'One Bed and Bedstead, one Chair and some very old things.' As Table 3.3 indicates, the standard items recorded in Norfolk pauper inventories were bedding, hearth gear, kitchen utensils and work tools. Bedding varied in quality, but curtained bedsteads (unknown in cottage inventories before 1650) were common from the later seventeenth century. Hearth tools and cooking implements also show considerable continuity through to the later eighteenth century. Pewter and wooden vessels were more prevalent before 1750, while throughout the period earthenware was ubiquitous, and only a tiny minority of pauper inventories refer to delft or blue-and-white china. Work tools comprised labouring or craft implements for men, with spinning wheels, laundry tubs and smoothing irons common means of income for women. All these household items also appear in Durham inventories, though regional differences in household economies are evident: spinning wheels were a rarity in Durham, while the use of coal for fuel was less commonplace in Norfolk.[51] Overall, the inventories document a strong degree of continuity in humble domesticity over the long eighteenth century.

Two items, in particular, indicate change in the domestic experience of the eighteenth-century labouring poor. Firstly, tea kettles confirm that tea-drinking was universal among pauper cottagers from the mid-eighteenth century. This was more of an addictive necessity than a luxury, and was partly adopted to offset deficiencies in diet; at Sedgefield 'many of the poor declared that they had been driven to drinking tea from not being able to procure milk'.[52] Secondly, 16 per cent of Norfolk inventories (and 27 per cent in Essex) refer to a looking glass. These were not display items but small – sometimes broken – pieces of mirror which the poor used to check their appearance before leaving the house. The 'one small Looking-Glass' and 'Looking-Glass-frame with a Drawer' in Widow Searls' kitchen in 1739 possibly had a comb or hair pins in the drawer, while a 'Broken Looking-Glass' perhaps sat on one of the three shelves 'in ye Low Room' Richard Hammond occupied in the Town House at Redenhall in January 1741. It was the very poverty of these households which made personal appearance so important to their dignity.[53] Drinking tea and checking appearances in the mirror were ultimately about ameliorating lives of toil.

Yet, signs of cheerfulness are not absent from pauper inventories. Elias Bygrave at Carrow Abby near Norwich had a 'Caniva bird and cage' worth one shilling and six pence in 1754. Nor was display absent – Isaac Day in 1742 had a 'Plate-Rack with six Delf Plates'. Godphrey

Table 3.3 Selected goods in Norfolk pauper inventories, 1690–1810

	1690s	1700s	1710s	1720s	1730s	1740s	1750s	1760s	1770s	1780s	1790s	1800s	Norfolk 1690–1810	Essex 1710–1819
Bedding	29	10	22	42	28	23	12	9	13	8	4	1	98%	–
Cooking equipment	25	7	17	30	26	21	8	9	11	8	4	1	81%	–
Pot hook	15	5	16	24	24	20	8	9	7	2	4		65%	–
Coal items						1		1	4	2	1		4%	7%
'Old' furniture	15	5	1	6	6	1	1			1			18%	–
Chest of drawers	1					3	5	3	3	3			9%	32%
Desk	1	1	2	2	1								3%	–
Corner cupboard			1		1				1		2		2%	–
Candlesticks	3	1	4	1	18	7	4	1	3	1	1		21%	49%
Looking glass	1	2	2	2	11	8	1	1	2	2			16%	27%
Books				2	2								2%	0%
Window curtains				2	2	2							3%	–
Pictures, prints					3								2%	10%
Clocks, watches													0%	20%
Hour glass			1			2							2%	–
Tea items						2		4	4	5	2	1	9%	46%
Coffee items									1				0.5%	10%
Tobacco items						2							1%	0%
Salt			2	2	3	2							4%	12%
Spice			1	2	2	1		1				1	3%	–

(*continued*)

Table 3.3 Continued

	1690s	1700s	1710s	1720s	1730s	1740s	1750s	1760s	1770s	1780s	1790s	1800s	Norfolk 1690–1810	Essex 1710–1819
Knives & forks											1	1	2%	0%
Silver		1											0.5%	0%
Brass	5	3	5	7	1	5	3	1	2		1	1	17%	–
Pewter	3	2	2	6	7	4	1	1			1	1	13%	–
Earthenware	3	1	2	3	15	9	1	3	3	4	1	1	21%	61%
China										1			0.5%	–
Delft plates						2							1%	–
Wooden vessels	3		2	3	11	9		3	2	1	1		17%	–
Chamber pot	4	2		1	2	2							5%	–
Smoothing iron	4	1	1	3	2		1						6%	–
Spinning wheel	2	1	7	14	14	10	6	6	2	4	3	1	34%	–
Work tools	1			6	5	1	2	2		1	3	1	11%	–
Livestock								1					0.5%	–
Value (lowest)	1-14-0	2-12-0	1-3-8	10-0	1-9-0	–	2-1-0	–	1-11-6	2-5-0	–	–	10-0	10-0
Range (highest)	5-14-0	9-19-0	5-3-6	4-9-6	3-13-6	3-17-9	2-2-6	3-19-6	1-12-6	3-1-0	3-14-10		9-19-0	(Average)
No. inventories	29	10	22	43	29	24	12	10	1w3	9	4	1	206	41

Source: Norf.RO PC 88/1; PD 50/71; 83/15; 88/1; 88/2; 100/140; 111/114; 111/170; 122/54; 193/93/1; 193/93/2; 216/90; 218/3; 236/51; 295/102; 316/46; 326/58; 326/59; 337/158; 358/41; 358/61; 421/133; 477/43; 489/29; 489/51; 575/128; 611/37; 629/50; MC 76/50, 534X10. Essex data from P. King 'Pauper inventories', pp. 162–5.

Goodrum in 1738 occupied two rooms – a well-equipped living room and a sleeping chamber:

> In the Kitching there is 23 Earthen plates and 3 earthen Dishes some pictures; a Dresser with Drawers two Tables 9 Chairs one Boyler and one pot one Hake a pair of hand Irons and tongs; a pair of Spice drawers, a Corner Cubbart with small Earthenwear; two Doz. of Glass Bottles and old Cubbert two Brushes, a Looking Glass plateshelf and a pair of Window Curtains a Killer a pail and old Rubbish. In the Chamber One Bed Bedstead etc. one pair of sheets.[54]

Elias, Isaac and Godphrey's possessions indicate that homely comfort was present in pauper households, and that this was not exclusively female. But the 'luxury' items that might be taken to signify cheerful endurance are offset by the basic necessities in the majority of inventories.

Sixty-five per cent of pauper inventories from Norfolk parishes include 'a hake', the Norfolk term for hook. These indicate that cooking was done over the fire, with porridge pots and tea kettles suspended from the hook. This was distinct from the adoption of more complicated cooking technologies by middling households, where cuts of meat rather than single-pot meals, and the adoption of cutlery, were increasingly the norm from the later seventeenth century. Adam Smith in *The Wealth of Nations* (1776) included knives and forks in his list of common possessions in a cottage, but cutlery is rarely recorded in Norfolk or Durham pauper inventories, and George Gascoign of Diss in 1795 was unusual in having 'some odd knifes and forks'. Widow Burroughs, in a two-hearth house, was also exceptional in having 'a cole range' at Gissing in 1742.[55] Most inventories document single-hearth households cooking over an open fire. These cottages invariably consisted of one main living room with a secondary space for sleeping and storage. Living in a house of one bay, focused on a single hearth, these households maintained continuities from the seventeenth century and earlier. There is very little sign, however, that eighteenth-century cottagers were living in a manner directly similar to the medieval house space with a central hearth. In both East Anglia and the North-East, excavated and surviving buildings indicate that hearths had generally moved to a chimney-wise position – even if they only had rudimentary smoke-hoods – by 1650 if not 1600.[56]

While the abandonment of central open-hearths occurred over several generations up to 1650, the mid-seventeenth century witnessed a more

decisive alteration in the position of entrances. Adam Longcroft's analysis of smaller house-plans has shown that opposed entrances (following
the medieval use of space, with the cross-passage at the low-end of the
hall) were still commonplace in Norfolk houses constructed between
1600 and 1650, but that after 1650 a lobby-entry arrangement against
the chimney was the norm (see Plate 3.4). This paralleled the adoption of lobby-entries by more affluent households in the early-to-mid
seventeenth century, which facilitated the separation of guests received
in the parlour from servants in the hall and service areas. Such social distancing was not a concern for poorer households with one main room,
though their lobby-entry does indicate the same privileging of front
access. Land-less households had little need of rear access and wished
to maximise floor space. Although the adoption of a lobby-entry was
often the decision of commercial landlords and builders, particularly in
towns, poorer households themselves had pragmatic reasons for depart-
ing from customary practice in having an entrance that maximised
the space available for furniture and household activities. Eighteenth-
century cottagers had too much free-standing furniture – including tables,
chairs, cupboards and bedsteads, as well as spinning-wheels and laundry
tubs – to have an open hearth in the middle of the floor. Moreover,
as Table 3.2 shows, their main living space, after 1700, was called the
kitchen rather than the 'hall' or 'fire house' of previous generations.
These folk were living in the eighteenth century and pursued their own
version of the changes in living practices better known for more affluent
households.

For housing conditions across the period 1650 to 1850 it is plausible
to suggest a broad pattern of improvement in the earlier part of the
period followed by deterioration. Neighbourhood housing from the
thirteenth to the seventeenth centuries was frequently constructed at
low-cost but would stand for generations with regular maintenance.
From the mid-seventeenth century, however, conditions favoured more
thorough rebuilding by husbandmen and craftsmen. A reduction in
the rate of marriage and household formation, along with rising real
wages and surplus income for rebuilding, all point to an improvement
in housing conditions nationally for the securely employed in the late
seventeenth century.[57] Many of these well-constructed houses were
occupied by poorer folk a generation and more later. The seventeenth-
century rebuilding of houses for the securely employed, moreover, was
not a straightforward improvement since the wage-dependent population had increased and many were descendants of those who raised
their own food on small-holdings a generation earlier. Rural rebuilding

replaced the sort of house documented for Frances Karrington at Shelton in 1700, whose goods totalled 9*l.* 9*s.* on his 'takeing ye patch upon himself and family'. The Karringtons occupied 'ye Fire room' (a common alternative to 'hall' in humble seventeenth-century households) 'and closet by it'; 'ye other room' (an inner room, equivalent to the 'parlour' in more affluent households) which contained the marital bed as well as 'a great Wicker Chayr and cushion', earthenware, pewter, candlesticks, a warming pan, household linen etc.; and 'ye chamber' (containing a table and two stools, seemingly used as a work space).[58] Artisan housing, meanwhile, was constructed on a commercial basis in the larger towns. On St Martin's Lane and Timberhill in Norwich, two pairs of houses built in the late seventeenth century survive. Two storied, with one room per floor, they were built by commercial landlords taking advantage of the rental market.[59] Many such one-up one-down houses were built in the late seventeenth century, sometimes with architectural embellishments to their door cases and facades. They did not originally contain the poor, who were more likely to occupy lodgings in sub-divided older houses. Population increase and price inflation over the mid-to-later eighteenth century created an increase in poverty, placing pressure on the housing stock. By the later eighteenth century many of these artisan houses had slipped in status, and were now occupied by poorer households, often with one household per floor, as at The Rows in Great Yarmouth (see Plate 3.5). The commercial sensitivity of their builders to changes in the rental market is revealed by the fact that multiple occupancy was anticipated at their construction. Some of the late seventeenth-century houses on The Rows were constructed with external entrances leading directly onto the staircase, facilitating separate households on each floor.[60]

The deterioration in housing conditions during the eighteenth century was exacerbated as poorer folk found it increasingly difficult to achieve piecemeal repair of older housing. Records of thatching decline around 1800 in the rural churchwarden records and the urban-industrial settlements on Tyne-side witnessed a parallel switch from gathered to permanent roofing materials. This prompted antiquarian comment. Thomas Bell collected descriptions of Gateshead Fell between 1825 and 1841, recording William Potts, aged 60 in 1747, as winning stones to build a cottage with 'duffetts' (turf sods) for covering it, and describes conditions a generation earlier:

At that time, and indeed at a much later period, the cottages were principally of the most miserable description, being built with 'mud' and covered with turf or 'sods', but these have gradually given place

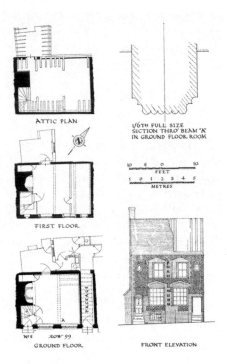

Plate 3.5 A late seventeenth-century house on The Rows, Great Yarmouth. (B. H. St. J. O'Neil, 'Some Seventeenth-Century Houses in Great Yarmouth', *Archaeologia* XCV (1953), p. 157, fig. 2 'Row 99, No.5' © The Society of Antiquaries of London)

to other buildings of a better description and a sod cottage is now a rarity even on Gateshead Fell.

While housing in the urban-industrial areas of the North-East was being modernised, higher population densities meant worsening sanitary conditions. A report on the 'shameful dirty state' of a privy and yard at South Shield's in 1831 was written the year cholera reached Britain through Sunderland. Even in urban-industrial districts, however, people wished to hang on to what little they had. One woman from All Saints parish in Newcastle on entering the workhouse in 1836 protested that '... it would be an act of oppression on the part of the vestry. In the event of my death my children ought to have my household goods'.[61]

The evidence from the North-East and East Anglia points to a number of conclusions. Local demographic and employment patterns, along with the available housing stock, did much to determine the quality of poorer dwellings. The agency of poorer folk lay in their ability to do what they could to maintain the fabric of their dwellings. Household efforts were supplemented by direct assistance from the parish and in some instances landlords, who together ensured that the physical fabric of dwellings was maintained, at least among the deserving poor within rural settlements and market towns. Those in regular employment from the late seventeenth century witnessed an improvement in housing and furnishings, as the value of wages and availability of affordable consumer goods increased. In both regions throughout the eighteenth century many households in relative poverty were able to accrue a range of goods beneath a durable roof during their working life and remain in their own homes in old age. Their ability to do so often depended on more than parish relief; particularly the assistance of kin or their substitutes.[62] In 1778, Jo Vipond, yeoman, of Craggshield in Cumberland, bequeathed house-space for his mother Elizabeth in that part of the 'Dwelling House' 'wherein I now live consisting of an upper and lower Room'. He also left £1 to his three brothers Joseph, Jacob and Thomas a 'superintendant over lead mines', and his married sister Mary, as well as £5 to each of their children at the age of 21. 'But if in Case it shall happen that my said Brothers and Sister or any of them shall at any time be likely to become chargeable to the said parish of Alston Then in Ease of the said parish and for the better maintenance and Support of such of them as shall happen to be likely to become chargeable' he bequeathed £3 to be paid to each of them yearly, 'for so long as they shall otherwise be unable to support themselves and no longer, such Inability to support themselves to be determined by the Overseer of the poor'.[63] Charity really might begin at home, even if it ended with assistance from the parish.

There were certainly many less salubrious dwellings in the later seventeenth century, though their exclusion from hearth tax lists makes it doubtful whether they counted as households at all. The proportion of those in poverty generally increased as the eighteenth century progressed, and housing conditions deteriorated where population increased or wages fell. This was the scenario that reformers became alert to across the country from about 1760 and struggled to ameliorate through to 1850. One Norfolk account published in 1773 echoes Goldsmith's *Deserted Village* (1770):

> In passing through a village near Swaffham, in the County of Norfolk a few years ago, to my great mortification I beheld the houses tumbling into ruins, and the common fields all enclosed; upon enquiring into the cause of this melancholy alteration, I was informed that a

gentleman of Lynn had bought that township and the next adjoining it: that he had thrown the one into three, and the other into four farms; which before the enclosure were in about twenty farms: and upon my further enquiring what was becoming of the farmers who were turned out, the answer was that some of them were dead and the rest were become labourers.[64]

Conversely, farm workers in the estate-villages of Norfolk and the commercial farms of Durham and Northumberland experienced an improvement in housing where tied-cottages were rebuilt as an expression of patrician concern. But it was the later eighteenth-century genteel sensibility towards the homes of the poor – distinct from the pious charity of seventeenth-century almshouse building – that altered most.

Dependent on wage labour, and frequently occupying older housing built for more self-sufficient households in earlier generations, the eighteenth-century rural poor did experience some deterioration in housing conditions. Even the apparent continuity in many aspects of pauper domestic life through to the early nineteenth century represented a 'falling behind' in living standards. This was not by any means offset by the widening range of consumer goods available to the poor, as the age and condition of furnishings and utensils marked out their poverty. The aspirations and disappointments expressed in pauper letters compliment the evidence of pauper inventories. Hopefully Hugh Constable's request in 1827 for 'Getting a few Household Goods' was met, as 'if the Gentlemen will advance a little money to finish furnishing a place it is my intention to marry if I possibly can raise Sufficient money'. Harsh treatment, however, might have dire consequences. William James wrote in 1821, 'I hope Sir – something will be done for me, to stop the threatening proceedings of my Landlady to take away the Comfort of our few goods from us in which case I see no remedy to keep us from utter ruin'.[65]

We are left with a mixed picture of continuity and change. Concern for the deserving poor enabled some dignity in old age, which was distinct from the treatment faced by those in difficulties (supposedly of their own making) during middle age. Already by 1650, there was a distinction between the respectable working poor keeping their heads up and the disrespect of the underemployed, who may have preferred to raise an ale pot. The following two centuries saw little alteration in this basic division, though the forms of housing occupied by the poor meant this social cleavage was not always clearly reflected in distinctions between dwellings. Those in relative poverty were not always in desperately worse accommodation than the industrious workers whose small houses might place them on the lowest rung of the middling sorts. Many occupied well-constructed housing built for those who could afford higher rents a generation or more earlier. Sub-division of these properties, alongside tiny cottages and the occupancy of lofts and cellars in towns, perpetuated single-room dwelling spaces, though even the smallest usually had a secondary space for sleeping or storage. Rents certainly forced some of the poor into cramped housing, but the contents of the home probably distinguished degrees of poverty more precisely than the outward appearance or size of dwellings, since moveable goods were easily pawned, sold or never purchased in times of crisis, while rents were more difficult to negotiate.[66] Even the most meagre of goods mattered to those who failed to lead orderly lives: 'My old Great Coat, wich hides the Rufull tokens of want and Poverty – will take 2/6 to Redeem, our Blanket and Meny other things are away By Reason of want [...] Putting them away will Bear Reflection – No Drunkness, No Disorderly Life'.[67]

Posterity should avoid the condescension of assuming that poverty prohibited people from finding consolation at home. Tending the hearth is a very ancient means of fulfilling humans' need of security, comfort and sustenance. And paupers were acutely distressed by the loss of a home. David Rivenall in 1827 suffered so, that 'my fits have been Such as to dissable me from Workin to keep my Family [...] I have 7 in family With my Wife Self and No house to Be in I am distresst Beyound and all I Ever met With'. Sarah Withnell, a young widow with children, wrote in 1815 'pray Sir for god Sake help me at this time or it will So destress Me I think it will break my Heart'.[68] Yet the very ideas of unhomely misery versus homely comfort – which paupers and polite commentators shared to some degree – were largely a creation of the period under study; emerging in the later-eighteenth and reaching their apogee in the nineteenth century, they have framed understandings of domesticity ever since. Historians' discovery of an economy of make-shifts that tended to maximise resources, means that assumptions of universal squalor and misery for the poor in their own homes are not sustainable. Misery certainly arose where landlords or employers failed to fulfil patrician values or assistance from family, neighbours and the parish was lacking. Squalor could also arise where deprived families failed to maintain conventions governing food preparation, ventilation and waste disposal, which only reinforced their social isolation. But most households coped with material, physical and spatial constraints, and actively sought to avoid the psychological deterioration that

followed from a disrupted domestic economy. There were few, if any, hearth-less houses between 1650 and 1830 and for some of the poorest households we can connect with via documentary and archaeological evidence there are signs of homely comfort. Where this is lacking, and only basic cooking utensils and bedding are recorded, the effort to avoid actual squalor is palpable. Even the most impoverished inventories record pewter and wooden chamber pots.[69] It is not flippant to conclude that the eighteenth-century poor, when in control of their own dwelling-space, usually had a pot to piss in.

Notes

I am grateful for the British Academy research grant (SG:35465) that enabled me to work in Norfolk, and to the staff of Norfolk and Durham Record Offices for help with finding pauper inventories. Joanne Bailey, Chris Brooks, David Craig, Matt Greenhall, Matthew Johnson, Leona Skelton, Judith Welford and Keith Wrightson provided helpful discussion and references. Meanwhile, my grandparents, in their determination to tend their own hearth at an advanced age, have been an inspiration.

1. J. Tosh, *A Man's Place: Masculinity and the Middle Class Home in Victorian England* (New Haven & London: Yale University Press, 1999), pp. 27–50; A. Vidler, *The Architectural Uncanny: Essays in the Modern Unhomely* (Cambridge & London: MIT Press, 1992); V. Smith, *Clean: A History of Personal Hygiene* (Oxford: Oxford University Press, 2007); A. Mayne & T. Murray (eds), *The Archaeology of Urban Landscapes: Explorations in Slumland* (Cambridge: Cambridge University Press, 2001).

2. L. Cowen Orlin, *Private Matters and Public Culture in Post-Reformation England* (Ithaca & London: Cornell University Press, 1994), pp. 2–11; C. Brooks, *Law, Politics and Society in Early Modern England* (Cambridge: Cambridge University Press, 2008), Chapter 12.

3. D. A. Kirby (ed.), *Parliamentary Surveys of the Bishopric of Durham* (Durham: Surtees Society, 1968), I, p. 8 & 84; D. Levine & K. Wrightson, *The Making of an Industrial Society: Whickham 1560–1765* (Oxford: Oxford University Press, 1991), pp. 83–151; see also J. H. Bettey, 'Seventeenth-Century Squatters' Dwellings: Some Documentary Evidence', *Vernacular Architecture* 13, (1982), 28–30.

4. J. Thirsk & J. P. Cooper (eds), *Seventeenth-Century Economic Documents* (Oxford: Oxford University Press, 1972), p. 781; L. Stone, *The Family, Sex and Marriage in England 1500–1800* (Weidenfield and Nicolson, 1977); R. B. Shoemaker, *Gender in English Society, 1650–1850: The Emergence of Separate Spheres?* (Longman, 1998), pp. 15–58.

5. A. Ballantyne, 'Joseph Gandy and the Politics of Rustic Charm', in B. Arciszewska & E. McKellar (eds), *Articulating British Classicism: New Approaches to Eighteenth-Century Architecture* (Aldershot: Ashgate, 2004), pp. 163–85, quoting Kent at p. 166; J. L. Hammond & B. Hammond, *The Village Labourer* (1911), (Stroud: Nonsuch, 2005), p. 172; S. Lloyd, 'Cottage

Conversations: Poverty and Manly Independence in Eighteenth-Century England', *Past & Present* 184, (2004), 69–108; J. Crowley, *The Invention of Comfort: Sensibilities and Design in Early Modern Britain and America* (Baltimore & London: Johns Hopkins University Press, 2001), pp. 203–29; *Idem*, 'From Luxury to Comfort and Back Again: Landscape Architecture and the Cottage in Britain and America', in M. Berg & E. Eger (eds), *Luxury in the Eighteenth Century: Debates, Desires and Delectable Goods* (Basingtoke: Palgrave Macmillan, 2003), pp. 135–50.

6. Norf.RO, PD 218/3; A. Green, 'Confining the Vernacular: The Seventeenth-Century Origins of a Mode of Study', *Vernacular Architecture* 38, (2007), 1–7; J. Barrell, *The Dark Side of the Landscape: The Rural Poor in English Painting, 1730–1840* (Cambridge: Cambridge University Press, 1980).

7. The following draws on A. Green, E. Parkinson & M. Spufford, *County Durham Hearth Tax Assessment Lady Day 1666* (British Record Society in association with British Academy Hearth Tax Project, 2006); R. Welford, 'Newcastle Householders in 1665', *Archaeologia Aeliana* 3, VII (1911), 49–76; P. Seaman et al., *Norfolk Hearth Tax Exemption Certificates 1670–1674: Norwich, Great Yarmouth, King's Lynn and Thetford* (British Record Society, 2001); T. Ashwin & A. Davison (eds), *An Historical Atlas of Norfolk* (Chichester: Phillimore, 2005), p. 109; A. Longcroft, 'The Hearth Tax and Historic Housing Stocks: A Case Study from Norfolk', in P. S. Barnwell & M. Airs (eds), *Houses and the Hearth Tax: The Later Stuart House and Society* (York: Council for British Archaeology, 2006), pp. 62–73; 'Norfolk Hearth Tax Assessment, Michaelmas 1664', *Norfolk Genealogy* 15, (1983); 'Norfolk and Norwich Hearth Tax Assessment, Lady Day 1666', *Norfolk Genealogy* 20, (1988).

8. In 1800, 9.3 per cent of Durham's population was in receipt of poor relief versus 15.2 per cent in Norfolk (K. Williams, *From Pauperism to Poverty* (Routledge, 1981), pp. 149–50).

9. Great Yarmouth North Ward in 1664 contained 37 single- and 49 two-hearth households exempt; Hartlepool in 1666 had 30 single and 12 two-hearth households exempt.

10. By 1801 urban overcrowding was worse in Newcastle (8.6 inhabitants per house; the highest nationally) than Norwich (4.6) (J. Ellis, 'The Black Indies', in R. Colls & B. Lancaster (eds) *Newcastle upon Tyne: A Modern History* (Chichester: Phillimore, 2001), p. 14; P. Corfield, *The Impact of English Towns, 1700–1800* (Oxford: Oxford University Press, 1982), p. 183).

11. Seaman, *Norfolk Hearth Tax*, pp. x–xli; see also T. Arkell, 'Understanding Exemption from the Hearth Tax', in Barnwell & Airs, *Houses and the Hearth Tax*, pp. 18–21; A. Green 'The Durham Hearth Tax: Community Politics and Social Relations', in Barnwell & Airs, *Houses and the Hearth Tax*, pp. 144–54.

12. 'Non-solvent' was the term used in the 1674 Durham Return (TNA, E179/106/25); A. Everitt, 'Farm Labourers', in J. Thirsk (ed.), *Agrarian History of England and Wales, V 1640–1750* (Cambridge: Cambridge University Press, 1967), pp. 396–465.

13. Green, *Durham Hearth Tax*, p. lxxxiv; S. Pearson et al., *Kent Hearth Tax Assessment Lady Day 1664* (British Record Society, 2000), pp. c–cii; N. W. Alcock, 'Housing the Urban Poor in 1800: Courts in Atherstone and Coventry, Warwickshire', *Vernacular Architecture* 36, (2005), 49–60; even 'one

room' pit-men's dwellings in Northumberland usually had a loft above, E. Mercer, *English Vernacular Houses* (HMSO, 1975), p. 77.

14. *Historical Atlas of Norfolk; An Historical Atlas of County Durham* (Durham: Durham County Local History Society, 1992); S. Pincus, *1688: The First Modern Revolution* (New Haven & London: Yale University Press, 2009), pp. 54 and 62.
15. E.g. Norf.RO, MC 72/3–5, 520X4, Division of farmhouse into three dwelling-houses, 1811; M. H. Johnson, 'A Contextual Study of Traditional Architecture in Western Suffolk, 1400–1700' (Unpublished University of Cambridge PhD Thesis, 1989).
16. Norf.RO, MF/X/140/13, Holt Manor Court, 23 December 1734.
17. R. I. Hodgson, 'Demographic Trends in County Durham, 1560–1801', *University of Manchester School for Geography Research Papers* 5, (1978).
18. *Historical Atlas of County Durham*, p. 40. R. W. Brunskill, 'Vernacular Architecture in the Northern Pennines', *Northern History* 11, (1975), p. 109.
19. N. Emery, 'Materials and Methods: Some Aspects of Building in County Durham, 1600–1930', *Durham Archaeological Journal* 10, (1994), p. 114.
20. M. J. Tillbrook, 'Aspects of Government and Society of County Durham, 1558–1642' (Unpublished Liverpool University PhD Thesis, 1981), II, p. 810.
21. A. Green 'Houses and Landscape in Early Industrial County Durham', in T. Faulkner, H. Berry & J. Gregory (eds), *Northern Landscapes: Representations and Realities* (Woodbridge: Boydell, 2008); Levine & Wrightson, *Whickham*, pp. 238–9.
22. J. U. Nef, *The Rise of the British Coal Industry* (Cass, 1966), I, p. 176; W. Page (ed.), *Victoria History of Durham* (Constable, 1905–28), II, p. 37.
23. *Newcastle Courant*, 6 July 1723, 5 October 1728 and 24 May 1729; J. Ellis, 'The Decline and Fall of the Tyneside Salt Industry, 1660–1790: A Re-examination', *Economic History Review*, 2nd ser., 33, (1980), 45–58.
24. Dur.RO D/St/B3/1–4, 'List of new tenants in Pickering's house, South Shields', mid-eighteenth century.
25. A. Green, 'Houses and Households in County Durham and Newcastle-upon-Tyne, *c.* 1570–1730' (Unpublished Durham University PhD Thesis, 2000), pp. 217–21.
26. Dur.RO, EP Pi/22 v. 129–130.
27. At Long Newton officers identified three sorts of poor in the 1660s: those in receipt of relief; those who kept livestock 'and so maintained themselves and their families, but that employment being taken away by the inclosure [...] are likely to be wholly burdensome to the town' and those 'with divers children and nothing to maintain them but the poor man's hand labour' (Dur.RO, D/Lo/F 196(2)).
28. L. A. Botelho, *Old Age and the English Poor Law, 1500–1700* (Woodbridge: Boydell, 2004), pp. 104–52.
29. Dur.RO, EP/Di 7/1.
30. Dur.RO, EP/Ha 7/1, Hart Overseers' Accounts, 1736–1809, 'Repairing the Poor's houses'; EP/Ha 7/2, Hart Overseers' Accounts, 1810–1839, documents a decline in thatch. See also, R. Lucas, 'The Disappearance of Thatch from Norfolk', in A. Longcroft & R. S. Joby (eds), *East Anglian Studies* (Norwich: Centre for East Anglian Studies, 1995), pp. 141–54.

31. Norf.RO, PD100/140; also, MEA 3/239, 654X7, Tenants' bills for cottage repairs, 1804.
32. Norf.RO, MC 343/112/1–7 735X8; PD 264/45,50,51.
33. On parish relief, see P. Rushton, 'The Poor Law, the Parish and the Community in North-East England, 1600–1800', *Northern History* 25, (1989), 135–52; T. Wales, 'Poverty, Poor Relief and the Life-Cycle: Some Evidence from Seventeenth-Century Norfolk', in R. M. Smith (ed.), *Land, Kinship and Life-Cycle* (Cambridge: Cambridge University Press, 1984), pp. 351–404.
34. K. Wrightson, 'The Decline of Neighbourliness Revisited', in N. Jones, N. Leslie & D. R. Woolf (eds), *Local Identities in Late Medieval and Early Modern England* (Basingstoke: Palgrave Macmillan, 2007), pp. 19–49; On the 1550 Act for 'the improvement of commons and waste', which protected small cottagers by enabling them to build a tenement and take up to three acres, see J. Thirsk (ed.), *The Agrarian History of England and Wales IV, 1500–1640* (Cambridge: Cambridge University Press, 1967), pp. 224–5.
35. J. Sykes, *Local Records* (Newcastle upon Tyne, 1833), p. 101; Dur.RO, M7/2, Quarter Sessions, 13 July 1681 and 16 November 1686 (also, 12 July 1676, Brancepeth overrun with poor); D/Wat Box 61, 23 October 1691. I am grateful to Matt Greenhall for allowing me to cite this evidence from his 'The Use of Communal Space as a Sphere of Social Relations in County Durham, 1600–1700' (Unpublished Durham University MA dissertation, 2006).
36. Dur.RO, M7/2, Quarter Sessions, 4 July 1675.
37. J. J. Dodd, *The History of the Urban District of Spennymoor* (Spennymoor, 1897).
38. Norf.RO, PD 300/16; PD 297/79.
39. J. T. Smith, 'Short-Lived and Mobile Houses in Late Seventeenth-Century England', *Vernacular Architecture* 16, (1985), 33–4; C. Carson et al., 'Impermanent Architecture in the Southern American Colonies', *Wintherthur Portfolio* 16, (1982), 135–92.
40. N. Pevsner & B. Wilson, *The Buildings of England: Norfolk 2: North West and South* (Penguin, 2000), p. 572, 'this is the smallest kind of permanent house to have survived in the county'; North Lopham's Townhouse (alias Workhouse Row and Weavers Cottages) also survives (partially rebuilt): 'the churchwardens in the early nineteenth century had to look after its reed thatching and other repairs' (M. F. Serpell, *A History of the Lophams* (Chichester: Phillimore, 1980), pp. 127–8).
41. A. Longcroft, 'Plan-Forms in Smaller Post-Medieval Houses: A Case Study from Norfolk', *Vernacular Architecture* 33, (2002), 34–56; Idem. 'The Hearth Tax and Historic Housing Stocks'.
42. P. King, 'Pauper Inventories and the Material Lives of the Poor in the Eighteenth and Early Nineteenth Centuries', in T. Hitchcock, P. King & P. Sharpe (eds), *Chronicling Poverty: The Voices and Strategies of the English Poor, 1640–1840* (Basingstoke: Macmillan, 1997), pp. 155–91; B. Cornford, 'Inventories of the Poor', *Norfolk Archaeology* 35, (1973), 118–25.
43. Norf.RO, PD 295/102.
44. The details of 209 Norfolk pauper inventories (1690–1810) have been incorporated into Norfolk Record Office's online catalogue: http://nrocat. norfolk.gov.uk. Durham parish records yielded only Dur.RO, EP/Rom 4/8,

Cotherstone, 1754; EP/BO 42, Boldon, 1761; EP/Stai 554i–ii and EP/Stai 7/576–8, Staindrop, 1788 and *c*. 1810.

45. Norf.RO, PD 295/102.
46. Norf.RO, PC 88/1; PC 88/2.
47. Norf.RO, PD 358/41, 1670 and 1676.
48. M. Spufford, 'The Limitations of the Probate Inventory', in J. Chartres & D. Hey (eds), *English Rural Society, 1500–1800: Essays in Honour of Joan Thirsk* (Cambridge: Cambridge University Press, 1990), pp. 139–74. P. Slack, *Poverty and Policy in Tudor and Stuart England* (Harlow: Longman, 1988), p. 84, notes that 'in the later seventeenth century, the old were sometimes encouraged to make over their own houses to the parish, in return for a weekly allowance'. Norf.RO, PD 295/102; PC 88/2; PD 358/61; NCR Case 15c–f, schedules of goods for discharging debtors in Norwich gaol, 1678–1781; PD 575/28, Hingham, 1706, John Sterman for county court writ of *venire facias*. Also, Dur.RO, EP/Gr 9/46a, Thorp Thewles, *c*. 1788, Thomas Tailford's household goods seized.
49. Norf.RO, PD 100/140; PD 50/71.
50. Norf.RO, PD 575/128; PD 358/61; PD 122/54.
51. Norf.RO, PD 575/128; PD 295/102; PD100/140; PD 50/71, nd. Gissing, Widow Watling's goods included '10 Trenchers 8 Wooding Dishes' and '1 wooding Chamber Pot'; DRO EP/Stai 7/577, Staindrop *c*. 1810 includes '23 woden plats'. No Durham lists included spinning wheels. Dur.RO, EP/Wi, p. 59 instances the prevalence of coal in Durham: Winston, 1705 'five loads of coal to Elizabeth Garthwaite given to her at several times when in childbed 4*s*. 6*d*.'.
52. Hammonds, *Village Labourer*, p. 109, citing *Annals of Agriculture*, vol. xxv, pp. 367–8; E. J. Hobsbawm, *Labouring Men: Studies in the History of Labour* (Weidenfield and Nicolson, 1964), pp. 94–104.
53. Norf.RO, PD 295/102; T. Sokoll, *Essex Pauper Letters, 1731–1837* (Oxford: Oxford University Press, 2001), p. 67; J. Styles, *The Dress of the People: Everyday Fashion in Eighteenth-Century England* (New Haven & London: Yale University Press, 2007).
54. Norf.RO, PD 216/90; PD 295/102.
55. A. Smith, *The Wealth of Nations* (1776), (Oxford: Oxford University Press, 1993), p. 19; Norf.RO, PD 100/140; PD 50/71.
56. S. Wrathmell, 'The Vernacular Threshold of Northern Peasant Houses', *Vernacular Architecture* 15, (1984), 29–33; L. Butler & P. Wade-Martins, 'The Deserted Medieval Village of Thuxton, Norfolk', *East Anglian Archaeology*, (Report 46, 1989), 58–62; P. Wade-Martins, 'Excavations at North Elmham, 1969: An Interim Report', *Norfolk Archaeology* 35, (1970), 25–78; P. Wade-Martins, 'Fieldwork and Excavation on Village Sites in Launditch Hundred, Norfolk', *East Anglian Archaeology* (Report 10, 1980); Mercer, *English Vernacular Houses*, p. 27.
57. R. Machin, 'The Great Rebuilding: A Reassessment', *Past & Present* 77, (1977), 33–56; Green, *Durham Hearth Tax*, pp. lxxvi–lxxxix.
58. Norf.RO, PD 358/41. Also HARE 4837, 215X5, Winbotesham, Ingaldesthorpe Manor Court, 22 October 1665, admission of Paul Wilson on surrender of Thomas Wilson his brother for part of a cottage then fallen down, 44 feet by 35 feet; GUR 100, 146X2, Hempnell manor court, 8 May 1667, licence for John Tyrrell to demolish ancient cottage in Tasburgh.

59. Illustrated in *Norfolk Hearth Tax*, p. liii; see also U. Priestley & P. Corfield, 'Rooms and Room Use in Norwich Housing, 1580–1730', *Post-Medieval Archaeology* 16, (1982), 93–123.

60. B. H. St. J. O'Neil, 'Some Seventeenth-Century Houses in Great Yarmouth', *Archaeologia* XCV, (1953); P. Guillery, *The Small House in Eighteenth-Century London* (New Haven: Yale University Press in association with English Heritage, 2004), pp. 269–70. *Idem*, 'Housing the Early-Modern Industrial City: London's Workshop Tenements', in A. Green & R. Leech (eds), *Cities in the World, 1500–2000* (Leeds: Maney, 2006), pp. 117–131.

61. Dur.RO, EP/Star 7/22; TWA, DT.BEL/4/1 Thomas Bell, Collections relative to the Parish of Gateshead Fell, pp. 28 and 51; ACC T241, All Saints Parish Poor Relief.

62. M. Pelling, 'Old Age, Poverty and Disability in Early Modern Norwich: Work, Remarriage and Other Expedients', in *The Common Lot: Sickness, Medical Occupations and the Urban Poor in Early Modern England* (Longman, 1998), pp. 134–54; Botelho, *Old Age*, p. 102.

63. Durham University Library, Probate Registry I/ 1/ 1778/VI/ 1–2.

64. F. Moore, *Consideration on the Exorbitant Price of Proprietors* (1773), quoted in Hammonds, *Village Labourer*, p. 86; Marshall, *Review of the Reports of the Board of Agriculture for the Northern Department* (York, 1808); Sir J. Walsham, *Three Reports on the State of the Dwellings of the Labouring Classes in Cumberland, Durham and Westmorland* (1840); T. Dodds, 'The Cottages of Northumberland', lecture to the Alnwick Institute, printed in *Gateshead Observer*, 17 November 1838; J. Hodgson, *History of Northumberland* (Newcastle upon Tyne, 1827), I, part 2, esp. p. 189.

65. Sokoll, *Essex Pauper Letters*, pp. 258 and 409–10.

66. Pawnbrokers were prevalent in north-east towns, (Durham Probate Registry, wills for Lewis Chapman, Newcastle, 1792; Sam Wear, North Shields, 1794; William Cellar, Sunderland, 1797; George Burrell re. Jo Welch of Durham, 1798; Richard Brown, North Shields, 1801).

67. Sokoll, *Essex Pauper Letters*, pp. 131–4; *Idem.*, 'Negotiating a Living: Essex Pauper Letters from London, 1800–1834', *International Review of Social History* 45, (2000), 19–46.

68. Sokoll, *Essex Pauper Letters*, pp. 257 and 297–8.

69. Norf.RO, PD 295/102, Redenhall 1731, 'one pewter Chamberpott' among Lina Lason's goods; PD 50/71, Gissing, nd. '1 wooding Chamber Pot' among Widow Watling's.

4
Joys of the Cottage: Labourers' Houses, Hovels and Huts in Britain and the British Colonies, 1770–1830

Sarah Lloyd

When the Board of Agriculture systematised its enquiries into the state of British farming during the 1790s, it instructed its county surveyors to investigate local housing, specifically cottages.[1] Arthur Young, who had decided views on the importance of land management as a means to improve the lot of agricultural labourers, increase productivity and enhance national prosperity and security, yoked the two issues together in his study of Lincolnshire. He reported that Sir John Sheffield, member of the Board of Agriculture and advocate of enclosure, had kept rents down and let dwellings directly to the poor, by-passing those tenant farmers who might manipulate housing to oppress their labourers. Young remarked that such indulgence 'has no ill effect; they are very clean in everything; remarkably well cloathed; no children in rags; their beds and furniture good; are very sober, and attentive to church'. Pigs and children were numerous and poor rates low; with only one pub in twenty square miles, inhabitants kept to their own hearths, conserving time, energy and money.[2] And since security of tenure depended on good behaviour, employers were guaranteed a supply of industrious and uncomplaining labour. By the end of his account, Young had recommended a general extension of Lincolnshire's cottage system to deliver the ultimate political goal: the poor 'inevitably' felt committed to their country when they were able to 'partake thus in the property of it'.[3] Land and dwellings were both an economic resource and imbued with meanings.

Encapsulated here were the main features of a new interest in the dwellings of the poor (taken in the general eighteenth-century sense of those who had to work daily for their daily survival). Agricultural improvers, poor law commentators, moralists and architects now believed that it was possible to 'read' labourers' circumstances from the details of their material surroundings and to reform their moral character through the domestic environment. Although differing in opinion about whether the cottage should come with enough land for a cow or a vegetable garden or less, the general principles were clear. On Sussex, Young commented that 'too many of their houses are the residence of filth and vermin; their dress insufficient; their minds uneducated, uninstructed; and their children, from insufficiency of earnings, trained to vice'.[4] By contrast, well-ordered and comfortable dwellings spread virtue, encouraged self-reliance and eradicated disaffection. None of this had been particularly obvious to observers earlier in the century: they had had other criteria for assessing the condition of the poor and proposed different methods of improving it.

So where did the cottage scene come from? Ideas developed through the century. Discussions of the poor laws, widening consumerism, agrarian improvement, theories of sentiment and picturesque aesthetics all played a part.[5] A series of assumptions about 'human nature' as played out in humble life made a commentary on the agricultural labourer available as an analysis of the poor in general: 'it is admitted, on all hands, that the more the comforts of their *homes* are increased, the more likely they are to become industrious, sober, and good'.[6] In a significant departure from earlier commentaries on poverty, imagined cottage scenes systematised ideas about the 'natural' differences between men and women, promoting them as an antidote to rising poor rates, pauperism and social unrest. As the 'monarch of his mansion', the poor man's identity grew out of the authority he had over his 'family'.[7] English liberty now secured a distinctive form of property: domestic happiness in evenings before the fire and a 'homely board ... spread [with] wholesome but frugal plenty!'[8] In theory too, such manly independence required no relief from parish funds. And since the British were better off than 'occupiers of the miserable unadorned huts in other countries', housing became a measure of national well-being and constitutional security.[9]

By the twentieth century what had once been a novel approach to poverty, to be worked through and elaborated, had become a self-evident and immemorial truth:

> There is probably no object so much a natural part of the English landscape, nor which makes such a direct appeal to the heart and the imagination, as the old country cottage ... the appeal of the country cottage is universal.[10]

Emotions and gender distinctions so central in the eighteenth-century account had lent themselves to totalising claims that concealed the very specific contexts out of which such formulations emerged. The eighteenth-century cottage scene was infused with elite pleasures derived from viewing or imagining an orderly lower class. Assumed differences between women and men, poor and rich, complemented and reinforced one another; good effects rippled outwards. But to what extent was this anything more than elite discourse; did any of it match the poor's experiences: shivering, demoralised and sexually irresponsible in 'shattered', leaky, crowded and dirty hovels; or sitting warm and comfortable, sober and industrious, before the fire?[11] And what should we make of anomalies where details departed from the model? In Lincolnshire, Mr Goulton had followed Sheffield's cottage system on his own estate. For all its profusion, conformity and contentment, however, parents were still not very conscientious in ensuring that their children were industrious. 'The women are very lazy', Young also reported. 'I have noted their indolence in spinning; Mr Goulton's expression was, "they do nothing but bring children, and eat cake"; nay, the men milk the cows for them; but the men very sober and industrious'.[12] That domestic order of the sort theorised by numerous commentators did not necessarily issue from correct social and spatial arrangements, invites us to read between the ideological lines and to distinguish lower-class decisions and adaptations from other people's wishful thinking.

Shelter, or lack of it, was important in the experience of poverty throughout the century, but the power of the cottage argument lay in its specific promise to coax occupants towards prudence and self-reliance. Was this, therefore, an ideal that the poor shared, and if so was it for them too a newly minted possibility and goal? Jonathan White, for example, has proposed that 'proletarian' forms of domestic respectability, which commodified feelings of connection and loss, developed during the later eighteenth century in response to the displacement of older customary practices.[13] Board of Agriculture surveyors certainly recorded many instances of labourers keen to occupy dwellings with some land attached.[14] Although agronomists thought this proved the value of cottages as a mechanism to eradicate pauperism and ensure a valuable supply of labour, the dynamic was less reliable and the evidence more equivocal if those Lincolnshire women were anything to go by. Observers nevertheless sought out signs of affection, of tender and patriotic feelings, privileging occupants' love of cottage, family, land and, by extension, nation. For all its sentimentality and doubtful authenticity, this focus does foreground emotion, a topic that historians of poverty tend not to investigate and often take for granted. But was a yearning for domestic delights an aspect of 'human nature' that in reality had to be learnt, as John Crowley has argued for the eighteenth-century invention of comfort in general?[15] What uses, meanings and rituals did plebeian occupants create around their dwellings and gardens? The following discussion offers some tentative answers to such questions. Labouring and elite interests were not congruent. Although poor people often recognised the terms of cottage debate, their sense of place had distinctive components, notably land, food, specific objects and a freedom to close doors or roam abroad.

Evidence heard at the Old Bailey indicates that from the late 1770s it became increasingly common for poor people around the metropolis to use the term 'cottage' to describe a small dwelling. This chronology closely followed the expansion of cottage literature and reflected widespread disregard of the Elizabethan requirement, repealed by Parliament in 1775, that four acres of land should be attached to certain categories of new cottage.[16] Giving evidence in a trial for highway robbery, John Neller of Ashford in Surrey, for example, related how one of the accused wanted directions to Hounslow and 'a place to lie in; I told him I had no such place; I have only a little cottage, I am a day labouring man'.[17] In 1788, Mary Sadler stated that she paid a shilling a week for two rooms. Asked whether this included an outside door, she relied: 'My door comes into a field ... it is a cottage divided'.[18] In 1792, William How went out at six in the morning: 'I fastened the house by driving a large nail in the shutter; it is a cottage'. He also locked the door, but a thief got in through the window leaving damp marks over the 'one boarded floor'.[19] Gardeners, building labourers and hay binders lived in cottages; some were rented, others went with the job.[20] Never more than a couple of rooms, they might include wash houses, cellars, staircases and sheds. As was the case with the timing of this language, descriptions of the cottage in these records closely mapped the discourse of professional men. In their extension of a term, which once carried very specific legal and economic associations, to the urban environment of Paddington and Marylebone as well as to the metropolitan fringe and its agricultural hinterland (Wilsden and Hendon, for instance), plebeians participated in a wider cultural shift. They too understood the cottage generically, as the abode of the poor.

The language of the cottage was therefore adopted by labourers as well as by gentlemen. One indirect sign that the poor had very definite feelings about housing was their well-known – and long-established – reluctance to enter the workhouse.[21] Richard Burn, author of the definitive legal handbook for local officials, advised: 'Let the poor themselves be consulted, and they will chuse houses like unto those they formerly inhabited'.[22] Cottage and family became powerful arguments for using the workhouse to deter claimants for relief and for keeping out of it those who are 'wedded to' their dwellings 'by a long continued residence, an association of ideas, a partial affection to one particular spot'.[23] Burn's conclusion does not however require us to accept the detail of his contemporaries' explanations. Cottage exponents at the turn of the century may have built great hopes on 'independence', but their anodyne version co-existed with more anarchic forms. Runaway convicts, for example,

> will submit to live in the state of the most abject wretchedness *in the enjoyment of liberty*, rather than feast upon sumptuous fare to which the bare name of work or control is attached.[24]

What we are looking for, therefore, is not simply evidence that poor people were attached to their dwellings, led emotional lives or were self-reliant, elements that Adrian Green has already established in this volume,[25] but signs of that distinctive cluster of cottage associations which emerged in print during the second half of the eighteenth century.

In 1832 William King, an Essex pauper, described to the overseers of Braintree his great suffering the previous winter:

> By Reason if a Cold and Shattered Covering But we have Remooved to a Better Dwelling though Under Much <u>Imbarisments</u> Sirs tis with the Greatest Humility and Respect that I thurs Apeel to you But tis to My own Beloved Birth Place on wich I think with P[eculiar] Delight Under a Mind Sometimes Bent down with Sadness and Distress.[26]

Whoever the author was (and for pauper letters this is often difficult to establish), the text demonstrates a working knowledge of cottage clichés: the 'cold and shattered covering', the 'beloved birth place' and 'sadness and distress'. It is, however, a late and atypical example. When other Essex paupers referred to housing, they were often living together in single rooms and preoccupied with rent, clothes and bedding. George Craddock wrote that his children were now too big to share a bed with their parents, but if this was an appeal to contemporary anxieties about separating sexes and generations, the reference is very oblique.[27]

Ann Candler (1740–1814), 'a Suffolk cottager' and poet was much more explicit. For more than 20 years she lived in the Tattingstone House of Industry and from 'within these dreary walls', the cottage represented the life and 'liberty' that she had lost. She had given up a 'comfortable cottage, and kind friends' and 'goods, which were very decent' to follow her feckless and drunken husband to London. He had subsequently persuaded her with 'prospects of comfort', specifically the hope of settling in a cottage. Her daughter was more fortunate. She was 'I believe in the true sense of the words, the contented happy cottager! Her husband is a very sober industrious man'.[28] John Clare (1793–1864), poet and agricultural labourer, remembered the thatch, smoking chimney, garden and hearth of his childhood home; a section of his *Shepherd's Calendar* (1827) conjured with an imagined scene of 'Cottage Evening' and fireside.[29] Labouring poets however made complex compromises with elite culture and sponsorship; in speaking between worlds, their words were distinctive. Popular songs of the 1820s expressed in a different register the labourer's desire for beer, bread and bacon, for economic self-sufficiency through hard work and small holdings. This 'cottage charter' rejected recent economic changes and detected a social decay that cut the labourer adrift from his employer.[30] It emphasised the status of the adult male, but significantly this was a vision centred in land, not dwellings; it departed robustly from the subservience demanded by moralists and agronomists. The cottage praised by Arthur Young is there, but has been significantly re-worked.

So what happened when the idea of the cottage was exported? Again we know about enthusiasts and administrators. In the early nineteenth century, proponents of assisted emigration promised 'domestic happiness' and 'comfortable habitations' in new lands.[31] In Australia, the concept of the cottage and its garden shaped elite ideas about colonisation as governors experimented with allotments and household arrangements to improve convict behaviour.[32] An order of 1810 instructed settlers to pay more attention to 'domestic comfort ... by erecting commodious residences for themselves' out of brick and weatherboard, and conforming to an official design.[33] But how did plebeians respond when voluntarily or forcibly removed from British shores? Separation sharpened experiences of belonging and identity, but had these people assimilated cottage sentiments and commitments to home and hearth? Since colonisation is a process of making a place and establishing a life, did lower-class migrants carry those lessons of neatness, prudence, comfort, conjugal harmony and provision that the authors of improving tales were so keen to press on them?[34] These are tricky questions. Britons had fashioned domestic and economic lives for themselves in other countries long before poor-law reformers became entranced with the possibilities of the cottage. The first emigrants to the new colony of Georgia in the 1730s – as previous generations of migrants and many British contemporaries – lived in houses without glazed windows, cooked in outside ovens and made do with 'plain and needful' furniture.[35] Direct plebeian testimony is less plentiful than that of well-resourced migrants, but we should not assume that people simply tried to reproduce old arrangements when adapting to new environments: some clearly broke with the past.[36] Furthermore, even for a group whose economic freedom of action in Britain was limited, the physical and cultural challenges of re-settlement entailed constrained choices; the presence of indigenous peoples, for instance, might set different priorities. However in negotiating unfamiliar places, settlers drew on habits and memories; decisions made under pressure have the potential to reveal what was fundamental to physical and emotional survival.

Poor landless labourers and artisans sent to Upper Canada in the early 1830s echoed the cottage charter. Writing to their relations back in England, they were certainly enthusiastic, returning again and again to employment, wage rates, firewood, and the prices of land, animals and food. They had far less to say about dwellings, even when they invoked comfort: 'the houses are not so comfortable as at home, as they are all wooden ones, or mostly so'.[37] Charlotte Willard, her husband, who was a carpenter, and seven young sons arrived in Canada as a result of a settlement dispute between a number of parishes. She wrote to her sister at some length about their new life – the garden, harvesting maple sap and attending chapel. She listed the prices of land, mutton, pork, veal, butter and sugar. She offered advice on what to bring on the ship: a chest, dishes, pots and 'embden grits'. But despite wishing that she had brought a grate, an item that spoke volumes to cottage commentators with their idealised scenes of contented sociability before the fire, she said nothing about her house or its domestic arrangements.[38] For Willard, like many others, success and happiness lay in things, notably food. It was a 'beautiful spring of water like your orchard water at Milton' that connected her through a recollection of taste and place back to life in Surrey. Abundance mattered, not that curious 'frugal plenty' quoted earlier. Many male correspondents echoed the cottage charter's masculinist assertions. William Clements, a day labourer, revelled in his 'liberty' to shoot turkeys. John Down, a weaver, noted that servants ate at the same table as their masters and were welcomed to the farmer's house: this was a country 'where a man can stand as a man'. Thomas Hunt, another day labourer enjoyed 'plenty of good fire and grog'.[39] Wild gooseberries, pheasants and mushrooms in the woods, repeated requests for seeds and plant cuttings – through individual acts of collecting, gardening and eating, migrants' habits and memories created a sensory landscape that was transnational.[40] In short, they knew the signs of prosperity or joy but did not replicate conventions of cottage cosiness.

What preoccupied the mainly male correspondents from Upper Canada was the price of land. In the same decade, it was reported that in England the labouring poor would rent potato grounds 'on the most exorbitant terms'.[41] This was not new. At the turn of the century, during an earlier period of economic strain, Charles Vancouver noted that in Devon the prospect of enclosing a patch of land had drawn labourers from the village to the fringe of a common.[42] In Australia, where the British confronted all the complexities of establishing a new society on penal principles on a continent with no European presence and few familiar resources, land and housing raised unique issues.[43] Convicts differed from the Canadian migrants in their social origins and urban and maritime experiences. Manly independence, which so interested poor law reformers, was especially problematic in a system confronted by male resistance, where liberty and hard work had overtly political meanings, and where there were so few women.

The First Fleet – 'each Ship like another Noah's Ark' – sailed into Port Jackson in January 1788. It landed nearly a thousand people and their presumed material requirements, together with philosophical ideas about utility and improvement.[44] The cargo included nails, panes of glass, hinges and locks[45] but for the first six months, soldiers and convicts lived under second-hand canvas from the Portsmouth dockyards; the governor occupied a portable canvas house, while his officers sheltered in 'marquées'.[46] Europeans struggled with the materials they found. Timber split awkwardly; there was no lime for building until convicts collected and burnt oyster shells. Settlement began on barrack principles; on Norfolk Island a few months later, women swept around the tents, cooked and washed for the men.[47] Subsequently, rough dwellings of cabbage palm, mud and brushwood became standard, with huts 'still more slight' for the convicts.[48] Indeed when Watkin Tench surveyed the scene from Rose Hill (Parramatta) in December 1791, he remarked,

> In a colony which contains only a few hundred hovels, built of twigs and mud, we feel consequential enough already to talk of a treasury, an admiralty, a public library and many other similar edifices, which are to form part of a magnificent square.[49]

In these early years, dwellings were frequently 'huts' and to be housed was the military term of being 'hutted'.[50] Before the fleet had set sail, plans for creating a society of independent, hard-working, self-sufficient cultivators were in the air.[51] In July 1790 Governor Phillip planned to allot garden ground at Parramatta to groups of ten convicts. They would 'live more comfortable' than in larger numbers, with the gardens providing a 'spur to industry' and good behaviour.[52] The first issue of the *Sydney Gazette and New South Wales Advertiser* in 1803 re-published advice from the Society for Bettering the Condition and Increasing the Comforts of the Poor on the advantages of cottage pig-keeping.[53] By the 1820s, the cottage informed aesthetic responses to an Antipodean environment and provided a measure of success: the cottages of Parramatta were 'purest white, shining in our clear cloudless sky'; the great majority of houses may have looked 'mean' on the outside, but 'cleanliness and comfort' were evident inside.[54]

In the short term, however, food was of greatest concern. When stores ran low, convict gardens were of vital importance. They expressed other desires too. By 1790, John Fuller, a Kent carpenter, had grown 1500 cabbage plants in the poor Sydney soils, as well as kidney beans, French beans, turnips and potatoes. In Alan Atkinson's analysis 'his rows of cabbages were a kind of signature on the Australian soil'.[55] Jeremy Burchardt has also argued that in England during the same period allotments brought considerable benefits 'in material form and in less tangible ways'.[56] Plots of land gave their cultivators a sense of control, self-respect and mental stimulus and opened up complex community relationships of exchange and gifting.[57] Gardens contributed variety and supplied the pot during winter months.[58] Scarcity and military discipline set different parameters in Australia, but the few hundred convicts sent to Norfolk Island in February 1788 may have shared this understanding of land as security and source of identity as they felled trees and planted fruit and vegetables. A later, highly sentimental, account claimed that they developed a 'parental fondness' for the island where they achieved 'all the comforts, and most of the luxuries of life'. Shipped off to Van Diemen's Land in 1811, they left well-worked and fenced gardens in 'a spot endeared to them by so many cherished recollections'. It was 'heart-rending' to see them 'with their wives and children, quitting abodes in which they had spent so many years of felicity, to go and raise, in their old age, new habitations', to clear and cultivate 'new fields in an uninhabited country'.[59] In this version of place, Aboriginal people never featured.

Gardening thus offered an important arena for convict autonomy. Again land emerges as a focus for lower-class aspirations and culture, not least perhaps because the earliest housing resources were so unpromising: what one convict woman described as 'most miserable huts', their unglazed windows filled with 'lattices of twigs'.[60] Convicts allowed time to gather materials and construct huts for themselves in 1788

> for the most part ... preferred passing in idleness the hours that might have been so profitably spent, straggling into the woods for vegetables, or visiting the French ships in Botany Bay.[61]

Their physical responses to loss and separation speak of sociability and hopes of escape;[62] habitual acts of provisioning, 'vegetables' not shelter, orientated them in an unknown environment. Watkin Tench thought the houses they eventually built were 'wretched hovels three-fourths of them'.[63] Although cottage discourse distinguished between the neat cottage and the nasty hovel, hut or cabin, this taxonomy with all its moral resonances was very shaky in the earliest years of settlement. Europeans thought their own societies the most advanced, but the first British dwellings – their cabbage tree rooves, rough-hewn walls, twigs and mud – were perhaps not so different from those of indigenous people.[64] Several decades later, the system was more securely in place, with gentlemen settlers building ornamented cottages, marvelling at the improvements evident in housing and judging Aboriginal 'progress' according to standards of cleanliness and tidiness.[65] From the outset, however, indigenous land practices provided certain and stark grounds of difference: the exploitation of land would allow lower-class (male) Britons to share in a very particular understanding of their place in the world.

Direct and indirect evidence therefore confirms that the occupation and cultivation of land was important economically and culturally for many labourers, but they did not immediately adopt eighteenth-century talk of hearths, domestic conjugality and plain comforts. Cottage morality struggled against other notions of survival or abundance. Governor Phillip 'strongly inculcated the absolute necessity that existed for every man to cultivate his own garden, instead of robbing that of another'. He grumbled that some men 'preferred any thing to honest labour'; on Norfolk Island, soldiers and sailors were said to be so accustomed to daily rations that they were unable to toil for themselves. When convicts plundered gardens or wandered into the bush to pick 'sweet tea' (and we might pause here to consider how they, like the Canadian migrants, recreated familiar tastes through naming alien flora and resuming foraging habits learnt elsewhere), they reacted to an environment where ownership, belonging and dependence were open questions: questions that Phillip wished to close by developing in them a sense of what was their 'own'. His was the world of huts, gardens and boundary fences evident in early views of Sydney. Major Ross wanted the inhabitants of Norfolk Island to live independently on small holdings. He allocated pigs and encouraged relationships favoured by cottage proponents in Britain: such male convicts 'as are desirous to maintain the females, such females shall not be called upon by the public to do any work'. But for a substantial group, fear of losing government stores outweighed any of the material or personal advantages in allotments, and they rejected Ross's plan as impossible.[66]

Amid dislocation, makeshift accommodation and homosociality, British cottage associations may seem largely irrelevant to those low in the new social order. Forms of domestic life and households were nevertheless attempted from the outset, and adapted and re-imagined in these new situations.[67] Convicts accommodated under canvas (and separated by sex) in the west of Sydney Cove in 1788 soon built huts with water cisterns, yards, vegetable gardens and privet hedges, without any reference to official planning or policy. What they created in these first years perhaps comes closest to a demotic sense of home. Strikingly, their dwellings looked out to sea; only later were they turned to face inwards onto pathways. What Grace Karskens takes as a sign of early Sydney's maritime character, also manifested the occupants' cultural orientation, their backs turned literally on this new place.[68] We can only guess at the value to their inhabitants of what were, in Tench's eyes, 'wretched hovels'. Crimes centred on huts establish them as places of privacy away from prying official eyes. Gardens outside and things stored indoors – notably foodstuffs and clothing – had heightened meaning in a land where the stock of recognisably European goods was very meagre. Rather than lose the social connection represented by a 'comfortable hut and garden' within range of Sydney, one man banished to the 'New Grounds' in 1792 attempted suicide.[69]

Cottage scenes travelled out to Australia in plebeian minds and memories. Pricked onto the metal surface of a cartwheel penny, which had been rubbed smooth, was 'the cotage of peace'. 'E.A.' – and that is all that is known about the creator – may have made the object herself or asked someone to do it for her while she awaited transportation, probably sometime in the early years of the nineteenth century. With its trees and dog, it resembles an image from a sampler and heads the text: 'This was once/my cotage/of peace' and on the reverse 'This is/for my dear/farther from .is/unfortalnate/datuer who is going out/of her

cotage/for life'.[70] 'E.A.' may have made the object herself or asked someone to do it, but its basic literacy and personal immediacy suggest that for
her – as for Ann Candler – affective and imaginative qualities saturated
material life. The lines of a cottage could carry all the emotion of exile.
The token's biblical echoes recall forms of home-based, female-centred
religion which flourished in the late eighteenth and early nineteenth
century and put the household at the centre of social, religious and
economic life.[71] E.A. evoked places that might have existed, or perhaps
never did, to leave behind her a material trace of who she was or would
have liked to have been, and what mattered to her. On the inaccessi-
ble far west coast of Van Diemen's Land, convicts exiled to Macquarie
Harbour, a site of secondary transportation, decorated their cells with
'very fairly executed drawings of cottages with enclosing gardens'. The
prison opened in 1821 and closed in 1834, but the sketches could still be
seen when Henry Button, a prosperous settler, visited the ruins in 1854.
Button imagined 'unfortunates who beguiled their sorrowful solitude
by reproducing faded scenes of happiness and comparative innocence',
but their images also resonated with land-hunger and allotments.[72]

E.A. and the convicts of Macquarie Island return us to issues that
hover through the Canadian migrants' accounts, the cottage charter
and the female convict's complaint about twiggy windows. In a period
when cottage discourse was increasingly deployed to address problems
of poverty, how did gender politics figure in a demotic culture of home?
Although scholars have associated a sense of 'home' and domestic
privacy with modern and industrialised societies, recent research suggests how eighteenth-century women and men expressed personal
identity, forged relationships, carried emotion and embodied memory
in fragmented household spaces and through material possessions.[73]

Pauper inventories demonstrate that the quantity and type of goods
possessed by the poor, whether agricultural workers or not, increased
during the eighteenth century and included decorative items. What
these lists do not reveal are the precise circumstances in which goods
were acquired and used, and the meanings their owners attached to
them.[74] Looking back to the 1790s, that atypical plebeian, Francis Place,
attached so much importance to the city lodgings he took with his wife
that he not only included a plan in his autobiography, but described
their fittings in some detail:

> Along the space where the dotted line is placed [referring to the
> plan] we put an Iron rod close up to the cieling, on which ran a
> couple of curtains ... I bought a stove and had it set on a plan of

Count R[umford's], our little furniture was good enough for our circumstances and the room was especially neat and clean ... our neat
place, the absence of want, and the expectation of continuing to do
well, the persuasion that our days of suffering were at an end, and
our mutual affection made us, perhaps, as happy as any two persons
ever really were.[75]

Place shared the vision, if not the politics, of moralists and improvers
who used the cottage to promote exactly this domestic setting with its
icons: mutual affection and a Rumford stove.

Place was well-attuned to cultural developments and there are limits
to what we can generalise from his reflections on lower-class life. More
direct, if enigmatic evidence comes from the Old Bailey where women as
well as men gave evidence of life indoors and in the house's immediate
vicinity. Their detailed descriptions of cottage interiors ran counter to
many idealised scenes, and suggest that material objects provided more
significant social markers than the house itself as a domestic setting;
that what mattered were things, not some greater whole created through
assembling items. That last conclusion is of course skewed by the context
which generated the evidence – overwhelmingly trials for theft – but it
sits well enough with other material.[76] Accusing Richard Bowerman of
stealing from her 'little house' in 1810, Ann Codgell reported that

He took two waistcoats, and a pair of nankeen trowsers off the line
in the room; there were two shirts and a pair of cotton stockings,
wrapped up in an old table cloth at the end of the table ... [He]
took down my clock, after that he took down my husband's leather
breeches from a nail, and then he took a bason with a saucer at the
top, that contained a bit of victuals.[77]

William Kenton confronted a thief he found in his house in Paddington
in 1815, asking

What could you expect to find in a poor man's cottage like this? He
said, he was searching for money and victuals. He had tied up in a
clean white napkin, a coat, waistcoat, and breeches, of mine; they
were tied up on the bed ... I found that the drawers in my house had
been rummaged.[78]

Legal process elicited descriptions of interiors somewhat different
from those found in cottage literature. While the clean white napkin,

described by its owner in terms that might have pleased Hannah More, fitted well with the rhetoric of homely repasts and neat inhabitants, such scenes did not accommodate clothing hung about the room.

Cottage sociability was evident from a copper tea kettle Catherine Fosmiere hung up to dry in a wash house after breakfast in 1799. But according to the 'cottage charter', sermonisers and many political economists, tea represented enervation and the decadence that radicals pinned to the farmer's wife and daughters; in a highly gendered debate, it was beer that was healthy.[79] Complaints from all directions hinted at the ways the poor preferred to live and their selection of new domestic products. William Cobbett – opponent of enclosure and champion of the 'cottage charter' – recommended what was plain, durable, strong and warm: wood, pewter, wool. He favoured home production and fulminated against 'crockery-ware', coloured textiles and glassware, exactly the sort of thing the poor owned and lost.[80] In Sydney, where the government supplied sturdy wooden platters and bowls, plebeians exercised diverse choices.[81] Frequently living in the single-room huts so detested by cottage improvers, early white settlers crammed their cooking pots full of meat; within 15 years of the First Fleet's arrival, some convicts had furnished their huts with tea sets, delft ware, prints and glassware.[82] Abundance, comfort and prosperity led in various directions.

In 1783, a clergyman weighed into a recurrent, highly-clichéd debate over luxury and moral decline, complaining that the lower ranks lived from hand to mouth on unwholesome white bread, tea, sugar, tobacco and snuff.[83] A decade later the poor of Selkirk were said to be more interested in finery, pleasures and wandering about than in settling themselves and being 'cleanly and neat in their persons, their tables, their furniture'.[84] In Sutherland, the poor's behaviour was no more acceptable as it threatened to escape the market economy altogether: 'they all return before winter, and are said to pass their time round good fires of peat, which the country everywhere furnishes, and do very little work'.[85] This, like convict independence, was nothing like the scene of domestic sufficiency imagined by moralists and agronomists. Commentators, who had long deplored a lower-class preference for leisure over income, and now complained about lack of decency, comfort or cleanliness, detected alternative systems of values, habits and tastes circulating among those they investigated.

This essay has probed the degree to which the poor could or did engage with ideas that became important in debate about the poor laws. Cottage discourse attached weighty social meanings to particular living arrangements as if they were a natural and inevitable match. In thinking about housing, therefore, we need to unpick these associations and distinguish between physical spaces and social life; tidiness, for example, was prized for historical and political reasons; it is in time, not timeless. We need to explore what occupants found in their dwellings and how they used them. Labourers registered cultural shifts, often through exposure to metropolitan change; they responded to experience of economic – especially agricultural – restructuring, and to the availability of specific consumer goods. The cottage was itself deeply embroiled in these trends. Professional expertise fashioned it into a desirable commodity, while broader developments transformed the household from a site of production into a place of consumption and source of labour.[86]

In championing self-sufficiency and independence, proponents of the 'cottage charter' like Cobbett were fighting a very particular tide, a tide championed by agricultural experts who argued that the cottage and its garden would keep occupants available for wage labour and that their vegetables would never free them from the market. But as that example also demonstrates, the idea of the cottage was recruited to serve varied and sometimes contradictory ends: its meanings were much less fixed than commentators implied when they argued from 'human nature'. Print was crucial in communicating ideas to plebeian as well as to elite audiences, a point recognised by publishers like Robert Sayer, who in the 1790s marketed radical political images of cottages ravaged by the demands of war, and by loyalist organisations that pressed a contrast between prosperous British homes and Parisian squalor and madness.[87] Plebeian awareness of cottage discourse probably had regional dimensions closely mapping the availability of other types of commodity; age, gender, occupation and particular events shaped reactions here as in other contexts.[88] Autodidacts, like Place, found much of interest. Its promises, like that of 'cottage religion', could appeal strongly to the dispossessed or economically stressed. However many sources also indicate the importance of land and material objects in anchoring experiences of place and belonging. Those with limited resources crafted relationships and maintained a sense of decency through things.[89] Tastes and everyday routines – making tea, collecting food and water, foraging, going out and closing the door – were the stuff of memory, human connection, sensory life and survival. Clothes, food and utensils were central, but did not necessarily serve as props in the creation of domestic cosiness and a specific sort of social space. And there are obvious reasons for this too: assets were commonly stored in the form of movable goods and urban accommodation in particular was transitory.

The miserable convict's hut was a woman's complaint; much of the desire for land was expressed by and mediated through men. If the cottage charter mapped a demotic politics of the cottage, with a clear gender dynamic, Old Bailey evidence hints at rival cottage cultures. In this sense, debate about consumption habits[90] was closer to the dynamics of lower-class life than attempts to analyse poverty through those cottage emotions and conjugal comforts which supported 'frugal plenty'. So when Catherine Fosmiere set her kettle to dry, convicts wandered into the bush in search of tea, or the men of Lincolnshire milked the cows while their wives ate cake, their quotidian understandings of endurance, propriety or even happiness were far from simple replicas of other people's social imaginings.

Notes

1. For example, J. Holt, *General View of the Agriculture of the County of Lancaster* (1795), pp. iii–iv.
2. A. Young, *General View of the Agriculture of the County of Lincoln* (1799), p. 412; John, Lord Sheffield, *Remarks on the Deficiency of Grain, Occasioned by the Bad Harvest of 1799* (1800–1), pp. 159–60.
3. Young, *Lincoln*, p. 419.
4. A. Young, *General View of the Agriculture of the County of Sussex* (1808), p. 437.
5. S. Lloyd, 'Cottage Conversations: Poverty and Manly Independence in Eighteenth-Century England', *Past & Present* 184, (2004), 69–108.
6. W. Mavor, *General View of the Agriculture of Berkshire* (1809), p. 71.
7. R. Elsam, *Hints for Improving the Condition of the Peasantry in all Parts of the United Kingdom, by Promoting Comfort in their Habitations* (1816), p. 4.
8. E. Bartell, *Hints for Picturesque Improvements in Ornamented Cottages and their Scenery: Including Some Observations on the Labourer and his Cottage* (1804), p. 135.
9. For example, J. Sinclair, *The Code of Agriculture*, 5th edn (1832), Appendix XIII, p. 49.
10. C. Holme (ed.), *Old English Country Cottages* (1906), pp. 3, 5.
11. N. Kent, *Hints to Gentlemen of Landed Property* (1775), pp. 229–39.
12. Young, *Lincoln*, p. 413.
13. J. White, 'Luxury and Labour: Ideas of Labouring-Class Consumption in Eighteenth-Century England' (Unpublished University of Warwick PhD, 2001), pp. 143–4, 269–71.
14. A. Pringle, *General View of the Agriculture of the County of Westmoreland* (Edinburgh, 1794), p. 8; A. Young, *General View of the Agriculture of the County of Norfolk* (1804), p. 24; *Gentleman's Magazine*, August 1798, pp. 654–5.
15. J. E. Crowley, 'The Sensibility of Comfort', *The American Historical Review* 104:3, (1999), 749–82.
16. R. Burn, *The Justice of the Peace, and Parish Officer*, 7th edn (1762), I, pp. 354–5: 31 Eliz c. 7; *The Justice of the Peace*, 14th edn (1788), I, p. 434.

17. *OBP*, 15 Jan 1778, trial of Francis Green & Joseph West (t17780115-5).
18. *OBP*, 25 June 1788, trial of John Greenaway (t17880625-5).
19. *OBP*, 31 October 1792,trial of Martha Marshall (t17921031-6).
20. *OBP*, 30 October 1799, trial of Isabella Whitehead (t17991030-72); *OBP*, 25 Feb 1784, trial of John Pond (t1784, t17840225-36); *OBP*, 31 October 1792, trial of Martha Marshall (t17921031-6).
21. *An Account of Several Workhouses for Employing and Maintaining the Poor* (1725), p. 35.
22. R. Burn, *The History of the Poor Laws* (1764), p. 233.
23. R. Potter, *Observations on the Poor Laws, on the Present State of the Poor, and on Houses of Industry* (1775), pp. 53–4. See also [J. Scott], *Observations on the Present State of the Parochial and Vagrant Poor* (1773), pp. 47–8.
24. P. Cunningham, *Two Years in New South Wales; Comprising Sketches of the Actual State of Society in that Colony*, 2nd edn (1827), I, p. 20.
25. See Chapter 3.
26. T. Sokoll (ed.), *Essex Pauper Letters, 1731–1837* (Oxford: Oxford University Press, 2001), p. 133.
27. Sokoll (ed.), *Essex Pauper Letters*, pp. 298, 317–8, 444.
28. A. Candler, *Poetical Attempts by Ann Candler, a Suffolk Cottager with a Short Narrative of her Life* (Ipswich, 1803), pp. 4, 9, 14, 15, 53, 64. I am grateful to Tim Hitchcock for this reference.
29. J. Bate, *John Clare: A Biography* (Picador, 2003), pp. 13–14, 310.
30. I. Dyck, 'Towards the "Cottage Charter": The Expressive Culture of Farm Workers in Nineteenth-Century England', *Rural History* 1:1, (1990), 95–111. See also: J. Styles, *The Dress of the People: Everyday Fashion in Eighteenth-Century England* (New Haven & London: Yale University Press, 2007), pp. 199–202.
31. C. Barclay (ed.), *Letters from the Dorking Emigrants, who went to Upper Canada in the Spring of 1832* (1833), p. 7; G. Powlett Scrope (ed.), *Extracts of Letters from Poor Persons Who Emigrated last year to Canada and the United States*, 2nd edn with additions (1832), p. 10.
32. *Historical Records of Australia*, Series I, (Sydney, 1914), I, p. 198; K. Reid, *Gender, Crime and Empire: Convicts, Settlers and the State in Early Colonial Australia* (Manchester: Manchester University Press, 2007).
33. F. M. Bladen (ed.), *Historical Records of New South Wales* (Sydney, 1893–1901), VII, pp. 468–70.
34. For example, H. More, *Black Giles the Poacher; With Some Account of a Family who had rather Live by their Wits than their Work. Part I* [1796?], pp. 3–4.
35. W. A. Knittle, *The Early Eighteenth-Century Palatine Emigration* (Philadelphia: Dorrance & Co., 1937), pp. 197–8; T. M. Harris, *Biographical Memorials of James Oglethorpe, Founder of the Colony of Georgia in North America* (Boston, 1841), p. 318. See also, J. E. Crowley, *The Invention of Comfort: Sensibilities and Design in Early Modern Britain* (Baltimore: Johns Hopkins Press, 2001), p. 80.
36. D. Maudlin, 'Architecture and Identity on the Edge of Empire: The Early Domestic Architecture of Scottish Settlers in Nova Scotia, Canada, 1800–1850', *Architectural History* 50, (2007), 95–123.
37. W. Cameron, S. Haines & M. McDougall Maude (eds), *English Immigrant Voices: Labourers' Letters from Upper Canada in the 1830s* (Montreal & Kingston: McGill-Queen's University Press, 2000), p. 47.

38. Barclay (ed.), *Letters from the Dorking Emigrants*, pp. 15–20.
39. Powlett Scrope (ed.), *Extracts of Letters*, pp. 11, 18, 20, 23.
40. Cameron, Haines & McDougall Maude (eds), *English Immigrant Voices*, pp. 17–8, 23, 98, 149,180.
41. Labourers Friend Society, *Cottage Husbandry: The Utility and National Advantage of Allotting Land for that Purpose* (1835), pp. 11–13.
42. C. Vancouver, *General View of the Agriculture of the County of Devon* (1808), p. 98.
43. M. Lewis, 'Making Do', in P. Troy (ed.), *A History of European Housing in Australia* (Cambridge: Cambridge University Press, 2000), pp. 41–56 (p. 41).
44. G. Worgan, *Journal of a First Fleet Surgeon*, p. 1 on http://setis.usyd.edu.au; J. Gascoigne, *Science in the Service of Empire: Joseph Banks, the British State and the Uses of Science in the Age of Revolution* (Cambridge: Cambridge University Press, 1998).
45. *Historical Records of New South Wales*, I, pt.2, pp. 15–7, 156. See also W. Bell, *Hints to Emigrants; In a Series of Letters from Upper Canada* (Edinburgh, 1824), p. 74.
46. J. White, *Journal of a Voyage to New South Wales* (1790), p. 122, 172; *Extracts of Letters from Arthur Phillip Esq ... to Lord Sydney* (1791), p. 22.
47. J. Hunter, *A Historical Journal of the Transactions at Port Jackson and Norfolk Island* (1793), p. 308.
48. White, *Journal*, pp. 3, 133, 177, 188; *The Voyage of Governor Philip to Botany Bay* (1789), pp. 124–5.
49. W. Tench, *A Complete Account of the Settlement at Port Jackson in New South Wales* (1793), p. 140.
50. *Voyage of Governor Philip*, p. 126. For the importance of British military influence on housing types in different colonial settlements see: L. D. Distephano, 'The Ontario Cottage: The Globalization of a British Form in the Nineteenth Century', *Traditional Dwellings and Settlements Review* 12:2, (2001), 33–43.
51. A. Atkinson, *The Europeans in Australia* (Oxford: Oxford University Press, 1997), pp. 67–70, 72–8.
52. *Historical Records of Australia*, Series I (Sydney, 1914), I, p. 198.
53. *Sydney Gazette and New South Wales Advertiser*, 5 March 1803.
54. Cunningham, *Two Years in New South Wales*, I, p. 93; II, p. 55. See also, Bell, *Hints to Emigrants*, pp. 72, 88.
55. Atkinson, *Europeans in Australia*, pp. 125–6. See also, G. Karskens, *Inside the Rocks: The Archaeology of a Neighbourhood* (Alexandria: Hale & Iremonger, 1999), p. 33.
56. J. Burchardt, *The Allotment Movement in England, 1793–1873* (Woodbridge: Boydell Press, 2002), pp. 5, 136–40. See also, D. C. Barnett, 'Allotments and the Problem of Rural Poverty, 1780–1840', in E. L. Jones & G. E. Mingay (eds), *Land, Labour and Population: Essays Presented to J.D. Chambers* (Edward Arnold, 1967), pp. 163–83 (p. 170); K. D. M. Snell, *Annals of the Labouring Poor: Social Change and Agrarian England 1660–1900* (Cambridge: Cambridge University Press, 1985), pp. 10–14.
57. Burchardt, *Allotment Movement*, pp. 153–4, 164–72.
58. J. Thirsk, *Food in Early-Modern England: Phases, Fads and Fashions 1500–1760* (Hambledon Continuum, 2007), pp. 201–2.

59. J. Wallis, *An Historical Account of the Colony of New South Wales and its Dependent Settlements* (1821), pp. 12–3.
60. Atkinson, *Europeans in Australia*, p. 124.
61. D. Collins, *An Account of the English Colony in New South Wales* (1798), p. 15.
62. G. Karskens, '"This Spirit of Emigration": The Nature and Meaning of Escape in Early New South Wales', *Journal of Australian Colonial History* 7, (2007), 1–34.
63. Tench, *Complete Account*, p. 148.
64. W. Tench, *A Narrative of the Expedition to Botany Bay* (1789), pp. 80–1.
65. Cunningham, *Two Years in New South Wales*, I, pp. 37,55, 59, 87; II, pp. 5–6, 62, 65–6. H. Home, Lord Kames, *Sketches of the History of Man* (Edinburgh, 1788), I, p. 164.
66. Collins, *Account of the English Colony*, pp. 57, 109, 234–5; *Historical Records of Australia*, I, p. 198; *Historical Records of New South Wales*, I, pt.2, pp. 445–7, 562; A. Frost, 'The Growth of Settlement', in B. Smith & A. Wheeler (eds), *The Art of the First Fleet and other Early Australian Drawings* (Melbourne: Oxford University Press, 1988), pp. 109–39 (p. 117): 'A View of Sydney Cove – Port Jackson March 7th 1792', (p. 124): G. Raper, 'Chief Settlement at Norfolk Island, April 1790'; Atkinson, *Europeans in Australia*, pp. 77–8.
67. K. Daniels, *Convict Women* (St Leonards: Allen & Unwin, 1998), pp. 24–25, 62, 153.
68. G. Karskens, *The Rocks: Life in Early Sydney* (Melbourne: Melbourne University Press, 1997), pp. 18–28.
69. Collins, *Account of the English Colony*, pp. 139–40, 148, 153, 213. See also, G. Davison, 'Colonial Origins of the Australian Home', in Troy (ed.), *History of European Housing in Australia*, pp. 6–25 (p. 20); A. Vickery, 'An Englishman's Home is his Castle? Thresholds, Boundaries and Privacies in the Eighteenth-Century London House', *Past & Present* 199, (2008), 147–73 (162, 170).
70. I am grateful to Tim Millett for showing me this token. M. Field & T. Millett (eds), *Convict Love Tokens: The Leaden Hearts the Convicts Left Behind* (Kent Town: Wakefield Press, 1998), pp. 73, 111. See also, Cunningham, *Two Years in New South Wales*, II, p. 51.
71. D. Valenze, *Prophetic Sons and Daughters: Female Preaching and Popular Religion in Industrial England* (Princeton: Princeton University Press, 1985), p. 22.
72. Reid, *Gender, Crime and Empire*, p. 2; H. Button, *Flotsam and Jetsam: Floating Fragments of Life in England and Tasmania* (Launceston, 1909), p. 230.
73. J. R. Gillis, *A World of their Own Making: Myth, Ritual, and the Quest for Family Values* (New York: Basic Books, 1996); D. Miller (ed.), *Home Possessions: Material Culture Behind Closed Doors* (Oxford: Berg, 2001); Vickery, 'An Englishman's Home is his Castle?'; L. Auslander, 'Beyond Words', *American Historical Review* 110:4, (2005), 1015–45.
74. P. King, 'Pauper Inventories and the Material Lives of the Poor in the Eighteenth and Nineteenth Centuries', in T. Hitchcock, P. King & P. Sharpe (eds), *Chronicling Poverty: The Voices and Strategies of the English Poor, 1640–1840* (Basingstoke: Macmillan, 1997), pp. 155–91.
75. F. Place, *The Autobiography of Francis Place (1771–1854)*, ed. by M. Thale (Cambridge: Cambridge University Press, 1972), pp. 124–5. See also, Crowley, 'Sensibility of Comfort', p. 750.

76. Examples include: *OBP*, 25 June 1788, trial of John Greenaway (t17880625-5); OBP, October 1792, trial of Martha Marshall (t17921031-6); *OBP*, 30 October 1799, trial of Isabella Whitehead (t17991030-72); *OBP*, 18 September 1802, trial of William Stevens (t18020918-23).
77. *OBP*, 18 July 1810, trial of Richard Bowerman (t18100718-10).
78. *OBP*, 25 October 1815, trial of Thomas Smith (t18151025-2).
79. *OBP*, 20 February 1799, trial of Thomas Wheeler (t17990220-16); White, 'Luxury and Labour', pp. 269–71.
80. W. Cobbett, *Cottage Economy*, stereotype edn (1822), pp. 197–8. These complaints had a long history and Cobbett himself would have come under attack in the late sixteenth century for his preference for pewter: C. Shammas, 'The Domestic Environment in Early Modern England and America', *Journal of Social History* 14:1, (1980), 3–24 (6). See also, King, 'Pauper Inventories', p. 170; J. Styles, 'Custom or Consumption? Plebeian Fashion in Eighteenth-Century England', in M. Berg & E. Eger (eds), *Luxury in the Eighteenth Century: Debates, Desires and Delectable Goods* (Basingstoke: Palgrave Macmillan, 2003), pp. 103–15.
81. *Historical Records of Australia*, I, p. 86.
82. Karskens, *Inside the Rocks*, pp. 48–52, 70–2.
83. A Clergyman, *Useful and Practical Observations on Agriculture. With Some Essays Annexed, on Inclosures, the Improvement of the Country and the Poor* (1783), p. 219.
84. R. Douglas, *General View of the Agriculture in the counties of Roxburgh and Selkirk* (Edinburgh, 1798), pp. 248, 333.
85. J. Sinclair, *General View of the Agriculture of the Northern Counties and Islands of Scotland* (1795), p. 130.
86. On the links between consumerism and household production, see Styles, *Dress of the People*, Chapter 8, pp. 135–51.
87. J. Barrell, *The Spirit of Despotism: Invasions of Privacy in the 1790s* (Oxford: Oxford University Press, 2006), pp. 226–31.
88. Styles, *Dress of the People*.
89. Styles, *Dress of the People*, pp. 6–7, 248, 325.
90. White, 'Luxury and Labour'.

Part II
Mobility and Household Composition

5
Vagrant Lives

Tim Hitchcock

Simon Eedy and his dog lived for years 'under a staircase in an old shattered building called 'Rats' Castle', in Dyot Street' in St Giles in the Fields. In the next century the building would become a byword for rough living and the model for that Victorian nightmare, the 'Rookery'. But Eedy found it comfortable enough. He was born in Thrapston, Northamptonshire, in 1709, and by the beginning of the 1780s was a familiar figure on the streets of London.[1] Following his death in Bridewell on 25 April 1788 several newspapers printed an obituary notice describing him as having, 'for many years ... gone about this city covered with rags, clouted shoes, three old hats upon his head, and his fingers full of brass rings'.[2] In his *Book for a Rainy Day*, John Thomas Smith, as well as confirming the newspapers' account of his clothing, provides further details of his appearance and behaviour:

> Old Simon ... had several waistcoats and as many coats, increasing in size, so that he was enabled by the extent of the uppermost garment to cover the greater part of the bundles containing rags of various colours; and distinct parcels with which he was girded about, consisting of books, [a] canister containing bread, cheese, and other articles of food, matches, a tinder box and meat for his dog; cuttings of curious events from old newspapers; scraps from *Fox's Book of Martyrs* and three or four dog's-eared and greasy thumbed numbers of the *Gentleman's Magazine*.[3]

At the same time, while Simon Eedy was a well-known and established figure, liked by many such as John Thomas Smith, he was also a vagrant. The year before his death, in April 1787, he was brought before

Alderman Townsend, sitting in judgement at the Guildhall, and convicted of vagrancy:

> On searching him, a considerable quantity of money was found. The Alderman ordered him to be shaved and washed clean and then committed him to Bridewell for one month, and to be whipped going in and coming out, and his money then to be restored, and to be stripped of his ragged and patched apparel, and to have others in their room.[4]

A year later, and just before his death, he was again charged in the City of London with

> being an imposter, and going about as if he was insane; he was committed to Bridewell for one month to hard labour. He had sold the things the City bought for him when he was before taken up, and instead of a shirt had on an old sack, and for a waistcoat a piece of carpet.[5]

He was dead within the month, the coroners' inquest bringing in a verdict of death by a 'visitation of God'.[6]

The apparent contradiction between Eedy's repeated prosecution as a 'vagrant' and his public stature as an accepted local figure highlights a historiographical problem. Most histories of vagrancy focus on the sixteenth and seventeenth centuries, and are primarily concerned with vagrants as travellers – the unwanted and the unknown. The relatively little work we possess detailing the history of eighteenth-century vagrancy has also tended to focus on the removal of vagrants rather than on their mode of living, or the characteristics that led to their prosecution.[7] As a result, while we know a fair amount about vagrancy (particularly when it involves the prosecution of unwelcome travellers), we know very little about eighteenth-century vagrants. At the same time, we are possessed of an excellent and detailed history of settled, parochial poverty and its relief. Paul Slack, Steve Hindle, Steve King and Lynn Hollen Lees, among a host of equally sophisticated historians, have charted the workings of the Old Poor Law, and of charities and institutions. By extension, these historians have also charted the experience of a privileged subset of paupers – parish pensioners.[8] Falling between these two literatures, however, the 'vagrant poor' have been largely ignored. Those who failed to squeeze the smallest alms from the parish, or who did not need to – the 'successful' beggars and mendicants able to secure an adequacy from casual begging alone – are essentially absent from the literatures on both poverty and vagrancy.

This chapter explores the experience of the successful settled beggar and the unhindered pauper migrant in an attempt to rebalance our view of the experience of plebeian men and women in the eighteenth century – to refocus our attention from the systems of poor relief and vagrant regulation, to the experience of the settled beggar and seasonal migrant. It will use the autobiographies of individuals who fell within the definitions incorporated in the vagrancy acts to look at vagrant life-styles: how they lived and travelled, where they stayed, and how they were received. It will contrast the image found in the thick legal aspic of the dozens of vagrancy acts passed during the eighteenth century with the picture found in our most extensive and personal non-legal sources.

The legal framework for the prosecution and removal of vagrants evolved incrementally over the course of the eighteenth century, with some 28 different pieces of legislation passed between 1700 and 1824.[9] Of these Acts of Parliament, the most significant was the Vagrant Removal Costs Act of 1700 which shifted the expense of removing vagrants from the parish to the county.[10] This was followed by a range of further acts of Parliament directed primarily at codifying and consolidating the law, rather than fundamentally changing policy. In particular, the 1714 Vagrancy Act effectively widened the definition of a vagrant; bundling together in this single category settled paupers who were thought in danger of deserting their wives and children, those who refused to work for the usual wages and those 'wandring abroad, and lodging in alehouses, barns, outhouses, or in the open air, not giving a good account of themselves'.[11]

The 1714 Act was in its turn superseded by the 1744 Vagrancy Act, which again added little that was entirely new, but provided the legal framework for the policing and punishing of vagrants for the next 48 years.[12] The 1780s also saw the passage of two further Acts reflecting explicitly metropolitan concerns. In 1783, individuals found in possession of either small arms or burglary implements were encompassed within the vagrancy acts, and in 1787 those running unlicensed lotteries and similar games of chance were also explicitly defined as vagrants.[13]

In this flurry of legislation, and following sixteenth- and seventeenth-century practise, vagrants were associated with a series of specific occupations and activities. The 1744 Vagrancy Act, for instance, provided a long list of who could be prosecuted under the law. It included

- Patent gatherers, gatherers of alms under pretence of loss by fire, or other casualty;
- Collectors for prisons, goals or hospitals;
- Fencers and bear wards;
- Common players of interludes;
- All persons concerned with performing interludes, tragedies, comedies, operas, plays, farces or other entertainments for the stage, not being authorised by law;
- Minstrels and jugglers;
- Persons pretending to be Gypsies, or wandering in the habit of Gypsies;
- Those pretending to have skill in physiognomy, palmistry or fortune telling;
- Those using subtle crafts to deceive and impose, or playing or betting on unlawful games;
- All persons who run away and leave their wives and children;
- Petty chapmen and pedlars, not duly licensed;
- All persons wandering abroad and lodging in alehouses, barns, outhouses or in the open air, not giving a good account of themselves;
- All persons wandering abroad and begging, pretending to be soldiers, mariners, seafaring men, pretending to go to work in harvest; and
- All persons wandering abroad and begging.[14]

On the face of it, this dense blanket of definitions would appear to encompass just about everyone. And yet there were a range of caveats and exceptions, both legal and cultural, which effectively permitted a large number of men and women to live on the roads, and at the interstices of a growing urban and industrial world.[15]

At one level the characteristic randomness of this list can be seen in the light of an extension of judicial and parochial discretion. The distinction between those subject to the law, and those who simply wandered through, was located squarely in the mind's eye of the constables and justices charged with labelling travellers and the disorderly. But, by 1744 these labels were largely meaningless, and increasingly difficult to apply to real individuals. There is no evidence that by eighteenth century bear wards and jugglers could be found on the roads of England. The list also contains its own caveats and exceptions, which gave authority to the wandering poor, in opposition to that of the justice and his officers. For everyone 'pretending' to be a gypsy, a fortune teller or possessing a skill in physiognomy, with its implication of a false claim to professional authority, many others were perceived as legitimate claimants to be gypsies, fortune tellers and readers of physiognomy. Making a distinction between an 'authorized' chapman or pedlar and the unauthorised variety required a nicety of judgement that was beyond most eighteenth-century justices of the peace. As one beggar remarked in 1745, he adopted the guise and profession of a rag-gatherer, precisely because 'this branch of travelling is a very safe one, for it is neither obnoxious to the laws against strolling, nor to those of buying or selling without license'.[16] And while 'lodging in old houses, barns, outhouses' seems a clear enough talisman of a vagrant, the large body of evidence suggesting that the barns and outhouses of most pubs and alehouses, farms and larger businesses, were readily available for such rough sleeping, suggests that this was a sign that had become de-coupled from the state it was thought to signify.[17] And finally, the proviso that a certificate issued under the hand of their commanding officer, if a seaman or soldier, or their minister or local justice, if a simple traveller, negated much of the effect of the legislation.[18] With one simple sub-clause travellers were provided with a means of circumventing all the rest at the minimal cost of asking for a certificate.

Several historians, most notably Nicholas Rogers, have counted the poor men and women transported about the country through the agency of the laws against vagrancy, and clearly demonstrated that relatively large numbers of people were affected, but this work necessarily leaves uncounted the larger number who went about their business unmolested.[19] If we look even briefly at the careers of men and women who both identified themselves with the professions and activities listed above as illegal, who left detailed life histories and who at some point in their lives were in fact prosecuted or threatened with prosecution under the vagrancy laws, a more nuanced and difficult picture emerges.

***

Mary Saxby was born in London to poor parents in 1738.[20] After the death of her mother, and her father's remarriage, she ran away from home at the age of 11:

> I was forced to creep under bulks, or any where, to hide myself from the watchmen; and as soon as day broke, I went into the markets to pick up rotten apples, or cabbage-stalks; as I had nothing else to support nature. At length ... [I went] ... into the country .... I can recollect sitting in a black-smith's shop, and holding my feet in my hands, to get some warmth into them. One night, I crept under a

hovel for shelter, and there came an old beggar-man to lie down; seeing a child by herself, he asked me where I came from? ... Poor as he was he had pity on me; and gave me a piece of fat bacon, which I ate, without bread as greedily as if it had been the finest food.[21]

She later fell in with 'a poor travelling woman, who had three daughters [who] washed, combed and fed me, and took as much care of me as if I had been her own'. For the next few years, through her early teens, Mary made a living singing ballads in partnership with the youngest daughter of her protector, 'singing in alehouses, at feasts and fairs, for a few pence and a little drink'. Eventually, the two fell in with a 'gang of gypsies', whom the two girls joined. In the succeeding years Mary Saxby co-habited with one of the men, learned a gypsy 'cant', and 'was every way like them, excepting in colour'. At this point, however, being proposed as the 'second wife' to a member of the group, Mary struck off on her own:

I travelled as far as Dover in Kent, with a very little to support me; stopping, at times, to ask for a bit of bread, to keep me from starving. When I reached the coast, I met with a woman who sung ballads, which was a profitable trade in those parts; and she took me into partnership, till we had some words and separated. ... A vessel was, at this juncture wrecked near Sandwich; and the cargo consisting of checks and muslins, was sold cheap; which afforded opportunity to me, and many more, to get clothed for a trifle. Soon after this, having made myself clean and smart, I joined company with a decent woman, who had some small children. ... she sold hardware.[22]

For the next 20 years Mary lived what she herself described as a 'vagrant' existence. She co-habited with at least three different men, married one of them, and had a slew of illegitimate children. She earned her living first as a ballad singer and seller, and later as a seasonal harvest worker and unlicensed pedlar. She lived for many years with groups who identified themselves as gypsies, who moved about the country, setting up temporary tent encampments. In this generation of mobility she was subject to the force of law only once, and in her own recollection clearly blamed the incident on her own naiveté. After a long stay in hospital in London, she 'set out and went into Kent, to pick hops':

Out of Kent, I went into Essex; where they would not suffer any one to travel without a licence, except they could give a very good account of themselves. I, not knowing the rules of the country, sung ballads in Epping market. In the course of the day, I became acquainted with a middle-aged woman who looked like a traveller; and we went to sleep together at an alehouse. For this I soon smarted; as she proved to be a common woman, though I did not know it. Being in her company, and having been seen with her in the market, the constable came in the night, obliged us to leave our bed, and secured us till morning; when we were taken before a justice, who committed us both to Bridewell, ordering us both to be repeatedly whipped.

Mary had fallen in with an identified woman of poor repute, and had failed to acknowledge, 'the rules of the country'. But, even in this solitary instance of punishment, the treatment she received was, in her own estimation at least, relatively mild:

> The keeper heard my story very candidly; and I believe he was a good man. Observing my youth and inexperience, he pitied me; and remonstrated with the woman for drawing me into a snare. We were to be confined there six weeks, without any allowance. She was a good spinner; and he made her work, and give me half her earnings. As to being whipped, I knew little but the shame of it; for he took care not to hurt me.[23]

By her own account, Mary was never subject to a bastardy examination, despite her multiple illegitimate births (which legally ensured that her children were the responsibility of the parish in which they were born). She was never 'moved on', or subject to legal harassment after the one unfortunate incident in Epping Forest. And although she frequently begged for her bread, this did not result in further punishment. Her greatest self-confessed fear was the unwanted attention of the men who listened to her ballads and assumed that she was sexually available. On the one occasion on which she was actually subjected to an attempted rape, however, the incident was taken up by the local authorities, and serious (though unsuccessful) endeavours were made to bring the perpetrators to justice.

Mary and her by-then-legally sanctioned husband finally came to rest in Stony Stratford, Buckinghamshire, in the early 1780s, and with some difficulty established a legal settlement by virtue of renting a part of a house.[24] But, even later in life she continued to travel long distances to undertake harvest work, and to perform the services of an unlicensed pedlar to the more isolated communities of the Midlands.

The image of eighteenth-century society that emerges from Mary's religious autobiography and conversion narrative is one which is willing to encompass a substantial migratory minority. Despite the fact that Mary could easily have been shoe-horned into any number of the categories of 'vagrant' specified in the 1744 Vagrancy Act, neither she, nor the large troupe of migratory families she accompanied, people who self-identified as 'gypsies', seem to have caused the least local difficulty. Her descriptions of where she lodged are also significant. Bulks and barns, outhouses, the stables of pubs and inns, and the very public roadsides of rural England, seem to have been available for the asking; implying a high degree of tolerance for the mobile and the unsettled.

***

In part, Mary Saxby's experience suggests that the fragment of the lives recorded in the archives of crime and social policy are atypical and narrowly selective. When Mary Hyde, a seasonal worker and regular migrant, was examined by the Middlesex justice, Samuel Bever, in 1756, she patiently explained her circumstances:

> She is about 35 years of age. ... She hath a mother now living and married to George Floyd in the parish of Dawley in ... Shropshire, with whom [she] hath for fourteen or fifteen years past resided and lived with them in the winter season and hath usually come every year to or near London to work in the summer season, and hath constantly about Michaelmas gone to the said parish of Dawley aforesaid, of her own home. And should have done the same at Michaelmas last had she not been afflicted with sore eyes. And [she] hath lately been discharged out of St Georges Hospital, blind and incurable.[25]

As a result of her blindness she was temporarily and unusually exposed in the role of a vagrant, but this came at the end of a period of 14 years, during which she apparently progressed across the length of the country twice a year without hindrance. Armed with a vagrants' pass her progress homeward would have been equally unmolested.[26]

***

A vagrants' pass, a soldier's or clerk's certificate, the ability to give a 'good account' of oneself, a useful service, and non-threatening demeanour, seem in most cases enough to prevent the migratory poor from attracting unwanted attention. It is the sheer variety of guises, however, in which one could legitimately wander the roads of England that is remarkable. This variety is reflected in perhaps our most complete (though difficult) eighteenth-century vagrant narrative – the picaresque autobiography of Bampfylde-Moore Carew, the 'King of the Beggars'.

The two editions of Carew's autobiography, published in 1745 and 1749, contain a complex amalgam of literary invention and bald description. Much of the information contained in the first edition is verifiable from other sources, and certainly many of Carew's encounters with the law, and career as a transported vagrant, certainly are. But other elements seem at best unlikely. The second edition, bowdlerised and embellished by its editor Robert Goadby, is much further from an autobiographical narrative, and much more a literary concoction created in response to the contemporary evolution of the picaresque novel.[27] Nevertheless, Carew's account remains a valuable historical document, and one that seems to reflect powerfully on both how contemporaries viewed the migratory and unsettled, and also on the workings (or otherwise) of the vagrancy laws.

Born in Bickleigh, near Tiverton in 1693, Bampfylde-Moore Carew fell into a vagrant mode of life at school, when he and two companions joined a band of gypsies. For the next 30 years he lived a begging, vagrant life, spending the majority of his time (interspersed with voyages to Newfoundland) roving through the Southwest of England, begging for a living. Eighteenth-century readers of this autobiography were probably most struck by the shams and guises that Carew adopted in his ever more elaborate attempts to prise a few pence from the communities through which he passed. And there is little doubt that he could count himself among the small number of 'professional' beggars who worked the streets and roads of Britain. But, the range and variety of disguise and account that Carew uses to justify his vagrancy also act as a clear census of legitimate reason for travelling and justifications for begging. The *Life and Adventures of Bampfylde-Moore Carew, the Noted Devonshire Stroler and Dog Stealer* is a ribald tale of how to sin against agreed standards of behaviour, but in the process of transgressing those standards, Carew effectively illuminates them.

Early in his wandering career, Carew takes on the guise of a gypsy, and returns to it on several occasions during the next three and a half decades. Armed with a skilfully forged series of passes, he repeatedly pretends to be a shipwreck sailor: 'The news-papers which they constantly and carefully perused, continually furnished them with some melancholy and unfortunate story fitting for their purpose.'[28] At other times, Carew took on the character of a 'Grazier dwelling in the Isle of Sheepy in Kent, whose grounds were overflowed and whose cattle were drowned.'[29] He travelled as a rat-catcher, 'On the outside of his coat he always wore a large buff girdle, stuck thick with the largest and most terrible rats he destroyed, which served as a badge or ensign of his profession'; and a rag-gatherer, dressed in 'an old red Soldier's coat, ... a counterfeit sore on his right hand, and ... his beard ... very long, pretending he had been disabled in the Flanders wars.... Crying, *rags for the ragman, rags for the ragman*'.[30] At other times, Carew pretended to be a 'ragged old clergyman' turned out of his parish as a result of a religious dispute.[31] He was lunatic on license from Bedlam; a cripple, a match seller, a seller of 'songs and little two-penny histories, *Tom Thumb, Jack the Giant-Killer*, and such other little romances'.[32] He pretended to be a Quaker on several occasions; and regularly cross-dressed, begging with a borrowed child on his hip for verisimilitude.

In a text that rapidly becomes dull through repetitious renditions of one disguise after another, the boundaries of legitimate begging and migration are rapidly set. If you could 'give a good account of yourself'; if you were useful; if you were a gyspy; or woman and child; if you sold a commodity that people wanted to buy; if you could demonstrate a disability; or a tragic accident; or simply a real need to be in one place over another, movement was relatively unhindered, and uncomplicated.

The remarkable thing about Carew's 30 year vagrant career is that despite being 'famous' as the 'king of the beggars' (he was described as 'a most notorious common vagrant' in the records of the Exeter Quarter Sessions),[33] despite being widely believed to lead a gang of impostors and frauds, and despite committing a series of felonious criminal acts (he was a serial deserter from the army and navy), Carew was only punished on a handful of occasions prior to his transportation to Maryland in 1739. The first of these dated to around 1724 when he appears in the records of the combined house of correction and workhouse at Exeter for the first time. In Carew's explanation, he was 'Committed to Bridewell as a vagrant and impostor', when, after having been mistaken for a local malefactor, he was discovered on examination to be the 'famous' Bampfylde Carew. But, after two weeks in chains, the justices sitting in quarter sessions, simply,

> turn'd it off with a joke, respectively bowing to him, and expressing great joy in seeing a man who had rendered himself so famous and

of whom the world so loudly talk'd.... Without any trial they there fore discharged him.[34]

On two later occasions in the late 1720s and 1730s he was apprehended and whipped. First at Great Torrington, where the mayor's wife was tricked into providing relief, only to discover her error, and fly into a self-righteous rage; and the second at Chard, where a dispute about the ownership of two dogs led to Carew's persecution by a local JP.[35]

Carew's final run-in with the law, as recounted in the first more reliable edition of his life, occurred at Exeter, and resulted in transportation to North America. In Carew's rendition, his predicament was the result of ill-luck and poor judgement. On visiting one local magistrate with whom he had an excellent relationship, a fellow justice, who knew Carew and had vowed vengeance on him after a previous encounter, happened to be visiting:

> as ill-luck would have it, in comes Justice Lethbridge, ... he therefore now secured Bampfylde and sent him to St Thomas's Bridewell near Exeter. After two months confinement there he was brought up to the Quarter Sessions held at the Castle, where justice Beavis was Chairman, to whom he [Carew] used some abusive and opprobrious language, and the Justice ordered him seven years transportation.[36]

The remarkable element of this story is not Carew's punishment, or his professional character as a vagrant and beggar, but that he appears to have avoided any minor or substantial punishment for the vast majority of the over 30 years spent on the roads of Southwest England. His eventual punishment was not a result of his vagrant and begging habits, or even his undoubted forgery of official documents (in the form of a justice's pass, among several others items), but his notorious character in combination with his inability to keep his mouth shut in court. Like most able-bodied men and women, Carew appears to have been free to travel and migrate as he wanted, regardless of the blanket of laws and regulations which supposedly policed just this sort of thing. Despite Crew's claims to have perfected his many disguises, and the work he purports to invest in his many hard-luck stories, it is difficult to believe that a figure of his sort could escape censure and suspicion. The fact that he appears to have done so reflects more on the apparent tolerance of eighteenth-century communities than on Carew's inherent skills. If we turn to other, less substantial narratives, this same sense of a freedom of movement in the face of apparent legal obstacles emerges again and again.

***

When John Harrower set out from home in search of work in December 1773 he carried almost no cash. Instead he hawked knitted stockings in exchange for accommodation, food and money. Although technically this meant that he fell under the heading of an 'unlicensed pedlar' and therefore subject to arrest and punishment,[37] he travelled unmolested from Lerwick in the Shetland Islands to Leith, and on to Newcastle, and then to Portsmouth, begging free passage on a coaler on his way to London. The last three days of his journey to London from Portsmouth were undertaken on foot through some of the most travelled, crowded and rigorously policed parishes of Southern England. In his own terms, he was 'like a blind man without a guide, not knowing where to go'. His accent, if not his clothing and manner, must have marked him out as a member of the unsettled poor, but nevertheless, he came across little but good cheer and friendliness from the people he met on the way.[38]

A few years later, Israel Potter reproduced, in more difficult circumstances, the last leg of Harrower's journey from Portsmouth to London (see Plate 5.1). A prisoner of war, he escaped from a prison ship at Spithead, and proceeded directly towards the capital, where he hoped the anomity of a great city would protect him from re-capture. As a man on the run, dressed in a naval outfit, he stood out in the agricultural parishes of Sussex, but he nevertheless proceeded with remarkably little trouble. His first encounter after securing his escape was with 'an old man... tottering beneath the weight of his pick-ax, hoe and shovel, clad in tattered garments'; with whom Potter rapidly struck a deal. He traded his navy 'pea-jacket, trousers, &c.' for the man's Sunday suit. Dressed in a less attention grabbing attire, Potter made rapid progress:

> I travelled about 30 miles that day, and at night entered a barn in hopes to find some straw or hay on which to repose for the night, for I had not money sufficient to pay for a night's lodging.

The next day, in order to further justify his vagrant presence on the roads, he fashioned a crutch and pretended to be a cripple. This allowed him to progress through towns along the way, 'without meeting with any interruption'. He hitched a lift with 'an empty baggage wagon, bound to London', and again, 'sought lodgings in a barn; which containing a small quantity of hay, I succeeded in obtaining a tolerable comfortable night's rest'. It was only on the third day that he met with any trouble.

At Staines he was arrested and thrown into the roundhouse, but not on account of his vagrant behaviour or feigned lameness. Instead, he was arrested because his shirt (with which he had refused to part when he exchanged clothes with the elderly labourer), 'exactly corresponded with those uniformly worn by his Majesty's seamen' and 'not being able to give a satisfactory account of myself', he was 'made a prisoner of, on suspicion of being a deserter from his Majesty's service'.[39] He escaped a second time, and was soon mending chairs on the streets of London, an occupation he pursued in combination with outright begging, for the next 40 years.

For Israel Potter, as with Mary Saxby and Bampfylde-Moore Carew, it was the ability to both give a good account of one-self, and to travel

Plate 5.1   Israel Potter, 'Old Chairs to Mend', c. 1819; Plate xvi of John Thomas Smith, *The Cries of London: Exhibiting Several of the Itinerant Traders of Antient and Modern Times. Copied from Rare Engravings, or Drawn from the Life* (John Bowyer Nichols & Son, 25 Parliament Street, 1839). From the Author's Private Collection

unremarked that ensured they arrived safely. This was a point John Brown learnt early in life. As a young teenager in Cambridge, he was apprenticed, thrown into a local house of correction for insubordination, released from his master's authority, and set on a vagrant's road to London in the course of just a few months. At his first stop, just 18 miles from Cambridge, he 'pulled up at a roadside public house ...', and was almost immediately challenged by the local constable: 'a tall rough-looking fellow', who asked, 'how far I had come?' What ensued was a veritable interrogation, in which Brown's profession, home and destination were all assayed. In his somewhat breathless autobiography, Brown describes how he gave what he thought was a full and detailed account of his circumstances, 'having nothing to fear'. Nevertheless, he was rapidly labelled 'a runaway apprentice' by the constable, and threatened with arrest. It is what happened next, that speaks most clearly to what it meant to give a 'good' account of oneself. All of Browns recent troubles spilled from his lips, with details and names and relationships. And it was finally the landlady of the public house who declared: 'it was impossible I could make up such a tale if it were not true', on which the constable withdrew, and allowed Brown to continue to London.[40]

Although from a relatively comfortable background, Charlotte Charke also travelled through the English countryside, and occasionally attracted the censorious attentions of the authorities. Charke fell within the terms of the vagrancy acts, at least between 1746 and 1754, when she made a precarious living as a 'strolling player' in the Southwest. In this capacity she fell within the definition of a 'Common players of interludes, and all persons who shall for hire, gain, or reward, act, represent, or perform ... any interlude, tragedy, comedy, opera, play, farce or other entertainment of the stage'.[41] Her position was even more difficult than other vagrant travellers as the successful pursuit of a livelihood as a strolling player demanded maximum publicity. But, as with the other individuals discussed above, her single run-in with the law was the result of ill luck rather than the effective implementation of a legal precept. At Minchinhampton in Gloucestershire, she (although crossed-dressed as man throughout this encounter), along with one companion, was arrested for vagrancy, as part of an attempt to 'apprehend all persons within the limits of the act of Parliament'. According to her autobiography, this policy was implemented by an 'ignorant blockhead' who 'carried his authority beyond legal power', and who apparently did so in order to solicit bribes from his victims. The resulting night in gaol and appearance at the quarter sessions caused a local uproar in which various factions within the town appear to have been at loggerheads.

Charke's landlord and the Lord Mayor intervened repeatedly on her behalf, and she was eventually released, having spent a long night in a holding cell, entertaining her fellow prisoners with renditions of 'all the bead-roll of songs in the last act' of Gay's *Beggars Opera*.[42]

***

Like Saxby and Carew, Potter, Harrow, Brown and Charke were largely able to avoid the attentions of the systems intended to control internal migration, and to quietly meld into the constant stream of men and women who populated the roads; who slept in the barns and haylofts and who helped break through those parish boundaries that have generally been used to define the communities England. When Carl Philip Moritz undertook his travels 'chiefly on foot' in 1782, he fully reported the unusualness of a 'gentleman' travelling in this way, and by the end of his journey believed:

> that, in England, any person undertaking so long a journey on foot, is sure to be looked upon as either a beggar, or a vagabond, or some necessitous wretch, which is a character not much more popular than a rogue.[43]

But, he also noted with real surprise how differently parish and town officers treated travellers when compared to their German equivalents:

> It strikes a foreigner as something particular and unusual, when, on passing through these fine English towns, he observes none of those circumstances, by which the towns in Germany are distinguished ... no walls, no gates, no sentries, nor garrisons. No stern examiner comes here to search and inspect us, or our baggage; no imperious guard here demands a sight of our passports: perfectly free and unmolested we here walk through villages and towns, as unconcerned, as we should through an house of our own.[44]

The heavy coins and letters of introduction secreted in Moritz's pockets no doubt contributed to the warmth of his welcome and ease of travel, but the general point remains that despite the vagrancy acts and system of settlement, movement through the English countryside was largely unregulated.

In part, this conclusion must be the result of the many loopholes built in the vagrancy acts, and the 1744 Act in particular. While, 'pretending to go to work in harvest', for example, certainly fell within the Act, it was remarkably simple for either a legitimate or roguish traveller to circumvent:

> this shall not extend to any person going abroad to work at any lawful work in the time of harvest so as he carry with him a certificate signed by the minister and one of the churchwardens or overseers where he shall inhabit, that he hath a dwelling place there.[45]

Similarly, the Act authorised justices to issue a certificate that allowed a vagrant

> to pass the next and direct way to the place where he is to repair, and to limit so much time only, as shall be necessary for his travel thither; and in such case pursuing the form of such licence, he may for his necessary relief in his travels, ask and take the relief that any person shall willingly give him.

Richard Burn claimed that such certificates represented, 'the sole clause in any act of parliament, by which power is given to a justice of the peace to license any person to beg'. But, in Burn's opinion the existence of this extended system of certificates essentially created what amounted to an administrative chaos that was easily manipulated by the poor themselves. By way of illustration, Burn reported how he

> procured the hand writing of the mayor of Newcastle upon Tyne; by which I compared the passes of sailors said to be landed there that year; and out of eleven passes of that kind which came to my hands, the mayor's own proper hand writing was but set to two, and the other nine were forged.[46]

But in truth it was almost as easy to obtain a legitimate pass as it was to forge one. In the early nineteenth century, James Dawson Burn's mother was of the settled opinion that the vagrancy and settlement legislation posed little obstacle to her own travel arrangements. In around 1810 he accompanied his mother to the Mansion House, in London, where she spoke to the Lord Mayor:

> My mother took the whole of the children into her charge, and made application at the Mansion House for a pass to Hexham, in Northumberland, as a soldier's widow, which she had no difficulty in

obtaining; with this pass we visited nearly all the towns and villages on the east coast of England between London and Newcastle-upon-Tyne. As my mother preferred taking the journey at her ease, and her own time, she frequently had the benefit of the cash that the overseers would have had to pay for sending us forward in a conveyance, and at the same time she had the advantage of the intermediate relieving officers, who were often glad to get clear of us at the expense of a shilling or two.[47]

***

There is no doubt that large numbers of men and women fell foul of the vagrancy and settlement laws, and that huge efforts and substantial resources were dedicated to their implementation. The thousands of vagrancy and settlement examinations, certificates and passes that litter our archives are testimony to this. But, this does not imply that the eighteenth-century state (either national or parochial) was actually successful in regulating migration, or that the poor were unwitting 'victims' of this system. The apparent contradiction between the findings of most demographers that up to 40 per cent of people born in even rural parishes disappeared within a generation; and the belief expressed by historians of social policy that domestic migration was subject to severe restriction, can only be resolved by assuming that the legal framework just did not work.[48] The evidence of pauper autobiographies suggests that while the unlucky and the ill-informed, the positively recalcitrant and obviously vicious, might find themselves subject to the full and painful obloquy of the law, it required a certain wilfulness. These autobiographies also suggest that to fully understand the experiences of the eighteenth-century poor we need to move beyond an analysis of the settled poor, of pensioners and almshouse dwellers, to the rough sleepers and seasonal workers, to the men and women for whom barns and out-buildings, the roadside verge and quiet copse formed their only shelter.

Notes

1. 'Old Simon' of St Giles in the Fields was sardonically mentioned as the originator of a new fashion in hoop skirts in *Morning Chronicle and London Advertiser*, 25 July 1781.
2. *The Times*, 29 April 1788, p. 3. The same notice was also printed in *General Evening Post*, 26 April 1788; *London Chronicle*, 26 April 1788; *Whitehall Evening Post*, 26 April 1788; and the *Public Advertiser*, 29 April 1788.

3. J. T. Smith, *A Book for a Rainy Day: or, Recollections of the Events of the Last Sixty Years* (1845), (1905 edn), pp. 86–7.
4. *London Chronicle*, 24 April 1787.
5. *London Chronicle*, 3 April 1788.
6. *General Evening Post*, 26 April 1788.
7. See, for example, N. Rogers, 'Policing the Poor in Eighteenth-Century London: The Vagrancy Laws and Their Administration', *Histoire Sociale / Social History* 24, (1991), 127–47; N. Rogers, 'Vagrancy, Impressment and the Regulation of Labour in Eighteenth-Century Britain', *Slavery & Abolition* 15:2, (1994), 102–13.
8. P. Slack, *From Reformation to Improvement: Public Welfare in Early Modern England* (Oxford: Clarendon Press, 1999); S. Hindle, *On the Parish?: The Micro-Politics of Poor Relief in Rural England, c. 1550–1750* (Oxford: Oxford University Press, 2004); S. King, *Poverty and Welfare in England, 1700–1850* (Manchester: Manchester University Press, 2000) and L. Hollen Lees, *The Solidarities of Strangers: The English Poor Laws and the People, 1700–1948* (Cambridge: Cambridge University Press, 1998). A notable exception to this emphasis on the settled poor can be found in the growing literature on unmarried motherhood, whose objects of study were significantly migratory and socially dislocated. See for example L. Forman Cody, *Birthing the Nation: Sex, Science, and the Conception of Eighteenth-Century Britons* (Oxford: Oxford University Press, 2005); and T. Evans, *'Unfortunate Objects': Lone Mothers in Eighteenth-Century London* (Basingstoke: Palgrave Macmillan, 2005).
9. Rogers, 'Policing the Poor', p. 128. The most detailed account of the evolution of vagrancy legislation remains, B. Webb & S. Webb, *English Local Government: English Poor Law History: Part 1. The Old Poor Law* (Longmans, 1927), pp. 350–6.
10. 11 William III c. 18.
11. 13 Anne c. 26. This phrase is repeated through the rest of the eighteenth century in the numerous editions of Burn's Justicing Handbook. See for instance, R. Burn, *The Justice of the Peace and Parish Officer*, 18th edn, (1797), p. 489.
12. 17 George II c. 5.
13. 23 George III c. 88; and 27 George III c. 11. For a discussion of the 1787 Act see A. Eccles, 'A Superior Kind of Vagrant: Middlesex Lottery Vagrants in the 1790s', *Transactions of the London and Middlesex Archaeological Society* 60, (2008), 213–20.
14. 17 George II c. 5; for the continuing relevance of this list, even at the end of the century, see for example, R. Burn, *The Justice of the Peace and Parish Officer*, 18th edn (1797), IV, pp. 410–11.
15. The survival of an increasing number of 'pauper letters' from the 1780s onwards reinforces the impression of eighteenth-century England as a society in which migration was commonplace. For a comprehensive collection of one county's letters see, T. Sokoll (ed.), *Essex Pauper Letters, 1731–1837* (Oxford: Oxford University Press, 2001).
16. C. H. Wilkinson (ed.), *The King of the Beggars: Bampfylde-Moor Carew* (Oxford: Clarendon Press, 1931), p. 17.
17. For sleeping rough in London see, T. Hitchcock, *Down and Out in Eighteenth-Century London* (Hambledon, 2004), Chapter 2.

18. For a comprehensive overview of the law following the passage of the 1744 Vagrancy Act, including the role of certificates, see R. Burn, *The Justice of the Peace and Parish Officer*, 1st edn, (1755), II, pp. 486–91.
19. Rogers, 'Vagrancy, Impressment and the Regulation of Labour'; and Rogers, 'Policing the Poor'.
20. M. Saxby, *Memoirs of a Female Vagrant Written by Herself* (1806). Saxby's autobiography needs to be viewed in the light of at least two different and rapidly evolving literary forms, and treated with care. It is both an example of a 'conversion narrative' and an 'autobiography' showing clear literary influences. For a discussion of the evolution of the Methodist conversion narrative, see I. Rivers, 'Strangers and Pilgrims: Sources and Patterns of Methodist Narrative', in J. C. Hilson and others (eds), *Augustan Worlds* (Leicester: Leicester University Press, 1978). For a detailed analysis of the rise of plebeian autobiography see J. S. Amelang, *The Flight of Icarus: Artisan Autobiography in Early Modern Europe* (Stanford: Stanford University Press, 1998).
21. Saxby, *Memoir*, p. 6
22. Saxby, *Memoir*, p. 11.
23. Saxby, *Memoir*, p. 14.
24. Saxby, *Memoir*, p. 26.
25. T. Hitchcock and J. Black (eds), *Chelsea Settlement and Bastardy Examinations, 1733–1766* (London Record Society, 1999), no.308.
26. For a rare attempt to chart the interrelationship between the evolution of social policy and migration see D. Feldman, 'Migrants, Immigrants and Welfare from the Old Poor Law to the Welfare State', *Transactions of the Royal Historical Society*, 6th ser., 13 (2003), 79–104.
27. For an account of the evolution of these texts and supporting scholarship on Carew's life see Wilkinson (ed.), *Carew*, Introduction; G. Morgan & P. Rushton, *Eighteenth-Century Criminal Transportation: The Formation of the Criminal Atlantic* (Basingstoke: Palgrave Macmillan, 2004), pp. 78–85; and M. A. Nooney, *The Cant Dictionary of Bampfylde-Moore Carew: A Study of the Contents and Changes in Various Editions* (Unpublished University of Florida MA dissertation, 1969).
28. Wilkinson (ed.), *Carew*, p. 30.
29. Wilkinson (ed.), *Carew*, p. 14.
30. Wilkinson (ed.), *Carew*, pp. 16–17.
31. Wilkinson (ed.), *Carew*, p. 19.
32. Wilkinson (ed.), *Carew*, pp. 19–21.
33. Dev.RO, QS 1/18 Order Book, 1734–45, Easter 1739, pp. 105–7. Quoted in Morgan & Rushton, *Eighteenth-Century Criminal Transportation*, p. 81.
34. Wilkinson (ed.), *Carew*, pp. 38–40. For an excellent piece of historical detective scholarship tracing aspects of Carew's career in the local records of Devon see Morgan & Rushton, *Eighteenth-Century Criminal Transportation*, pp. 78–85.
35. Wilkinson (ed.), *Carew*, pp. 115–16, 131–2.
36. Wilkinson (ed.), *Carew*, pp. 134–5.
37. Burn, *Justice of the Peace*, 1st edn, (1755), I, 'Hawkers and Pedlars', pp. 504–5.
38. E. M. Riley (ed.), *The Journal of John Harrower: An Indentured Servant in the Colony of Virginia, 1773–1776* (Williamsburg: Colonial Williamsburg, 1963), pp. 3–14.

39. I. Potter, *Life and Remarkable Adventures of Israel R. Potter* (1824), ed. by L. Kriegal (New York: Corinth Books, 1962), pp. 27–32.
40. J. Brown, *Sixty Years' Gleanings from Life's Harvest. A Genuine Autobiography* (New York, 1859), pp. 29–30.
41. Burn, *Justice of the Peace*, 15th edn, (1785), IV, p. 335.
42. C. Charke, *A Narrative of the Life of Mrs Charlotte Charke* (1755), ed. by R. Rehder (Pickering & Chatto, 1999), pp. 109–12.
43. C. P. Moritz, *Travels of Carl Philipp Moritz in England in 1782* (1795), ed. by P. E. Matheson (Humphrey Milford, 1926), p. 152.
44. Moritz, *Travels*, p. 114.
45. Burn, *Justice of the Peace*, 15th edn (1785), IV, p. 343.
46. *Ibid.*, p. 342.
47. J. D. Burn, *The Autobiography of a Beggar Boy*, ed. by D. Vincent (Europa, 1978), p. 58.
48. For a recent survey of the literature on 'movers and stayers' see Hindle, *On the Parish*, pp. 304–5.

6
The Residential and Familial Arrangements of English Pauper Letter Writers, 1800–40s

Steven King

6.1 Introduction

On 30 November 1841, Thomas Pitt came before the Malmesbury (Wiltshire) Coroner to give evidence about his recently deceased father, Joseph Pitt, aged 82. His testimony is worth quoting at length:[1]

> *No person lived in the House with him. He was capable of taking care of himself up to the last 10 days* and within that time he was able with help to get out of bed. *I attended him three or four times a Day and sent others.* He had an Allowance from the parish of one shilling per week and two loaves which were supplied to him by the relieving officer. His pay for one week was stopped to induce him to go into the Union workhouse during which times *I relieved him.* I went down to the Deceased's house on the 15 November where I saw Edwin Bishop the Relieving Officer who was endeavouring to persuade the deceased to go to the House, meaning the Union Poor House but deceased then made no answer. On other occasions he expressed a willingness to go but when I went to accompany him he refused to go and said 'let me die here'. I took him a supper on Saturday Night between 9 and 10 0' clock … *When I left him that night I locked the Outer Door as I had been in the Habit of doing. Next Morning, Sunday, my little Girl who had gone down to make the deceased's fire* came crying and said she believed her Grandfather was dead.[2]

Ann Fry, a neighbour, noted 'I never heard him complain and I do not believe he died from want.'[3]

Several important lessons can be drawn from this episode. *First*, Thomas Pitt opened his testimony with the observation that his father lived alone and was capable of doing so. Perhaps he expected otherwise to be asked the question why he, as a son, had not either sent someone to live with his father or moved him into his own house.[4] The fact is, however, that father and son had worked out a system of support that allowed him to keep his residential independence, and this chimes with Robin's much underused study of later nineteenth-century Colyton which suggests that not until individuals reached the most advanced old age (like Joseph Pitt) did the intergenerational contract switch from care-giving to care receiving.[5] *Second*, it is definitively clear that Joseph Pitt did not want to end up in the workhouse. This observation fits very well with recent revisions to the literature on the residential arrangements of the elderly poor. While these have tended to play down the scale of solitary living of the sort experienced by Pitt, they have shown consistently that the aged poor tried every strategy to avoid institutional confinement.[6] *Third*, whatever his preferred residential arrangements it is clear that Joseph was tied into complex care-giving family and neighbourhood arrangements. Thomas Pitt interrupted his work regularly to visit his father, and he notes that he sent others including family members. Presumably too Ann Fry must have been in regular contact with the old man in order to make the assertion that he never complained. Even if care-giving did not involve co-residence it did mean helping the old man out of bed, setting fires, sending food, seeing to security and staying well into the long nights at that time of year. Such observations fit well with a literature that has emphasised both the complexity and fluidity of household arrangements amongst the poor and the value of care provided by families, neighbours and others.[7] They also chime with recent revisionist literature on kinship, which has questioned older assertions about the isolation of families and laid ever greater emphasis on the residential propinquity and even co-residence of kin.[8] *Finally*, while the Union officers tried to get the old man to enter the workhouse during his last weeks, when he would not go their only sanction was to briefly suspend relief. Having failed to get him to move, officials continued his allowance, which, though clearly insufficient, thus helped him to maintain his independence.[9] While capable of several readings, this course of events might point to an ingrained communal acceptance of the basic right to independent living.

Of course, the lessons drawn from the experiences of the Pitt family seem familiar. A more nuanced appreciation of the residential and familial arrangements of the poor has been creeping into the historiography since the 1980s, as the focus of poor law research moved from the law, institutions and basic practice, and towards the experiences, language and sentiments of paupers.[10] Thus, Sokoll has challenged the notion that pauper households were small and simple;[11] Sharpe and Cooper and Donald have shown that even poor households were remarkably open to migrant kin, poor lodgers and others;[12] Snell has emphasised the obligations that parishes felt towards the poor who belonged;[13] Hollen Lees has suggested that parishes had perceived moral obligations towards paupers, at least until the final decades of the Old Poor Law;[14] and I have argued variously that residential arrangements in the north-west of England were more fluid than has usually been allowed and that the poor law actively sought to shape the residential arrangements of the poor.[15] Yet, the evidential basis for discussion of issues such as pauper attempts to ensure residential independence; durability of housing arrangements; the size, structure and fluidity of pauper households; interactions between paupers and family and neighbours; official attitudes towards pauper housing; and the rhetorical and strategic place of housing as a distinct motif in pauper attempts to establish entitlement, remains relatively thin.

This chapter focuses on one source – the pauper letter – that, on its own and in tandem with other records, can begin to fill this gap.[16] Such letters survive in rather greater numbers than their early users could have imagined. While they are by no means easy to use – questions of representativeness, orthography, provenance and accuracy abound – Thomas Sokoll has created a framework within which pauper letters should be interpreted.[17] Moreover, he, Pamela Sharpe and others have shown persuasively that such letters can generate the sort of nuanced discussion about negotiation strategies, pauper and parish sentiment and detailed pauper experiences that would otherwise be missing from the historiographical debate on poverty and welfare.[18] They can also, when systematically used, fill the gap between the static portrayals of pauper household arrangements found using census material and the flowing portrayals of household and family provided by individual narrative sources. Accordingly, the chapter will draw upon some 3000 pauper letters and associated items of overseer correspondence that have been collected for 78 communities in Berkshire, Lancashire, and Northamptonshire,[19] dating mostly from the period 1810–40.[20] Of course, the issue of how to make sense of so much data and to generalise from the multiple life-cycle perspectives contained therein is potentially problematic. For this reason we will focus on the residential and familial arrangements of paupers who wrote multiple letters to their parish of settlement, and particularly on three sets of correspondence that appear to exemplify key regularities in such arrangements in the wider letter sample. Such an approach raises several issues of representativeness: Were multiple letter writers likely to emerge in particular socio-economic locations? Were multiple letter writers really representative of all letter writers in terms of life-cycle stage and the rhetorical and strategic content of narratives? Do the concerns, approaches and strategies of a set of non-resident letter writers accurately reflect the experiences and tactics of the settled and locally resident poor? These questions cannot be answered definitively, but it is certainly possible to overplay them. Thus, as Alannah Tomkins and the current author have clearly shown, multiple letter writers exist in very different topographical and socio-economic settings and that there are good reasons to think that the range of concerns expressed in letters more widely, and the way that those concerns were rhetoricised, carry a wider representativeness.[21] Accepting the idea that pauper letters can tell us something meaningful and portable about the residential and familial arrangements of the poor, this chapter will be underpinned by three key questions: First, and focusing particularly on the aged, how durable was a model of independent living for the poor? Second, how porous were the household boundaries of poor people and how fluid was their family size and structure? Finally, did the poor use the rhetoric and symbolism of household, housing and family as a distinctive motif – as opposed, for instance, to the rhetoric of unemployment or widowhood – in their efforts to establish or maintain entitlement to poor relief? It will be argued that we see a dogged attachment of the poor to independent living, volatility in the household size and structure of poor people and a distinctive place for the rhetoric of house and housing in their claims-making infrastructure.

6.2   A model of independent living

Joseph Pitt, with whose story we opened this chapter, clearly had very durable housing arrangements, living independently, presumably in a house that he had rented for some time and resisting any changes in these arrangements. Such residential independence has become an increasingly common observation in the secondary literature on poverty and welfare and it is reflected strongly in our letter sample for all places and all life-cycle groups. Its importance to the aged pauper is particularly pronounced, something that we can exemplify using a series of letters written on behalf of Jane Higginson, resident in Leeds but with a settlement in Hulme, near Manchester, in the 1830s. On 9 September 1835, William Hudswell, Minister of George Street Chapel Leeds, wrote to the overseers of the poor of Hulme on behalf of Higginson whose regular allowance had not been paid. He asked them 'Please to send it immediately and you will relieve the mind of the poor old woman. If you direct for Jane Higginson, *14 Bean Street, York Road, Leeds, it will find her as your last to her did.'*[22] A second letter on 2 October 1835 reminded the overseer 'her rent is due and she is in debt, and she does not know what to do'.[23] The money was clearly paid, because the next we hear from Hudswell is 21 May 1836 when, asking for an increase in her allowance, he reminded the official that Higginson was 81 and that 'She has only lately had to apply for parish relief when her husband died. ... *She lives in a little cot by herself no 14 Bean Street York Road. A few of her old neighbours have occasionally helped her a little* or the 2/6d per week would not have done'.[24]

In turn, written on the back of the original and dated 24 May 1836, was a reply from the Hulme overseer:

> Our township is one almost entirely of cottages and we are at times as much pained at compelling payment of rates as we are in withholding in cases like this now before us. *Might not Jane Higginson economize by lodging with some relation or friend – it seems a small waste of money to pay rent for a single individual. If there be neither relations nor friends she might probably be admitted into the Poor's House* and kept comfortable on her present allowances.[25]

Hudswell retorted on 19 August 1836 that 'she is an object worthy of attention and *it is thought by all who are acquainted with her a scandal that she be left in such a deplorable condition'*. Written on a slip attached to the letter was a comment from the Hulme overseer:

> Sir, we have been at pains to consider your request for Widow Higginson, but must refer you to our previous reply. *Consider, would it not be better for a woman of such age and with so much misfortune heaped up around her to lodge in the house of another or to apply to the Poor's House*, where we should be glad to meet her board and grant a small allowance, *for this is the custom with our own poor who live further than their independence allows.* Yet we enclose a note for her rent.[26]

Hudswell's reply had to wait until 10 December, when he noted that Higginson was firmly cemented into her community and that 'She has lived in her cott for four years since and has no family to go to'.[27] Nonetheless, he added 'I shall talk to the old woman about quitting her place for some other where she might be better attended'. His persuasion clearly worked; on 4 July 1837 Hudswell warned the overseer that

Higginson's creditworthiness was under threat but added as a postscript *'if you send it by post to the old woman she lives near the top of Ward's Fold, Mabgate, Leeds'*.[28] Higginson had moved from her dilapidated cottage, and Hudswell's last letter of 3 November 1837 (after which the New Poor Law had settled upon both places) noted, 'The old woman is at present very well but says she will be 84 next February. *She lives with Mrs Marshall* No. 36 top of Ward's Fold, Mabgate.'[29]

At the most human level, Higginson's story is both touching and interesting. It also resonates with key themes in the recent literature on the housing and household arrangements of the poor in general and the aged poor in particular. Through the opening letters in the sequence we learn that Jane Higginson was living as a solitary householder. She was aged, infirm and in debt, but had only recently applied for relief after the death of her husband, who, while presumably of an equal age, had clearly worked to support her. The latter observation is consistent with a growing literature that has emphasised the surprising resilience of the household economies and continued residential independence of old couples. However, a close reading of the letter of 21 May 1836 suggests that Higginson was not resident in the same house that she occupied with her husband. It was after all her *old* neighbours who helped her when the allowance from Hulme parish proved inadequate. Perhaps, then, the widow had moved to new (and cheaper) accommodation after the death of her husband in an attempt to maintain her residential independence? Such a strategy sits well with Botelho's analysis of the attitudes of the seventeenth-century aged poor towards their housing, and even more firmly with Robin's observation about the tenacious independence of the aged poor in later nineteenth-century Colyton.[30] However we read the evidence, for Jane Higginson residential independence was clearly very important even in the face of explicit suggestions from the overseer that she lodge with family or neighbours. This dogged attachment to residential independence can be seen throughout the thousands of pauper letters in the wider sample.

Other evidence from this particular series of letters suggests that an underlying belief in the need to maintain the residential independence of the poor in general and the aged poor specifically was widely shared. Widow Higginson was often in arrears with her rent, a common feature of pauper letters. Her landlord could on several occasions have either distrained or forced the old woman to quit the house. Yet, he took neither course of action. Perhaps he was afraid of upsetting Higginson's neighbourhood, or indeed incurring the displeasure of William Hudswell.

The fact that the neighbourhood was willing to pitch in to support the old widow certainly suggests strong support for her continued independence. There must, however, be a more general explanation, because while rent arrears are a consistent feature of the letters of paupers in the underlying sample, an equally consistent theme is the rarity of landlords evicting paupers or distraining their goods. Perhaps there was an inbuilt expectation that poor law officials would eventually pay up, yielding guaranteed rent payments into which delays could be built as a premium. However we explain it, even where officials were convinced of the moral or (in the case of Higginson) physical frailties of letter writers they nonetheless persistently paid for rents. Overseers were, in other words, sensitive to the housing needs of the poor in general and the need to support the continued independence of even the frailest of the aged poor, in particular.[31] This is not to say, of course, that poor law officials invariably supported residential independence but that they did not seek change lightly. The Hulme overseer suggested that Widow Higginson might lodge with kin or friends, or alternatively that she might go into the poor house. However, this was a suggestion, not a demand, and the overseer still paid her rent arrears. In the event, the old woman was clearly prevailed upon over a period of several months to give up her cottage and independence and lodge with Mrs Marshall in nearby Mabgate, and this episode goes at least a little way towards exemplifying the slow and non-linear move from independent living to co-residence with others among the aged poor, snapshot evidence of which we see in census returns.

Whether paupers had the advantage of proximate kin (like Joseph Pitt) or whether, in the absence of kin, they were obliged (like Widow Higginson) to substitute being known and visible in the neighbourhood and thus able to draw on the help of friends, there is clear, substantial and persistent evidence in pauper letters of an ingrained attachment to residential independence. Next to sickness, help in getting or maintaining a house was the single biggest issue prompting pauper letters. There was an equal concern with securing housing among the settled poor.[32] Moreover, the persistent failure of officials to force residential changes on the part of paupers (something that we see consistently in pauper letters) suggests persuasively that there was a durable notion of residential independence that they simply could not override. Only by looking at pauper letters can we get a real sense of the processes, negotiations, compromises and customs that hedged around and supported that durability.

6.3 The fluidity of household boundaries and structures

While residential independence seems to have been the ideal to which paupers like Joseph Pitt and Jane Higginson clung, this does not mean that the household boundaries of paupers were impermeable or household structures static. Indeed, the literature on household size and structure in general, and pauper households in particular, has emphasised that static snapshot sources such as censuses yield only a partial representation of the nature of the household life-cycle.[33] Yet, it remains true that we have a patchy appreciation of the processes by which households were supplemented, shrank, broken and reformed. Pauper letters afford a window into these issues. Naturally, to explore in detail the fluidity of household boundaries and structures in the thousands of letters from our underlying sample would require a separate chapter, since experiences varied according to life-cycle stage, location and chance events. For one group of paupers, however – parents with children – the data is very rich, with some 900 letters attributed to this group. Of particular interest, intrinsically and because they represent so well other (multiple and single) letter writers in exactly the same position, are the experiences of James and Frances Soundy. Their settlement was in Pangbourne, Berkshire, but they were resident in and around Battersea at the time they were writing a long series of 38 letters between 1818 and 1832. This series is worth considering at length, because it epitomises some of the variation in household arrangements that we often see in pauper letters but so little in static surveys of the poor or household censuses.

We first hear of the Soundys on 22 December 1818, when Frances wrote to Pangbourne from Battersea asking for a little extraordinary relief, noting that her husband had abandoned her after an argument and had gone to stay with an elder daughter.[34] The overseer did not reply and on 9 January 1819 we find a note in the parish collection that 'James Soundy [back with his wife either voluntarily or forced by the overseer], wife Frances and three children John (9), Frances (7) and Emma (2) removed from Battersea St. Mary to Pangbourne'.[35] Whether they were ever *physically removed* is unclear, but certainly by 29 September 1823 they were back in Battersea, from where the overseer of Pangbourne received a letter asking the parish to help with the clothes or apprenticeship fee for their son (presumably John, now almost 14). Frances Soundy informed the overseer that the £5 they had saved to pay for these things had been lost a year previous

> to pay for counsel for his unfortunate [previously undetected] brother and other exspences wich was vary hevey for *we ad his wife*

and child with us from the time she came from you and my son must have starved in prison if we ad not assised him.

The implication is that a daughter-in-law had lived with Frances and James for some time, converting a standard nuclear family into a complex family household. Frances added by way of a parting comment the prospect that their younger son would be resident with them forever because 'this poor boy John Soundy as got an empedement in his speech so that he can not vary wall be understood so that he can not git his living by servitude'.[36]

The family still had no answer on the apprenticeship by 30 January 1824 when Frances Soundy wrote seeking relief because James has smashed his thumb. Her letter noted 'my famely his *3 girls* and 1 boy and I my salf as bene hill som time'.[37] John (now 14) was clearly still co-resident and the implication is that the elder daughter that had offered sanctuary to her father in 1819 was also once again resident in the household. By 13 February 1826, the situation had changed again, and Frances Soundy wrote that they were

> *surporting our son his wife and child* gentillmen I would not have trobelled you a gain could i by any meanes have avoided it but throw my husband illness at Christmas and keep in of them as inthralled us so much in debt that i can not assist them any longer ... *they have now lived with me 11 weeks.*[38]

The return of the eldest son (later identified as Charles Soundy), a daughter-in-law and a grandchild had made this a multiple family household, pointing to a fluidity that is often suspected and hinted at in the secondary literature but rarely elaborated with empirical substance. The son and his wife were probably still co-resident (the letter is capable of several readings) on 16 November 1826 when Frances Soundy wrote to ask if her son should ask for relief from Battersea, for

> *it do not lay in my power any longer to surport them* I have dun a grat deal an none to my husband and distressed my salf and other children till we have nothing now left ... unles that we hear from you by monday *my son and his wife and child must com on tuesday as they will nither have home or habataion to hide thar unfortunate heads* gentellmen i humbly pray that you will whea [weigh] their misfortunes in your hone brast [breast] and *think wot a Mother must feel in seing her children starving and naked.*[39]

Despite these dire predictions, Charles and his wife did not remove. On 3 May 1827, Frances was about to become a grandmother and wrote to ask for the money for a midwife because

> intirely to surport her throu her trobell i can not for *I have my elldist darter at hom who ad lost the youse of her lims with the rumaxtick fever* and nou she is gitin better i can not git her the norris[ment] that she requires.[40]

Whether Frances had provided a home for her two elder children, grandchildren and a daughter-in-law throughout the period from November 1826 to May 1827 is uncertain, though the fact that the overseer of Battersea wrote on 16 June 1827 that 'he [James Soundy] also has been obliged to support his Son and his Wife for the last *12 weeks*', suggests that the family had got at least a little relief during the period.[41] By 7 June 1828, Charles and Mary Soundy had definitely removed from the household, but had left 'a little *grand darter darter to our son Charles soundy* your perrishoner'.[42] On 24 September 1828 Charles returned home to try and avoid an arrest warrant, but Frances Soundy warned the Pangbourne officials that she 'could not surport them *i allrady have one of his chilldren with me and a nother son* [presumably John, now 18] *and wife and child and have found tham a home for this last 3 months'*.[43] It is unclear whether the sick elder daughter remained co-resident, but whatever the case we can see clearly that the household boundaries of the Soundys were extremely permeable and that household and family size and structure could vary significantly.

Sometime between November and December one of the sons (probably John given the internal evidence of later letters) clearly removed, but this left the Soundys with his wife to support.[44] Charles, meanwhile, had returned by 2 February 1829, when Frances wrote to say that it was 'vary hard that 2 old popell shuld be brote in to the *gratest disstrees and trobell throu finding a home for thar children'*. Asking for help with the rent, she went on to observe that if it was not paid 'we must turn out wich *after being under one landlord for 22 years* to be turned in to the street for 14 shillings and seek a home ware we can'. By way of support to her claims, she recorded that

> *my famely consist of my dear darter wich we have exspeted her death hourly for this 7 weeks* she is quit confined to her bed and cannot be left day or night her illness is a decline and dropsey wich as soune as the warter overflows the last she will be gorn momently and *my*

2 youngest girls and my son John soundy wife and child wich i wrote to you stating that he ad left his home wich he as this 7 weeks last thursday we are told he his gorn to the south amaraky [south America] or vandemans land this we no to our sorro that he is gorn tho we can not for truth say ware so that his wif can not have any support from him and have not any think but wot she have from us and have ad for som months as he was vary vile and thortles.[45]

This letter reveals very clearly the fragility of young households, the potential impact of family breakage and the ongoing impact of illness, debt and life-cycle circumstances on the household size and structure of poor people. While it is easy to think that the poor had little to offer other poor relatives at times of economic or demographic crisis, the experiences of the Soundy family clearly locates co-residence as a viable collective coping strategy.[46] By 22 October 1829, Frances had been 'oblige to send *my son Charles soundy littell girl home*', and warned that if no relief were forthcoming '*I must give up my youngest son child and wot littell I do for his wife* and then wot she is to do i can not tell'.[47] This letter implies that both Charles and the abandoned daughter-in-law were no longer resident, and on 14 November 1829 a further letter stated that John Soundy's girl had been returned to the mother, leaving Frances resident with just her two daughters and husband. The nuclear family was not to stay that way for long. A penultimate letter of 11 October 1831 recounted the impending homelessness of Charles Soundy and his family. Frances wrote: '*if thay do not pay thar rant by next tuesday oct[r] 17 thay will take thar goods for the same and then gentellman i have not room to take them to my house.*'[48]

It would be easy to regard this long series of woes as part of the inbuilt rhetoric of pauper letters, a definitive strategy for establishing individual and familial entitlement. Indeed, the narratives of household fluidity and porous household boundaries constructed largely by Frances seem to have had a particular claim on officials in Pangbourne, who expended considerable sums on the Soundy family. It would be equally easy to question the representativeness of the Soundys given that they were based in London, which might predispose them to have proximately resident kin who could converge on the parental household in troubled times.[49] An alternative interpretation is, as Thomas Sokoll suggests, that we regard these narratives and their writers as essentially emblematic of the core experiences of the poor.[50] This is certainly true of the sample of letters underpinning this chapter. While there are variations of emphasis between county-based letter collections, in places such as Pangbourne, Hulme, Peterborough, Oundle or Lancaster the fluidity of household boundaries is a consistent theme whatever the socio-economic or life-cycle circumstances of the paupers concerned.

In this sense, the Soundy letters are both intriguing and fit snugly with recent speculation in the wider historiography. Thus, many of the Soundy experiences echo those of Widow Higginson, including long-term residence in a single property (in this case 22 years), persistent rent problems and yet a landlord that lets them remain, and an essential unwillingness on the part of the Pangbourne vestry to see the family unhoused. Moreover, and in contrast to Joseph Pitt, the direction of family support was clearly (in terms of both co-residence and support offered to non-resident children) from parents to children, suggesting just how complex the material aspect of intergenerational relationships could be. Yet, it is the fluidity of the Soundy household in the face of life-cycle crisis that is the most important observation here. The letters open with Frances Soundy effectively heading her own household having been abandoned by her husband who went to live with a daughter some-where else in London. She may have been the eldest daughter that later joined the family after a bout of serious illness. By the time we hear of the family in 1823 the eldest co-resident son, John, would have been 14, Frances would have been 12 and Emma seven. Around December 1822, the household had been joined by Charles Soundy, the eldest (and previously proximate rather than co-resident) son and his wife. This might explain why the Soundys then sought to apprentice John in 1823, though by January 1824 John was still resident. At the same date the two daughters recorded at the time of a removal order in 1819 had clearly been rejoined by an elder sister, because the number of girls in the household was three and there is no evidence that Frances had been pregnant in the intervening period. How any of these children interacted in their own right with officials in Pangbourne is unknown, but it is clear that it was the narratives of Frances Soundy that got them relief.

In turn, the co-residence of Charles and Mary Soundy was intermit-tent. They came in December 1822, but must then have left because a letter of February 1826 suggests that at this point Charles and Mary had lived with Frances for only the last 11 weeks. Twelve months later they had been co-resident again, while some time in-between the eldest daughter had left the household and returned again to be nursed through a rheumatic fever. By 7 June 1828 Charles and Mary had removed from the household but left behind a granddaughter. However, when Charles was pursued for a debt in September 1828, we learn that John Soundy had previously left the household, got married and that he, his wife and child had moved back into the parental home. The household became temporarily more crowded as Charles fled a debt and Mary also co-resided with Frances and James, three younger children, John Soundy and his wife and a further granddaughter. Mary had left by February 1829, when Frances wrote to say that John Soundy had gone to Australia or America, leaving his wife and child in the Soundy household. Not until November 1829 had the family become nuclear again. In short, over a decade between 1819 and 1829, the household of Frances and James Soundy had fluctuated wildly in size, complexity and structure. The boundaries of the household were notably porous in response to life-cycle crisis. Little wonder, then, that Frances Soundy persistently refers to the stresses and jealousies that co-residence caused. In this sense the experiences of the Soundys offers interesting nuance since census schedules and listings are static, reactive and reflective sources that give little sense of the complex processes of negotiation, despair and duty/obligation that generate the household formations detected in them. What these and other pauper letters show very clearly are that pauper house holds were in, or in expectation of, constant flux.[51]

Of course, demography and migration shape what was possible in family and household terms for pauper letter writers, and it is uncommon (but by no means unheard of) to find a series of pauper letters that so clearly relates household size, complexity and composition to the maximum available networks of proximate kin. Yet, just over 30 per cent of all letters in the underlying sample make reference to fluid household boundaries, and for this reason analysis of the Soundy letters are an important advance in our understanding of the residential and familial arrangements of the poor. There is also another factor to consider: at no point do the vestry or overseers of Pangbourne counsel Frances Soundy against taking in her children and their wives and children. They do not refuse to pay contributions to rent, doubt her stories about the family suffering or send inspectors to see if she is telling the truth about the desperate state that co-residence, illness and underemployment forces the household into. Rather they pay, albeit not on time and in full or enough. One reading of this situation is that the vestry clearly thought household fluidity among the poor not unusual, which in turn sits well with the idea that officials might seek to engineer (by law or, more usually, by bargain) such fluidity.[52] Porous household boundaries, in other words, were, and were expected to be, part of familial coping strategies, and our evidence from pauper letters suggests that this was true irrespective of the socio-economic or cultural setting in which we find poor people.

6.4   Housing as Rhetoric[53] and Symbol in Establishing Entitlement

Whatever the expectations of officials it is also clear from our pauper letter sample that the rhetoric, symbolism and actuality of housing could play a significant part in the process of negotiating with them. We have already seen something of this in Widow Higginson's attempts to secure regular or increased relief payments, or in Frances Soundy's multilayered rhetoric of home, homelessness and family. However, it is important to note that the tendency of paupers to invoke the symbolic and rhetorical value of housing, household or family and (potential) homelessness in their strategic and linguistic engagement with officials is very common indeed. In the underlying sample of pauper letters, 46 per cent mention these issues as part of the negotiation process, though such rhetoric is often tied up with other yardsticks of need such as an inability to provide proper care for children, sickness, old age or even unemployment. Housing was a distinctive motif, drawing, as we shall see, on a rhetoric which combined plea, fear, demand, expressions of rights and duties and threats (often to return home at great expense to the parish of settlement). Sickness, widowhood or simple old age were approached, described and rhetoricised in quite different ways.[54] For many of our pauper letter writers (and presumably too for poor law officials) housing was the last bastion of respectability. To be split asunder from house and neighbourhood was symbolically and practically (because it disrupted networks of credit and trust) one of the last stages of the descent into abject dependence. To be unemployed, naked, sick or a widow also threatened abject dependence, but such threats were met with rather different rhetorical reference points.

We might look at this issue through the letters of the Curchin family. Settled in Thrapston (Northamptonshire) but living in Wisbech (Cambridgeshire), the Curchins are one of the most richly documented of all pauper families in the underlying sample with 71 letters by or about them copied into the Thrapston letter books between 1824 and 1835. The family first appear in the records through a reply (17 June 1824) by the Thrapston overseer to his counterpart for Wisbech who had asked for permission to relieve Jacob Curchin. Robert Colls of Thrapston was scathing, suggesting that 'I beg to observe that he is a very troublesome and imposing man, and therefore shall be obliged by your being guarded against his crafty insinuations'.[55] So began a long engagement between Thrapston and the Curchins. Thus, on 26 September 1824, Jacob Curchin reported that he could not both pay rent and support his family, adding that his wife was pregnant.[56] This theme of encroaching maternity was taken up again by Jacob Curchin on 25 December 1824. He noted, 'my wife is confined and I had not a shilling nor nothing in the house, and no nurse, therefore she must be lost … *my wife is in a lost state and my quarters rent is due* today'.[57] While maternity may be the proximate reason for the application, the request itself is for help with rent rather than a nurse or food. The central claims-making rhetoric is an elision between the threat of homelessness (which the provision of relief will prevent) and the potential impact of homelessness (Sophia would be 'lost') on the family.

By 30 December 1824, the overseer had not paid the rent and Curchin claimed that 'I must sell my goods and *come home*, if you think I am telling you an untruth *I should be glad if you would inquire* of any of Wisbech as *it* [his housing situation] *is no secrete there*'. Here there is a multilayered language of home as the central rhetorical apparatus, with Curchin melding the rights conferred by his settlement to come home with a community appreciation (something we also saw in the letters written on behalf of widow Higginson) of his desperate housing situation. He was not in fact evicted; a letter of 12 March 1825 from Sophia Curchin refers to a rent payment by Thrapston, but continues that she was

> sorry to say there is another quarter due and we have not one shilling to pay it as my husband has no work or any jobs that he can meet with, the Rent due to Mr Dixon is one pound twelve and sixpence which I should be greatly obliged to you to send him or us, or we shall have our things sold and *as for my poor children … I hope you will do something for them to keep out the cold*.[58]

Once again, help with house rental is the central purpose of this letter, but in rhetorical terms the issue of housing is tied seamlessly into the implicit calls of duty that the parish officers should feel in providing a roof over the heads of helpless children. By the 25 April 1825, the overseer had not paid the arrears, and Sophia wrote again to say

> *we are almost starving as to pay the rent* … I hope your goodness will do to *keep me a home as I am not willing to go to a workhouse if I can help it* but I must if you do not pay my Rent.[59]

The issues of rent, housing and family are used as a rhetorical and strategic vehicle, with Sophia writing in her capacity as a mother to plead the case of her four children. She implies that a small expenditure will keep her out of the workhouse, and the way in which the sacrifices of the family (going without food) are related to keeping a roof over their heads and the household together is, as Sokoll has suggested, a rhetorically powerful model.[60]

The family continued to use housing as a touchstone for their appeals. Sophia wrote on 19 July 1825 to say that if Thrapston 'pay the rent what is due they [her landlords] have another tenant that will take it [the house] off our hands'.[61] The house, from being a refuge, a place on which the overseers must pay the rent in order to secure a mother and her four children, had become a burden, a millstone to be jettisoned if the Thrapston overseer would just pay the arrears of rent. By 1 June 1826 the rhetorical cycle had come full circle, with Jacob Curchin noting that

> my wife is very bad and expects to be confined every day which you must know what *an expensive time and my Rent day is past* and *my Landlord is at me every day as Mr Nixon tould him he had no orders to pay this Quarters rent* I hope your goodness will *send me a trifle to get me through*.[62]

As with his opening narrative, Curchin elided maternity with the issue of his rent, calling on the experience of Thrapston officials as fathers who must know that a man such as himself could not meet the bills attendant upon his wife's confinement. He faced a battle to survive and, like the enemy, his landlord was 'at him'. The house was crucial to his very existence. Sophia Curchin adopted a less positive tone on 26 June 1826, saying that the landlord threatened distraint and

> Though at the same time I am willing to shift all I can but I hope you will have the goodness to pay my Rent and *assist me a Trifle*[63] more a week in my confinement as *every one of feeling will allow it a shocking thing to want at such a time as I expect very shortly*.[64]

Thus, while for Jacob the house was a sanctuary in a troubled time, for Sophia it was a burden and a worry.

Jacob's letter of 8 November 1826 took up the housing thread, noting that 'my Landlord is quite out of patience about his rent and I am Greatly in Fear I shall lose the house If that was the case I am sure I could not get another so cheap in Wisbeach'.[65] Here we see a further rhetorical shift. His house is neither sanctuary nor burden, but an opportunity – an opportunity for the overseers to retain the family in a low rental house, which would be cheaper than the alternatives in Wisbech and, by inference, cheaper than bringing them back to Thrapston. His bluff was called and Thrapston refused to pay.[66] By 1 July 1829, Sophia was again writing to the overseer. She noted that

> our landlord has sold our furniture but we are not willing to leave here where we can get a bit of Bread though we are obliged to lay on straw as we have promise of another house if we can get a few things to put into it therefore if you would have the goodness to assist us with a trifle of money it will be the means of keeping us from you in future.[67]

Once more, their current house had become a burden, one that has resulted in them losing their goods and having to lie on straw. Yet, they had the prospect of a new beginning if only the overseer would give them the money to buy a few things for the new house, and the search for money allowances was thus firmly intertwined with the threat to housing and the fragility of household structures. Whether the parish paid or not is unclear, but a further six letters followed during 1830. The series resumed in February 1831, when Jacob Curchin wrote

> it is *thought a great disgrace* that our family is once again put before the bailiffs [sic] for want of a few shillings of rent, when we have shown the greatest economy and salved our Landlord so often.[68]

Here Curchin drew together his housing situation and a wider public opinion of his case, which, while it might have been an empty rhetoric nonetheless demonstrates his perception that the issue of housing, when laid bare, was a crucial one to exploit in establishing entitlement. This rhetorical line was developed in other letters, for instance on 11 September 1831, when Sophia wrote,

> Our case is a hopeless one unless your Goodness will find us a little rent as with past favours, for *what is a family such as ours to do when sick and then so many small mouths to feed* that I am driven quite to disracion [distraction] and we cannot put aside the money for the rent when my husband has so little work, but consider how it is for such a family as ours and a Landlord that threatens us with the street if you do not pay and with Christian duty oblige your poor parishoners and *keep a roof over the heads of these small children*.[69]

There are good reasons to doubt the thrust of Sophia's argument, and these doubts were shared by the overseer, who replied 'Madam, we are convinced that you manage very ill'.[70] For our purposes, however, the point is that Sophia brought together rent, housing, and the threat to the integrity of the household with claims – moral, logical and theological – for a general entitlement to relief.

Taken together, we can see that the rhetorical infrastructure of the Curchin letters varies in emphasis across a complex matrix running between: attempts to generate their own resources/the threat to their housing; housing as sanctuary/millstone; the economy of their housing/ the economical spending of small sums to keep them in their place; the dependency and chronic situation (illness, maternity, young children, nakedness) of the couple and their children/the central importance of maintaining a roof over their heads; and rent versus general entitlement. In a rhetorical and strategic sense, the central use of the linguistic register of housing or dispossession and its secondary fusion with some of the key grey areas in poor law entitlement (were the sick poor morally entitled to relief? How should parishes deal with unemployment? Should parishes attempt to lift children out of poverty as a way of keeping down future bills? Were out-parish paupers best relieved in parish of settlement or parish of residence?) are key observations. While it is tempting to suggest that these constructs and links are made by accident, they recur too regularly in the underlying sample of pauper letters for us to accept this view. Rather, the Curchin letters show that some paupers had a keen appreciation of the power of housing as a symbol in their confrontation with the authorities over entitlement. And in this sense it is important to recognise that whatever the officials in Thrapston and Wisbech thought of Curchin, they still paid rent. Housing, in other words, must have been an accepted and expected point of negotiation for both paupers and officials, one of the last bastions of independence.

6.5   Conclusion

We have seen that the literature on the housing, family size and structure and household boundaries of the poor in eighteenth- and nineteenth-century England has become much more sophisticated at the same time as its evidential base (at least before the mid-nineteenth century census) has grown only slowly. The experiences of our paupers both confirm some of the recent trends in this historiography and suggest important new departures. Thus, Widow Higginson, the Soundys and the Curchins all demonstrate a remarkable tenacity in their attempts to stay in their homes. While eviction and downsizing appear to be a constant threat (certainly in the minds of letter writers) what is remarkable is that the paupers stay in their homes (often for many years) and with the support of the overseers. Even where officials had real doubts about the character, morals and truthfulness of paupers (as with the Curchins) they generally still paid. Moreover, they appear to have been susceptible to a language and strategy that tied up entitlement with fluid household boundaries, the particular need to ensure that a roof was kept over the head of infants, and the inability of families to meet lump-sum payments such as rent. While overseers may have wanted to wind down the residential independence of old people in particular, neither Widow Higginson nor Joseph Pitt were forced from their homes and out of solitary living.

At the same time, complex families and households are also significant in the letter sample deployed here and the wider database from which it was chosen. The Soundy family are perhaps the epitome of the fluidity of household boundaries, and in this sense they mark an advance in the literature which, by nature of the sources involved, has tended to focus on snapshots of structure rather than the processes that generate complexity. However, the Soundys are by no means unique in their porous household boundaries. Whether they lived alone, with partners and children or in households with a fluid structure, it is clear that all of our multiple letter writers tied up their appeals for casual or permanent relief with the language of household, house and family. For Widow Higginson the language was that of solitary living, rootedness in locality, the threat of lost credit and the desire to hang onto residential independence notwithstanding the poor state of her house; for the Soundys, the language was that of fluid household structures and the emotional and financial stresses that such fluidity brought; for the Curchins their housing was elided constantly with household structure (young children), life-cycle (confinement and illness) and the inability to pay rent in a linguistic repertoire that shifted between housing as salvation to housing as millstone.

It is not, of course, easy (or indeed uncontentious) to draw wider lessons from such a small sample of records. While the life stories dealt with here are representative of the sorts of people and the sorts of issues they deal with in the wider sample, they are in the end just individual examples. At the very least they bring to life the processes that generate the particular household forms observed in census and other static data. Widow Higginson moved (literally and figuratively) from being married, to living as a solitary in a different house to that she occupied with her husband but still tied in with her neighbourhood networks, to living as a lodger in a private house. These individual stages are well established in the literature but it is less clear how the individual moved through them and whether that process was linear. The experiences of the Soundy family certainly do not suggest linearity. At their best, however, these letters can and must stand for more than just elaborating process. They provide perhaps the only way that we can systematically (especially if linked to census-type sources and other forms of poor law data) investigate issues such as housing and household structure among the poor in eighteenth- and nineteenth-century England, because residential and familial arrangements comprise a substantial concern for the poor and poor law officials, a distinctive motif for those on the edge of total dependence.

Notes

This research is funded by the Wellcome Trust. I am grateful to Elizabeth Hurren, Anne-Marie Kilday and Alysa Levene for their perceptive comments.

1. On the wider potential of such records see J. Sim & T. Ward, "The Magistrate of the Poor?' Coroner's and Deaths in Custody in Nineteenth-Century England', in M. Clarke & P. Crawford (eds), *Legal Medicine in History* (Cambridge: Cambridge University Press, 1994), pp. 245–67.
2. J. Cole (ed.), *Coroners' Inquisitions for the Borough of Malmesbury, Wiltshire, 1830–1854* (Trowbridge: Wiltshire Family History Society, 1994), pp. 16–17. Emphasis is mine.
3. Cole, *Coroner's*, p. 17. The reference to want is significant as from 1839 families could be prosecuted for neglect.
4. On the legal duties of care see D. Thomson, 'The Welfare of the Elderly in the Past: A Family or Community Responsibility', in M. Pelling & R. M. Smith (eds), *Life, Death and the Elderly: Historical Perspectives* (Routledge, 1991), pp. 194–227.
5. J. Robin, 'Family Care of the Elderly in a Nineteenth-Century Devonshire parish', *Ageing and Society* 4, (1984), 505–16. On the gradual and non-linear separation of the households of parents and children, see the excellent discussion by W. Coster, *Family and Kinship in England 1400–1800* (Longman, 2001), p. 24.
6. Both Peter Laslett and David Thomson have argued that the aged had little choice in this matter given nuclear hardship, familial poverty, shallow kinship networks and increasingly individualistic attitudes towards provision of care by children. See D. Thomson, 'I am not my Father's Keeper: Families and the Elderly in Nineteenth-Century England', *Law and History Review* 2, (1984), 265–86, and P. Laslett, 'Family, Kinship and Collectivity as Systems of Support in Pre-industrial Europe: A Consideration of the Nuclear Hardship Hypothesis', *Continuity and Change* 3, (1988), 201–32. Others have argued that the aged poor had more choice and that kinship care was a very important part of the economy of makeshifts. See S. Barrett, 'Kinship, Poor Relief and the Welfare Process in Early Modern England', in

S. King & A. Tomkins (eds), *The Poor in England 1700–1850: An Economy of Makeshifts* (Manchester: Manchester University Press, 2003), pp. 199–227. For the most recent analysis of workhouse residents, see N. Goose, 'Poverty, Old Age and Gender in Nineteenth-Century England: The Case of Hertfordshire', *Continuity and Change* 20, (2005), 351–84, who, while arguing that workhouses became care homes for aged males particularly in rural areas, nonetheless shows that even in extreme old age a minority of any cohort entered the workhouse.

7. P. Thane, *Old Age in English History: Past Experiences; Present Issues* (Oxford: Oxford University Press, 2000); T. Sokoll, *Household and Family among the Poor: The Case of Two Essex Communities in the Late Eighteenth and Early Nineteenth Centuries* (Bochum: Verlaag fur Regionalgeschichte, 1993). However, see the work of Susannah Ottaway which has suggested that poor relief – the community – became a much more central component of this network over the eighteenth century: S. Ottaway, *The Decline of Life: Old Age in Eighteenth-Century England* (Cambridge: Cambridge University Press, 2004).

8. D. Kertzer, 'Living with Kin', in D. Kertzer & M. Barbagli (eds), *Family Life in the Long Nineteenth Century, 1789–1913* (New Haven: Yale University Press, 2002), pp. 40–72; N. Tadmor, *Family and Friends in Eighteenth-Century England: Household, Kinship and Patronage* (Cambridge: Cambridge University Press, 2000); D. Cooper & M. Donald, 'Households and Hidden Kin in Early Nineteenth-Century England: Four Case Studies in Suburban Exeter 1821–1861', *Continuity and Change* 10, (1995), 257–78; D. Mills, 'The Residential Propinquity of Kin in a Cambridgeshire Village', *Journal of Historical Geography* 4, (1978), 265–76.

9. As Tim Harris has suggested, in some situations (particularly perhaps in their dealing with the aged and sick), officials had to listen to the wishes of the powerless. See T. Harris, 'Introduction', in T. Harris (ed.), *The Politics of the Excluded, 1500–1850* (Basingstoke: Palgrave Macmillan, 2001), pp. 1–29, 12–13.

10. Epitomised by J. Taylor, *Poverty, Migration and Settlement in the Industrial Revolution: Sojourners' Narratives* (Paolo Alto: Stanford University Press, 1989) and T. Hitchcock, P. King & P. Sharpe (eds), *Chronicling Poverty: The Voices and Strategies of the English Poor 1640–1840* (Basingstoke: Macmillan, 1997).

11. Sokoll, *Household and Family*. For the nineteenth century: Goose, 'Poverty, Old Age and Gender', has argued that in 1851 St. Albans and Royston, 21 per cent and 20 per cent respectively of pauper households were extended.

12. P. Sharpe, 'Survival Strategies and Stories: Poor Widows and Widowers in Early Industrial England', in S. Cavallo & L. Warner (eds), *Widowhood in Medieval and Early Modern Europe* (Longman, 1999), pp. 220–39; Cooper & Donald, 'Households and Hidden Kin'.

13. K. D. M. Snell, *Parish and Belonging: Community, Identity and Welfare in England and Wales, 1700–1950* (Cambridge: Cambridge University Press, 2006).

14. L. Hollen Lees, *The Solidarities of Strangers: The English Poor Laws and the People, 1700–1948* (Cambridge: Cambridge University Press, 1998).

15. S. King, 'The English Proto-industrial Family: Old and New Perspectives', *History of the Family* 140, (2003), 1–23.

16. For the context in which such letters were created and an argument that we should consider them as representative of wider pauper experiences, see S. King, T. Nutt & A. Tomkins, *Narratives of the Poor in Eighteenth-Century Britain* (Pickering and Chatto, 2006). For the view that the Scots, Swedes and English were by far the most literate countries in Europe, such that the existence of pauper letters in some numbers should not surprise us, see Coster, *Family and Kinship*, p. 75.

17. See T. Sokoll, *Essex Pauper Letters, 1731–1837* (Oxford: Oxford University Press, 2001); *Idem*, 'Old Age in Poverty: The Record of Essex Pauper Letters, 1780–1834', in Hitchcock, King & Sharpe (eds), *Chronicling Poverty*, pp. 127–54; *Idem*, 'Writing for Relief: Rhetoric in English Pauper Letters, 1800–1834', in A. Gestrich, S. King & L. Raphael (eds), *Being Poor in Modern Europe: Perspectives 1800–1949* (Bern: Peter Lang, 2006), pp. 91–112.

18. P. Sharpe, 'The Bowels of Compation: A Labouring Family and the Law c. 1790–1834', in Hitchcock, King & Sharpe (eds), *Chronicling Poverty*, pp. 87–108; J. Taylor, 'A Different Kind of Speenhamland: Non-resident Relief in the Industrial Revolution', *Journal of British Studies* 30, (1991), 183–208; *Idem*, 'Voices in the Crowd: The Kirkby Lonsdale Township Letters, 1809–1836', in Hitchcock, King & Sharpe (eds), *Chronicling Poverty*, pp. 109–26.

19. The wider project involves collection of poor law data for these counties along with Leicestershire, Oxfordshire, Norfolk, Warwickshire, West Yorkshire and Wiltshire. The three counties that are the focus of this chapter were chosen mainly because of their excellent pauper letter survival.

20. On the development of the out-parish system in this period, see S. King, '"It is impossible for our vestry to judge his case into perfection from here": Managing the Distance Dimensions of Poor Relief, 1800–40', *Rural History* 16, (2005), 161–89.

21. King, Nutt & Tomkins, *Narratives of the Poor.*

22. MCL, M10/815, 'Letters'. MCL M10/808–15 comprises large A3 books into which the letters were originally pasted. Subsequently many have worked loose and there is no established ordering. All italics here and subsequently are mine.

23. MCL, M10/815.

24. MCL, M10/808.

25. *Ibid.*

26. MCL, M10/812.

27. *Ibid.*

28. MCL, M10/815.

29. *Ibid.*

30. L. Botelho, '"The old woman's wish": Widows by the Family Fire? Widows' Old Age Provisions in Rural England, 1500–1700', *History of the Family* 7, (2002), 59–78; L. Botelho, *Old Age and the English Poor Law, 1500–1700* (Woodbridge: Boydell, 2004).

31. Indeed, the parson William Holland suggests that the poor facing distraint of their goods had a 'right' to relief, which might have ratcheted up pressure on the overseer to pay arrears. J. Ayres, *Paupers and Pig Killers: The Diary of a Somerset Parson 1799–1818* (Stroud: Alan Sutton, 1984), p. 183. Contrast Higginson with R. M. Smith, 'Charity, Self-interest and Welfare: Reflections

from Demographic and Family History', in M. Daunton (ed.), *Charity, Self-Interest and Welfare in the English Past* (UCL Press, 1996), pp. 23–49, 40, who argues that the poor law consciously set out to from the later eighteenth century to undermine the independence of female pensioners.

32. J. Broad, 'Housing the Rural Poor in England, 1650–1850', *Agricultural History Review* 48, (2000), 151–70.
33. See, for instance, Cooper & Donald, 'Households and Hidden Kin'.
34. Berk.RO, D/P 91/18/6. All italics here and subsequently are mine. This letter describes a situation in which one nuclear family had become, temporarily, a female-headed household and a lodging household consisting of father and elder daughter.
35. Berk.RO, D/P 91/13/1/4.
36. Berk.RO, D/P 91/18/4.
37. *Ibid.*
38. *Ibid.*
39. *Ibid.*
40. *Ibid.*
41. *Ibid.*
42. Berk.RO, D/P 91/18/10.
43. *Ibid.*
44. *Ibid.*
45. *Ibid.*
46. See P. Horden, 'Household Care and Informal Networks: Comparisons and Continuities from Antiquity to the Present', in P. Horden & R. M. Smith (eds), *The Locus of Care: Families, Communities, Institutions and the Provision of Welfare Since Antiquity* (Routledge, 1998).
47. Berk.RO, D/P 91/18/4.
48. There is no evidence of the Soundy family having moved to smaller lodging, and hence this inability to provide room is a rhetorical device.
49. Lack of housing, the tendency for migrant kin to cluster near those already resident in towns and the fact that up to one sixth of the entire population may have lived at one point in eighteenth-century London all made potential kinship networks more extensive than might be the case in rural areas. See Coster, *Family and Kinship*, p. 105.
50. Sokoll, *Essex Pauper Letters*.
51. Though see Coster, *Family and Kinship*, pp. 24 and 43 who, while acknowledging the complex links between related households nonetheless feels that co-residence was exceptional.
52. King, 'The English Proto-industrial Family'.
53. For a discussion of the nuanced differences between rhetoric, strategy and negotiation, see Sokoll, 'Writing for relief', and J. Hanley, 'The Public's Reaction to Public Health: Petitions submitted to Parliament 1847–1848', *Social History of Medicine* 15, (2003), 393–411.
54. On sickness rhetoric see S. King "Stop this overwhelming torment of destiny': Negotiating Financial Aid at Times of Sickness under the English Old Poor Law, 1800–1840', *Bulletin of the History of Medicine* 79, (2005), 228–60. On narratives of widowhood, grounded in the language of respectability, custom and self-help, see Sharpe, 'Survival strategies', p. 235.
55. North.RO, 325P/193/3. All italics are mine.

56. North.RO, 325P/193/22.
57. North.RO, 325P/193/42.
58. North.RO, 325P/193/50.
59. North.RO 325P/193/53. See also North.RO, 325P/193/63, dated 22 April, in which the overseer warns Curchin that 'the parish has tyred with your applications and letters'.
60. Sokoll, 'Writing for relief'.
61. North.RO, 325P/193/80. Also North.RO, 325P/193/83, dated 13 August, which is a copy of a letter to Sophia noting 'we are convinced you must manage very bad, or are extravagant'.
62. North.RO, 325P/194/5.
63. Taylor, 'Voices in the crowd', p. 21, suggests a widespread contemporary belief that casual relief – the trifle – did not equate to chargeability and thus removability for the non-settled poor, potentially explaining the frequency with which we see this rhetorical device.
64. North.RO, 325P/194/7.
65. North.RO, 325P/194/35.
66. North.RO, 325P/194/69.
67. North.RO, 325P/194/134.
68. North.RO 325P/194/201.
69. North.RO 325P/194/216.
70. Loose draft reply found in North.RO 325P/193.

7
Labour Discipline, Agricultural Service and the Households of the Poor in Rural England, c. 1640–1730

Steve Hindle

In *The Great Law of Subordination Consider'd* (1724), Daniel Defoe was delighted to report to his (fictional) French correspondent that 'we have Laws here [in England] for regulating of servants'. In particular, he was pleased to observe that magistrates were empowered not only to force poor children to work, but also to specify the spaces and places where that work should be undertaken: a Justice of Peace, he noted,

> may oblige young People who are idle, and live, as 'tis call'd, at their own Hands, to go to Service, and may, if they refuse it, send them to the House of Correction.[1]

This spatial regulation of the labour market was, he argued, borne of a

> [c]oncern which the law takes for parents, whose Circumstances being but mean, and their children lying heavy upon them, are willing to be maintained in Idleness and Sloth, and refuse either to Work for themselves, or go out to Service.

'In such a case', Defoe reported, the magistrate 'may oblige [the child] to go out' to apprenticeship in the household of a master.[2] By contrast, however, magistrates enjoyed no such freedom when confronted with idle spinsters. Defoe was disappointed to note that if a single young woman was challenged by a justice about living out of service, and answered that 'she work'd and maintains herself, and is able to maintain herself without being a Charge to her Parents, or the Parish', then there was no law that could compel her into service.[3] The result, thought Defoe, was dangerous flexibility in a labour market where the project of employing the offspring of the rural poor, especially through

169

the institution of agricultural service regulated by the 1563 statute of artificers, was already being undermined by the penetration of industry, with its associated wage labour and piece work, into the countryside.[4] The consequences were all the more perilous because households were not simply units of production (of manufactured goods) or of reproduction (of children), but also of socialisation, in which habits of industry and deference ought to be inculcated among the poor.

Defoe argued that wages in the textile industry had risen so high by the early 1720s, that 'the Poor all over England, can now earn or gain twice as much in a day, and in some places more than twice as much, as they could get two or three years ago'. In the regions where the wool industry was most concentrated (and especially in the West County and East Anglia), 'the poor women now get 12*d*. to 15*d*. a day for spinning, the Men more in proportion, and are full of work whereas before they could not get half so much, and very often not find Employment either'.[5] This new-found prosperity might be expected to promote a rise in living standards, perhaps even the purchase of consumer goods, but Defoe was convinced that it induced nothing but 'Sloth, Idleness, Drunkenness, and all manner of Wickedness'. The labouring poor had, he thought, begun to 'slight their work, and bully their Employers'. They would work long enough to earn sufficient cash to spend in the alehouse and nothing would recall them to labour 'while they have a farthing of it left'.[6] Defoe believed, moreover, that spiralling wages had devastating consequences for the institution of agricultural service. In the countryside, he observed, 'the Farmers Wives can get no Dairy-Maids, their Husbands no plowmen'. Young women protested that 'they won't go to Service at 12*d*. or 18*d*. a week while they can get 7*s*. to 8*s*. a Week at Spinning'; and the men insisted that

> they won't drudge at the Plow and cart, hedging and ditching, threshing and stubbing, and perhaps get £6 a Year, and course Diet, when they can sit still and dry within Doors, and get 9 or 10s a week at Wool-combing, or at carding and such work about the Woollen Manufacture.[7]

Defoe hinted that he might be persuaded by the economic logic, and perhaps even by the justice, of the social consequences of this textile boom if the labouring poor really did intend to live lives of industry and thrift. But the realities of a flexible labour market were very different from the 'diligent application to business' and 'frugal, honest virtuous life' to which he thought the labouring poor should aspire. On the contrary, he argued, these 'Wenches and Fellows run to the Manufacturing-Towns' where 'they Spin and Work, and when they have a got a little Money in their Pockets before-hand, then they turn Vagrant and Idle, spend the little they have got in revelling, drinking, and by consequence something worse', by which he implied sexual promiscuity, and perhaps even prostitution. Eventually, Defoe suggested, the magistrates would be 'call'd upon to rout them out' and 'secure the Parishes from the charge of their Debaucheries' [i.e., the burden of their illegitimate offspring].[8] These vicious habits, congenital in the households of the idle poor themselves, subsequently became contagious in the households of the un-contracted young. Idle youths 'spread themselves about the Villages, where they draw in other young People, (till then Sober and diligent,) into the like wickedness'. In some cases, Defoe reported, he had seen 'six or seven of them in a House with big-Bellies, to the shame and Affliction of their poor Parents, and the scandal of the whole Country'. The inevitable *denouement* was that as soon as they these single mothers 'can drop their Burthen [i.e., give birth], they fly, for fear of the House of Correction' to London, which was accordingly, Defoe believed, filled with a generation of whores and thieves.[9]

Defoe doubtless exaggerated the idleness and mobility of these poor young men and women for rhetorical – perhaps even for satirical – effect.[10] His analysis of the working habits, leisure preferences and living accommodation of the labouring poor is, nonetheless, entirely characteristic of a growing consensus, emerging among the propertied elite in the century after 1650, about the 'utility of poverty'. This was a period when labour was in relatively short supply, when it was believed that 'the very fabric of society could be threatened, not just by rising wages and costs, but by a swelling independence among the working masses, which commonly manifested itself in a refusal to engage wholeheartedly in unremitting toil'.[11] Employers, magistrates and political economists alike agreed that 'the higher the wages labourers and artisans received, the less they worked, and that, while low wages bred industry and diligence, high wages bred laziness, disorderliness and debauchery'.[12] One of the recurrent themes of this discourse was the question of where the offspring of the labouring poor were, or should be, employed and accommodated: if they thought they could make a living more easily elsewhere, service contracts would become unenforceable, and young men and women would flee the household discipline of their masters to drift in and out of wage-labour, living all the while idly at home with their parents or 'friends'.[13] To be sure, housing the aged deserving poor of the parish was a very significant item on the policy agenda of overseers and vestrymen, and a substantial body of housing stock, into which deserving paupers might be rotated, was gradually accumulated in some local communities.[14] But the labouring poor were far more problematic in this regard, and magistrates frequently wrestled with the problem of where they were, or should be, domiciled. By the end of the seventeenth century, magistrates were arguing that the children and youths of poor labouring families were, in fact, more usually located not in the household of their master or employer but in one part or other of a matrix consisting of the parental home, the alehouse, and the house of correction – all of them places which figured prominently in Defoe's analysis of the 'insolence and unsufferable behaviour of servants'.

It is not the purpose of this essay to test the accuracy of Defoe's analysis against the realities of labour discipline and agricultural service in late seventeenth and early eighteenth-century England.[15] After all, with its titillating references to hovels full of big-bellied wenches and its 'realistic' reportage of encounters between magistrates and labourers, *The Great Law of Subordination* (like its overtly fictional counter-part *Moll Flanders*) sometimes seems to have more in common with the older tradition of rogue literature than with the developing genre of social investigation.[16] But, in articulating so vividly the difficulties faced by employers and magistrates in policing the residential arrangements of the poor at a time when young men and women were able to find work relatively easily, Defoe's portrait of the 'lab'ring poor' as 'saucy, mutinous and beggarly' surely had to be plausible to his readers. The following discussion of the administration of the laws of apprenticeship and service in the century after 1650 therefore takes up several themes of Defoe's analysis – the powerful sanctions that might be deployed against the feckless parents of pauper children; the ineffectiveness of wage regulation; the failure to enforce service contracts which were intended to fix the young in the households of their employers – to suggest that the limitations of a social policy developed at a time of labour surplus were rapidly exposed at a time of labour shortage; and that these limitations had profound consequences for the shape, size and character of the households of the poor.

7.1   The legal context of the spatial regulation of labour

The Elizabethan poor laws were codified in the late sixteenth century at a time of labour surplus, when the ranks of the impotent life-cycle poor and the wilfully idle had been swollen by large numbers of under- and unemployed labourers who could not earn enough to support themselves or their children.[17] The authors of the 1598 legislation accordingly placed enormous emphasis on the provision of work for this newly-discovered group who would, by the early eighteenth-century, become familiar to Defoe as the 'labouring poor'.[18] In practice, however, the under-employed seem to have been far more commonly supported not by overseers' payments for beating hemp or the making of yarn and thread in their own homes but by being relieved of the obligation to support their own children, who were sent out to be trained and maintained in the households of their betters.[19] From the early seventeenth century onwards, therefore, the households of the poor were frequently fractured by the intervention of parish officers who removed, often in the teeth of parental resistance, the children of those labourers who they deemed unable to provide for them appropriately, and exported them into the households of their more prosperous neighbours, sometimes even across the boundaries of the parish. This widespread campaign to apprentice children at parish expense was motivated both by the desire to lessen the burden of expenditure in poor households and by the imperative to inculcate labour discipline in a plebeian class whose idleness appeared to be inherited, perhaps even congenital.[20] The policy was targeted at the parents of the very young, the statute providing for the binding out of boys and girls aged as little as seven, in the hope that they were still sufficiently amenable to socialisation.

Neither the Elizabethan relief statutes, however, nor the advice which was subsequently given to overseers, made any reference to the fate of these children once their often very prolonged period of parish apprenticeship had ended (theoretically at the age of 24 for boys and, unless they married first, 21 for girls).[21] Indeed, although late eighteenth-century settlement examinations sometimes disclose details of the subsequent careers of those bound apprentice by parish indenture, our knowledge of the employment histories of seventeenth- and early-eighteenth-century pauper apprentices is almost negligible.[22] The unspoken assumption was that these youths, now with a dozen or so years of 'training' in (or at least experience of) husbandry and housewifery behind them, would enter the world of work and service under the terms of the 1563 statute of artificers, which provided a comprehensive framework for the negotiation of labour relations and the annual assessment of maximum wage levels by county magistrates.[23] The statute stipulated that the young and unmarried were to be forced into compulsory residential agricultural service; that they were to be hired for a year; that they were to give their employers a three-month period of notice; and that they were to carry a testimonial from their masters when they moved on. The institution through which this transition from apprenticeship into service was regulated was the annual statute sessions or 'hiring fair', at which masters and servants were informed by the high constables of the wage-rates stipulated by the justices; and accordingly ratified their contracts of employment, which had generally been agreed informally beforehand.[24] The 1563 statute of artificers and the 1598 poor law, therefore, dove-tailed to create a policy platform from which children and youths could initially be socialised into habits of industry in the household of a master; and subsequently contracted into the labour market in the household of an employer. At both stages of this process – parish apprenticeship at the age of seven or older; contracted service in the mid-to-late teens – the residential arrangements of the labouring poor were subject to the intervention of parish officers, magistrates and employers. Until they crossed the threshold of adulthood represented by marriage, therefore, poor children and youths were generally accommodated by their masters or employers rather than by their parents. The households of the poor ought, it was argued, to be denuded of children in the interests of parish economy and labour discipline.[25]

In the second half of the seventeenth century, a long period of falling living standards – during which Elizabethan labour and poor law policy had been formulated – came to an end. The structural characteristics of this new economic context were demographic stagnation, falling grain prices, and significantly improved real wages.[26] Whether or not the very poorest households might share the increased purchasing power which enabled their more prosperous neighbours to engage in conspicuous consumption is open to doubt, but at the very least they were insulated from the worst extremes of indigence.[27] The consequences of all this for labour policy in general, and for the composition of poor households in particular, were complex and ambiguous.

7.2   Children and parish apprenticeship

On the one hand, pressure was maintained on poor parents to reduce their household expenditure by agreeing to have their children apprenticed by the parish. Late seventeenth-century magistrates accordingly spent endless hours co-ordinating, supervising and enforcing those clauses of the Elizabethan relief statutes which empowered overseers both to extract poor children from their parental home and insert them for a protracted period into the household of a master or employer, usually without payment of a premium. This concern with the residential arrangements for the training of children aged as young as seven continued, despite the fact that the very young were becoming, by the end of the seventeenth century, a far less significant proportion of the population than they had been at the time that the apprenticeship clauses of the poor laws had been introduced.[28] Indeed, if anything, the powers of compulsion implied by the 1598 statute were strengthened and made more explicit in one of the very few seventeenth-century statutes that amended the Elizabethan relief system to any significant extent: the 1697 statute, which empowered overseers to withhold pension payments from any pauper who refused to wear the parish badge, also insisted that recalcitrant parents and reluctant masters could be committed to bridewell for refusing to consent to the enforcement of the terms of a parish apprenticeship indenture.[29]

So thoroughly institutionalised had pauper apprenticeship become by the mid-seventeenth century that some parents were actually prepared to plead not for cash relief but to have their children removed into an employer's household at parish expense on their behalf. Thus, the widower Robert Barrowclough of Smalley (Derbyshire) pleaded with the magistrates in the late 1640s that he was 'unable in respect of his extreame poverty' to put any of his six young children 'to trades', and requested either that they pay him relief or that they apprentice out his children. The justices considered that the four Barrowclough children aged ten or older were 'serviceable', and two of them, a boy aged 15 and a 'wench' aged 11, were promptly removed and accommodated elsewhere.[30] Sarah Knowles of Hognaston (Derbyshire) was even more explicit in 1681, directly requesting that 'an order may be taken to sett forth my boy to apprentice'.[31] Whether these parents genuinely believed that a parish apprenticeship in the household of a master was likely to be advantageous to their offspring is unclear, but they nonetheless saw the strategic advantages of telling magistrates what they wanted to hear. Yet for every Robert Barrowclough or Sarah Knowles there was an Elizabeth Taylor, who in Little Bedcombe (Wiltshire) in 1647, allegedly told the ratepayers that she would take back the two children who had forcibly been apprenticed away from her at parish expense. The magistrates complained that Taylor, 'being her self of base and evill life', had 'endeavoured to bring up her children (that were well provided for) in base and evill manners', and the bench accordingly committed her to the house of correction in the hope that they might 'prevent her children from being rogues'.[32] Even those who apparently recognised the virtues of pauper apprenticeship might find themselves on the receiving end of labour discipline. When Samuel Bennett pleaded with the Derbyshire justices to persuade reluctant parish officers to bind out his son William in 1708, the bench ordered that Bennett's pension was to be stopped as soon as *both* his sons could be apprenticed; that he was to be set on work 'at the rate of other persons'; and that any refusal on his part would result in his committal to the house of correction.[33]

This very close correlation between the value of the pension and the number of resident offspring in the households of the poor is nowhere more evident than in the 1698 order of the Lancashire justices in respect to Dorothy, the deserted wife of William Lund of Overwyversdale, which stipulated that the overseers were to pay her two shillings week while her three children remained with her, but that '9*d*. a week upon each putting apprentice out [was to be] taken off'.[34] The sanctions that might be applied to those labouring parents who had children of serviceable age are all too apparent: forced apprenticeship; reduction – perhaps even cancellation – of the parish pension; and committal to the house of correction. The concern to re-locate the children of the labouring poor from a domestic environment in which idleness was contagious to one in which industriousness could be inculcated resulted in the very peculiar age structure of poor households, as measured in surviving parish listings or censuses. Although such data are notoriously difficult to interpret, in late seventeenth-century Swindon (Wiltshire), for instance, only 50 per cent of girls and 58 per cent of boys were apparently still living with their parents by the time they reached the age of 15, and it is almost certain that these figures would be lower still in the households of labourers as opposed to farmers.[35]

By the late seventeenth century, the institution which had been described by Michael Dalton in 1635 as a 'seminary of mercie' had been institutionalised across the country: in Leeds, apparently, there was even a local proverbial expression for the parish- or 'town-apprentice', who was colloquially referred to as a 'Godsake'.[36] That the experience of pauper apprenticeship might fall well short of charity is, however, demonstrated by the very large number of cases of abuse, abandonment and neglect with which Restoration and Georgian magistrates had to deal. The widowed mother of Matthew Holdsworth of Sherburn in the East Yorkshire of Riding was not the only anxious parent who had to plead for magisterial intervention: in 1724, she explained that Matthew's master, a Rillington shoemaker, had absconded and that his mistress would not release him. 'He has been very unmercifully used for five years, both for food and raiment': 'please Sir', she argued, his mistress should be compelled to 'throw in his Indentures'.[37] Nor was Nicholas Edon, a Cooper from Appleby (Westmorland) found guilty in 1756 of the 'ill usage and neglect' of his parish apprentice, the only master to have to answer to the justices when the victim plausibly accused him of abuse.[38] The relocation, whether forced or semi-voluntary, of a pauper child as young as seven from the parental home to a master's household was bound to involve as many risks as rewards.

7.3   Youths and agricultural service

In parallel with their ongoing concern to ensure the socialisation of the very young, late seventeenth-century magistrates devoted considerable energy to the enforcement of service contracts for an older age group of the labouring poor. Three sets of issues loomed particularly large on the agenda of those magistrates seeking to co-ordinate the administration of the 1563 statute: the regulation of wages; the flight from service to wage-labour; and the residential patterns of the labouring poor. In respect of wages, the changed economic context of the late seventeenth century ensured that the cards were increasingly stacked in favour of servants rather than masters when it came to negotiating the terms of employment. Indeed the increase in rural wage rates in the decades after 1650 is to be explained partly by the fact that labourers, however organisationally outflanked they might have been by the provisions of the 1563 statute, began to bargain successfully with their employers over terms and conditions, secure in the knowledge that their fellows could do likewise: a young man 'could hold his hat in his hand and still find ways to remind a farmer of what his neighbour paid'.[39] Although this process of individual wage bargaining is visible in the historical record only in those rare cases where witnesses were present and were subsequently called to give evidence in the law courts when a breach of contract was alleged, it is probable that the length of the contract was as controversial an issue as the level of remuneration. At a time of rising money wages and falling food prices, it was in the interests of a servant to renegotiate terms as frequently as possible, and a contract of more than a year (the minimum stipulated for agricultural servants), let alone the three or even five that a farmer or a master in another trade might prefer, was emphatically not in his or her interest. While individual servants could bargain over wages and terms, others appear to have entered into illegal combinations to do so. Norwich weavers gathered at the Unicorn in 1635 to discuss how the Journeymen would 'holde all together concerning the mendinge of their wages' and 'promised one another that they would have no lesse then 6*d*. a weeke more then nowe they have if they could gett itt'. In 1655, John Sanders of Harbourne (Warwickshire) incited all the nail-makers of the surrounding villages to strike for at least two weeks or preferably even a month to force Birmingham ironmongers to offer better wages to 'poor workmen'. Whether the higher wages that were being offered within and beyond the agricultural sector in the late seventeenth century generally owed something to collusion of this kind is open to question, though it is clear that the institutions through which collective bargaining might take place were emerging in this period.[40]

As wages rose, the authorities became increasingly concerned about the attitudes of the poor towards work.[41] Among the earliest statements of the view that servants were exploiting labour scarcity to drive up wages originates in the West Riding of Yorkshire in 1641, where the justices noted a 'general complaint of the inhabitants of these parts that servants refuse to work for reasonable wages, and cannot be hired for competent allowance as formerly, making advantage of the much business of the times'.[42] In Wiltshire in 1655, it was argued that

> young people, both men and maids, fitting for service, will not go abroad for service without they may have excessive wages, but will rather work at home at their own hands, whereby the rating of wages will take little effect.

The magistracy therefore insisted that

> no young men or maids fitting to go abroad to service (their parents not being of ability to keep them) shall remain at home, but shall with all convenient speed betake themselves to service for the wages aforesaid, which if they refuse to do the justices shall proceed against them.[43]

In Worcestershire in 1661, the grand jury pleaded that 'servants' wages may be rated according to the statute because they regarded the 'unreasonableness' of servants wages as a 'great grievance': 'servants are grown so proud and idle', they feared, 'that the master cannot be known from the servant except it be because the servant wears better clothes than his master'.[44] In 1664, the East Sussex JPs were forced to reiterate the central provisions of the labour laws that were being honoured more in the breach than the observance.[45] The parish officers of Bolton (Lancashire) complained in 1674 that 'when demanded by the Overseers if they will bee set to worke', the poor responded that they 'have other Masters' and that 'they will worke, when and with whome they please'.[46] The bargaining power implied by these orders is demonstrated by the case of Elizabeth Gooch of Caxton (Cambridgeshire) who was contracted – at the public hiring sessions in 1670 – for an annual wage of fifty shillings, some 25 per cent above the rate stipulated by the justices only three years previously. Even more tellingly, Gooch had broken the contract because she could secure more favourable terms still in the household of another master.[47]

High wages, it was believed, undermined service contracts and created dangerous mobility among the labouring poor. The Kent justices argued in 1682 that too many men and maidens either lived at their own hands 'or else put themselves to service for a year and a half or three quarters of the year as they see good, and then lie at their own hands again, whereby they get a habit of idleness, laziness and debauchery'.[48] In Essex in 1684, magistrates knew both 'by their own experience' as well as by 'the daily complaint of their neighbours, that the insolence and disobedience of servants was grown almost insufferable', especially in 'exacting greater wages' than those stipulated by justices' assessment. 'Farmers and others', accordingly, 'were much imposed upon, and their work never the better done'.[49] In Hertfordshire in 1687, the magistrates complained that the 'licentious humours of some servants have prevailed so far upon the Lenitic and good nature of their masters, that they have advanced the charge of their wages and the expense of their diet above their masters farms'. 'To heighten this grievance', servants had been 'so exorbitant' in their demands that 'they will not work but at such times, and such matter as they please; and when their work is most necessary, they often-times leave the same, if not their services'.[50]

Throughout this discourse, rehearsed by magistrates in response to the complaints of constables, jurymen and employers, the concern that the labouring poor held the whip hand in wage-negotiations was entwined with anxiety about the consequence of their independence and mobility. How could the loyalty and residence of servants be secured? One obvious solution was to raise wages, sometimes above the legal maxima stipulated by statute, as occurred in Warwickshire in the 1730s.[51] Another was to differentiate the wages of agricultural as opposed to non-agricultural workers, as also occurred in Warwickshire in 1672.[52] A third was to promote labour mobility by relaxing the terms of the settlement laws, especially by relieving poor migrants of the obligation to indemnify the parish.[53] But the usual fallback was to insist on the letter of the law, by compelling the idle to work and by enforcing the public hirings which ought to prevent the giving of higher wages. Late seventeenth-century magistrates accordingly insisted that servants carry testimonials, as in Cambridge in 1670,[54] and even punished both those employers who paid wages above the going rate, as in Essex in 1684, and those servants who accepted them, as in Cambridge in 1670.[55] Before long, however, the entire project seems to have been abandoned. Neither the Cambridge nor the Kent magistrates, it seems, were making rigorous attempt to regulate wages by the early eighteenth century, leaving the labouring poor to take advantage of the laws of supply and demand, and the opportunities for mobility and household formation that they created.[56]

7.4   A restoration magistrate on labour (in)discipline

One of the most vivid analyses of the causes, nature and significance of plebeian assertiveness in the labour market, and especially its consequences for the socialisation of the rural poor, was provided by the Norfolk magistrate Robert Doughty.[57] Writing in the early 1660s, Doughty argued that the roots of the problem of plebeian idleness lay in a shortage of labour, but argued that, far from being the consequence of the stagnating population levels identified by modern historical demographers, it was caused by the proliferation of masters, many of whom were ill-equipped to set themselves up in trade.[58] There were simply too many masters seeking too few men. Over-supply of employers, he believed, had been encouraged by the maladministration of the apprenticeship clauses of the statute of artificers through which the right to practice a trade was supposed to be regulated. Most indentures issued under the terms of the 1563 statute stipulated service contracts of seven years, but Doughty was well aware that apprentices' terms frequently expired before the young man had reached the age of 24. 'In too many [cases]', he wrote, 'the indentures be antidated and the apprentices really serve but three foure or five yeares of the seaven'. Because the indentures were not usually enrolled, and too little care was taken to ensure accurate recording of ages, the satisfactory completion of apprenticeship contracts was virtually impossible to enforce. The consequence, he believed, was that 'few fully & perfectly learne their trades And yet sett upp their trades before they be settled in their judgement or able to deale in the world for or about their owne concernements'. The inevitable consequence of so many young masters who 'have non of their owne wherewithall to sett up their trades', was business failure. Desperate indebtedness, Doughty believed, was driving large numbers of bankrupt tradesmen to abscond to the army, to the plantations or to lives of crime.[59]

Those tradesmen who did make a go of it were competing for too little business. So many apprentices were becoming tradesmen, Doughty argued, 'that there is no worke for them on their trades for above three or fower dayes in the weeke'. This was especially problematic, in turn, for the tradesmen's own servants who were, through their own under-employment, driven into a 'blind [i.e., hiding place] or other Alehouse' where they

> spend the beginning of every weeke, if not the Sundayes & holy-dayes, & thither they draw in other mens sons & servants which occasions also the loss of their tyme and money & generally (through custome and their and others evill examples) the corrupting depraving and debauching of all youthe.

Just as Defoe was to do some 60 years later, Doughty therefore drew a straight line from the ineffective regulation of service contracts in the households of masters to the drunkenness and debauchery associated with 'Saint Monday' spent in the alehouse.[60]

In describing the conduct of under-employed servants, however, Doughty was convinced that significant distinctions of gender were at play. Indeed, he seemed particularly interested in the behaviour of mobile young women, whose loyalty in domestic service, he thought, was virtually impossible to secure. Those 'wenches (or mayds) as are ablest to performe services', he argued, 'give over service and gett into their friends houses & there live at theire owne handes'. Their flight from service back to the parental home was, he suggested, motivated by their confidence that they could 'make far better earnings then by [servant's] wages'. His list of alternative sources of income for young women seems initially ('spinning & knitting') to reflect a realistic under-standing of the demand for labour in the local textile industry;[61] gradu-ally ('gleaning & stealing in harvest') to disclose authoritarian paranoia about the threat of social crime;[62] but ultimately ('secret whoredoms all the yeare') to bear little but the hallmarks of a fevered sexual imagina-tion.[63] Even those young women who were prepared to hold to their service contracts for more than a few months 'either bargaine att first to goe away, or els quarrell with their Masters & Dames & so breake away in or aboute harvest when theire service is most needed'. A servant girl with an eye for the main chance would, Doughty suggested, adjust her working and residential arrangements in line with the seasonal demand for her labour. By contrast, Doughty seemed altogether less interested in the fortunes of poor young men. He noted that for lads the most attractive alternative to service in husbandry (in his coastal part of Norfolk at least) was to go to sea 'where they make good voyages & best earnings'. Seafaring work was also, however, seasonal and Doughty was convinced that runaway servants would during the winter 'play smoake & slaver away' most of what they were able to earn aboard ship during the summer and that they would do so in the alehouse.[64]

Doughty believed that the net result of these structural problems was that 'both for husbandry & housewifery Masters, Mistresses & Dames are brought to that passe [where] they can scarce get servants'. In an analysis which converges with that subsequently presented by Defoe, Doughty went on to argue that the shortage of domestic and agricultural labour shifted the terms of negotiation not only over rates of remuneration but also over the very fact of subordination.[65] To those men and women whose service they could secure, masters were forced to 'give great wages' and even greater latitude, permitting them 'to take what libertyes they list'. Reproof or discipline of these employees was out of the question, since 'upon any check or discontent they are gone'. Similar problems prevailed with waged labour, which Doughty thought had once been abundant both 'for ourselves and for others'. But now agricultural labourers in particular were 'very scarce', and 'will have great wages'. If labourers were employed by the day, they would hardly 'do one dayes worke in twoe', but if they were employed to do piece work, 'then on the contrary they wil as hastily slubber itt over'.[66] Most of all, there was a flight from residential service in husbandry to waged agricultural labour: 'single persons', Doughty feared, 'begin to give over serving by the yeare to live by day labour' in the homes of their parents or friends.

Doughty's was a lengthy diagnosis of the ills of the labour market, and its detail only serves to throw into greater relief his lack of conviction in possible solutions: he closed his memorandum by very briefly pondering what might be done 'in these exigents'. Most of his attention was focused on the possibilities presented by the house of correction. He conceded that the vagrancy and poor relief statutes stipulated that committal to bridewell was appropriate punishment only for rogues and vagabonds; for the poor who refused to be set on work by the overseers; for bastard bearers; or for parents who had abandoned, or absconded from, their children.[67] He nonetheless wondered whether the most appropriate solution was to command the bridewell master 'to require loose persons to serve & retayne them into his service'. In doing so, he was anticipating by over half a century the kind of arrangement usually negotiated between parish officers and those workhouse masters who were contracted to employ the labouring poor under the terms of the Workhouse Test Act of 1723. Even so, Doughty was not optimistic that bridewell masters would find the prospect attractive. The idle poor were so inured against labour that even governors of houses of correction would not 'be troubled with them'.[68]

Robert Doughty's analysis of the shortcomings and consequences of labour policy is therefore both thoroughgoing and vivid, bearing the authentic stamp of the experience of having tried to enforce the letter of the law during his brief and frustrating career as a magistrate. Doughty's insights are particularly useful for social historians investigating the possibilities and pitfalls of labour discipline precisely because his analysis extends beyond the economic consequences of the weakness of the 1563 legislation into a remarkably far-sighted discussion of its social ramifications, not only at the aggregate level of the local economy but also at the micro-cosmic level of the household. In this respect, as in so many others, Doughty was deploying an idiom deployed to such dazzling rhetorical effect 50 years later by Daniel Defoe.

7.5 Novelists, magistrates and the households of the poor

By contextualising Robert Doughty's and Daniel Defoe's views on the behaviour of the idle poor in the contexts both of existing statutory provision for labour discipline and of the changed economic circumstances of the late seventeenth and early-eighteenth century, this essay has suggested that the terms on which labour was contracted and the poor were accommodated had shifted in favour of servants at the expense of their masters. By implication, it has been argued that the late seventeenth-century flight from service which loomed so large on the agenda of both men was not simply a product of their imaginations, and that this phase at least of Ann Kussmaul's celebrated 'cycles' in the incidence of agricultural service is not illusory.[69] The concerns of magistrates, jurymen and constables discussed here reflect genuine fears about the supply of labour, the rate of wages, and the concomitant difficulties in accommodating, socialising and governing the rural poor.

To be sure, both men exaggerated the laziness, idleness, drunkenness and debauchery of the labouring poor in their efforts to reinforce a popular consensus about the desirability of labour discipline. What little evidence we do have of the actual behaviour of servants and apprentices in alehouses, for instance, suggests that the drunkenness, gambling and promiscuity imagined by the authorities was not by any means universal.[70] Indeed, the references to alehouse visits in the diary (written at precisely the time that Doughty was fulminating about wenches' secret whoredom and lads' drunken slavering) of Roger Lowe, the mercer's apprentice of Ashton-in-Makerfield (Lancashire), have been taken to suggest that 'despite the concerns of governors and moralists, alehouses were benign institutions rather than nests of satan'.[71] It is, moreover, striking that both Defoe and Doughty should offer such highly gendered, even explicitly sexualised, accounts of the implications of the flight from service. To be sure, analysis of patterns of prosecution has suggested that living at one's own hand was one (along with witch-craft and scolding) of a small but highly significant group of gender-specific offences that preoccupied the authorities at a time of social and economic change.[72] In their references to promiscuity and prostitution both men made explicit the kind of concerns that underpinned the anxieties of moralist and authorities about masterlessness, especially among young women. In suggesting that wenches flitted from one lover to the next, just as they flitted from one household and one employer to the next, Doughty and Defoe not only suggested that labour mobil-ity implied promiscuity, but that these servants were as casual in their attitudes to sex as to employment.[73]

In sum, the discourses of labour discipline by definition implied the spatial regulation of the idle poor. The polemicists of the late seven-teenth and early eighteenth century harked back to an era in which the master's household was a unit geared for work, lubricated with discipline and deference. Instead, they felt that were confronted only with an idle, debauched underclass of drunken lads and promiscuous wenches who endlessly orbited the poles of the family home, the alehouse and the house of correction in ever-widening circles of independence and insolence. From a twenty-first century perspective, it is clear to economic historians that the laws of supply and demand had rendered the provisions of Elizabethan labour policy virtually unenforceable, and created a liminal space in which the young might exercise some agency in the nature and location of their employment opportunities. To contemporaries, this was nothing less than a threat to the great law of subordination, a masterlessness whose symptoms included not only independence but residential mobility. The social policy imperatives of late seventeenth-century magistrates helped ensure the young were conspicuously under-represented in the households of the poor, but economic realities meant that they were not always to be found in the workshops of their masters or the households of their mistresses where the authorities hoped to find them. The century or so after the reservation may well therefore have been a brief but particularly troubling moment in the long history of relations between master and man, a moment in which the labouring poor were able to carve out a psychological, social, and residential space of their own.

Notes

1. A. Moreton [Daniel Defoe], *The Great Law of Subordination Consider'd; or, The Insolence and Unsufferable Behaviour of Servants in England Duly Enquir'd Into* (1724), pp. 86–7. Defoe's attitudes to servants are contextualised in J. Richetti, 'Class Struggle without Class: Novelists and Magistrates', *The Eighteenth Century: Theory and Interpretation* 32:3, (1991), esp. pp. 205–8; S. Sherman, 'Servants and Semiotics: Reversible Signs, Capital Instability, and Defoe's Logic of the Market', *English Literary History* 62:3, (1995), 551–73.
2. For the powers of overseers and magistrates to apprentice pauper children, see S. Hindle, *On the Parish? The Micro-Politics of Poor Relief in Rural England, c. 1550–1750* (Oxford: Clarendon Press, 2004), pp. 195–203.
3. [Defoe], *The Great Law of Subordination*, p. 87. The best discussions of master and servant law in this period are D. Hay, 'England, 1562–1875: The Law and its Uses', in D. Hay & P. Craven (eds), *Masters, Servants and Magistrates in Britain and Empire, 1562–1955* (Chapel Hill: University of North Carolina Press, 2004), pp. 58–116; S. Deakin & F. Wilkinson, *The Law of the Labour Market: Industrialisation, Employment and Legal Evolution* (Oxford: Oxford University Press, 2005), pp. 61–74. The gendered language of this passage is significant, a point to which we will return. See section 7.4.
4. The classic study of agricultural service is A. Kussmaul, *Servants in Husbandry in Early Modern England* (Cambridge: Cambridge University Press, 1981), but see the recent critiques in S. Caunce, 'Farm Servants and the Development of Capitalism in English Agriculture', *Agricultural History Review* 45, (1997), 49–60; D. Woodward, 'Early Modern Servants in Husbandry Revisited', *Agricultural History Review* 48:2, (2000), 141–50; and S. M. Cooper, 'Service to Servitude? The Decline and Demise of Life-Cycle Service in England', *History of the Family* 10, (2005), 367–86. For rural industry, see J. Thirsk, 'Industries in the Countryside', in F. J. Fisher (ed.), *Essays in the Economic and Social History of Tudor and Stuart England in Honour of R.H. Tawney* (Cambridge: Cambridge University Press, 1961), pp. 70–88; E. Kerridge, *Textile Manufacture in Early Modern England* (Manchester: Manchester University Press, 1985); M. Zell, *Industry in the Countryside: Wealden Society in the Sixteenth Century* (Cambridge: Cambridge University Press, 1994); J. Walter, *Understanding Popular Violence in the English Revolution: The Colchester Plunderers* (Cambridge: Cambridge University Press, 1999), pp. 243–56; and D. Rollison, 'Discourse and Class Struggle: The Politics of Industry in Early Modern England', *Social History* 26:2, (2001), 166–89.
5. [Defoe], *The Great Law of Subordination*, p. 83. For the power of spinners to command high wages, see Kerridge, *Textile Manufactures*, pp. 210–12. The maximum daily wage rate identified by Peter Bowden for agricultural

labourers in the 1720s is 12*d.* (in Suffolk and Sussex) though the 'national' average was less. P. Bowden, 'Agricultural Prices, Wages, Farm Profits and Rents: Appendix III Statistics', in J. Thirsk (ed.), *The Agrarian History of England and Wales, Volume V: 1640–1750: II, Agrarian Change* (Cambridge: Cambridge University Press, 1985), p. 877. Live-in servants would earn less still, of course, being remunerated partly in room and board. For servants' wages, see Kussmaul, *Servants in Husbandry*, pp. 35–9.

6. [Defoe], *The Great Law of Subordination*, p. 84. The term 'labouring poor' itself first appears in Defoe's early-eighteenth-century works: 'Of Banks', in *Essays Upon Several Projects: or, Effectual Ways for Advancing the Interest of the Nation* (1702), p. 83; *Giving Alms No Charity, and Employing the Poor a Grievance to the Nation*, (1704), p. 27.

7. [Defoe], *The Great Law of Subordination*, pp. 84–5. For wool-combers and carders, and their wages, see Kerridge, *Textile Industry*, pp. 152–8, 159–62, 207.

8. [Defoe], *The Great Law of Subordination*, p. 85.

9. [Defoe], *The Great Law of Subordination*, pp. 85–6.

10. For an astute discussion of Defoe's motives in writing *The Great Law of Subordination Consider'd*, see M. E. Novak, *Daniel Defoe, Master of Fictions: His Life and Ideas* (Oxford: Oxford University Press, 2001), pp. 625–30.

11. J. Hatcher, 'Labour, Leisure and Economic Thought Before the Nineteenth Century', *Past and Present* 160, (August 1998), 64.

12. Hatcher, 'Labour, Leisure and Economic Thought', p. 69.

13. Living at one's 'own hand' was, it has been suggested, a major concern in late Elizabethan and early Stuart towns, even during a period of labour surplus. P. Griffiths, *Youth and Authority: Formative Experiences in England, 1560–1640* (Oxford: Clarendon Press, 1996), pp. 351–89.

14. J. Broad, 'Housing the Rural Poor in Southern England, 1650–1850', *Agricultural History Review* 48:2, (2000), 151–70. For a particularly nice example of the rotation policy in early eighteenth-century West Harptree (Somerset), see Somerset Archives and Research Service, Taunton, D/P/w.harp/13/2/1, unfol. (entries of 3 Apr. 1716, 15 Apr. 1718).

15. For the view that Defoe 'meant every word of [the *Great Law*] literally', even though he held contradictory positions elsewhere, see H. Gladfelder, *Criminality and Narrative in Eighteenth-Century England* (Baltimore: John Hopkins University Press, 2001), p. 119.

16. Cf. the essays in C. Dionne & S. Mentz (eds), *Rogues and Early Modern English Culture* (Ann Arbour: University of Michigan Press, 2004), esp. T. Kuhlisch, 'The Ambivalent Rogue: Moll Flanders as Modern *Picara*', at pp. 337–60.

17. 39 Elizabeth c. 3 (1598); 43 Elizabeth c. 2 (1601); P. Slack, *Poverty and Policy in Tudor and Stuart England* (London and New York: Longman, 1988), pp. 27–32.

18. Hindle, *On the Parish*, pp. 171–2.

19. Hindle, *On the Parish*, pp. 174–226.

20. Hindle, *On the Parish*, p. 225; see also B. Stapleton, 'Inherited Poverty and Life-Cycle Poverty: Odiham, Hampshire, 1650–1850', *Social History* 18:3, (1993), 339–55.

21. *An Ease for Overseers of the Poore: Abstracted from the Statutes* (Cambridge, 1601) is conspicuously silent on this issue.

22. For a rare early eighteenth-century example, see W. Stout, *The Autobiography of William Stout of Lancaster, 1665–1752*, ed. by J. D. Marshall (Manchester: Manchester University Press, 1967), p. 154 (the case of John Robinson, apprenticed in 1706). See also the parish records of Combeinteignhead (Devon), for instance, which contain the settlement examinations, taken between 1796 and 1824, of 19 young men and women originally bound out as parish apprentices: Dev.RO, 3419 A/PO9/18, 20, 22, 4–25, 26, 28, 31, 32, 33, 36, 37, 38, 41, 46, 53, 54, 63, 64, 66.

23. 5 Elizabeth I, c. 4 (1563), conveniently printed in *Tudor Economic Documents*, R. H. Tawney & E. Power (eds), (Longman, 1924), I, pp. 338–50. For the origins of the legislation, see D. Woodward, 'The Background to the Statute of Artificers: The Genesis of Labour Policy, 1558–63', *Economic History Review*, 2nd ser., 33, (1980), 32–44.

24. Kussmaul, *Servants in Husbandry*, pp. 60–1; M. Roberts, '"Waiting Upon Chance": English Hiring Fairs and their Meanings From the Fourteenth to the Twentieth Century', *Journal of Historical Sociology* 1:2, (1988), 119–60.

25. For the difficulties of enforcing parish apprenticeship in the 1630s especially, see Hindle, *On the Parish*, pp. 206–12.

26. E. A. Wrigley & R. S. Schofield, *The Population History of England, 1541–1871: A Reconstruction* (Cambridge: Harvard University Press, 1981), p. 210; P. Bowden, 'Agricultural Prices, Wages, Farm Profits and Rents', in J. Thirsk (ed.), *The Agrarian History of England and Wales, Volume V: 1640–1750: II, Agrarian Change* (Cambridge: Cambridge University Press, 1985), pp. 1–118; K. Wrightson, *Earthly Necessities: Economic Lives in Early Modern Britain* (New Haven: Yale University Press, 2000), pp. 227–48, 307–30.

27. L. Weatherill, *Consumer Behaviour and Material Culture in Britain, 1660–1760* (Routledge, 1988); P. King, 'Pauper Inventories and the Material Lives of the Poor in the Eighteenth and Early Nineteenth Centuries', in T. Hitchcock, P. King & P. Sharpe (eds), *Chronicling Poverty: The Voices and Strategies of the English Poor, 1640–1840* (Basingstoke: Macmillan, 1997), pp 155–91. Defoe, incidentally, was sceptical of the idea that the poor spent their increased wages 'furnishing themselves with Conveniences, Cloaths, and Necessaries': *The Great Law of Subordination*, p. 83.

28. On the changing age structure of the population, see Wrigley & Schofield, *Population History*, p. 448.

29. 8 & 9 William III, c. 30 (1697); Hindle, *On the Parish*, p. 203; S. Hindle, 'Dependency, Shame and Belonging: Badging the Deserving Poor, c. 1550–1750', *Cultural and Social History* 1:1, (2004), 6–35.

30. Derb.RO, Q/SB/2/157.

31. Derb.RO, Q/SB/2/331.

32. Wiltshire and Swindon Record Office, Trowbridge, A1/110/1647M/206.

33. Derb.RO, Q/SB/2/691.

34. Lanc.RO, QSP/813/1.

35. See Kussmaul, *Servants in Husbandry*, pp. 77–8; and the various analyses of household structure by R. Wall, 'The Age at Leaving Home', *Journal of Family History* 3:2, (1978), 181–202; 'Leaving Home and the Process of Household Formation in Pre-Industrial England', *Continuity & Change* 2:1, (1987), 77–101; 'Leaving Home and Living Alone: An Historical Perspective, *Population Studies* 43:3, (1989), 369–89. See also the overview offered by T. Sokoll,

'The Pauper Household Small and Simple? The Evidence from Listings and Inhabitants and Pauper Lists of Early Modern England Reassessed', *Ethnologia Europaea* 17, (1987), 25–42. The figures from Swindon (1697) are from Wall, Age at Leaving Home', p. 194 (Table 4).

36. R. Thoresby, *Ducatus Leodiensis: Or, the Topography of the Ancient and Populaous Parish of Leedes* (1715), p. 620.
37. East Yorkshire Archive Service, Beverley, QSF/69/E/11.
38. CRO, WQ/SR/254/43.
39. Wrightson, *Earthly Necessities*, pp. 326–7.
40. Norf.RO, NCR 20A/10, fo. 60^{v}; J. Sanders, *An Iron Rod for the Naylors and Tradesmen neer Brimingham* (1655) [Wing S574A]. See M. Chase, 'Covins and Fraternities: A "Prehistory" of Trade Unionism', [Chapter 1] in Chase, *Early Trade Unionism: Fraternity, Skill and the Politics of Labour* (Aldershot: Ashgate, 2000), pp. 6–32.
41. As Hatcher, 'Labour, Leisure and Economic Thought', pp. 76–9 demonstrates, this chorus echoes that of a previous generation which was similarly concerned, in a period of labour shortage some three centuries previously, with the evil consequences which were believed to flow from excessively high wages.
42. *West Riding Sessions Records, 1597–1642*, ed. by J. Lister (Leeds: Yorkshire Archaeological Society, 1888–1915), II, p. 333. For more widespread concerns about the capacity of 'dependants to frustrate their masters' during the crisis of the early 1640s, see D. Cressy, *England on Edge: Crisis and Revolution, 1640–42* (Oxford: Oxford University Press, 2006), p. 359.
43. HMC, *Reports on Manuscripts in Various Collections, Volume I* (1901), p. 131.
44. HMC, *Various*, I, p. 322. This comment pre-figures Defoe's conviction that 'it is a hard matter to know the Mistress from the Maid by their dress': A. Moreton [Daniel Defoe], *Everybody's Business is No-Body's Business, or Private Abuses, Publick Grievances* (1724), p. 24.
45. A. Fletcher, *Reform in the Provinces: The Government of Stuart England* (New Haven: Yale University Press, 1986), p. 223.
46. Lanc.RO, QSP/413/14.
47. E. M. Hampson, *The Treatment of Poverty in Cambridgeshire* (Cambridge: Cambridge University Press, 1934), p. 55.
48. D. C. Coleman, 'Labour in the English Economy of the 17th Century', *Economic History Review* 2nd ser., 8:3, (1956), 291.
49. ERO, Q/SR D/DCv2/4.
50. *Hertford County Records*, ed. by W. Le Hardy (Hertford, 1905–39), VI, p. 406.
51. A. W. Ashby, 'One Hundred Years of Poor Law Administration in a Warwickshire Village', *Oxford Studies in Social and Legal History* 3:VI, (1912), 175.
52. *Warwick County Records*, ed. by S. C. Ratcliff, H. C. Johnson, & N. J. Williams (Warwick, 1935–64), V, p. 183.
53. *Quarter Sessions Records of the County of Somerset*, ed. by E. H. Bates-Harbin (Taunton: Somerset Record Society, 1907–19), IV, pp. 190–1.
54. Hampson, *Treatment of Poverty*, pp. 55–6.
55. ERO, Q/SR D/DCv2/4; Hampson, *Treatment of Poverty*, p. 55
56. Hampson, *Treatment of Poverty*, p. 55; N. Landau, *The Justices of the Peace, 1679–1780* (Berkeley, University of California Press, 1984), pp. 246–7.

57. For Doughty himself, see J. M. Rosenheim, 'Robert Doughty of Hanworth: A Restoration Magistrate', *Norfolk Archaeology* 38, (1983), 296–312; Rosenheim, 'Introduction', in *The Notebook of Robert Doughty, 1662–1665*, ed. by J. M. Rosenheim (Norwich: Norfolk Record Society, 1989), pp. 7–12; Rosenheim, 'Documenting Authority: Texts and Magistracy in Restoration Society', *Albion* 25, (1993), 591–604.

58. Norf.RO, MS Aylsham 304, unfol. ([undated memorandum on] '5 Eliz c. 4'). Unless otherwise noted, all subsequent quotations are taken from this source, which is *not* among those printed in Rosemheim (ed.), *Notebook of Robert Doughty*.

59. For the enforcement of apprenticeship in the period after 1660, see C. W. Brooks, 'Apprenticeship, Social Mobility and the Middling Sort, 1550–1800', in J. Barry & C. W. Brooks (eds), *The Middling Sort of People: Culture, Society and Politics in England, 1550–1800* (Basingstoke: Macmillan, 1994), esp. pp. 62–9. The dynamics of apprenticeship and its associated rural-urban migration in late seventeenth-century Norfolk are explored in P. Corfield, 'A Provincial Capital in the Late Seventeenth Century: The Case of Norwich', in P. Clark & P. Slack (eds), *Crisis and Order in English Towns, 1500–1700* (Routledge, 1972), pp. 273–4; J. Patten, 'Patterns of Migration and Movement of Labour to Three Pre-Industrial East Anglian Towns', reprinted in P. Clark & D. Souden (eds), *Migration and Society in Early Modern England* (Hutchinson, 1987), pp. 77–106.

60. E. P. Thompson, 'Time, Work-Discipline and Industrial Capitalism', reprinted in *Customs in Common* (Merlin Press, 1991), esp. pp. 372–80; A. D. Reid, 'The Decline of Saint Monday, 1766–1876', *Past & Present* 71, (1976), 76–101.

61. For the Norfolk worsted industry in the early modern period, see Kerridge, *Textile Manufacture*, pp. 145, 152, 159.

62. Doughty's own notebook contains several examples of women suspected of theft during harvest: Rosenheim (ed.), *Notebook of Robert Doughty*.

63. Though, it has been suggested that the idiom of prostitution loomed large in political discourses about the textile industry. M. Mowry, 'Dressing Up and Dressing Down: Prostitution, Pornography and the Seventeenth-Century English Textile Industry', *Journal of Women's History* 11:3, (1999), 78–103.

64. The realities of life for a poor apprentice who ran away to sea in the 1660s are vividly described in P. Fumerton, *Unsettled: The Culture of Mobility and the Working Poor in Early Modern England* (Chicago: University of Chicago Press, 1996), Part II ('The Case of Edward Barlow').

65. See D. Levine & K. Wrightson, *The Making of an Industrial Society: Whickham, 1560–1765* (Oxford: Clarendon Press, 1991), p. 348; M. J. Braddick & J. Walter, 'Introduction. Grids of Power: Order, Hierarchy and Subordination in Early Modern Society', in M. J. Braddick & J. Walter (eds), *Negotiating Power: Order, Hierarchy and Subordination in Early Modern England and Ireland* (Cambridge: Cambridge University Press, 2001), p. 42.

66. For the significance of piece-work, see Kerridge, *Textile Industry*, pp. 207–09.

67. J. Innes, 'Prisons for the Poor: English Bridewells, 1555–1800', in F. Snyder & D. Hay (eds), *Labour, Law and Crime: An Historical Perspective* (Tavistock, 1987), pp. 42–122. This list clearly reflects the influence of Dalton. See Hindle, *On the Parish*, p. 379.

68. Doughty was not alone in believing that idle servants and disobedient apprentices were best accommodated in the House of Correction. William

Wilson of Underbarrow (Westmoreland) explained in 1741 that he had been forced to commit his parish apprentice to the house of correction for 'certain roguish actions and misdemeanours', though it turned out that the neglect of the Bridewell mast resulted only in making the boy 'more hardened in his rogueries'. CRO WQ/SR/135/3 (1741).

69. See the reservations expressed by Woodward, 'Early Modern Servants in Husbandry Revisited', which are based on analysis of parish registers and account books, to the exclusion of any reference to the difficulties of wage regulation.

70. P. Clark, 'The Alehouse and the Alternative Society', in D. Pennington & K. Thomas (eds), *Puritans and Revolutionaries: Essays in Seventeenth-Century History presented to Christopher Hill* (Oxford: Clarendon Press, 1978); K. Wrightson, 'Alehouses, Order and Reformation in Rural England, 1590–1660', in E. Yeo & S. Yeo (eds), *Popular Culture and Class Conflict 1590–1914: Explorations in the History of Labour and Leisure* (Brighton: Harvester, 1981).

71. A. L. Martin, 'Drinking and Alehouses in the Diary of an English Mercer's Apprentice, 1663–1674', in M. P. Holt (ed.), *Alcohol: A Social and Cultural History* (New York: Berg, 2006), pp. 93–105.

72. D. Underdown, 'The Taming of the Scold: The Enforcement of Patriarchal Authority in Early Modern England', in A. Fletcher & J. Stevenson (eds), *Order and Disorder in Early Modern England* (Cambridge: Cambridge University Press, 1985), p. 119; Griffiths, *Youth and Authority*, pp. 359–589. It is nonetheless striking that both these discussions are confined to the period of labour surplus before 1640.

73. C. Steedman, 'Lord Mansfield's Women', *Past and Present* 176, (2002), 105–43.

8

'I was Forced to Leave my Place to Hide my Shame': The Living Arrangements of Unmarried Mothers in London in the Early Nineteenth Century

Samantha K. Williams

In November 1814, when she was working in a South Lambeth household as a servant of all work, Alice King became acquainted, while walking in the street, with Richard Hains, a sailor on the Trabella of Hull. They decided to meet on their days off, once a month. In March he seduced her in a 'strange house' near Westminster Bridge. She saw him two months later but did not mention the pregnancy and she never saw him again, despite writing to him when his ship was in dock. When her employer Mr Tooch discovered she was pregnant, he 'told his Wife and desided her to turn her away'. Alice was forced to leave both her place of work and her residence. She moved into lodgings in Blackfriars Road and was delivered of a baby boy in Westminster Lying-in Hospital. Alice managed to find herself a new position and put her child out to nurse. By contrast, in January 1816 another woman, Mary Ann Jackson, chose to conceal her pregnancy from her master and mistress for fear of losing her residence. She did so with the help of an old friend, Mrs Gregory, who

> hearing of her Misfortune contrived the Scheme of her Journey to Ireland to deceive Mr & Mrs Morris – She allowed Petitioner to live in her House for Seven or Eight months and also to be delivered there – Petitioner had saved some money in her Services – with which and the help of a few Compassionate friends she maintained herself while she returned to her services.

This chapter explores the living arrangements of unmarried young women who found themselves pregnant in the metropolis during the early nineteenth century. It explores the role of residence in courtship and the impact of an unplanned pregnancy upon women's security of accommodation. These issues are placed within the context of the mobility of plebeian women, the wider metropolitan labour market and the living conditions and household composition of the poor. The findings have implications for other debates within the historiography of plebeian sexuality and the role of sexual reputation and 'respectability' in class formation, changing notions of the 'household-family' and the extent to which domesticity was a working-class, as well as a middle-class, aspiration and reality.[1] In order to do so, this chapter analyses a sample of the petitions written by unmarried, pregnant women to the London Foundling Hospital in the early nineteenth century.[2] The hospital was a charity that offered to take in infants and provide them with education and training. Unmarried mothers put forward their case for the admission of their child to the Hospital in their 'petition', as well as answering the questions of the hospital enquirer concerning their situation and providing the name of a character referee.[3] The enquirer then carefully checked these statements by visiting previous employers and lodging-house keepers. His findings were written up into a report and collated with the petitions. Since children over the age of 12 months were not admitted, this effectively means that we can only examine the households of these women until this point.[4] Other studies have found that unmarried mothers tried to support themselves and their children for some time before they approached either the Hospital or the parish authorities.[5]

The petitions and reports offer the historian a unique source of evidence on the residence of pregnant single women in the metropolis in this period. They provide detailed information on where the petitioners were living when they became acquainted with their lovers, where they lived throughout their pregnancies, where they laid in, where they resided once their children were born and up until the time they approached the hospital. It is unlikely, however, that these cases provide us with a representative sample of all unmarried mothers in the capital and the wide variety of their living circumstances. It is probable that the situations of some women prevented them from applying, since their circumstances could in no way fit the criteria of eligibility of the Foundling Hospital.[6] These cases might include prostitutes and those living in a 'Lodging House of loose Women', those who had given birth to more than one bastard, those cohabiting with the fathers of their children, those who left their husbands to live with another man, and those whose situations were more appropriately handled by the parish authorities. Many women were given outdoor relief by the parochial authorities (either within London or they were removed back to their parish of settlement) and parish officials sought to recoup costs through affiliation orders on the putative fathers. Other women whose circumstances might not feature in the petitions include women whose infants had died before they were 12 months old and, conversely, those whose children were more than 12 months old. Women who could not obtain a good reference from their employers might not have applied, as too might mothers in better economic circumstances and residential situations, such as those receiving more generous assistance from their friends. Some women in these situations did apply to the Hospital, and, while many were rejected, some were successful (and rejected petitions are a part of the archive). As the nineteenth century progressed, however, applicants did become more self-selecting and did conform more fully to the admission regulations.[7]

The Foundling Hospital archive has been used by a number of other historians in order to comment upon a wide range of historical issues, including the institutional provision for unmarried mothers in the metropolis; the emergence of new forms of sexuality (male aggressive-ness and female passivity), which were accompanied by a breakdown in traditional forms of courtship; the extent and nature of sexual assault and rape; the occupational make-up of petitioners and the fathers of their children; and the increasingly insecure metropolitan labour market for female labour.[8] While a few of these studies do briefly consider the living arrangements of unwed mothers, their analyses are largely anecdotal and there is little quantification of the incidence of differ-ent living situations. Evans and Barret-Ducrocq provide a close reading of individual petition cases, and in doing so describe examples of the household situations of pregnant women and unmarried mothers, but they provide no systematic discussion of these arrangements. Gillis also generalises from his assessment of a large number of petitions over the entire nineteenth-century, while Clark's assertions are based on only one or two examples. Trumbach presents an analysis of the financial strategies and support networks exploited by petitioners, but he does not include specific information on residence.[9]

This chapter examines whether, like Alice King, pregnant servants were thrown out of their employers' houses and went into lodgings; whether some women were able to remain in service once their preg-nancies were discovered; and whether, like Mary Ann Jackson, some women managed to conceal their pregnancies from their employers and return to work, either for their existing employers or for another employer. The cost of lodgings would quickly consume all of the savings accrued from years in service and young mothers had to find the means of supporting themselves, either by going back into service or, for instance, taking in needlework. Infants could not live with their mothers when they returned to work as live-in servants and the expense of putting their child out to nurse was substantial. All of the petitioners would have been in considerable material distress and many stated that they had only approached the charity once they could no longer 'make shift'.[10]

8.1   Households and domestic space: Service, courtship, lodgings and family

Domestic service was central in the lives of the young women who approached the hospital; service was the main source of employment for women in the capital and the majority of applicants to the Hospital were in service.[11] For many women, particularly those from outside the metropolis, domestic service was an attractive form of employment because it provided accommodation and meals; there was no worry about finding a place to live or eat, and, in time their annual wages might allow for modest savings. Joining another household as a servant was a life-cycle stage for young and unmarried women in their teens and early twenties. Domestic service and service-in-husbandry facilitated the movement of young women and men from one household to another. The young were the most mobile section of society and many servants moved from place to place frequently.[12] Most servants had migrated long distances to the metropolis in search of work, with petitioners travelling from Northampton, Dorset, Hertfordshire, Exeter, Berkshire, Yorkshire, Southampton, Norfolk and Surrey. It was the custom of mistresses to meet the wagons which brought country girls to London to find and engage servants.[13] Domestic service incorporated an immense variety of situations, living conditions and forms of household composition.[14] Some servants were employed in large houses, such as Margaret Weir, who worked as a kitchen maid in St James' Palace among a large staff. Wealthy households would be in London for 'the season' between February and August, and then they travelled back to their country residences for the rest of the year. Such mobility disrupted servants' social networks, making bonds within each neighbourhood more difficult to maintain.[15] Most servants, however, worked in single-servant households as maids-of-all-work and were the lowest paid and hardest worked. These servants could feel lonely and isolated.

Such variety in the nature of service meant very real differences in the living conditions and domestic spaces of different types of servants. Servants' quarters could be small attic rooms or even just spaces on landings or virtual cupboards without windows or doors. Wherever their quarters were, something that was common to them all was that they could rarely be locked, since servants had to be accessible at all times. Servants rarely enjoyed any privacy in their quarters and privacy might only be extended to the possessions in their locked boxes, trunks or chests.[16] Thus the very nature of servants' quarters could contribute to their vulnerability to the sexual advances of male members of the household.[17] In addition, servants were far from home and the protection of family, friends and community, and this made abandonment by lovers all the more likely, as did the relative immobility of domestic servants and the rapidity of movement of their lovers between jobs or even across the seas.[18] And, while domestic service offered a woman a place to live, if a servant lost her job, she also lost her home.

The extent to which domestic servants were seen as an integral part of the household of their employers was changing during this period. Naomi Tadmor has described the 'household-family' of the eighteenth century, which incorporated not just the nuclear family, but other relatives, servants, apprentices and lodgers. The term 'family' was inclusive and referred to all members of a household. The household head held authority over all other household members and was in a position of *loco parentis* for any servants and apprentices. However, the nineteenth century witnessed the transition towards the term referring to the nuclear family only, as other members were increasing excluded and the 'household-family' became the 'family'.[19] Alongside this transition, live-in service-in-husbandry was in sharp decline, as the provision of accommodation, meals and annual wages became more expensive than weekly or daily hiring, and as middling sort wives withdrew from the communal kitchen to the privacy of the parlour.[20] Domesticity and 'separate spheres' were nineteenth-century ideals that were aspired to by the emerging middle class and some sections of the working class.[21] Domestic service became more regimented, there was an emotional distancing between the employing family and their servants, and servants became more isolated.[22] The relationship between employers and servants most probably changed, with a shift away from the role of *loco parentis* by masters and mistresses to a more formal authority. The emerging middle class also used sexual morality as a marker of class differentiation; it provided a dividing line between the 'dissolute aristocracy' and the 'debauched plebeians'.[23] Clark argues that sexual morality was far from the most important element in reputation for plebeian women and that an alternative sexual morality allowed for premarital sex, illegitimacy and common-law marriage, although certain sections of the working class were far less tolerant. Illegitimacy rates were rising rapidly in the early nineteenth century and there is evidence that the number of common-law marriages was also increasing.[24] The extent to which masters and mistresses extended their view of sexual morality to the servants in their households requires further exploration, but it is likely that these wider changes affected the extent to which masters and mistresses were willing to help a servant in distress. The extent to which they were prepared to help, and the assistance that they provided, is a central theme of this chapter.

Little is known about the practicalities and spatial dimensions of courtship in early nineteenth-century London, yet place of residence undoubtedly influenced where young men and women met and conducted their relationships. The demands of service and, in particular, long working hours in one household meant that it could be very difficult for servants to meet men.[25] In households employing more than one servant, women and men could meet this way and in almost half of petition cases the young man and woman either met in service or met through other servants in the household. Margaret Weir, the kitchen maid at St James' Palace, met Henry Julian there, who was the footman, and Charlotte Winds met Edward Kenward, the gardener, when she was in service with Mrs Newport. In other cases, petitioners met the fathers of their children in their place of work, such as Sarah Barber, who met Charles Collis in the ham shop where she worked.[26] Another 12 per cent of couples met while living in lodgings.[27] Lovers could also meet through family, friends and neighbours, and 23 per cent of petitioners met in these circumstances. In the final 16 per cent of cases petitioners lived or worked nearby to their lovers or they met in the street. Mary Farman, for instance, met Joseph Baite, a Musician of the Band of the First Regiment of Foot Guards, in her local park. The housekeeper told the hospital enquirer that

> She thinks Nursery Maids sho[d] not be supposed to visit the Park as they generally do, without some one to attend them – on Acc[t] of the Danger of red Coats and Music which are tempting Things to inexperienced Girls.

These findings confirm those of Black and Evans, who also found that couples usually met in and around the places where they lived and worked.[28]

Where a couple were living had a huge influence upon their court-ship and where they had sex. One would think that if the couple both worked in service then finding a private place for sexual activity might be difficult; not only was servants' access to private spaces restricted but they were also under the surveillance of other household members and the authority of the household head. Yet many couples did manage to have sex in their rooms: over half of cases where place of sex is known were in service residences. The enquirer reported that 'Connection took place' between Harriet Dore and Richard Hornblow 'in her Masters House', and while John Daves seduced Jane Craston 'at Lady Corks during the Absence of the Family', Henry Julian was bolder in his con-duct and 'seduced [Margaret Weir] in Oct 1839 in her Bed Room in her Masters House They used adjoining Rooms as Bedrooms' while 'All the family was at home'. If the petitioner and/or her lover lived in lodgings, then sex could take place there, frequently without the surveillance of others. In one-fifth of cases couples had sex in their lodgings. William Wood, for instance, visited Elizabeth Crest in her lodgings, while Mary Neill and Edward Bicknell had been courting for several years when Edward 'Seduced her with her Consent Con[nection] took place in his Lodgings on the Wandsworth Road'. Sarah Thompson's lover was a sailor and they conducted their courtship between her lodgings and his ship. Sarah told her landlady that 'She had been on board Ship to visit him and this Child was the consequence of that visit'. A similar proportion of couples went to local pubs in order to have sex. This was the case with Mary Ann Jackson's lover, who 'One night he took her to the [public house] and under a pretence of giving her Refreshment took her to a House and Seduced her', while the man courting Elizabeth Edgeley 'appointed a meeting at Public House in Lucen Sq Westminster and seduced her there'. Such descriptions appear to support middle-class contemporaries' fears that many pubs were dens of immorality.[29] In one case John Robinson and Sarah Watson were 'connected' in Earl's Park. These findings are largely in line with those of other research on sexual activity in the metropolis. Black's study of metropolitan bastardy examinations found that couples had sex in the households of employ-ers, the lodgings of one partner in the couple, or another unrelated house.[30] Residential arrangements were, therefore, critical to where cou-ples conducted their courtships and the vast majority of sexual activity took place indoors and on private territory. All the women considered here were unlucky and became pregnant.

Continuing to provide a pregnant servant with a place to live was the single most important form of assistance that an employer could give.

Residence and meals were worth a considerable sum in kind and servants who left their place of service to move into lodgings could quickly use up their savings. However, only a handful of servants were offered this form of assistance during the crises of their unplanned pregnancies. Just five petitioners (12 per cent) were kept in their employers' homes throughout their pregnancies and deliveries. Mr and Mrs Green kept a ham shop on Chandors Street and they were so pleased with the conduct of Sarah Barber, who they described as 'sober, honest, and industrious', that not only did they agree to retake her into their service if she was relieved, but she lay in there and she and her child were still there when she applied to the hospital. Mr Green was sympathetic to the petitioner's plight due to a number of mitigating circumstances: Sarah's mother 'has been well known to us upwards of 25 years' and was a 'Poor destret widow much afflicted ... and is uncapable of rendering her any assistance', while Sarah was just 17 and was also subject to fits. The father of the child 'had seduced several young Woman' and had absconded to America. Likewise, Ann Tolmadge's employers wished to keep her in their service. Mr and Mrs Mackenzie, of Finsbury Place, Finsbury Square, who, 'pittying her situation, have received her again in consequence of her conduct having in many points deserved their approbation'. Ann was delivered in the Westminster Lying-in Hospital and then returned to her post and placed her baby with a nurse. In another case, Sarah Harding 'was delivered suddenly in the house' and her mistress allowed her and her child to remain there. Ann England, who worked in the house of Lord Montgomery for a year, was described as 'a very good servant, she had no fault, but her present misfortune', and apparently, 'She behaved so well that she was kept in the house as long as possible before her delivery'.

For the vast majority of servants, however, continued residence in their employers' homes was not possible. In 36 cases (88 per cent) pregnant servants left their positions, some before their situation became known to their employers, while others did not leave until later in their pregnancies when their masters and mistresses must have known of their situations. Sixteen petitioners explicitly stated that they had decided to quit before their master and mistress found out. The primary motivation for leaving was to retain their good character references for future employment. Elizabeth Edwards, for instance, informed the hospital enquirer that

> your petitioner has been in service in a respectable family which she was obliged to leave four months since, in order to prevent a discovery of her unfortunate situation.

Likewise, when Hannah Jones requested a character reference from her previous employer, she replied, 'she refers to Mr Bond who is ignorant of her crime-nality'. Mary Woodward made sure that not only her employer, but also all her friends, were ignorant of her pregnancy. After the birth she took a new domestic service post under another name. Ann Blagg, a bar maid at the King's Arms in Sheffield, had a similar experience. When she 'discovered pregnancy in two months', she 'did not reveal her Situation to ... Mr Walker her Master' and quietly left her post. A servant tried to conceal her pregnancy from her employer for as long as possible because it was of vital importance for continuing to be able to support herself. If dismissed, pregnant servants had little or no chance of finding another situation. Betrothed couples also arranged for the woman to stay in domestic service up to the last possible moment so that employers absorbed the cost of room and board.[31]

In order to obtain a new place, good character references were vital. When Mary Ashford, who described her life as a domestic servant in her autobiography, wanted to leave her place she discovered just how important her employer's opinion was; she stated that whenever 'ladies came for my character' her mistress 'always said something that broke it off'.[32] The petitioner Mary Wells secured her post as a wet nurse due to the 'very good Character' she provided, while Cecilia Quigley's application to the Foundling Hospital was rejected due to a very poor reference from her employer Frances Armitage, who told the enquirer that, 'she is a most undeserving impertinent Hussey as ever enter'd any Person's House, mine being the Second Place she has quitted when Wet Nurse, owing to her bad Behaviour'. The majority of referees promised their former servants a good character, but this should not surprise us as in order to qualify for admission of their child to the Foundling Hospital, petitioners had to able to provide good character references.[33] With this bias in mind, it is therefore difficult to estimate the extent to which sexual morality was an integral part of employers' assessments of the reputations of their servants and the extent to which such assessments were translated into character references. On the one hand, most servants left their service position, which implies some level of judgement and stigma. On the other, employers were still willing to write a good character reference, which suggests that they continued to prize other qualities, such as industriousness and honesty. This is an issue that we shall return to after we have explored in total the range of support offered by masters and mistresses.

In some cases, employers later found out that their servants were pregnant and offered support rather than condemnation. One such case is that of Mary Ann Jackson, outlined at the beginning of this chapter. We have noted how she contrived a journey to Ireland 'on account of indisposition' so that she might conceal her pregnancy, but when Mr and Mrs Morris found out about her situation they offered her considerable assistance. Mr Morris told the hospital enquirer:

> That on her return they by accident discovered she had a Child – and were on that Account very kind to her – but never mentioned the Subject to her on Account of her relations in Fleet Market who as well as Ten Brothrs and Sisters Know nothing of her misfortune ... She is now in her Place at Mrs Morris and will remain there if Child is received.

It would certainly appear that Mary Ann had not thought that her master and mistress would be so sympathetic or as kind as to retake her into their service, but Mr and Mrs Morris recognised just how important a secure (and free) place to live was to a young mother. It was not unusual for employers to offer some other form of material assistance. In a similar case, Mrs Thorald offered her former servant material assistance when she most needed it. Ann Smith had left service before her condition was apparent, but her mistress called on her and 'She discovered her condition and was in great distress'. She paid the 2s. a week for Ann's lodging 'from motives of compassion'. Ann acknowledged this great kindness in her petition: 'but for the kindness of the Lady she lived with must have wanted the Comon nessary of Life'. Like Mary Ann Jackson, Mary Neill also left her position so that her employers might not discover her pregnancy, but when they did find out they were less sympathetic. She left her post as a house maid to Colonel Williams 'in an ill state of health, the Col & his Daughters being at the time ignorant of the cause' and went to Devon, where she 'placed herself under the protection of [her brother's] Wife who was very kind to her and laid in – Staid there 2 months'. She also wished to keep knowledge of her pregnancy from her brother and so, 'being apprehensive her Brother would discover her Sickness she left without informing her Sister in law of her intention' and moved back to London and into lodgings. However, Colonel Williams did find out about Mary's situation and told the enquirer that

> As the head of a family of four Daughters he has not thought it right to see her since her misconduct was discovered, but he is anxious for her wellfare and would willingly assist in promoting it.

Of the 36 servants who left their positions, ten left after their pregnancies were discovered.[34] We have already seen that Alice King's employer Mr Tooch immediately dismissed her, but she was the only petitioner who was treated in this manner; most other employers offered at least some form of assistance. Such help included giving money and paying rent, the giving of a good character reference, help with writing a petition to the Foundling Hospital, gaining the mothers-to-be a ticket to a lying-in hospital and, in some cases, offering to retake the servant into service. For instance, Mrs Even, who employed Mary Wheeler, 'has from motives of compassion contributed much towards her support' and she said that she would take her back into her service. Offering to retake a servant solved the petitioner's immediate and pressing problems of accommodation and wages, but it also required the separation of mother and child. The help provided by Mr Ash was quite exceptional. He had thought his two servants Charlotte Smith and Thomas Walker so good that, when they intended to marry, he began 'looking for a Shop to put them into business', but Walker absconded.

Other employers also offered some help but stopped short of retaking the petitioners into their service. Mr Morris offered help to Mary Farman in a number of ways. He had advised her against courting Joseph Baite (the musician of the band of the First Regiment of Foot Guards), who was already married with a child. Mr Morris told the enquirer that Baite 'is a profligate Character and having a good person debauched the Petitioner who did not know he was marr^d'. Mr Morris wrote the petition for Mary and also obtained her a ticket of admission to the Westminster Lying-in Hospital. He would not, however, retake her into his service, although he would give her a good character reference so that she might get another situation elsewhere. In another case, once Jane Lomax's pregnancy became evident her master John Slee felt he could no longer keep her in his service, despite the fact that 'She was the best servant he ever had'. He stated, 'I should not have discharged her had it not been for this her misfortune. I do entertain a high opinion of her Honesty'. Instead, he provided her with a strong character reference. It is clear that some employers, such as John Slee and Colonel Williams (see above), felt that their reputations had been sullied by the pregnancy of a servant in their households and that they could not sanction the return of these women. But although they felt that they could not offer such servants a place to live, they did offer help – primarily good character references – either for the Foundling Hospital or for potential employers. This reaffirms the importance of references for the rehiring of servants.

Another way in which employers assisted their servants was in the pursuit of the men who had abandoned their lovers. In six cases employers made enquiries after the men involved. In the case of Elizabeth Paine, her employers Mr and Mrs Ryan of 50 Chequer Alley told the enquirer that, 'they have assisted the Petitioner in a search after the Father of the Child without effect', as did Mr Paty, Sarah Samuel's employer, who made a search for the reputed father of her child. Mr Paty,

> has wrote to Bridport and Bristol and caused an enquiry to be made through the Trade in Order to discover Wm Smith, he thinks he must have gone to Sea or he should have found him.

Although Alice King was thrown out of her post upon the discovery of her pregnancy, her mistress Mrs Tooch still assisted in the search for the Richard Hains and 'enquired at Chumberlains Wharfe and elsewhere but could not gain any intelligence of father.' Employers hoped that by tracking down the fathers they might facilitate the marriage of these couples, who could then set up a home of their own.

Those petitioners who were not in domestic service were either already living in lodgings or were residing with relatives.[35] A number of women lived in hired lodgings and took in out-work. Elizabeth Williams and Mary Ann Stellings took in needlework to earn their living, while Sarah Thompson was given government slop work by her employer Mrs Turner. Since they already lived in lodgings, these women did not experience the abrupt change in residential arrangements that were the lot of many of the pregnant domestic servants who left their positions. All three women spent their pregnancies there, lay-in there and continued to live there afterwards, paying their way by continuing to take in work. Mary Wells, Bridget Edwards and Mary Snowden also lived in lodgings but chose instead to be delivered in the Westminster Lying-in Hospital. They did not return to their rooms but took wet nursing positions instead. Such positions are discussed in more detail below.

Of those residing with kin, Ann Hawkes, Maria Bigg and Sarah Fay lived with their parents, Elizabeth Church lived with her uncle (since her parents were dead), and Eleanor Pratt lived with her sister-in-law. Maria received the kind of treatment we might expect from a reading of Victorian novels. Maria was living at home with her parents when she became engaged to James Long. The enquirer found that 'a day was fixed upon for the Marriage – the ring bought, and every thing prepared except the purchase of the License', but a few days before the day of the wedding, the groom 'ceased his visits and had not since been seen or heard of'. Once her father realised that his daughter was also pregnant, he threw her out and 'has refused to see her since, and has not assisted her except in a trifling way'. Maria was forced to take lodgings and gave birth there. It is possible that Elizabeth Church's uncle also insisted she leave his house, since she was admitted to the Westminster Lying-in Hospital for her delivery and then went on to a post of wet nurse. The reactions of these men would seem to have been fairly extreme, given Anna Clark's finding that premarital sexual activity was largely tolerated by the working classes.[36] On the other hand, Ann Hawkes continued to receive the support of her parents and lived with them, and Eleanor Pratt left her sister-in-law's house to lie in at her sister's.

Accommodation played a central role in the courtships of servants: many met their lovers within, or just outside, the household in which they were employed and living, and it was in their rooms that the couples frequently had sex. Service provided women with free bed and board, but, once pregnant, the majority of women had to leave these households. In order to secure future employment, it was essential for servants to keep their good character. Many employers offered at least some help to their pregnant servants, but this rarely extended to continued residence in the household. Other women – who lived in lodgings or with kin – retained a little more independence and experienced continuity in their residential arrangements.

8.2 Childbirth, survival strategies and residence

Once a woman had left her place of domestic employment and residence, where did she go for the later stages of her pregnancy? In roughly half of the cases (16) women went into lodgings, nine went to live with relatives and two with friends.[37] Women shared the domestic space of other families as a lodger or went to live in a common lodging house that catered for a number of lodgers. A large proportion of the poorer classes in London lived in ready-furnished rooms, paying a weekly rent. Rooms contained little but necessities. At the end of the eighteenth century, Colquhoun blamed the frequenting of alehouses to the experience of living in 'a miserable half-furnished lodging from week to week'.[38] It would seem reasonable to suppose that there was less surveillance by landlords and landladies of their lodgers than by employers of their domestic servants, but this would depend upon the exact living arrangements. Joanne McEwan's chapter suggests at least a level of privacy behind the locked doors of some lodging rooms. Some pregnant women tried to conceal their situations from their landlords and landladies. Jane Craston, for instance, pretended to be married when she lodged with Mrs Brayley for seven weeks and laid in there: '[Jane] represented herself to be a Married Woman that her Husband was a Coachman and gone to France'. Her housing situation was very precarious and she complained to the Hospital, 'Gentlemen I have Now selled place At present'. When she took lodgings with her brother and sister, Mary Aldridge was obviously pregnant and, on being questioned ˙ by the woman who kept 29 James Street, confessed she was not married. The cases suggest that these women feared that if the lodging housekeepers knew that they were unmarried then they would face not only disapproval but even reluctance to let them rooms. On the other hand, Mary Woodard's landlady, Miss Dibble, was the only other person who knew of her situation. Like employers, landlords and landladies displayed a range of responses to the pregnancies of single women.

The petitioners who took lodgings had to rely upon savings accrued in service. These savings were intended, of course, to help servants and their future husbands to set up their own household and living space, but the crisis of an illegitimate pregnancy upset this. Boulton highlights in Chapter 1 how rent accounted for a very large proportion of income of plebeian men and women and that it was an important factor in the experience of poverty. For petitioners, domestic service had provided free accommodation and food, as well as wages, but lodgings had to be paid for as did one's own meals. When the hospital enquirer visited Hannah Jones in her lodgings in Worship Street Shoreditch, he reported that 'She appears to be distressed, she says she has spent all she had'. Hannah pleaded with the governors of the hospital:

> how to support my dear baby I do not know I am distressed to the last farthing in supporting myself and my baby trust your worthy Gentlemen will take it into consideration as I am no imposture I am nothing but a poor servant and no other prospect but my servitude to get my bread I am Loath to part with my dear baby but I cannot Look upon myself and my Infant Starving for bread.

Jane Craston lodged with Mrs Bayley, who observed that 'she lived very scantily to make her Money last'. Elizabeth Marks supported herself by 'a remnant of Wages', while Margaret Weir stated that, 'she has been maintained out of money saved by her whilst in Service & with the aid of her friends'.

Moving from service into lodgings did not necessarily mean that assistance was not forthcoming from kin. In some cases rooms had been taken by relatives. Lodgings were taken for Maria Bigg (whose father had thrown her out) by her elder sister and Maria was 'beholden to her chiefly for support'. Her brothers and sisters had visited her there, but her mother and father refused. In another case, Mary Aldridge took lodgings with her brother and sister. The lodging-house keeper said, 'That they are honest sober steady People and very industrious'. The father of the child was killed in the Battle of Waterloo and it was said of Mary that 'when by herself she is always in Grief'.

The pregnant servants who went to live with kin resided with parents, sisters, uncles and aunts, and a sister-in-law. Mary Cooke moved in with her grandmother and father. Margaret Weir's sister 'took her in and has had her under her charge ever since'. However, many women living with family and friends were still expected to earn their keep, such as Mary Farman who lived with her uncle and took in needlework. Clark has argued that while many female relatives offered shelter through-out pregnancy and birth, male kin tended to shun unwed girls. This assertion, however, is only based upon two examples.[39] The evidence provided here reveals that while female relatives might have been more likely to assist a pregnant daughter or sister, male relatives also took them in. Recent research on Scotland shows that many pregnant women returned to the households of their parents, and frequently left their children behind while they returned to work elsewhere.[40] Regarding friends, we have already seen how Mary Ann Jackson moved to Ireland to stay with her friend Mrs Gregory, while Elizabeth Edgeley went to live with friends in Ramsey, Huntingdonshire.

In two cases, petitioners cohabited with the fathers of their children (and this reveals that cohabiting couples are not necessarily missing from the petitions). Such a residential arrangement was immensely helpful for these women: they shared the cost of lodgings and day-to-day living expenses, while hoping that their lovers would eventually marry them. The enquirer's report for Isabella Wilson reads as follows:

> Lived at no 3 Unicon Buildings Dove Court Leather Lane as a Servant where she was seduced – on being pregnant she left her place and Fathr took Lodgings for her at Mrs Baynes N° 3 Dove Court – where they lived together as Man and Wife Fathr deserted her when she was within a Week of delivery Child 7 Months-old – fathr has been gone nearly 12 Months.

It seems probable that this period of cohabitation resulted in Isabella's application being rejected by the Hospital, but in the second case, similar in many respects, the petition was accepted. Mary Ann Stellings became acquainted with Thomas Nash, a hairdresser, when he visited a friend at Mary Ann's lodgings at Mrs Ginges, Little Coram Street. The report tells us that

> one day he called when she was putting her things on and her family abroad and seduced her and soon after he persuaded her to go into Yorkshire to Mrs Thompson of Sheffield 50 Bridge Street a Grocer – she remained there 6 months – but father left her deserted less than 2 months after their arrival.

She returned to Mrs Ginges pregnant and delivered her baby there. It is likely that such a residential strategy did work for many other women, who either went on to wed their lovers or continued living with them in an informal union (but did not come to the attention of the Foundling Hospital), a situation that was widespread in early nineteenth-century London and the country more generally.[41]

Many of those who went into lodgings also gave birth there: 39 per cent. The next most common place of delivery was the Westminster Lying-in Hospital, where 22 per cent of mothers were delivered. Seventeen per cent gave birth in the homes of relatives, 10 per cent gave birth in the homes of their service employers, and 7 per cent were delivered in either Marylebone or Lambeth workhouse.[42] Thus, for many petitioners pregnancy meant a move out of service, and childbirth might necessitate yet another move. Lying-in hospitals and workhouses offered women free accommodation and food, as well as medical care and the attention of a midwife during childbirth and lying-in; however, the length of stay was usually restricted to between three weeks and a month. Within workhouses, mothers were also expected to work when they were able and the institution was designed to be disciplinary.[43] Admission to the Westminster Lying-in Hospital required mothers to stay for a minimum of 14 days and visitors were not allowed. To gain admittance to the hospital petitioners would have required a letter of recommendation, probably obtained through those employers whom were willing to help their pregnant servants. Nearly 70 per cent of single women delivered in the hospital were domestic servants, as were over half of those giving birth in London workhouses.[44] The type of accommodation offered to unmarried mothers and their experiences of institutional life varied from workhouse to workhouse: St Luke's Chelsea and St Margaret's Westminster accommodated pregnant women within the workhouse, rather than admitting them into their infirmaries, whereas St Andrew Holborn had a specific lying-in ward.[45] Delivery in a lying-in hospital or workhouse was a transitional residence between the world of work and the new situation a mother would find herself in, either in lodgings, in another household as a wet nurse, or in a new domestic service position. Their experience inside the workhouse can be contrasted with the more preferential experiences of the elderly in St Martin-in-the-Fields' workhouse, examined in Chapter Nine by Boulton and Schwarz.

In general, most women were delivered at home within the female-only sphere of childbirth, attended by a local midwife and female friends and family, but it is not clear from the petitions whether the petitioners who gave birth in lodgings were able to draw upon this female network during confinement.[46] It seems likely that they were either attended by only one or two women or they gave birth alone. Maria Bigg was delivered in her lodgings and was attended by a doctor for a small amount. This was unusual, since only higher class women were usually delivered with the help of a male practitioner.[47] Those giving birth in the homes of relatives and employers were more likely to have had company during their delivery and lying in period. Thus, at the point of giving birth the living arrangements and household composition of the petitioners' residence had a direct impact upon her experience of the delivery.

The amount in savings dictated the length of time unmarried mothers in lodgings could live in their hired rooms and directly affected the security of their living arrangements. In the first decade of the nineteenth century the annual wages of Mary Ashford, a servant in modest London households, was between £2 10s. 0d. and 10 guineas. Wages of domestic servants also included pay in kind, the most important of which was accommodation, but servants also received tea and sugar, small beer, vails (tips) and the mistress's cast-off clothing. In 1814, after 13 years in service, Mary had savings of £9 and 'a good stock of useful clothes' in her possession.[48] Only one petitioner in the current sample gave the amount she had saved – Harriet Dore, who in 1805 had managed to save 12 guineas 'with which she supports herself'. Lodgings cost another petitioner, Ann Smith, 2s. per week. If savings paid for lodgings alone then these amounts would have covered rent costs for almost two and a half years; however, lodgers also had to pay for food and fuel, household sundries, and their lying-in expenses. In addition, these saving amounts seem high and, since most petitioners were younger than Mary Ashford by four years, it is unlikely that they accrued quite so much.[49] Indeed, the vast majority of petitioners, their employers and their lodging-house keepers complained that savings were all too soon used up. It was usually at the point of the exhaustion of these savings, when it became evident that they could no longer support their infants, that these women approached the hospital. These petitioners claimed to be at the point of destitution before their infants turned were 12 months old.

In order to pay for lodgings and food, Trumbach has found that almost a quarter of petitioners in his sample used up savings from years of service or sold or pawned their clothes. Only a small proportion received help from families or friends (6 per cent), with more (nearly 9 per cent) claiming that their families were too poor to help them and (presumably) could not offer their pregnant relative a place to stay.[50] Evans also describes the many strategies employed by unmarried mothers to make shift in the metropolis.[51] Moreover, recourse to savings, pawning and selling clothes were familiar strategies for servants, who also used them when they were out-of-place.[52] In 1800 there were around 10,000 servants of both sexes out of place. Because many were from the county, when out of place they were obliged to go into lodgings and to subsist on their little savings and take odd jobs until they found a new position. Servants could experience long periods without a settled place and residence.[53]

A number of mothers managed to take some form of employment and thereby stay in their lodgings in the longer term. Elizabeth Williams, Maria Bigg, Sarah Barber and Mary Ann Stellings took in needlework. Mary Ann's landlady stated that the 'Petitioner earns a scanty subsistence by working at her needle for the shops'. Sarah Thompson and Elizabeth Paine were employed in slop work, while Ann Sayer made straw hats, Ann Hawes was a mantua maker, and Eleanor Pratt earned 9s. a week making muffs. Dina Moody paid for her lodgings by helping her landlady with shoe binding and household chores, while Elizabeth Aris stated that she had supported herself through 'private subscriptions'. The Foundling Hospital offered emergency interim financial support to petitioners (the 'indigent fund') such as Ann Sayer, who was allowed '3/6 a week until Admission' and Charlotte Smith, for whom it was ordered one guinea and 3s. 6d. per week, and so the application process itself can be seen as a further way of making shift. The experiences of these women show that there was an alternative to a return to domestic service; Elizabeth, Maria, Sarah and Mary Ann all managed to live independently, earning their own living and paying for their lodgings.

Ann Blagg's story is very different to most of those discussed so far. Ann was living and working as a barmaid at the King's Arms in Sheffield when she met Mr Weaterley, a commercial traveller who was staying at the inn. Once she discovered her pregnancy she moved between jobs, as a barmaid in the Manchester Arms in Manchester and as a housekeeper to a linen drapers in Sheffield, and residing with her mother, who kept the Social Tavern in Sheffield. Ann and her mother travelled to London in search of the father of the child. Her pay as a barmaid had been 'very handsome' but, once she had given birth and gone into lodgings, her landlady reported that 'She had only half a sovereign which she offered to her – She is now in debt but is very industrious at her needle and in assisting in the house.' Ann had a reasonably secure place to live and her story confirms the finding that women could exist independently after the birth of a bastard child.

Many found themselves in debt, however, particularly to lodging housekeepers. When Elizabeth Weathrall died shortly after giving birth to twins she was in debt 'for necessaries during the time of her lying-in', despite the 'small pecuniary Relief' that her employer had given her. Mary Neill and Ann Blagg had also left their lodgings in debt. Others sold or pawned their clothes. It was stated that Elizabeth George, for instance, 'has subsisted herself by making away with her Clothes'. We have already noted the value of Mary Ashford's clothing and there was a ready second-hand market for clothing. The pawning or selling of clothes brought these women close to destitution, however, and could prevent them from recovering their situations, since to lose one's clothes made it difficult to regain employment. Mrs Paty acknowledged this when she told the enquirer that she had assisted her servant Sarah Samuel so that 'she might be enabled to save some of her Clothes to appear in to get her another situation'.

Maria Bigg combined a number of strategies, taking in needlework 'when she could get employment', accepting money from her sister and running up debts with her landlady. She also owed the doctor who attended her delivery 'for a small account'. Mary Ann Jackson, who we met at the start of this chapter, made shift from a combination of rent-free accommodation (in Mrs Gregory's house in Ireland), her savings from service, further assistance from 'a few Compassionate friends', and then a return to her post. Her determination to conceal her situation from both her employers and her family meant that she 'has suffered every privation'. In another case, Mary Metcalf became pregnant during her courtship with Joseph Longstaffe, a fellow servant to Dr Dodgson. When he procured his wages and left, Mary left her place shortly after-wards and stayed with her parents for a short time. She then started a new position, as servant of all work with Mrs Forsyth. Once her pregnancy was discovered she returned to her parents and gave birth there. She then returned to service with a new employer, Mr Cook. In the case of Ann Hawkes, although her settlement was in the parish of St George Hanover Square, she gave birth in Marylebone workhouse. She left the child there and returned to work but this arrangement had to come to an end because 'the Governors of the Work House directed her to take Child out'. Tim Hitchcock argues that cases such as Ann Hawkes' were far from unusual in eighteenth-century London; the metropolis offered considerable institutional provision for unmarried mothers and their infants and, he suggests, some women left their children in the workhouse in order to return to work.[54]

In a number of cases, the fathers offered some assistance to their pregnant sweethearts. The rules of admission explicitly stated: 'That the father shall have deserted his offspring, and be not forthcoming, that is, not to be found, or compellable to maintain his child'. Many of the petitions claim either that the whereabouts of the putative fathers is not known or that it is only vaguely known, such as 'fathr is now (she supposes) in Yorkshire' or that 'he was gone to the West Indies'. In two cases, however, the enquirer discovered that fathers had offered some financial help. Sarah Thompson and John Blackhall, a sailor on board The Glory, had been courting for four years when she became pregnant. Her landlady told the enquirer that, 'they were to have been married but to he was ordered to Sea'. When Sarah was eight months pregnant, John sent her £5 and Sarah added this to the income she made taking in slop work. In the other case, the father of Susan Poppleton's child paid for her lying in. Gillis found similar examples of fathers supporting the mothers of their children.[55] In most cases, however, the fathers offered no financial assistance and help was not forthcoming via maintenance orders through the parish authorities.[56]

The position of wet nurse was open to women once their children were born and seven petitioners took posts as wet nurses. Character references for these positions were forthcoming not only from previous employers but also matrons at the lying-in hospitals. Wet nurses were frequently retained in the household after the infant was weaned and at least three women were rehired in this way. In addition, at least four petitioners went into new service positions. While these positions solved the housing problems faced by unmarried mothers in the longer term, such live-in positions meant that their own infants were put out to nurse elsewhere, a separation which was both expensive and extremely distressing. Bridget Edwards told the enquirer that 'She has hitherto maintained her Child by her Wages as Wet Nurse, but they will soon be reduced, when She will be no longer able to pay for it'. Mary Rose complained that 'my wages is not half enough to pay the woman that has got my Child, which makes me very unhappy & at times very ill that I can hardly go through my work'. Ten women put their children out to nurse and the weekly cost of a nurse ranged from 5*s*. 6*d*. to 7*s*. These sums are far in excess than the 2*s*. a week paid in rent for lodging. Sarah Cape complained,

> as it nearly imposible for me to keep the Child any longer Im Considrable in debt for it already and so much troubled for the money that I fear I cannot keep my Situation for the an expence of Seven Shillings a weak for three or four months more I shall not recover for years by Servitude.

When Alice King, whose case is discussed at the beginning of this chapter, put her child out to nurse, there were fatal consequences. When Alice went to visit her baby she found him:

> not crying on a bed but flat on his back upon a chest on which an old coat was spread with not a single rag to cover him his dear hands perished almost with cold and in so weak a state that he is not able to suck. The woman said his bowells was bad. I returned home in the dark in almost a lifeless state and I think my heart will break. the woman had her bed in the room. I think she might laid him upon that. the room was a small dirty damp place full of wet linen and pots and pans. I shall never forget it. I expect the baby will die before he goes into the foundling.

Indeed, the enquirer wrote at the bottom of the petition: 'Child died previous to the day for admission'. Alice also stated that she moved with her employers between London and their other residence, which, if the child had not died, would have meant that she was a long distance from her child. These cases also shed further light on the issue of the importance of sexual morality for the reputations of servants. Employers must surely have known that they were taking single women into their households who had recently given birth and such evidence adds weight to the argument that the sexual morality of servants, and any lapses, did not bar future employment. Historians have also argued that, from the late eighteenth century, perceptions and ideals of mothering were shifting and, as part of the redefinition of good mothering, wealthier women were encouraged to breastfeed their own children.[57]

Nevertheless, despite such prescriptive advice, wet nursing continued for some time. In order to avoid poverty and potential destitution, these petitioners were prepared to breastfeed another woman's infant while placing their own out to another nurse.

In summary, the majority of women took lodgings after they left the households where they had been employed, gave birth there and lived on, and soon exhausted their savings. Relatives offered an alternative place to live for some women and kin sometimes provided other forms of assistance. Very few of those who approached the Hospital lived with their lovers. A small number of women managed to eke out a living by taking in needlework or other work which could be done from home. What all of these women shared, however, was that they – sooner or later – felt that they could no longer make shift and they all drew up their pitiful petitions and approached the Hospital.

8.3   Conclusion

Unmarried mothers in nineteenth-century London frequently found themselves in significant material distress and in uncertain residential arrangements. Although continuing to provide a place to stay was the single most important form of assistance an employer could give, very few actually did. The vast majority of petitioners had to leave their positions – which meant giving up their living quarters and board – and move into lodgings. Many petitioners had to move several times: out of their employers' household into lodgings or to the homes of kin or friends, or into the workhouse or a lying-in hospital, and then into new work or on elsewhere. A high rate of mobility was common among the young and servants were used to changing position frequently, especially in London, as well as spending periods between places in hired lodgings. This situation was not so dissimilar to other poor families in London, who also moved repeatedly (largely to save rent) and might also have had to share domestic space.[58] In her chapter, McEwan shows that lodging was particularly prevalent in London and that there was a variety of lodging arrangements, including short-term stays. Such mobility surely reinforces Sharpe's concept of the 'chain of poverty' (see 'Introduction').[59] However, the crisis of an illegitimate pregnancy necessitated a more rapid turnover of places of accommodation for these women that must have amounted to a traumatic and isolating experience. The 'chain of poverty' for at least some petitioners was necessary to avoid destitution. Nevertheless, a small number of young mothers did manage to remain independent. These women paid for their lodgings by taking in out-work – although they were all desperately poor – and lodgings were never an adequate substitute for the security of a domestic service post. A significant number of petitioners were taken in by family and friends. For others, their only choice was to put their child out to nurse and return to service. Such a post bestowed a respectable and secure residence once more. All these women approached the Foundling Hospital, however, claiming that they could no longer cope.

Within the employing household there was an implicit tension between female servants and their mistresses: unmarried, childless servants assisted their mistresses (who were wives and mothers) to run their households and bring up their children and such households could not accommodate the illegitimate children of servants. On the other hand, having a bastard child did mean that some of these unwed mothers could find a new position in other households as wet nurses, but this too required a separation from their infants and the breast-feeding of the child of another woman. Some of these women were able to place their infants out to nurse, but most felt that this too expensive to be a long-term solution. It does seem poignant that a woman had to have recently given birth to her own child in order to nurse another woman's baby and that she then, too, had to place her infant out to another nurse.

Joining another household as a servant was a life-cycle stage for young women and it was usually their own marriages that acted as the transition point between living in the household of others and that of their own (and with their own legitimate children). However, for petitioners to the Foundling Hospital there had been a breakdown of the informal contract between the betrothed lovers as future mothers/wives and fathers/husbands. The high rate of mobility among the young and the increasingly unstable London labour market contributed to the dissolving of these informal bonds, as did the distance between the petitioners and their families of origin. However, there is evidence in the petitions that women in the metropolis nurtured alternative urban support networks of employers, lodging-house keepers, neighbours, and friends, and many of the women were still able to draw upon the support of their relatives.

This brings us to the somewhat thorny issue of the extent to which employers, and possibly lodging-house keepers, judged petitioners on their sexual morality. Conflicting evidence is apparent in the petitions. The fact that so few women remained in their service households is important and would seem to imply that masters and mistresses were unwilling to keep 'fallen' women under their roofs. Certainly, Alice King's employer Mr Tooch felt strongly on the matter and dismissed her and Mary Neill's master, Colonel Williams, would not see her. A number of women kept their real circumstances from their lodging-house keepers, presumably fearing a negative reaction from them. On the other hand, a few employers did allow their servants to remain in their households or they agreed to retake them into service if the child was admitted to the Hospital, and many employers provided a range of other material or emotional assistance. In terms of references, many employers were prepared to provide good character references, presumably attesting to the industriousness of their former servants and with no reference to their recent predicament. Yet there was a group of petitioners who had deliberately left their positions before their conditions were known, fearing that their employers would not be so willing to write them such good references and that this would bar them from future employment. The evidence on the role of kin is also contradictory: some relatives offered substantial help while others refused to assist them, and in other cases petitioners hid their pregnancies from their mothers and fathers, uncles and aunts, brothers and sisters. The late eighteenth and early nineteenth centuries was obviously one of transition, when the reactions of others to an illegitimate pregnancy were still varied, both within plebeian culture and the emerging middle class. It is difficult to know whether the petitioners themselves had internalised notions of stigma. A much harsher attitude towards unmarried mothers certainly characterised Victorian society, with punitive Bastardy Clauses in the New Poor Law and a rash of charities and institutions designed to reform and redeem the fallen woman.[60] Moral as well as economic considerations impacted upon the living arrangements of poor unwed mothers in nineteenth-century London.

Notes

1. See, for example, T. Hitchcock, *English Sexualities, 1700–1800* (Basingstoke: Macmillan, 1997); A. Clark, 'Whores and Gossips: Sexual reputation in London 1770–1825', in A. Angerman, G. Binnema, A. Keunen, V. Poels, & J. Zirkzee (eds), *Current Issues in Women's History* (Routledge, 1989), pp. 231–48; A. Clark, *The Struggle for the Breeches: Gender and the Making of the British Working Class* (Rivers Oram Press, 1995); N. Tadmor, 'The Concept of the Household-Family in Eighteenth-Century England', *Past and Present* 151, (1996), 111–140; J. Tosh, *A Man's Place: Masculinity and the Middle-Class Home in Victorian England* (Yale University Press, 1999).
2. This chapter analyses a sample of 60 petitions and all accompanying reports between 1801 and 1840. Other petitions with insufficient information about residence were excluded (another 40). LMA, A/FH/A08/001/002/010-049, A/FH/A08/001/003/009-015.

3. LMA A/FH/6/2/4/2, 'Copy Book of Letters', 1795–1810. For more on the rules of admission and the content of the petitions and enquirers' reports, see S. K. Williams '"That the Petitioner Shall have Borne a Good Character for Virtue, Sobriety, and Honesty Previous to her Misfortune": Unmarried Mothers' Petitions to the Foundling Hospital and the Rhetoric of Need in the Long Eighteenth Century', in A. Levene, T. Nutt, & S. K. Williams (eds), *Illegitimacy in Britain 1700–1920* (Basingstoke: Palgrave Macmillan, 2005), pp. 86–101; T. Evans, *'Unfortunate Objects': Lone Mothers in Eighteenth-Century London* (Basingstoke: Palgrave Macmillan, 2005), Chapter 5.

4. Williams, 'A Good Character', pp. 87–9.

5. J. Black, 'Illegitimacy and the Urban Poor in London, 1740–1830' (Unpublished University of London PhD Thesis, 1999), p. 297; R. B. Outhwaite, "Objects of Charity': Petitions to the London Foundling Hospital, 1768–72', *Eighteenth-Century Studies* 32, (1999), 497–510; Evans, *Unfortunate Objects*, p. 132.

6. After 1801 the admission procedure required mothers to put forward their case in a 'petition', their children had to have been born in London, be illegitimate and be under 12 months old, and they were to give the name and address of a person who could verify the truth of what was contained in the petition and provide a character reference. The rules also required that as few people were to know about her situation as possible and that she had employment to return to if their child was admitted. See Williams, 'A Good Character', pp. 87–9 and R. H. Nichols & F. A. Wray, *The History of the Foundling Hospital* (Oxford University Press, 1935), pp. 98–9.

7. See Williams, 'A Good Character', pp. 94–100.

8. R. Trumbach, *Sex and the Gender Revolution. Heterosexuality and the Third Gender in Enlightenment London: Volume One* (University of Chicago, 1998); Outhwaite, 'Objects of Charity'; P. S. Seleski, 'The Women of the Labouring Poor: Love, Work and Poverty, 1750–1820' (Unpublished University of Stanford PhD Thesis, 1989); T. Evans, *Unfortunate Objects*; J. Gillis, 'Servants, Sexual Relations and the Risks of Illegitimacy in London, 1801–1900', in J. L. Newton, M. P. Ryan & J. R. Walkowitz (eds), *Sex and Class in Women's History* (Routledge & Kegan Paul, 1983), pp. 114–45; F. Barret-Ducrocq, *Love in the Time of Victoria: Sexuality and Desire among Working-Class Men and Women in Nineteenth-Century London*, translated by J. Howe (New York: Penguin, 1991); B. Weisbrod, 'How to Become a Good Foundling in Early Victorian London', *Social History* 10, (1985), 193–209; A. Clark, *Women's Silence, Men's Violence: Sexual Assault in England 1770–1845* (Pandora, 1987); Clark, 'Whores and Gossips'; Clark, *Struggle for the Breeches*.

9. Trumbach, *Sex and the Gender Revolution*, Chapter 9, especially Table 9.6, p. 281.

10. Evans, *Unfortunate Objects*, Chapter 5.

11. In the Foundling Hospital sample used in this chapter, occupations could be established in 52 cases, 41 of whom were servants (79 per cent). The others were employed as: stay maker (1), straw hat maker (1), slop work (1), mantua maker (1), dress maker (1), bar maid (1), took in needlework (1) or were recorded as living with family (4). The proportion of servants applying to the Foundling Hospital rose substantially between the eighteenth and nineteenth centuries, from around half (Evans) to three-quarters (Gillis),

while Seleski found that 90 per cent of petitioners had been employed at
some time or other as a domestic servant (1750–1820). Gillis found that
most of the remaining petitioners were employed in the clothing trades.
The rise in the proportion of servant-petitioners was the consequence
of the change in the rules for admission in 1801 which emphasised that
only 'respectable' petitioners, and those able to return to work, would be
successful. Servants were more able (than women employed in other trades)
to fulfil these criteria. Evans, *Unfortunate Objects*; Gillis, 'Servants', Table 1,
p. 117; Seleski, 'Women of the Labouring Poor', p. 15. On the changes in the
rules for admission and the consequences for the occupational make-up of
Foundling Hospital petitioners, see Williams, 'A Good Character'.

12. R. Wall, 'Leaving Home and the Process of Household Formation in Pre-
Industrial England', *Continuity and Change* 2 (1987), 77–101.

13. M. D. George, *London Life in the Eighteenth Century* (Kegan Paul, 1925),
pp. 112–13.

14. Gillis, 'Servants', pp. 119–21; B. Hill, *Servants: English Domestics in the
Eighteenth Century* (Oxford: Clarendon Press, 1996); P. Horn, *The Rise and Fall
of the Victorian Servant* (Stroud: Alan Sutton, 1975).

15. Gillis, 'Servants', p. 122.

16. See Chapter 2 in this volume.

17. George, *London Life*, Chapter 3.

18. Gillis, 'Servants', pp. 123, 133; George, *London Life*, Chaper 3; Evans,
Unfortunate Objects; Black, 'Illegitimacy in London'.

19. Tadmor, 'The Concept of the Household-Family'.

20. Snell, *Annals of the Labouring Poor: Social Change and Agrarian England 1660–
1900* (Cambridge: Cambridge University Press, 1985), Chapters 1 and 2; N.
Verdon, '"…subjects deserving of the highest praise": Farmers' Wives and the
Farm Economy in England, c. 1700–1850', *Agricultural History Review* 51:1,
(2003), 23–39.

21. Tosh, *A Man's Place*; Clark, *Struggle for the Breeches*.

22. Seleski, 'Women of the Labouring Poor', p. 149.

23. Clark, *Struggle for the Breeches*, p. 43.

24. Clark, *Struggle for the Breeches*, p. 48; A. Levene, T. Nutt & S. K. Williams,
'Introduction', in Levene, Nutt, & Williams (eds), *Illegitimacy in Britain*,
pp. 1–17; J. Gillis, *For Better, For Worse: British Marriages, 1600 to the Present*
(Oxford: Oxford University Press, 1985), Chapter 7.

25. George, *London Life*, pp. 202–3.

26. In 43 cases the place the lovers met was given. In 4 per cent of cases the
woman was in service and the man was a lodger in the same house.

27. This is known in 42 cases.

28. Black, 'Illegitimacy in London'; Evans, *Unfortunate Objects*.

29. Ducrocq, *Love in the Time of Victoria*, Chapter 1.

30. Black 'Illegitimacy in London', pp. 225–7. See also J. Black, 'Illegitimacy,
Sexual Relations and Location in Metropolitan London, 1735–85', in
T. Hitchcock & H. Shore (eds), *The Streets of London From the Great Fire to the
Great Stink* (Rivers Oram Press, 2003), pp. 101–18.

31. Gillis, 'Servants', p. 128.

32. Hill, *Servants*, pp. 48, 92–1, 200–1.

33. It is likely that petitioners were self-selected, with those women whose life
histories most closely conformed to the rules for admission being most likely

to apply. This made servants far more likely to be successful than women in other trades. See Williams, 'A Good Character'.
34. In the remaining petitions (10) it is not clear whether the petitioner left before or after her employers knew of her circumstances.
35. Seven lived in lodgings, five with relatives and one worked as a barmaid and lived above the pub; in the remaining six cases there was no information.
36. Clark, *Struggle for the Breeches*, p. 48.
37. In the remaining cases petitioners left their post but neither the petitions nor the reports state where they went.
38. George, *London Life*, pp. 91–3.
39. Clark, 'Whores and Gossips', pp. 237–8.
40. A. Blaikie, E. Garrett, & R. Davies, 'Migration, Living Strategies and Illegitimate Childbearing: A Comparison of Two Scottish Settings, 1871–1881', in Levene, Nutt, & Williams (eds), *Illegitimacy in Britain*, pp. 141–67.
41. A. Clark, *Struggle for the Breeches*, pp. 48–9; Gillis, *For Better, For Worse*, Chapter 7.
42. The place of birth was given in 41 cases. The remaining petitioners were delivered in 'hospital' (1) and 'Doclus Hayden House' (1).
43. Evans, *Unfortunate Objects*, pp. 150–1; WAC, 9.1.1728/9, 5.11.1730, St Margaret's Westminster, Workhouse Committee Minutes, E2633; LMA, P74/LUK/110-111, St Luke's Chelsea Workhouse Admission and Discharge Register, 1743–99.
44. Evans, *Unfortunate* Objects, p. 159; Gillis, 'Servants', p. 116. See Evans, *Unfortunate Objects*, Chapter 7, for further information on London lying-in hospitals.
45. WAC, St Margaret's Westminster, Workhouse Committee Minutes, E2633, 9.1.1728/9, 5.11.1730; K. Siena, *Venereal Disease, Hospitals and the Urban Poor: London's 'Foul Wards', 1600–1800* (Woodbridge: University of Rochester Press, 2004), p. 146; Evans, *Unfortunate Objects*, pp. 150–1.
46. I. Loudon, *Medical Care and the General Practitioner 1750–1850* (Oxford: Clarendon Press, 1986).
47. A. Wilson, *The Making of Man-Midwifery: Childbirth in England, 1660–1770* (UCL Press, 1995).
48. Hill, *Servants*, Chapters 4 & 10; Horn, *Victorian Servant*, pp. 142–51.
49. The average age of petitioners in the early nineteenth century was between 23 and 24. Gillis, 'Servants', Table 2, p. 118.
50. Trumbach, *Sex and the Gender Revolution*, Table 9.6, p. 281.
51. Evans, *Unfortunate Objects*, pp. 113, 132.
52. Outhwaite, 'Objects of Charity', p. 503.
53. George, *London Life*, pp. 112–13, 200–1.
54. T. Hitchcock, "Unlawfully Begotten on her Body': Illegitimacy and the Parish Poor in St Luke's Chelsea', in T. Hitchcock, P. King & P. Sharpe (eds), *Chronicling Poverty: The Voices and Strategies of the English Poor 1640–1840* (Basingstoke: Macmillan, 1997), pp. 70–86.
55. Gillis, 'Servants', p. 137.
56. This is probably because, after 1801, the rules for admission required that 'The birth is not known to any parish authorities' (although in the present study 7 per cent of women did give birth in the workhouse). It seems likely that many of the women who were not successful at the Foundling Hospital then approached the parish for assistance.

57. R. B. Shoemaker, *Gender in English Society, 1650–1850: The Emergence of Separate Spheres?* (Longman, 1998), pp. 126–8.
58. See the Introduction in this volume.
59. *Ibid.*
60. Williams, 'A Good Character'

Part III
Parochial Relief and Charity

9

'The Comforts of a Private Fireside'? The Workhouse, the Elderly and the Poor Law in Georgian Westminster: St Martin-in-the-Fields, 1725–1824

Jeremy Boulton & Leonard Schwarz

9.1 The elderly as an object of study

The history of the elderly has received a good deal of treatment recently. Susannah Ottaway, Margaret Pelling, David Thomson, Richard Smith, Lynn Botelho, Pat Thane and others have explored, often in great detail, the historical experience of growing old.[1] Ottaway's contribution in her book, *The Decline of Life*, in particular, has shed much valuable light on the history of old age in rural and provincial communities in the eighteenth century, on how age was defined and written about, what provision was made for the care and maintenance of the elderly and so on.[2]

Like many authors, Ottaway devoted a great deal of attention to the role of the poor law in providing for the elderly. This included both outdoor relief, and also relief given to the elderly in local workhouses. Informal charitable relief to the elderly in her communities, in contrast, was 'utterly dwarfed' by assistance funded via the parish poor rate.[3] According to Ottaway, the eighteenth century saw an increasing proportion of the elderly receiving parish pensions, at least in Puddletown and Terling, although the real value of such pensions fell during the last decades of the eighteenth century.[4] What of indoor relief? In Terling, the workhouse 'replaced outdoor relief for many of the elderly in the 1790s'. Ottaway argues that the increased use of workhouses contributed to, and was part of, 'an overall decline in the quality of care provided by the community' in the eighteenth century.[5] In Terling there was a dramatic increase in the proportion of aged people occupying the (small) local workhouse, in fact it became virtually an old people's home, with most inmates spending their last years there, and also dying

221

there.[6] In the Halifax township of Ovenden, in contrast, there was no visible trend in the proportions of elderly resident: 15 per cent of known inmates between 1773 and 1801 were aged 60 or more.[7] What proportion of the elderly population lived in workhouses in her two communities? In Ovenden in 1773, Ottaway estimates that between 6 and 9 per cent of the elderly population of that parish 'entered the workhouse for some amount of time'. In Terling the comparable figures ranged from just 2 to 14 per cent in the 1790s. Ovenden's workhouse appears to have been used more flexibly by elderly inmates, and was often used as a temporary refuge rather than as a 'long-term care facility or a hospice for dying' as in Terling.[8] Both usage patterns are observable in Eden's survey of the poor made in the 1790s.[9]

Ottaway's important work also raises questions regarding whether the elderly received special treatment. Many local vestries specifically exempted some local elderly poor from a requirement to enter the workhouse, often giving outdoor allowances instead. In others, workhouse regimes included special provision for the elderly, such as exemption from work, dining first, or extra rations. In the event, enduring hostility to entering workhouses and local poor law policy meant that 'most of the aged and even the great majority of the elderly poor remained outside of workhouse walls' in the eighteenth century.[10] Did this happen in the metropolis?

The introduction of the New Poor Law is said to have changed official policy in this regard. 'The use of workhouses for the aged poor was to become a hallmark of nineteenth-century social policy.'[11] Ottaway's statement, however, is not really supported by Thomson's work, who wrote more than 20 years ago that 'in the middle decades of the last century the aged formed a minor portion of any workhouse population'. It was only in the *closing* decades of the nineteenth century that the provision of more specialist care for other categories of inmates meant that 'the workhouse became, more by default than design, the institution of the aged'. In the middle of the nineteenth century, therefore, the proportion of the elderly who found themselves in an institution remained low. Nationally, in 1851, for example, only 3.43 per cent of males aged 65–74 inhabited a poor law institution, and for women the comparable figure is still lower: 1.95 per cent. Even the 'old old', aged 75 or more, had little likelihood of poor law institutionalisation in the mid nineteenth century: just 4.87 per cent of men aged over 75 and 3.16 per cent of women in 1851.[12] Their proportion of the workhouse population rose from 20 per cent in 1851 to 37 per cent in 1900.[13]

Thomson's work, however, also emphasises the distinctive role of London in the institutionalisation of the elderly: 'By the opening of the nineteenth century, London had already earned the dubious distinction of placing an extreme emphasis upon large institutions as being the answer to all welfare needs.' The 'huge and highly visible' London workhouses also had relatively large numbers of elderly inmates. Thompson states that in 1851, one in three of London's workhouse population were over 65 years old, compared to only about one in seven for the rest of the country.[14] In fact, Lynn Hollen Lees' one-in-ten sample of the metropolitan workhouse population, of both sexes, found that in 1851 over half were over the age of 60.[15] Moreover, 'London's workhouse record was never more atypical than with regard to aged women'. In 1851, 12.4 per cent of women aged 75 or more living in London lived in a workhouse: six times more likely than women of similar ages in other parts of the country.[16]

All of this presents important challenges to the London historian. Can we say much about accommodation of the elderly in London *before* the New Poor Law? What proportion of the elderly were incarcerated? What was their experience of workhouses and the welfare system, and can we say anything at all about the circumstances that drove them to seek relief from the poor law? Can we identify the workhouse acting as a 'hospice' or long stay care home, or did it approximate more to the flexible institution found at Ovenden? How common was experience of the workhouse? Did the elderly receive distinctively different treatment when inside?

Studying this is difficult and time-consuming, and is dependent on the quality of contemporary record-keeping and the chances of such records surviving. The Westminster parish of St.Martin-in-the-Fields is particularly fortunate in these respects. Covering the area between the Strand and Covent Garden and the subsequent Trafalgar Square, it had in the period under review a population probably between 25,000 and 30,000. There is one principal source deployed here. This is the series of workhouse admission registers and day books, which supply details on the age of admission, reason for discharge, ward number and other information about the 86,000 or so individuals who entered the workhouse between 1725 and 1824. These records have been supplemented by overseers' and churchwardens' accounts, vestry and overseers minutes, and other records generated by this heavily bureaucratised parish administration. Particularly useful is the series of settlement examinations that survive in an unbroken series between 1708 and 1795. These, which have been deployed here to build up some case studies of individual paupers, supply a great deal of information regarding matters such as marital status, settlement status, rent, marital and residential history in addition, sometimes, to giving more incidental information about family history, children and employment.

9.2   Defining the elderly

The first question has to be, of course, how many elderly were 'at risk'? And, for that matter, who exactly *were* the 'elderly'? Contemporaries (like today's historians) rarely agreed on any one age as defining the start of 'old' age. This study follows Ottaway and Thane in taking 60 to be the 'gateway to old age'.[17] In taking this as the starting point of the ageing process, one has to recognise the probability that age misreporting at age 60 will mean that this study includes some individuals who were actually in their mid to late 50s,[18] and omit others who claimed to be younger than they actually were. Moreover, it does not mean that the chronological age of 60 was necessarily associated in the contemporary mind with 'old age'. The fact that a person had reached the age of 60, of course, as Ottaway has pointed out, does not necessarily mean that he or she thought of themselves as elderly, or was perceived by others as such. In a society lacking a rigid notion of a retirement age, and where age reporting could be often less than exact, definitions of the elderly would have been subjective: 'with respect to the dilapidation of time, much will depend on constitution, mode of life, and climate: some are worn out at 60, whilst others at 70 are healthy and vigorous'.[19] Age reporting itself, of course, is 'subject to social pressures and community conventions. No "standard correction" of the nineteenth century figures … can be suggested'.[20] However, a comparison of age at death as given in workhouse registers with that given in the sextons' accounts of age of death from 1747 to 1758 reveals that they are very close. Of 83 people who died in the workhouse during this period and who can be connected with the sextons' burials, 75 had the same age of death in both registers, and for three it was only one year apart. At one level this is to be expected, as the sextons may have received age of death from the workhouse administrators. However, as will be shown, many who died in the workhouse had entered it on several previous occasions, and on each occasion they had given their age. These are usually internally consistent – somebody who claimed to be aged 62 on entering the workhouse would claim to be 65 when he entered it three years later. It is possible to demonstrate cases from other multi-linkage exercises using settlement examinations that some ascribed ages at entry were almost certainly exaggerated, but these were not very numerous and will not distort the figures to any significant extent.

9.3 Size of the population

Figure 9.1 presents some rough estimates of the total population of the parish, using baptism totals corrected for under-registration caused by the growth of religious dissent, delayed baptism and other factors. Three estimates have been calculated, using notional birth rates of between 30 and 35 per 1000. The lower the birth rate, the higher the estimated population. Although this technique is defensible, the reader should be aware that we have no direct evidence for the birth rate in eighteenth-century London. It is thought, however, that this range of population estimates provides reasonable approximations. The parish seems to have experienced a modest decline in population, from around 30,000–35,000 at the beginning of our period, to 22,000–25,000 in the late 1750s, and then a gradual recovery such that the population seems to have recovered to its original size by the 1820s. These figures are probably within the right general range, although they probably exaggerate growth in the nineteenth century. Our population estimates for 1801 range from 24,095 to 28,111, with the mid-point population being 25,948 . The 1801 census population was 27,437 suggesting that estimates based on the lower end birth rates are to be preferred.[21]

How many elderly people were there in this population? Landers has made ingenious estimates that suggest that, throughout the eighteenth century, between 5 and 6 per cent of London's inhabitants were aged

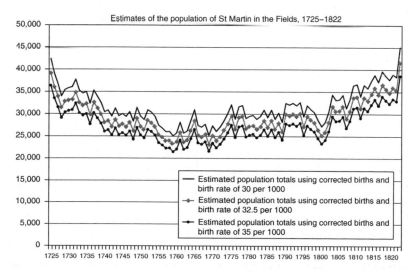

Figure 9.1 Estimates of the population of St Martin-in-the-Fields, 1725–1822

60 and over. This is significantly lower than that found in provincial England, where Wrigley and Schofield's estimates suggest that around 10 per cent of England's population in the late seventeenth and early eighteenth century were over 60. The age structure reflected the heavy immigration into London, and also, Landers estimates, a net *outflow* of people in the older age groups. London, then, may well have exported some of its older inhabitants.[22] The number of elderly inhabitants obviously track the changes in the overall population. Applied to the estimates above, this would suggest that there might, depending on the period, have been between about 1200 to perhaps 2000 elderly inhabitants in this urban district. Although small in percentage terms, the elderly still represented a sizeable welfare problem in the early modern metropolis.

9.4   Admission rates: How many elderly entered the workhouse?

The workhouse contained a cross section of the pauper population throughout the period. During the entire period the elderly formed between 6 per cent and 17 per cent of all individual admissions. The fluctuations are driven by the changing proportions of other age groups admitted.[23] Of course, the age composition of the workhouse *at any one point in time* cannot be deduced from these figures. As we demonstrate below, since the elderly stayed longer in the workhouse than younger age groups, they made up a larger proportion of the resident population than the proportions admitted would suggest.

As was the case at earlier ages, females predominated in elderly admissions, although there is a suggestion that this was beginning to change in the early nineteenth century when more elderly men were admitted. Our figures suggest there were, on average, between 40 and 60 males admitted per 100 females for most decades in the eighteenth century. It was during the early nineteenth century that the proportion of males aged 15–59 was rising among workhouse admissions, itself a complex procedure that needs to be analysed separately. From what we know of workhouses under the Old Poor Law, this female surplus was not unusual.[24]

9.5   The elderly in the workhouse

The elderly residents of the workhouse were even less likely to stay for long periods than the elderly inhabitants of the nineteenth-century

Bedford workhouse studied by David Thomson.[25] More than three quarters of the elderly stayed less than one year and many stayed only a month or so. Around 40 per cent of elderly inmates died rather than left the house. Females stayed a little longer than males in the workhouse, and were significantly more likely to stay for relatively long periods of time.[26] Data of this sort demonstrates that, even for the elderly, stays in the workhouse could often be relatively brief, and that long stays were the exception rather than the rule. What such an analysis cannot show, however, is that some elderly *individuals*, like other paupers, as our case studies below demonstrate, could be *serial* users of the workhouse, using the accommodation flexibly as their circumstances required.

Since we have admission dates, discharge dates and thus lengths of stay in the institution for most of the inmates, it is possible to consider the nature of the workhouse population in more detail. Here we use the workhouse admissions and discharge registers to generate snapshots of the workhouse at particular points in time. Some selected 'reconstructed censuses' are given below in Figure 9.2. This method is obviously sensitive to missing information, and the dates have been selected from periods when the workhouse registers are thought to be particularly reliable. They have also been tested against known summary totals of workhouse inmates, when the agreement is encouragingly close. Nonetheless, there must be some small margin for error since not all inmates had the necessary age information, and a few could not be included in the reconstructed 'census' because either their admission or discharge dates were missing.

Clearly, as suspected, the proportion of elderly in the workhouse admission registers is not a good guide to the proportion of the institution's

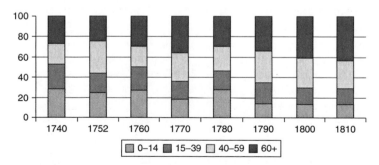

Figure 9.2 Estimated age distribution of workhouse population, 1 January, selected years
Source: Workhouse admission and discharge registers, 1725–1824.[27]

inmates they comprised at any one point in time. In fact, the elderly formed between one quarter and one third of workhouse inmates throughout the eighteenth century, and this proportion seems to have increased to over 40 per cent in the early nineteenth century. The proportion of inmates who were elderly increased still further in the first half of the nineteenth century.[28] It is likely that this ageing of the workhouse population owes something to new policies relating to the care of children and infants in the late eighteenth-century workhouse. Children were increasingly sent out to nurse, school or apprenticeship, and this naturally reduced their share of the workhouse population and might itself be one reason why the number of inmates in the institution was falling in the early nineteenth century. However, the increase in the early nineteenth century in the proportion of inmates in the 60+ age group was not matched by any increase in the 40–59 age group. This suggests that, for some reason, relatively more elderly men and women were entering the workhouse in that period, or perhaps (given that their proportion in the admissions registers do not increase that much in the early nineteenth century) they were staying for relatively longer.

An unusually detailed survey of the poor survives for St James Westminster, a neighbouring parish (Table 9.1).[29] St James workhouse had 31.6 per cent of its inmates aged over 60, entirely comparable with St Martin's at the same date. In fact, the age structure of St James's workhouse was entirely comparable with that of St Martin's in 1790. Our

Table 9.1   Age distribution of inmates in St James Workhouse, c. 1797

Age	Number and age of poor persons in the workhouse of St James, January 1797	%
Not exceeding 10	51	7.2
10–20	61	8.6
20–30	90	12.6
30–40	79	11.1
40–50	79	11.1
50–60	128	18.0
60–70	129	18.1
70–80	76	10.7
80–90	18	2.5
90–100	2	0.3
	713	100.0

Source: Sketch of the State of the Children of the Poor in the Year 1756, and of the Present State and Management of all the Poor in the Parish of St James Westminster, in January 1797 (London, 1797), p. 16.

reconstructed censuses, and the St James survey, thus confirm what others have found in London and elsewhere, that the workhouse usually accommodated paupers of all ages.[30]

9.6 The impact of the workhouse on the elderly population of the parish

It is also possible to relate a fuller version of the information used to construct Figure 9.2 to the age distribution for London as suggested by Landers. In essence, this relates the estimated number of individuals in the workhouse to our estimated size and age structure of the population. Readers should be aware that the figures here are estimates only. They depend on our estimates of the size of the total population of the parish (which themselves derive from another series of plausible assumptions about the underlying birth rate) as well as the applicability of Landers' estimates of the age distribution of the population. They are also maximum estimates, since they are based on winter occupancy, when workhouse admissions tended to be at their highest.

Table 9.2 represents an estimate of the percentage of each age group in the population housed in the workhouse at a number of selected dates in our period. This is in some ways more telling that looking only at the composition of the workhouse population in isolation. Table 9.2 reflects a number of things. For one thing, it represents the increased capacity of the workhouse after a rebuilding in the early 1770s. Following this

Table 9.2 Estimated percentage of the population of the parish in different age groups in the workhouse

	1740	1752	1760	1770	1780	1790	1800	1810
0–4	0.7%	0.6%	0.5%	0.2%	0.7%	0.5%	0.8%	0.8%
5–9	2.7%	1.9%	2.2%	1.8%	4.7%	2.0%	1.7%	0.9%
10–19	2.6%	1.4%	2.5%	1.8%	3.1%	2.0%	0.7%	0.5%
20–29	0.8%	0.6%	0.7%	0.5%	1.1%	1.3%	0.9%	0.5%
30–39	0.9%	0.5%	0.9%	0.7%	1.2%	1.3%	1.0%	0.8%
40–49	0.9%	1.2%	1.0%	1.4%	2.1%	2.2%	1.6%	1.4%
50–59	2.0%	2.5%	1.9%	2.9%	3.8%	5.2%	4.0%	2.5%
60–69	6.5%	3.7%	6.7%	9.4%	13.3%	15.7%	14.4%	10.2%
70–79	10.6%	9.9%	11.3%	15.1%	17.7%	20.0%	22.8%	16.7%

Source: These avowedly rough estimates have been produced by applying the age distributions estimated by Landers, *Death and the Metropolis*, p. 180, to the five-year average populations for the mid-point populations in Figure 9.1 for the particular census years. The resulting age distributions have then been compared to the raw number of inmates in the 'reconstructed censuses' shown in Figure 9.2.

growth in capacity more paupers could be housed at any one point in time. Most age groups thus see a jump between 1770 and 1780. This growth in workhouse capacity makes it still more striking that younger age groups (5–9 and 10–19) were less frequently found in the workhouse *per capita* after 1790 than before.[31] There was little apparent long term change in the representation of those in their 20s, 30s and 40s and even 50s. It also seems clear that more of those in their 60s and 70s would find themselves in the workhouse in the late eighteenth and early nineteenth century than ever before. It is worth noting, however, that these estimates, for what they are worth, do underline one important point, returned to later, namely that the vast majority of elderly people, even in the late eighteenth and early nineteenth centuries, lived in their own homes.

9.7   Leaving the workhouse

The reasons why the elderly *left* the workhouse reveal a great deal about their experience of the institution, their attitudes towards it, and some interesting things about their physical capabilities.[32] The workhouse registers provide some detail of the discharges of around ten and a half thousand paupers who left the institution aged 60 or more.[33] Some of the reasons were clearly ambiguous or tell us relatively little, and others may often have been simply a matter of phrasing. However, some are more revealing. Clearly and unsurprisingly, the biggest single cause of discharge was death, accounting for 43.3 per cent of all those leaving the workhouse aged 60 or over. However, this statistic also confirms that the majority of elderly people were not making a one-way trip – the workhouse did *not* act solely as a hospice for the elderly. The elderly were as likely as those in younger age groups to leave by absconding or 'absenting' themselves from the workhouse without permission. In most cases the reason was given solely as 'absented', but rare detail sometimes suggests an occasionally independent spirit. The 74-year-old John Orange, admitted in September 1800, 'ran away' in January of the following year. He 'got out at the Soup Kitchen by forcing himself by the cook'.[34] Similarly, Robert Cole, aged 64 on his admittance, in 1802 'forced his way out at the Dust Hole'.[35] Opportunistic flight occurred in the case of Mary Burk, a 60-year-old woman admitted in 1797; after eight months in the workhouse she, 'Eloped at ye Burying Gate while open in the morning'.[36] An element of desperation is suggested by the case of Dennis Coleman, a 60-year-old admitted in 1799, who broke out after less than two months residence. He 'Eloped by Forcing & Breaking the Locks of the two Doors leading to Hemmings Row'.[37] In another case a relative connived at the escape from workhouse life of Thomas Hitchens, a pauper then in his early 70s who, in 1808, 'absented with his Daughter who appy'd to have him out for the Day only'.[38] In only one case was an elderly person recorded as having left upon leave with workhouse property – an enduring problem in the eighteenth century. This occurred when the 65-year-old Mary Wilson absented herself in 1791 and 'took away a pr. of sheets with her'.[39]

Most recorded departures from the workhouse were less contentious. Most of the elderly, if they did not die, could expect to be simply discharged. From 1785, however, the workhouse authorities seem to have introduced a formal 'leave of absence' scheme, which was applied disproportionately to elderly residents. Such paupers were recorded as being discharged 'upon leave'. These individuals were allowed out for short periods, from a few days or weeks to a couple of months, presumably to visit friends or relatives, or to take up temporary employment. Only twice was a particular reason for this leave actually specified. Sarah Moxham, a 66-year-old inmate, left for a month 'upon leave to nurse a Lying in Woman by Order of Mr. Robinson Overseer'. Sarah is an example of someone with a historic connection to the workhouse. She had first entered as a 49-year-old woman in 1780, had returned in 1784 and thereafter spent the rest of her life in the institution, with only three short absences. She died 'aged' in the workhouse in 1798.[40] Mary Parsons, after a nine year stay, left 'Upon leave to the Dispensary in Nassau Street' in 1806 at the age of 65. Even the very old were granted such periods of formal leave. Thomas Laugher, said to be 83 years old at his first admission in 1798, was granted four formal periods of leave between 1799 and 1804, and was discharged to some unknown destination in 1805 at the age of 89.[41] Not only were the elderly more likely to be granted periods of leave – they were probably allowed more freedom of movement on a daily basis. Just as Ottaway suggested for the parishes she investigated, greater freedom of movement, the ability to come and go – known in St Martin's as liberty 'of the gate' – seem to have been a particular perk of old age. In December 1795 it was noted 'That no pauper be permitted to go out (except the Aged) only on Saturday Afternoon', suggesting more leeway for elderly inhabitants.[42]

Where did the elderly paupers go when they left the workhouse? Most of the discharged or dismissed must have returned to lodgings in the neighbourhood. Some elderly residents returned to outdoor relief, as discussed below. We do know that a few were sent to, or taken out by, relatives, although this is rarely made explicit and must have occurred far more often than the discharge registers suggest. It is noticeable that few of these elderly sent to relatives had been long in the workhouse, only three had been resident more than a year before being taken out, and 23 out of the 30 had been resident for less than three months. Mary Bailey, aged 75, admitted to the workhouse in October 1760, was 'Took out by her two Daughters the same Day'.[43] There was also a marked gender difference: of the 30 cases where the elderly were discharged explicitly to relatives, only four were men. All of these males were relatively young (60 or 61 at their discharge), and of these, three were sent home to their wives and one to his sister in Hampstead.[44] Women taken out by, or sent to, relatives had a greater age range (between 60 and 87 at discharge). This suggests that women might have had a greater economic utility at more advanced ages to those that took them in, performing tasks such as nursing, house-keeping or childcare that older men were not expected to fulfill. That said, one of these cases was clearly just a short visit lasting one week, and another elderly woman, 64-year-old Alice Durrance, was 'Took out by Her Daughter to be sent to Abthorp in Northam[pton]shire' early in 1741.[45] Those relatives taking in the 26 elderly women from the workhouse were mostly their own daughters (15) and sons (6), with only a few going to husbands (2), nieces (2) and a sister (1). Filial duty probably played some part in the care of elderly women, although reciprocity was probably expected, given the likely limited resources of their children. This is also suggested, as noted above, by the fact that few elderly men seem to have been discharged to relatives.

9.8   The outdoor poor: Payments to the aged poor living in their own homes, 1725–1824

The workhouse was by no means the only method by which elderly people were relieved by the parish. Although most parishes in eighteenth-century London operated workhouses by the mid-century, they all retained outdoor relief as well. The overseers of the poor in St Martin's, like all London parishes which erected workhouses in the eighteenth century, never abandoned outdoor relief. Such relief provided by overseers of the poor, probably by the early 1730s, had come to take the form either of regular payments, or less regular, casual payments. In September 1795, Frederick Eden could therefore report that

> The poor of this parish are partly relieved at home, and partly maintained in the work-house in Castle Street, Leicester Fields. There are,

at present, about 240 weekly out-pensioners, besides a considerable number of Poor on the casual list.[46]

St Martin's, even at the end of the eighteenth century, when the tide of opinion had swung against indoor relief, was a parish which relied unusually heavily on indoor relief – some 60 per cent of its 'permanent poor' receiving relief were in the workhouse at the time of the 1803 returns.[47] Most other London parishes relieved proportionately more people in their own homes. The balance between indoor and outdoor relief, of course, must have altered over time. This is demonstrably so in the case of St Martin's. Numbers relieved indoors varied according to both the prevailing levels of hardship, workhouse capacity, local poor law policy regarding workhouse admissions and one presumes the current state of parochial finances.

St James, Westminster, adjacent to St Martin's,[48] has left an unusually detailed picture of all those receiving poor relief which helps to illustrate the balance struck between indoor and outdoor relief. In addition to the published survey of inmates in its workhouse noted above (Table 9.1), it also counted different kinds of relief given to the elderly.[49]

There are a number of interesting features about this survey. First, it is clear that, at least in this parish, the elderly were somewhat more likely to be relieved in their own homes, than in the parish workhouse. Table 9.3 summarises their experience. The difference was not that large – 57 per cent of the elderly on parish relief were relieved outdoors rather than in the workhouse. Second, in percentage terms, the distribution of the ages of

Table 9.3 The relief of the aged poor in St James, Westminster, c. 1797

Age group	Indoor (work-house)	%	Outdoor (pension-ers on weekly allow-ances)	%	Ratio of out-door to indoor	Percentage of all those aged 60 and over on poor relief relieved outdoors	Total in age group on parish relief
60–70	129	57.3%	175	59.7%	1.36	58%	304
70–80	76	33.8%	94	32.1%	1.24	55%	170
80+	20	8.9%	24	8.2%	1.20	55%	44
	225	100.0%	293	100.0%	1.30	57%	519

Source: Calculated from *Sketch of the State of the Children of the Poor*, pp. 16–18. We have not included here those few inmates of lunatic asylums or wives of militiamen who might have been aged 60 and over.

those of the aged poor on indoor relief was very similar to those on out-door relief, at least in the harsh conditions of the 1790s. To understand the total experience of the elderly, we clearly need to know more about those on out relief. Those on out relief fell below what might be termed the minimum level of destitution that would have got them admitted to the workhouse. This is suggested by the fact that those on such outdoor pensions, the Ancient Poor, otherwise described as 'the Old, Blind, and Paralytic People' had their maximum pension *capped* at two shillings a week, 'except their case is attended with particular Circumstances of Distress'.[50] The St James survey, by itself, demonstrates quite clearly that studies that concentrate only on workhouse populations would give a misleading impression of the scope and extent of poor relief, just as studies that ignore the impact of workhouses on levels of pensions paid are almost certainly deeply flawed. So long as there was room in the work-house, the cost of keeping a person there set a ceiling for pensions.[51]

Unfortunately we do not have any record of the names of parish pensioners relieved by the parish after 1780.[52] Individuals receiving regular weekly allowances, pensions in all but name, are identified in the accounts by overseers as early as 1733.[53] What figures we do have suggest that there may have been an inverse relationship between the number of workhouse inmates at any one point in time, and the number of pen-sioners (sometimes with dependents) relieved in their own homes. The rebuilding of the workhouse in the early 1770s seems to have resulted in a fall in the number of recorded parish pensioners, as workhouse capacity virtually doubled. More of the aged and infirm must have been brought into the workhouse following the rebuilding.[54] Eden's reported figure of 240 as the number of out-pensioners in the parish in 1795, was at a time when numbers relieved in the workhouse were falling. The highpoint of workhouse capacity actually coincides with 'Gilbert's Act' in 1782. That Act is thought to have reflected a swing of opinion against workhouses and encouraged and facilitated the growth of out-door relief. Certainly there must have been a resurgence in outdoor pen-sions after 1780 in the parish, after what seems to have been a dramatic fall in those receiving regular outdoor relief in the previous decade. The relationship between the number of those on outdoor and indoor relief is not a straightforward matter, given the possible changes in the size and age structure of the population of the district, the vagaries of local poor law policy and fluctuations in the health of parochial finances.[55] Nonetheless, it is clear that those who study poor relief must be aware of the dynamic relationship between indoor and outdoor relief. More work is needed to illuminate this important subject.[56]

How many of those who received regular outdoor relief were 'aged'? The short answer is that we do not usually know, since age information was rarely given in the overseers accounts. However, the 1749 listings noted that 74 pensioners out of 204 were 'aged'.[57] Our 'reconstructed' census for 1752 suggests an elderly population in the workhouse of 88 persons; this suggests that just over half the elderly relieved by the parish were taken into the workhouse, the rest being relieved by parish pensions. However, since the latter figure *excludes* the almswomen of the parish and others on endowed charities, this must mean that, at least in the middle of the eighteenth century, the experience of the majority of elderly people who had contact with the local welfare system would have been outdoor, rather than indoor relief. A similar situation was evident in St James where over half the elderly relieved lived in their own homes (Table 9.3). However, this situation was certainly not a constant. The balance in St Martin's seems to have shifted in favour of indoor relief in the 1770s and early 1780s, before reversing as numbers in the workhouse dropped again from the mid 1780s. The experience of the elderly pauper was far from being a constant in the eighteenth century.[58]

9.9 Almswomen

In addition to outdoor pension payments, there were also groups of almswomen occupying the parish almshouses. There were two groups of these. The 'overseers' almswomen' numbered about 40 or so, until 1762 when the number seems to have been reduced to 32 or less (although on a number of occasions more women than received payments were listed). Overseers' almswomen received 8s. per month. The 'churchwardens' almswomen' numbered between 27 and 32 individuals throughout the eighteenth century and received pensions of equivalent value. Their pension was increased to 8s. a month on petition in 1726.[59] So, at least 55 to 80 or so women, most of them elderly, all supposedly of respectable backgrounds, were being relieved out of the workhouse as almswomen in the local almshouses, in addition to others who might have been relieved in their own homes.[60] A comparison of workhouse and almshouse population reveals that in fact there seems to have been relatively little overlap between these groups.

9.10 Ad-hoc poor relief payments

The most difficult task, for all poor law studies, is analysing the hundreds, sometimes thousands, of 'extraordinary' payments made on a daily or weekly basis to the parish poor. The reasons for such payments, recorded in overseer's accounts, are rarely given in any detail, and the recipients are often hard to identify or link to other records because they usually lack supporting detail. Even more seriously, in St Martin's, after the 1750s, there are apparently no itemised lists of such payments recorded in the overseer's accounts at all – those keeping the accounts merely summarised such payments. What can be stated, however, is that some elderly people would have received these casual small-scale payments, in addition to those who were identified as receiving regular allowances in the accounts. These would have been paid particularly at times of crisis, notably illness. The volume of such casual payments fluctuated considerably, like the numbers on regular outdoor relief. There seems to have been a surge in expenditure on the casual and settled poor in the early nineteenth century. In 1726–7, at a time when the workhouse was relatively small, and when there were few individuals clearly identified as receiving regular relief, the overseers of the poor were making thousands of these payments to large numbers of people. Since the accounts in this year contained more than the usual sparse detail, it is possible to estimate that some 1378 individual payments out of 4729 (29 per cent) were made to poor described at least once in these accounts as 'aged'.[61]

9.11   The elderly and the infirm: Some case studies

Poor relief policy and workhouse capacity clearly affected the lives of the elderly. Only very detailed research can uncover why particular aged individuals were admitted into the workhouse rather than relieved in their own homes, but it is likely that illness and disability, or perhaps the lack of a partner or carer, explain their different fates. At the point where the parish authorities considered that their independent existence was not economically viable, they would be admitted to the workhouse. Another possibility that might have applied to some of those maintained on outdoor relief was that the more 'respectable', perhaps the previous rate payers, could have been more likely to be funded to maintain an independent life. Occasional cases of this can be found in St Martin's, as discussed below. It would require a formidable linkage exercise to establish how discrete these two populations were. Both the overseers accounts and the churchwarden and overseers' minutes make it clear that individual payments were made routinely to adult paupers following a stay in the workhouse – the workhouse was part of a larger system of poor relief.[62] How often did those aged on regular out relief enter the workhouse? How often were they granted regular allowances, as opposed to one off payments, on leaving? For a tentative answer to some of these questions, case studies can be instructive.[63]

To begin with, it is clear that there *was* movement between the workhouse and those on regular outdoor relief. This can be demonstrated most clearly by considering the following case studies. In January 1767, a widow by the unusual name of Feveral Blinkhorn was admitted for the first time to the St Martin's workhouse. She had been examined under the settlement laws on the day of her entry, when she established a settlement in the parish by virtue of her marriage to her husband, who had rented a house of the appropriate value for two years in the parish 12 years earlier.[64] Feveral stayed just over five months and was discharged from the workhouse in June 1767. By the following year she was receiving a pension payment of 12*d*. a week, was resident in the Bedfordbury ward of the parish, and remained on the pension at that rate until 1773. In that year she received pension payments for only part of the year, which must have been because in November 1773 she was admitted into the workhouse again, this time giving her age as 64. Feveral was discharged from the workhouse after just under six months in May 1774. She appears again as receiving a weekly pension of 1*s*. a week in 1775 for 24 weeks, but this pension too stopped at her last and final admission to the workhouse in January 1776, at which point she was said to be 70. Feveral stayed almost exactly three years in the workhouse, dying there at the end of January 1779, when she was buried at parish expense, 'aged' and then said to be 78.[65] Apart from apparently ageing 28 years in only 12 actual years (such exaggerated ageing was not usually so blatant), Feveral's case illustrates nicely the important point that the aged poor could move between outdoor and indoor relief with some flexibility.

Another case where workhouse and outdoor relief were balanced would be that of a woman called Charity Pollard, born in 1725. This is an unusual case in that one can track Charity from her marriage to her death at a (possibly) relatively advanced age. She regularly entered the workhouse, and regularly received outdoor relief, but in later middle age she appears to have been relieved outdoors, receiving some clothing. In 1765 she appears as receiving a modest pension of 12*d*. a week, which she continued to receive until at least 1779, when our information ends. Charity spent the last 11 years of her life in the workhouse, since she (or someone with her relatively unusual forename) was admitted into the workhouse in November 1783, giving her age as 78 (rather than 58 or thereabouts). She died in the workhouse early in 1794, at the ascribed age of 88 (rather than 68 or thereabouts).[66] Like Feveral Blinkhorn, Charity might have exaggerated her age to gain entry to the workhouse, although it might also have been the case that she appeared to be physically older than she really was to her contemporaries.[67]

David Bevan was another long term parish pensioner whose case is similarly instructive was receiving a weekly pension of 18*d*. per week from 1750 until at least 1778. He had apparently no other contact with the parish relief system and there is no record of his death in the parish.[68] Another study demonstrates that it was equally possible to have contact *only* with the workhouse, perhaps especially if one's habits and behaviour were somewhat suspect. Charity Bevan (no known relation to David) who had an atypically long career in (and out of) the workhouse, never seems to have received any form of regular pension. She was admitted to the workhouse no less than 36 times between 1749 and 1768. She was unusual, too, in being subject to *four* settlement examinations. Her first, which is incomplete, took place in July 1726, when she was described as a 'singlewoman'. On oath, Charity said 'that she is about one & twenty years of age, and that she was never married', but 'possessed of child or children'.[69] Charity's second examination took place on the day of her recorded admission to the workhouse in July 1749, and for a third time, after her next admittance to the workhouse, in November of the same year. On this occasion, Charity was actually passed from the parish of Camberwell as a vagrant, which suggests an enduring problem with her settlement, or her ability to afford lodgings, or both. Her last extant examination took place on the day she was admitted on the first Day of November 1755, when she was described as 'aged 56 years destitute of lodging'. Unlike Feveral Blinkhorn and Charity Pollard, Bevan's ascribed ages increase appropriately with time, such that on her last admission to the workhouse she was described as 67 years of age, if anything a slight understatement. It is clear that the workhouse must have been the chief focus of Charity's life in this period. In fact she spent nearly half (47.8 per cent) of the period 1749 and 1769 in the workhouse, with an average length of stay of just over three months and a median stay of 56 days. Charity Bevan is a good example of a pauper with a tarnished reputation, itinerant and wandering habits, possibly even a local vagrant who never qualified for a regular pension, but was seen as a proper workhouse inmate.[70]

9.12   Conclusion: The elderly and the workhouse in the eighteenth century

This essay suggests the following important points about the experience of the elderly, and has wider implications for other poor law studies.

First, it is clear that, from the point of view of the elderly population of this large urban district, the chances of admission were relatively low. Most elderly people survived in their own homes, even in a parish like St Martin's where the workhouse was an integral part of the poor relief system. Elderly people could seek alternative welfare support, and many must have got by on the resources of friends, family and private charity. A related conclusion would be that many, almost certainly the majority, must have got by on the resources of friends, family and private charity rather than having any need to resort to public relief.[71] Experience of the workhouse, when it came, would often be for relatively short periods of time. For about four in ten of the elderly admitted it was a one-way trip – in some of those cases the workhouse was simply acting as an infirmary for the sick and dying aged paupers. For most, however, the workhouse was used with some flexibility, as part of that increasingly familiar strategy of 'makeshift and mend'.[72] For some elderly paupers, too, their experience of the workhouse was part of a larger engagement with the wider parochial welfare system. Cash doles might be juggled with periodic sojourns in the workhouse. The elderly were far from helpless pawns. We have noted a number of cases where the elderly worked, broke out of the workhouse, stole from fellow inmates or deliberately absented themselves. There is an ambiguity too in how the elderly experienced the workhouse. Separation of married couples was consistently practiced, but in other ways the workhouse regime of the later eighteenth century may have provided a few comforts, more freedom to come and go, possibly extra food or drink and of course, medical help from a resident apothecary and care from a ward nurse.

Another conclusion must be that the experience of the elderly, like that of all paupers, was far from uniform over time. As Ottaway has also found, experience of workhouse life and interaction with the poor law might change over time as local circumstances and policies developed or changed. The proportion of elderly residents increased over time, and the workhouse as an institution came to hold an increasing number of elderly residents in the later eighteenth century. In a very real sense, to understand how the elderly were accommodated and how their experience of the workhouse changed over time, we need to know more about how local policies dictated who was admitted and what alternatives were deployed.[73]

Lastly, this chapter suggests something of the complexity of studying poor relief before 1834. Those who look at the levels of pension payments, or who analyse the elderly inmates of eighteenth-century workhouses, need to pay much attention to the dynamic relationship that could exist between different parts of local welfare systems. Our cases studies by themselves suggest the very different histories and experiences that different pauper strategies and needs might produce at the local level.

Notes

The quote in the chapter title is from Frederick Eden's description of the treatment of the elderly in the Liverpool workhouse in 1795, quoted in P. Thane, *Old Age in English History: Past Experiences, Present Issues* (Oxford: Oxford University Press, 2000), p. 117.

This chapter presents some findings from our ESRC-funded project 'The Lives of the Poor in the West End of London, 1724–1867', RES-000-23-0250. We are grateful for that support. We are also indebted to our splendid research associates, John Black, Peter Jones and Rhiannon Thompson, who collected most of the data on which this chapter is based. We would also like to thank the participants of various seminars and conferences who have offered useful suggestions and comments.

1. N. Goose, 'Poverty, Old Age and Gender in Nineteenth-Century England: The Case of Hertfordshire', *Continuity and Change* 20:3, (2005), 379, nn.1–2 lists some of these.
2. S. R. Ottaway, *The Decline of Life: Old Age in Eighteenth-Century England* (Cambridge: Cambridge University Press, 2004).
3. *Ibid.*, p. 213.
4. *Ibid.*, p. 227.
5. *Ibid.*, p. 248.
6. *Ibid.*, pp. 250–9.
7. *Ibid.*, p. 260.
8. *Ibid.*, pp. 251, 261.
9. *Ibid.*, pp. 265–6.
10. *Ibid.*, pp. 270–2. Thomson reports similar perks for those classified as 'old' in the nineteenth century, D. Thomson, 'Workhouse to Nursing Home: Residential Care of Elderly People in England since 1840', *Ageing and Society* 3, (1983), 54–5.
11. Ottaway, *Decline of Life*, p. 275.
12. Thomson, 'Workhouse to Nursing Home', p. 46–51.
13. L. H. Lees, 'The Survival of the Unfit: Welfare Policies and Family Maintenance in Nineteenth-Century London', in P. Mandler (ed.), *The Uses of Charity: The Poor on Relief in the 19th-Century Metropolis* (Philadelphia: University of Pennsylvania Press, 1990), p. 75.
14. Thomson, 'Workhouse to Nursing Home', pp. 46–7.
15. Lees, 'The Survival of the Unfit, p. 73.
16. Thomson, 'Workhouse to Nursing Home', p. 51.
17. Ottaway, *Decline of Life*, p. 59.
18. Thomson points out that it may have been advantageous to claim old age when entering a workhouse, in order to qualify for a range of benefits, Thomson, 'Workhouse to Nursing Home', pp. 54–5.

19. W. Black, *An Arithmetical and Medical Analysis of the Diseases and Mortality of the Human Species*, 2nd edn (1789), p. 227.

20. D. Thomson 'Age Reporting by the Elderly and the Nineteenth Century Censes', *Local Population Studies* 25, (1980), 24. However, a comparison of age of death as given in workhouse registers with that given in the sextons' accounts of age of death from 1747 to 1758 reveals that they are very close.

21. The 1801 Census figure includes the population living in the Verges of the Courts of St James and Whitehall. In 1821 Westminster and the City had an age profile different from the rest of London. The dependency ratio in Westminster was below that of the rest of London, the reproduction level was low, and there is a suggestion of low nuptiality. If couples married, they frequently left Westminster for other parts of London. This is confirmed in 1841, using the Fifth Annual Report of the Registrar General giving all births 1840–2, compared with the 1841 census. Westminster and the City had a CBR of 25.3, the rest of London had 31.1. (L. D. Schwarz, 'Hanoverian London: The Making of a Service Town' in P. Clark & R. Gillespie (eds), *Two Capitals: Dublin and London, 1500–1840* (Oxford: Oxford University Press, 2001) pp. 93–110.

22. J. Landers, *Death and the Metropolis: Studies in the Demographic History of London, 1650–1830* (Cambridge: Cambridge University Press, 1993), pp. 180–3. However, Westminster parishes, from the evidence of nineteenth-century censuses, may have had their own characteristics. The proportion of population aged over 60 in 1821 was about half a percentage point below London as a whole, not enough to make a significant difference to the conclusions of this chapter. See Schwarz, 'Hanoverian London'.

23. The workhouse registers of St Marylebone for 1769–81 studied by Alysa Levene suggest that a lower proportion of elderly were admitted than in St Martin's, although her figures are not exactly comparable, A. Levene, 'Children, Childhood and the Workhouse: St Marylebone, 1769–1781', *London Journal* 33:1, (2008), 45.

24. A. Tomkins, *The Experience of Urban Poverty, 1723–82: Parish, Charity and Credit* (Manchester: Manchester University Press, 2006) p. 47 suggests a male:female ratio of between 2.5 and 5.0 in four Oxford workhouses in the 1750s, Shrewsbury and York in the 1740s, Chester in the 1730s. In the second quarter of the eighteenth century, the parishes of St. Giles-in-the-Fields, London, Chelsea, Middlesex and Cullompton, Devon had adult women outnumbering adult men by more than three to one; similar ratios applied to those over 55 years old, T. Hitchcock, 'The English Workhouse: A Study in Institutional Poor Relief in Selected Counties, 1696–1750' (Unpublished Oxford University D. Phil., 1985), p. 194. Ottaway, *Decline of Life*, p. 260 finds a fairly even sex ratio for the over 60s in Ovenden, but Ovenden may have been unusual in having a fairly even sex ratio until the 1790s. Terling's elderly do not appear to have become feminised: *Ibid.*, p. 260. The gender ratio of admissions to St Marylebone's workhouse was similar to St Martin's. See Levene, 'Children and the Workhouse', p. 44.

25. Thomson, 'Workhouse to Nursing Home', p. 61.

26. For comparable data on length of stay for St Marylebone, see Levene, 'Children and the Workhouse', pp. 49–50.

27. Sample size: 1740–499; 1752–371; 1760–394; 1770–435; 1780–764; 1790–771; 1800–589; 1810–523.
28. The count for the 1841 census of St Martin's workhouse, taken in June 1841, revealed an institution where more than half of the inmates were 60 or over. TNA, HO 107/740/35/9/1-17.
29. *Sketch of the State of the Children of the Poor in the year 1756, and of the Present State and Management of all the Poor in the Parish of St James Westminster, in January 1797* (1797), p. 16.
30. The proportions of elderly in the London workhouses in the late eighteenth century were greater than those found in workhouses analysed by Steven King. See, King, *Poverty and Welfare in England, 1700–1850* (Manchester: Manchester University Press, 2000), pp. 161 and 205.
31. The falling number of children as a proportion of all inmates almost certainly owes a lot to the policy of sending young children out to nurse in the country until the age of 7 or 8 at which point 'the children are taken into the house, and taught a little reading, &c for 3 or 4 years, and then put out apprentices'. F. M. Eden, *State of the Poor* (1797), II, p. 440.
32. For some useful comparable information, with some similar findings, see Levene, 'Children and the Workhouse', pp. 48–9.
33. This analysis therefore does not include those paupers for whom an age at admission not given, and also excludes those entries which lack either an admission date or a discharge date. Age at discharge was calculated by adding length of stay to the original age at admission. This analysis is based on all the surviving workhouse registers, together with some day books, for the period 1725–1824.
34. WAC, F4022/316.
35. WAC, F4022/87.
36. WAC, F4022/24.
37. WAC, F4022/80.
38. WAC, F4022/207.
39. WAC, F4022/447.
40. WAC, F4078/295, F4022/271, 278, 280, 281. For her burial, see burial entry for 19/01/1798, WAC, 241.
41. WAC, F4022/248, 249, 250, 253, 255.
42. WAC, F2075/120.
43. WAC, F4075 (unpaginated).
44. WAC, F4081/167; F4081/166; F4075; F4022/370.
45. WAC, F4022/387; F4073 (unpaginated).
46. Eden, *State of the Poor*, II, p. 440. The authorities of St Martin's were the only ones that cooperated with Eden's survey, *Ibid.*, p. 442. It is not clear whether Eden's 'out-pensioners' include almswomen or other poor relieved by charitable gifts and endowments. Here it is assumed it does not.
47. *House of Commons Accounts and Papers* (1803–4), XIII, pp. 724–5.
48. St James was originally part of St Martin's. It became a separate parish in 1685.
49. *Sketch of the Children of the Poor in the Year 1756*, pp. 16–18.
50. *Ibid.*, p. 17. This key statement runs 'Besides the Poor maintained in the Workhouse, the Old, Blind, and Paralytic People, have a Weekly Allowance of One Shilling, One Shilling and Sixpence, and some Two Shillings

per Week out of it, but none more, except their Case is attended with particular Circumstances of Distress'.

51. R. M. Smith, 'Charity, Self-Interest and Welfare: Reflections from Demographic and Family History', in M. Daunton (ed.), *Charity, Self-Interest and Welfare in the English Past* (UCL Press, 1996), pp. 36–43.

52. In what follows, only parish pensioners have been counted. Almswomen (some of whom were paid by the Churchwardens) and 'sacrament' pensioners have been excluded.

53. WAC, F2223. This is a paper book entitled 'A Register of all the Poor receiving Collection within the Parish of St Martin in the fields for the year 1749'. From the early 1730s overseers' accounts begin to identify separately those receiving regular allowances, listing them in groups in two-month blocks, by the then eight wards of the parish. See, for example, F487 and F490. One of the first uses of the term 'pension' after the erection of the workhouse was in 1741, when the Overseers of New Street Ward listed 'Hannah Scott for two Months Pension 5s', WAC, F514/125.

   Document F270 'Lists of paupers in Suffolk Street and New Street wards, with their ages and the amounts of their weekly pensions' for 1769–70, taken on the eve of the workhouse reconstruction, is no longer extant.

54. The last reference to regular allowances to itemised 'settled poor' occurs in 1780: WAC, F577. Such payments thereafter would have been subsumed among the payments to the 'casual' poor, which were not itemised in the accounts. A book for 1785 thus refers to expenditure on 'sundry Casual & settled Poor Persons as Per Book will appear': WAC, F587.

55. Between 1772 and 1774 St. Martin's spent over twice as much on indoor as on outdoor relief – and this was before the major extension to the workhouse had been completed: 'Report from the Committee appointed to inspect and consider the Returns made by the Overseers of the Poor, in pursuance of Act of last Session', *Reports from the Committees of the House of Commons Printed by Order of the House and not inserted in the Journals* (1777), IX, 22.

56. R. M. Smith, 'Ageing and Well-Being in Early Modern England: Pension Trends and Gender Preferences under the English Old Poor Law *c.* 1650–1800', in P. Johnson & P. Thane (eds), *Old Age from Antiquity to Post-Modernity* (Routledge, 1998), pp. 87–90. Smith reports, for example, that the opening of a workhouse in Tavistock produced a 'sharp decline' in the number of pensioners on out relief and a reduction in their average value, *Ibid.*, pp. 89–90. The elderly poor received *weekly* outdoor relief that was usually around three quarters of a *day's* pay of a London labourer. David Thomson has consistently argued that the Old Poor Law could be quite generous. Here it was not. If the weekly cost of upkeep exceeded a day's pay for a labourer by very much, it was tempting for the authorities to switch to indoor relief. This is precisely what was happening in the neighbouring parish of St James which, as we have seen, was capping pensions at 2s. a week. More work is needed on the 'depressing' effect that workhouses had on outdoor relief payments. See also, D. Thomson, 'The Welfare of the Elderly in the Past: A Family or Community Responsibility?' in M. Pelling & R. M. Smith (eds), *Life, Death and the Elderly: Historical Perspectives* (Routledge, 1991), pp. 194–221; D. Thomson 'Welfare and the Historians', in L. Bonfield, R. M. Smith, & K. Wrightson (eds), *The World We Have Gained: Histories of Population and*

244 The Workhouse, the Elderly and the Poor Law

Social Structure. Essays Presented to Peter Laslett on his Seventieth Birthday (Oxford: Blackwell, 1986), pp. 355–78.

57. WAC, F2223.
58. King, Poverty and Welfare, pp. 141–226; Ottoway, Decline of Life.
59. WAC, F2006/233. In July 1726 it was 'Ordered and agreed that the pay or allowance of the Almswomen in the Almshouses in Hogg Lane paid by the Churchwardens be (upon their Petition) advanced to Eight shillings a month'.
60. There appears to be no eighteenth-century age listing of the parish almswomen. The 1841 Census Enumerator's Book lists 62 'almswomen' and a few nurses occupying the parish almshouses. Of these all but five were 60 or over. The modal age was 75. TNA, HO 107/740/35/9/1-3.
61. This brief analysis rests on a database of the 4729 payments in the 1726/7 Overseers' accounts, WAC, F462/153-329. The data entry was carried out by Dr John Black, to whom special thanks are due. It excludes payments made in connection with sending paupers to Hospitals.
62. Thus, for example, 65 paupers are described as receiving a small payment (most commonly between 6d. and one shilling) on being discharged or dismissed from the workhouse in 1741/2: WAC, 514/1-141.
63. The case studies that follow are based in the main on the following classes of record: all those receiving regular allowances or pensions in the overseers (from 1749) and churchwardens' accounts; all known workhouse inmates recorded in the admission and discharge registers; all those mentioned in settlement examinations 1725–95; all inmates listed in the extant Churchwardens and Overseers Minutes 1755–64, 1774–78, 1792–1820, all burials recorded in the Sexton's notebooks, 1747–1824. Unfortunately, many of the overseer's accounts from the 1740s and 1750s appear to have been lost. There is a gap in the workhouse registers, 1730–1736.
64. WAC, F5055/347.
65. For Feveral's pensions, workhouse career and burial, see respectively: WAC, F567, F563, F561, F559, F553; F4076/30, F4077/50, F4077/65; 419/237.
66. Documentation for Charity Pollard: (Workhouse admissions) WAC, F4007/201, F4007/199, F4080/317, F4005/122; (Examination) F5040/380; (Churchwardens' and Overseers' minutes) F2070/86, 170; (Pensions) F2223/35, F526/55, F529/120–123, F535/73, F547/(unpag), F549/(unpag), F551/(unpag), F553/(unpag), F559/(unpag), F561/(unpag), F563/(unpag), F565/(unpag), F567/(unpag), F569/(unpag), F571/(unpag), F573/50, F575/illeg.; (Sexton's Day books) 419/240.
67. Thomson points out that it may have been advantageous to claim old age when entering a workhouse, in order to qualify for a range of perks and benefits, Thomson, 'Workhouse to Nursing Home', pp. 54–5.
68. WAC, F526/28, 30, 29, F529/80-83, F535/63-64, F547/(unpag), F549/(unpag), F551/(unpag), F553/(unpag), F559/(unpag), F561/(unpag), F563/(unpag), F565/(unpag), F567/(unpag), F569/(unpag), F571/(unpag), F573/42.
69. WAC, F5019/274.
70. WAC, F5040/ 83, 243; F5046/408; F4007/ 20, 27, 29, 30, 32, 33, 35-38, F4008/67, 152, 157,159, 194, 222, F4075/155, F4076/ 14,16,17, 20, 23, 25, 28, 29,35.

71. This is something argued strongly by Paul Johnson for the later nineteenth century. The 'most important conclusion' of work on the relief of the aged 'is often overlooked – that for most of the time aged people were not dependent on public support at all'. See P. Johnson, 'Risk, Redistribution and Social Welfare in Britain from the Poor Law to Beveridge', in Daunton (ed.), *Charity, Self-Interest and Welfare*, pp. 237–8. A similar situation probably existed in the eighteenth century. If our population estimates are within the right area, in 1750 there would have been perhaps 27,000 people in the parish. The age distribution constructed by Landers would suggest that 6 per cent or so would have been 60 and over, that is about 1600 individuals. If we make the defensible estimate that in the mid-eighteenth century in St Martin's there were approximately 250 elderly people (60 and over) relieved by the parish in total (in the workhouse, by outdoor pensions and in the parish almshouses), this would suggest that about 15 or 16 per cent of the elderly in the parish were receiving regular public relief. Even if another 150 were getting *ad hoc* payments as 'extraordinary' poor, that would still mean that *three quarters* of elderly people in the parish were getting by without *any* recourse to public welfare.

72. S. King & A. Tomkins (eds), *The Poor in England 1700–1850: An Economy of Makeshifts* (Manchester: Manchester University Press, 2003).

73. See also the discussion in Tomkins, *Experience of Urban Poverty*, pp. 36–72, particularly 38–41.

10
The Parish Poor House in the Long Eighteenth Century

John Broad

The rapid population growth and urbanisation in the century after 1740 may be regarded as the progenitor of a first great national housing shortage and crisis in England. We tend to concentrate on the miserable housing conditions for migrants to the new English industrial towns, but in many respects the problem in the countryside was at least as bad, because rising population, combined with structural changes in agriculture through both enclosure and the enlargement of farms, produced immiseration among rural labouring families, particularly in southern and midland England. In villages and small towns the parish authorities were central to solving it.

While historians debate the question of whether settlement in a parish entitled a settled person to relief in that parish, it was uncontested that a person settled in that parish was entitled to be housed there. In 1775 Nathaniel Kent wrote, 'if it were not for this excellent law, which obliges parish offices to find habitations for their poor, I am sorry to remark that in many parishes, they would literally be driven into the open fields'. The law did not mean the inhabitant had a right to a house, but to be lodged according to their needs. In the late seventeenth century the parish frequently provided them with a house. Quarter sessions orders across many counties show JPs requiring parish officers to provide individuals and families with houses, imposing punitive rates of relief to support the family on the parish until they were housed.[1] The surviving building accounts in the overseers' accounts for two such parish-built houses in Shropshire and Huntingdonshire indicate that they could be very basic one or two-roomed single storey dwellings. The Shropshire example shown in Table 10.1 shows no evidence of a window in the one-room dwelling, nor even a proper hearth and chimney, but probably a clay-lined smoke vent and single stone for a hearth.[2]

Table 10.1 Accounts for building of Parish house at Shawbury (Shropshire), c. 1650

Pd to Bayly Pidgen for Timber to build A house for Mary Hayes	£0 13s. 4d.
Pd to William Houlbrooke & William Davis for one dayes worke to Cutte oute timber to builde the a foursaid house	£0 2s. 0d.
Pd for Windeinges* & for ye windeinge of the house	£0 4s. 8d.
Pd for powles to latte ye howse & for ye settinge of them onne	£0 0s. 6d.
Pd for Broome to thatch the said howse & for ye the Cutteinge of ye Broome	£0 2s. 0d.
Pd to the Thatcher & one to serve him	£0 2s. 2d.
Pd for the Carryinge of ye Broome & for Carryinge of Claye & to A labourer to helpe them	£0 2s. 4d.
Pd for daubinge the house	£0 5s. 8d.
Pd for getteinge of stones for ye Asler	£0 0s. 6d.
Pd for Bordes to make A doore	£0 2s. 8d.
Pd for hinges & nayles	£0 1s. 0d.
Pd for ye Carriage of ffowre loades of timber for ye afoursaid house	£0 6s. 0d.
Pd to Richard Howlbrooke & William Davis for Buildinge ye Widdow Hayes house	£0 12s. 0d.
Total	**£2 14s. 2d.**

In the eighteenth century, the increasing number and cost of poor families led parishes to explore alternatives to building houses. At the most basic level, they either paid the rent of families who otherwise might have been evicted through poverty, or rented houses for them. Government collected figures that show that over 5 per cent of total poor law expenditure nationally was put to this use in 1776, and in some counties — Lancashire and Herefordshire for example – over 10 per cent. Table 10.2 gives the respective figures for the 15 counties that have been surveyed for information about their parish cottages *c.* 1834.

Elsewhere, parishes embarked on purchases of existing houses. More radical was the use of poorhouses and workhouses, concentrating the poor in one place and managing them institutionally. Though the number of places, particularly larger villages and small towns, adopting a workhouse/ poorhouse solution rose inexorably during the century, the process was as contested at a parish level as more generally poor law policy was debated nationally. The Midland villages whose poor law policy was examined many years ago by Emmison and Hampson, show frequent reversals of parish policy, introducing and then rejecting workhouses over decades and changing the regime between allowing poor families to live in their own homes, directly managing a poor or workhouse (perhaps targeted at

Table 10.2   Housing spend as a percentage of total poor law expenditure 1776[3]

	Housing spend	Total poor law spend	%
Bedfordshire	£486.00	£16,620.00	2.92%
Buckinghamshire	£1,194.00	£31,798.00	3.75%
Derbyshire	£1,373.00	£17,441.00	7.87%
Dorset	£1,163.00	£24,538.00	4.74%
Durham	£695.00	£14,441.00	4.81%
Hereford	£1,190.00	£10,193.00	11.67%
Lancashire	£7,435.50	£52,372.83	14.20%
Leics	£1,267.00	£24,399.00	5.19%
Norfolk	£3,737.00	£64,341.00	5.81%
Northants	£1,648.00	£35,342.00	4.66%
Staffs	£1,509.00	£32,088.00	4.70%
Suffolk	£1,558.00	£56,804.00	2.74%
Sussex	£3,915.00	£54,734.00	7.15%
Warwicks	£2,165.00	£44,070.00	4.91%
Westmoreland	£230.00	£2,834.00	8.12%
England	**£78,176.00**	**£1,523,163.00**	**5.13%**

the old, or orphaned children), and farming workhouse provision out to contractors: Eaton Socon in Bedfordshire and Linton in Cambridgeshire confirm the kind of pattern I have previously discussed in Ashwell in Hertfordshire.[4]

The scale of the rural housing problem was accelerating in the eighteenth century even before the rapid population growth of the last quarter of the century. A variety of legal and economic constraints exacerbated the problem. During the population expansion of the sixteenth century, the opportunities for individuals and families to carve new tenements from waste and forestlands were widespread. Squatter settlements were frequently condoned, or even welcomed, by manorial lords who saw in them a new source of income from short-term fines and long-term rental income. Examples can be found widely in for instance Rossendale (Lancs.), Myddle (Shropshire) and Brill (Buckinghamshire).[5] The famous, and much abused and ignored, Statute of 1589 requiring new houses be built with a smallholding of four acres attached to them defines a mindset that saw pioneering settlers subsisting on such a small plot, building their own houses from the wood, stone, mud and straw in the neighbourhood, and combining the small area of land attached to the homestead with the use of extensive additional common rights. It remained on the statute book until 1775, and a later commentator succinctly summed up the thinking behind those who initiated the change:

This statute has been repealed: four acres of land were too much for the
spade, and too little for the plough ... Yet perhaps it would have been
more advisable merely to have lessened the quantity of land required
for each cottage, than to have dropped this provision altogether.[6]

The onward march of enclosure and throttling of common rights
never eliminated such houses – waste-edge settlements continued to be
important. David Brown has shown in Staffordshire how in the eighteenth and nineteenth centuries the authorities came to regard them as
dangerously subversive and disorderly.[7] In Devon, Charles Vancouver
observed around 1800 that landowners allowed the poor to 'settle upon
the borders of the wastes', where

> The hovels ... are usually built with mud; the roof and other mate-
> rials are as commonly purloined from the adjacent woods, or any
> other place that will most conveniently supply it. The establishment
> is thus begun by plunder, and continued without controul, the seat
> of an idle, useless, and disorderly set of people.[8]

Wiltshire forest areas contain numerous hamlet settlements on parish
edges or straddling two parishes that can be dated from the eighteenth
and early nineteenth centuries, and were frequently named Cadley.[9]

However, in an age of expanding great estates, the combination of
changing estate practices and the effects of the Settlement Law of 1662
accentuated the process of immiseration. As farms were enlarged and
modern leasehold and rack-rent tenancies spread, so parishes with a
small number of large tenant farms emerged, farms that used farm
labourers more sparingly and efficiently, and the authorities sought to
persuade labouring families with insufficient work to move elsewhere
and lessen the parish's potential welfare. The open and closed village
paradigm that nineteenth-century commentators saw emerging from
these changes is simplistic: Sarah Banks used cluster analysis 20 years
ago to demonstrate empirically that landownership and social patterns
in rural parishes were far more complex.[10] Nevertheless the tendency for
'open' parishes full of small plots, poor labourers, dispersed landownership and weak control of migration, to expand their population rapidly
in the eighteenth century is well documented. Let us look at a graph
showing contrasting patterns of population change in two clusters of
adjacent villages (see Figure 10.1).

The first group of villages are the Claydons in Buckinghamshire,
where a falling population in the squire's village of Middle Claydon

contrasts with rapid expansion in Steeple Claydon, a community where enclosure and consolidation failed in the late seventeenth century and much land was sold off to the inhabitants. The other three are Bernwood villages that underwent disafforestation in the second quarter of the seventeenth century. There, the village of Brill apparently follows a roughly similar pattern to that of Steeple Claydon, with its population shooting ahead in the eighteenth and nineteenth centuries. Yet Brill was not a village of dispersed landownership with many small farms and agricultural holdings in the same way as Steeple Claydon. Although the 1798 Land Tax returns show many owners, they were almost exclusively within the village precincts. The farmland of the parish was owned by big landowners and farmed in large units. Here is another factor accentuating overcrowding in village houses. In the sixteenth century, the forest community of Brill expanded as families built new houses on the forest waste, creating a new settlement called Little London on the border of Oakley. In the enclosed world of the eighteenth century, Brill's expanding population could not encroach on the large farms, and was forced to use scarce land in the village centre, subdividing plots, building on gardens, infilling backsides, to the detriment of housing density, health and hygiene. Where they could not create a classic close village, estate managers could cynically allow

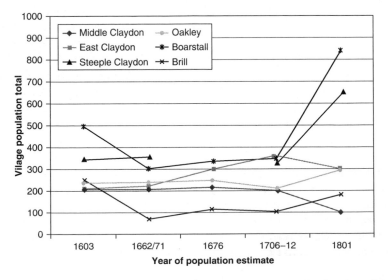

Figure 10.1 Population change and landholding in six Buckinghamshire Villages, 1603–1801

village centres, with their copyhold tenures, to decay while supporting
the expansion of tenant farms in outlying parts of the parish.[11]

Commentators began to acknowledge that the combination of poor
housing conditions and rural unemployment was widespread in the last
third of the eighteenth century. Rural poverty had long existed but the
mentality of the age brought it into sharper focus. The age's greater self-
awareness and ability to reflect on the human condition under the influence of enlightenment thinkers, and a rejection of older views of poverty
and vagrancy as a semi-criminal way of life both influenced this shift.
Equally important was the rise of the Georgian 'designed' house and the
contrast it pointed at traditional vernacular building. A good example of
this is Arthur Young's passing remarks in his autobiography disparaging
his father's decision in the 1740s to reject new fashions and to use a 'hedge
carpenter' to rebuild his farmhouse, while constructing modern brick farm
buildings for his horses and cattle, to the amusement of his neighbours.[12]
These elements helped articulate minimum design standards for the housing of the poor labourer, particularly when we add a further element, a
new awareness of privacy and sexuality within the family with its impact
on what were acceptable sleeping arrangements for a household.

John Wood's definition of the basic requirements for the cottage was
not published until 1788 but by his account had emerged from his
perception of the problem in the 1760s. He set out seven precepts for
designing a house for a labourer: (a) Dry and healthy – floors raised off
the ground; (b) Warm, cheerful and comfortable – thick walls, screened
entrances, south or east facing; (c) Convenient – porch, pantry, privy,
fuel store; (d) Stairs to upper storey not too steep; (e) Three bedrooms to
separate parents and children of both sexes and increase privacy; (f) No
more than 12 feet wide; and (g) Built in pairs to enable families to assist
each other in sickness.[13] Wood's seven precepts effectively set standards
that remained good into the twentieth century. The three bedrooms,
airiness and dryness, and the building of pairs of houses remain
central design precepts for the urban semi-detached house, and the
rural council house. Wood saw the construction of pairs of cottages
in social support terms, but Nathaniel Kent shrewdly appreciated the
considerable reduction in construction costs that went with it.[14] Wood's
was not the only view as to the specification of a labourer's cottage.
Kent's, the estate manager, had an eye to cost 20 years earlier that led
his specifications to be much more rough and ready:

> I am far from wishing to see the cottage improved, or augmented so
> as to make it fine, or expensive; no matter how plain it is, provided

it be tight and convenient. All that is requisite, is a warm comfortable plain room, for the poor inhabitants to eat their morsel in, an oven to bake their bread, a little receptacle for their small beer and provision, and two wholesome lodging apartments, one for the man and his wife, and another for his children. It would perhaps be more decent, if the boys and girls could be separated; but this would make the building too expensive, and besides, it is not so materially necessary; for the boys find employment in farm-houses at an early age.[15]

How did these precepts fare in the real world of the parish in the later eighteenth century? First, they were idealist solutions for landowners who had money to spare on enhancing the lives of labouring families on their estates. For every philanthropic landlord, there were many who supported their land agents' endeavours to pull down cottages and 'encourage' families to move to 'open' villages or towns. Farm rationalisation reduced the number of viable agricultural holdings, and falling real wages meant farm labourers found it increasingly difficult to make their rent. Moreover, estate stewards rationalising ring-fenced farms were fashionably convinced that it would be better to provide cottages by the new farmstead, allowing the farmer to have labourers to hand, dependent, and easy to supervise. Initially this was a position that Arthur Young supported and advocated, but after about 1800 he reversed his views and advocated giving labourers their own cottages and some land to help them be self-supporting and independent.

There were also changes in vernacular construction techniques and fashions that went against the grain of Wood's precepts. Wood's ideal cottage was raised on a plinth, high ceilinged and of clean brick roofed with tile or slate. Yet the eighteenth and early nineteenth century saw a continuation, even a revival of mud-walled construction, which continued the vernacular tradition of thick walls and thatched roofs. Cob construction was widespread in eighteenth-century Devon and in Northamptonshire, where the plebeian clergyman John Mastin praised the weatherproof and warm qualities of cob housing in his Naseby village, and recent re-evaluation has demonstrated the continued new building in cob through the eighteenth and early nineteenth centuries.[16] There was a fashionable appreciation of French pisé techniques that meant earth walling was used in architect designed buildings as well as by 'hedge' craftsmen, and additionally, in both areas, a use of large, unbaked, clay bricks in the construction mainly of low-status houses. Quite separately, another construction change in the period was the degrading of the quality of timbers used to frame houses, in which much thinner beams were used with struts to hold the frame square, and much flimsier wall infilling.[17] The fragility of new Hertfordshire roadside houses was commented on by Louis Simond recording his tour of England c. 1810: 'their walls are frightfully thin, a single brick of eight inches – and instead of beams, mere planks lying on edge'.[18]

Parish authorities were often providing housing on a hand-to-mouth basis. The buildings at their disposal could be medieval community space – church houses right across the country, parish guild buildings in East Anglia – or the freehold and copyhold houses exchanged by individuals in their declining years for a promise of lifetime support from the parish, or houses rented from villagers. In previous eras, poor people created makeshift structures themselves on common waste, using materials from woods and hedgerow trees and bushes. Now, these sources were under increasing pressure from enclosure and the squeeze on common rights. They were undoubtedly widely built, but by the second quarter of the nineteenth century, Liardet's contemporary analysis of social conditions in the Kent villages to the north west of Canterbury that rioted in the 1830s analysed not only the quality of housing, but the available carpentry skills to repair houses and even construct simple shelves and household furniture. In one village only three out of 51 families had competent skills, 24 some ability, but 26 none at all. In another it was four out of 50, and in a third three out of 50 had good carpentry skills while six had 'rough' skills and 37 none at all.[19]

Parish provision of housing, and intervention was probably the largest single source of new housing for the burgeoning numbers of poor rural families in the period from 1780 to 1834. Private investment in mass housing in the countryside was usually unprofitable, unless the parish could be persuaded to pay the rent, but some great estate owners who were cash rich and philanthropically inclined did occasionally build for their tenants and villagers. Another important source of village housing for the poor were the large numbers of property-owning charities for the poor which had previously taken house rent and redistributed it to the needy, but who chose in the late eighteenth century to allow the poor to live in their property rent free – perhaps because they were otherwise unable to collect the rent. These three sources were sometimes in conflict over who controlled access to the resource, but in the difficult first quarter of the nineteenth century, the boundaries between parish charity property and parish property could easily become blurred – especially if trustees overlapped.

There can be no doubt that huge responsibilities of, and monetary sums raised by, parishes and the farmer elites who ran so many of them, induced concerns on the part of the gentry and aristocracy. In 1790 a law was passed giving JPs powers to inspect parish poor houses and work-houses, and report to quarter sessions.[20] In 1819 the Select Vestries Act reaffirmed the statutory right of parishes to act as corporate bodies, but narrowed the responsible officers of the corporation to the churchwardens and overseers. It also stated the parish's right to raise loans secured on the poor rate.[21] This was widely used right across the country, and, after the 1834 Poor Law Amendment Act curtailed the parish right to be proactive in housing matters, a list of the debts and their purposes was drawn up parish by parish.[22] Over £350,000 had been raised, and about 91 per cent of it was for houses – though other uses included buying village fire engines. If we take the average price of a simple house for a poor family to be £50 (an estimate supported by the loan details, but also from parish accounts, and contemporary books and pamphlets), this gives a figure of over 6400 houses built on this basis before 1834. Many loans were for small sums of up to £100, but there were areas with a particular propensity to raise large amounts: Sussex, Hailsham, Hellingsley and South Malling all borrowed over £1000, the last 'to build cottages in lieu of a workhouse'. All areas of the country had their parish cottages, and in most areas borrowed to do so, though in Norfolk and Suffolk with their county workhouse systems, money was predominantly borrowed for the workhouses. In the eight years after the 1834 Act, the Poor Law Commissioners acted to encourage parishes to pay off their loans. They also exhorted them to sell up parish housing to pay for the new Union Workhouses, and over 3000 parishes (one in five) did so in that period, particularly in the early years as Figure 10.2 demonstrates.[23]

As Roger Wells has recently pointed out, many parishes managed to cling on to their houses through the nineteenth century,[24] and in Dorset, Martin Ayres' work shows how whole clutches of parishes delayed sales until the 1860s.[25] Wells' methodology does not permit quantification, and the numerous examples he cites may simply reflect those exceptional cases that reached the Poor Law Commission in London. His perceptions do, however, show how much greater the stock of housing available to poor families was than a simple aggregation of the post-1834 houses sold, and of those charity houses inhabited rent free, and listed in the Charity Commission surveys of the same period.

Given the pressures of rural population growth, parish house building and purchases in the late eighteenth century were unlikely to do much more than keep pace with the growth in families seeking accommodation. The 1831 census returns give us some measure of the scale of overcrowding, and these four county scattergrams (Figure 10.3) plot village size by number of families (above 200 population) against

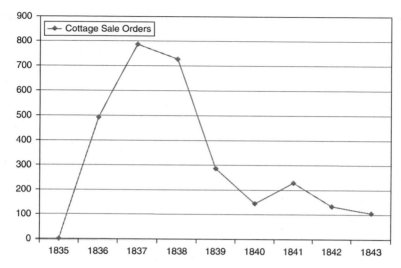

Figure 10.2 Cottage sale orders, 1835–43

the number of inhabited houses. To give some idea of the real situation shown by these figures, where number of families was 150 per cent of the number of houses, every other house in the village contained more than one family. On a county scale they show that smaller villages were at least as crowded, often more so, than small country towns, and, interestingly, that a new industrial area like Lancashire had relatively less housing overcrowding than many rural areas in the south.[26]

Statements about the condition of those parish houses sold after 1834 suggest that most were in poor repair and some virtually worthless. Tales of overcrowding and squalor were plentiful. Yet we should pause and consider what can be known about the basic quality of the houses built by parish authorities at that time. If we look at a row of cottages in Swanbourne (Bucks) that can be identified as parish-owned before 1834 (see Plate 10.1) we can see that it is not very different in basic design from the estate cottages of Nuneham Courtenay from a similar period, and a step change in quality compared to the seventeenth century parish houses whose building accounts are laid out above (see Plate 10.2).

Another set of parish cottages about which we have significant information is that at Bridestowe in Devon, just north of Dartmoor. Here Revd. Luxmore built simple houses, one up, one down (see Plate 10.3). There was a room 16ft square on the ground floor with a single storey lean-to at the back, and stairs to a similar-sized room above, used as a bedroom. Luxmore justified the single sleeping chamber by claiming it was customary for families to send their children into service or apprenticeship before

256

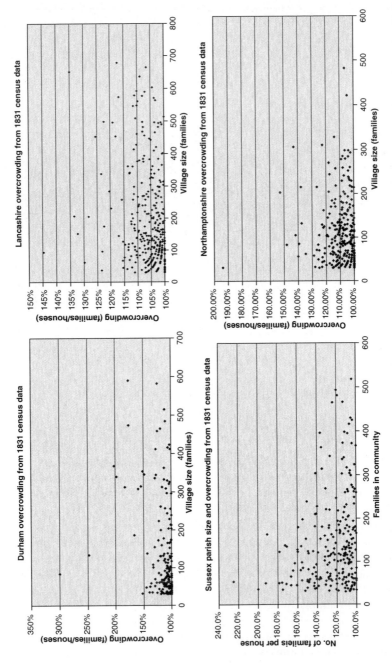

Figure 10.3 Village size by number of families against the number of inhabited houses in four counties. (Data from the 1831 census).

the age of ten, but the following quotation shows just how sensitive he was to changing design standards, and the new moral imperatives:

> I conceived that no evil could arise from each house being accommodated with one bedroom and the children sleeping in the same with their parents, but in so much request were these cottages, that they soon became tenanted by those whose industry kept them from the necessity of apprenticing their children, and I soon perceived that the want of a second room was a great evil.[27]

Another shaft of light on the reality of poor house conditions is shed by the reports on Bedfordshire houses made for the JPs (led by the philanthropically competitive Whitbreads and Howards) in the first decade of the nineteenth century. In the parish of Hawnes in 1801 the structure of the two poor houses was described as follows:

> The first part of the Poor house consists of a Dwelling Room 17ft by 11ft with a fire place; the Room 6ft high. 1 Sleeping Room on the

Plate 10.1 'The Barracks', Swanbourne, Buckinghamshire, built by the Parish Authorities c. 1800 to house Poor Families

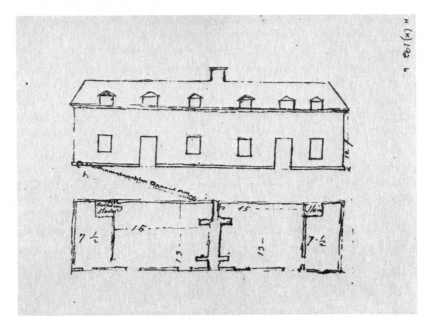

Plate 10.2   Plans for a Cottage Row in Nuneham Courtenay, Oxfordshire, built by the Harcourt Family, c. 1760–70. (Courtesy of Northamptonshire Record Office).

Ground floor 17ft by 14ft 6in with a dirt floor, the Rafters and Thatch on One side are unplaistered; 1 Sleeping Roome over the Dwelling Roome 17ft by 11ft to which they go up by a ladder. The second part of the Poor house Consists of, a Dwelling Room 17ft by 10ft 6 in with a fireplace and a Dirt floor. 1 Bed Room on the Ground floor 17ft by 13ft with a Dirt floor; the clay walls of this Roome are very bad. 1 sleeping Roome upstairs 17ft by 10ft 1 other sleeping Room up stairs 17ft by 13ft. No Windows in either of the Rooms upstairs.[28]

The first house was inhabited by a widow with five children aged three to 14, and a couple and their children, aged 12 to 23. The widow had a bed, two sheets and one blanket, but her children slept on straw on the floor, with no more than an old sack and a few rags to cover them. The couple had two beds, but their children included an 18-year-old boy, and a 23-year-old girl. Here were overcrowding and poor conditions, but each family had its own space, and the inspector had a sensitive eye with a shrewd appreciation of what was not acceptable. Here at least, the poorhouse did not break up family groups, as it certainly did in some places.

Plate 10.3 Revd Luxmore's Parish Cottages, c. 1800, Bridgestowe, Devon (Illustration from Vancouver, *A General View of the Agriculture of Devon*, 1808).

Parishes across England built thousands of houses, and bought and acquired thousands more in the period up to 1834, enabling them to fulfil their statutory obligation to house their settled inhabitants. Making an assessment of the total stock of parish owned houses in 1834 is difficult but provides a means of gauging the scale of the endeavour relative to that in more recent times. The Poor Law Commissioners in 1844 had agreed sale orders from some 3000 parishes from a total of 15,000 in the country. Working very conservatively, we can show from a sample of some 500 parishes, that the mean number of properties sold per parish was 4.9. If only half those parishes that owned houses sold them in the first ten years operation of the new poor law (I suspect an underestimate), then over 29,000 houses were owned by parishes in 1834. If we take the average numbers of charity houses being used to house the poor, often controlled by the same parish elites, we can add another 20 per cent, or 4800, making a grand total of 33,800 houses. This compares with a total of 15,245 council houses built in England with rural subsidies under government initiatives between 1918 and 1930.[29]

The achievement of parish elites in the century before 1834 was substantial, and the time and energy devoted to it by vestries and overseers must have been considerable. The New Poor Law reversed much of this.

Although parishes were not forced to sell houses, many of them did. Those that retained them did so to undermine and soften the attempt to shift the poor to the workhouse. The Poor Law Commission understood their thinking:

> Although the sales of this property have been much diminished for some time past, they have by no means ceased. We regret to find that, in many places there is a determined resolution on the part of the parishioners to retain their old workhouses, as receptacles into which they allow paupers receiving out-door relief to be crowded instead of such paupers being relieved by Guardians to the extent, or in the manner requisite to secure them adequate and proper lodging … The appearance of a saving to the parish by allowing a pauper to reside in such dilapidated buildings rather than supply the means of providing proper lodging, or causing them to be received into the Workhouse, proves an insurmountable barrier to the course which is obviously desirable, namely the disposal of such property to person competent and willing to attend to and improve it.[30]

But after 1834 parishes could no longer pursue an active housing policy: the occupants of parish houses had to pay rent, even rates, and parishes could no longer legally subsidise rental payments. Some tried to make poor families pay rent. Immediately after the passing of the Act, the vestry at Bridestowe in Devon found the occupants of the parish houses unwilling to pay rent, and voted to take legal action against them.[31] Far more often, parishes condoned the virtual autonomy of the occupants. They in turn could not expect help from the parish to keep their houses in repair. For the next 80 years, the English rural poor were left at the mercy of philanthropic landlords, or unscrupulous plebeian village landlords, to provide for their housing.

Notes

1. North.RO, QS Minute Book 1708–27, especially St. Thomas day 1 Geo. I, Michaelmas 4 Geo. I and Easter 4 Geo. I; W. Le Hardy & G. L. Reckitt (eds), *Buckinghamshire Sessions Records* (Aylesbury, 1939), III, Appendix 2, pp. 310–14; *Warwickshire Quarter Sessions Proceedings* 8, 1682–90, (1953), pp. 259, 263, 270; 7, 1674–82, (1953), p. 90; 9, 1690–96, (1964), pp. 21–2, 57–8, 65, 73, 131. See also the coverage in S. Hindle, *On the Parish? The Micro-Politics of Poor Relief in Rural England c. 1550–1750* (Oxford: Clarendon Press, 2004), pp. 268–70, 300–3.
2. Shropshire Record Office, 322/11/ Overseers' Accounts for Shawbury, 1649–64. Printed in *Salopian Record* 47, (Shrewsbury: Friends of Shropshire Archives,

2005), n.p. The other known account is from Overseers account for Dillington: Hunts Record Office, 2735/12/1, pp. 72–3 dated 1681, with a cost of over £5.

3. HLRO, Main papers, Parchment Box 162, 1776 returns of parish expenditure on the poor.

4. F. G. Emmison, 'The Relief of the Poor at Eaton Socon, 1706–1834', *Bedfordshire Historical Record Society* XIV, (1933), 23–6; E. M. Hampson, *The Treatment of Poverty in Cambridgeshire, 1597–1834* (Cambridge: Cambridge University Press, 1934), pp. 71–2; J. Broad, 'Parish Economies of Welfare, 1650–1834', *Historical Journal* 42:4, (1999), 985–1006.

5. G. H. Tupling, *The Economic History of Rossendale* (Manchester: Manchester University Press, 1927), esp. pp. 56–69, 127, 161; D. G. Hey, *An English Rural Community: Myddle under the Tudors and Stuarts* (Leicester: Leicester University Press, 1974); J. Broad & R. W. Hoyle (eds), *Bernwood: The Life and Afterlife of a Forest* (Preston: University of Central Lancashire, 1998), esp. Chapters 3 & 4.

6. *Communications to the Board of Agriculture on Cottages* (1796), p. 29 (from Robert Beatson).

7. D. Brown, 'Enclosure and Improvement: An Investigation into the Motives for Parliamentary Enclosure' (Unpublished Wolverhampton Polytechnic PhD, 1992), Chapter 6.

8. C. Vancouver, *General view of the Agriculture of Hampshire, including the Isle of Wight* (1813), p. 505.

9. D. A. Crowley (ed.), *VCH: Wiltshire*, (1999), XVI: Kinwardstone Hundred, pp. 110, 122, 131, 148, 209.

10. S. J. Banks, 'Nineteenth-Century Scandal or Twentieth Model? A new Look at "Open" and "Closed" Parishes', *Economic History Review* 41, (1988), 5–23.

11. Data from J. Broad, *Transforming English Rural Society: The Verneys and the Claydons 1600–1820* (Cambridge: Cambridge University Press, 2004), Chapter 9; Broad & Hoyle (eds), *Bernwood*, Chapter 5.

12. A. Young, *The Autobiography of Arthur Young, with Selections from his Correspondence*, ed. by M. B. Edwards (Smith, Elder & Co., 1898), p. 13.

13. J. Wood, *A Series of Plans, for Cottages, Habitations of the Labourer ... Adapted as well to Towns, as to the Country* (J. and J. Taylor, 1792), p. 8.

14. N. Kent, *Hints to Gentlemen of Landed Property* (1775), p. 243.

15. Kent, *Hints to Gentlemen*, p. 231.

16. J. Cox, 'Georgian Mud and Straw in Devon and Cornwall', in Neil Burton (ed.), *Georgian Vernacular: Papers given at a Georgian Group Symposium 28 October 1995* (The Georgian Group, 1996), pp. 19–26; J. Mastin, *A History of Naseby* (1792), (Northampton: Northamptonshire Record Society, 2004), p. 95; H. Bird, 'Seaborne Revisited: Cob Cottages in Northamptonshire 2004', *Northants Past & Present*, (2005), 54–69.

17. D. Martin, 'The Decline of Traditional Methods of Timber Framing in South-East England', in Burton (ed.) *Georgian Vernacular*, pp. 28–33.

18. L. Simond, *Journal of a Tour and Residence in Great Britain During the Years 1810 and 1811*, 2nd edn (Edinburgh: J. Ballantyne & Co., 1817), II, p. 259.

19. F. Liardet, *Riot in Kent. Report made to the Central Society of Education on the State of the Peasantry at Boughton, Herne-Hill, and the Ville of Dunkirk, near Canterbury. With a Paper upon Industrial Schools for the Peasantry, etc. Reprinted from the First Publication of the Society, etc.* (1838), pp. 23–46.

20. 30 Geo II, c. 49.
21. 59 Geo III c. 12, Poor Relief Amendment Act 1819, 31 March 1819; see Clauses 7 & 10.
22. *PP*, (1842), XXXV.
23. Figures derived from *PP*, (1844), XIX: 10th Report of Poor Law Commissioners, p. 16, 53–4.
24. R. Wells, 'The Poor Law Commission and Publicly Owned Housing in the English Countryside, 1834–47', *Agricultural History Review* 55:2, (2007), 181–204.
25. M. Ayres, 'Beyond the Rural Idyll: Housing Dorset's Labouring Poor in the Early Nineteenth Century' (Unpublished University of Leicester MA Thesis, 2000), Chapter 3.
26. From *PP*, (1831–32), XXXVI (67), which gives figures for parishes of over 40 families. It is important to notice the y-axis (left hand scale) varies between graphs, to accommodate the maximum figure for that county. Some high figures may be the result of terraces of cottages being considered as one building, which would greatly and misleadingly increase the implied overcrowding. However, it seems that many more small cottages were occupied by several families, as will be demonstrated below.
27. C. Vancouver, *General View of the Agriculture of Devon* (1808), p. 96.
28. Bed.RO, W1/762, 'Report on the State and Condition of the Poor Houses in the Parish of Hawnes in the County of Bedfordshire', 1801.
29. Data for 1834 based on detailed work done on six counties: Bedfordshire, Buckinghamshire, Dorset, Northamptonshire and Warwickshire. I am grateful to Meryl Wilson for her meticulous collection of much of the detailed data. The figures for rural council housing 1918–30 are drawn from TNA, HLG40/31, Agricultural Cottages Committee, 1930–1.
30. *PP*, (1846), XIX: 12th annual report of the Poor Law Commissioners, p. 19.
31. Dev.RO, PV/1, Vestry minutes for Bridestowe, dated 2 October 1834.

11

Retirement from the Noise and Hurry of the World? The Experience of Almshouse Life

Alannah Tomkins

Almshouse living has enjoyed a broadly positive image with historians and the public alike. The survival of attractive ranges of buildings, bearing tablets to commemorate founders' virtues, has ensured that the architectural features of almshouses provided an early focus for study.[1] Charities that remain operative tend to reinforce this perception; recently the Mary Feilding Guild residential home in north London was described as 'harder to get into than an Oxbridge college', emphasising both its exclusivity and its desirability.[2] The residential experiences of occupants in the past have been less well surveyed, mainly because obvious or concentrated sources of information remain sparse. As a result almshouses have been treated as individual institutions by local historians, but assessments of their collective impact are notably few.[3] The issue is complicated by terminology since the terms almshouse, poorhouse, and hospital were used variously by contemporaries. Other locally-derived terms include 'guildhouse', 'callis' and 'gift houses'.[4] Here, 'almshouse' is a generic label to refer to a house established by voluntary charity (rather than from local taxes) with a fixed number of spaces; they were probably founded most often by individual testators who wished to leave a permanent memorial to their own philanthropy, but almshouses were also established by monarchs, trade guilds and others. Some hospitals established under the pre-Reformation church continued to operate as almshouses in this period, while 1600–40 is regarded as a period of numerous foundations by bequest.[5]

This chapter will first consider the material lives of almshouse-dwellers in the period 1650–1850. This can be assessed via a comparison of the charities' capacity to house the poor, including their physical attributes of fabric and contents, along with the benefits they offered aside from accommodation (most importantly a stipend). It will go on to discuss the oversight of almshouse inmates or controls on their behaviour. It will argue that experiences were varied along a continuum that stretched from the comfortable to the impoverished. For every ancient pensioner maintained comfortably there was at least one almsperson whose entitlements and receipts were thin indeed. It will also consider the potential emotional freight attached to an almshouse place. Did people draw satisfaction and status from belonging to selected institutions? Given the paucity of first-person testimonies to draw on here, I will assess the potential for autonomy among inmates, and in particular will examine the scope of privacy for almspeople. Evidence on the aggregate desirability of an almshouse place is slight or oblique, but suggests that the value placed on admission was higher than material receipts alone would imply.

11.1   Material experiences of almshouse life

Almshouses often stood at the heart of a village or urban community; medieval foundations were often based around a central courtyard, while those founded after a facilitating Act of 1597 typically comprised a simple row of houses along a road close to the parish church.[6] Individual houses consisted of one or two rooms, on one or two storeys, with one or two hearths. This internal space was conceptualised by founders with limited variations; the almshouses founded by the Duke of Albermarle in Newcastle under Lyme provided a living room, bedroom and pantry to each woman, whereas in Theydon Garnon in Essex, the Lady Fitzwilliam almshouses had only one ground-floor room and an attic.[7] It was not uncommon to find communal spaces, too, especially in houses of ancient foundation. These might include a kitchen, bakehouse, hall or washhouse, or a chapel for all the almsfolk.[8] External space might be entirely communal, such as the gallery 'for walking exercise in bad weather' in Tiverton, or it might feature a separate garden for each inhabitant (permitting an early form of allotment).[9]

Almshouse living was defined partly by the number of the intended inhabitants. They were rarely built for fewer than four people, but were not designed for the masses. They might be substantial, with wings for both female and male beneficiaries, but they were not usually supposed to house more than around 50 people.[10] Experiences of almshouse living were also conditioned by the population regarded as eligible for admittance. Almshouse foundations tried to define people who would receive a place based on their age, gender, or personal attributes. Successful applicants were identified by honesty, poverty, local residence, former occupation or marital status. Of the 20 almshouses present in York by

1740, for example, nine preferred to admit widows (three of which aimed for a closer specification, such as Catholic widows or the widows of freemen).[11] This meant that new almspeople could expect to join a relatively elderly community, where the lowest ages were 50 or 60, with experiences in common. This did not inevitably make for harmonious living but it did at least ensure familiarity of knowledge or pursuits. Of the 13 almsmen in Seckford's almshouse in 1792 for example, nine had formerly followed just four occupations.[12]

A closer understanding of individual lived experience is generally precluded by the virtual absence of first-person accounts of life within an almshouse. Those very few that survive tend to derive from oral history projects, perforce drawing on twentieth-century accounts, or pertain to the wealthy, high-status almshouses where the prestige of residents was in little doubt. One that relates to the period before 1850 falls into this category.[13] James Lacy was probably around 62 years old when he was admitted to St Oswald's Hospital in Worcester in 1809. He began his diary 13 years earlier, while still working as a linen draper in the city. Spread across notebooks and loose sheets, Lacy appears to have kept a record of key events in his life. Prior to his admission, the focus falls on his working life and his involvement as a witness in two legal cases. After 1809 he concentrates on matters concerning the almspeople, among whom he was appointed as the vice-regent (possessing at least a notional supervisory role over the other inhabitants).

Lacy embraced almshouse life with considerable enthusiasm. On admission he made a careful note of the cash and other benefits he could expect, and a detailed account of his outlay furnishing his room. It is likely that he had previously lived in furnished lodgings, with insufficient possessions of his own. This implies, though, that either his almshouse room was bare or that he deemed the existing contents to be inadequate to his needs. It also indicates his own level of resources at the time of admission, since he spent £5 19s. 5d. on items other than food. His shopping list is dominated by a bed and bedding, but also features a candlestick, fire irons and cleaning brushes.[14] Thereafter he documented such diverse aspects of life as the value of the pews occupied by St Oswald's inmates, a list of inmates who died or were removed by relations, and the fabrics and tradesmen used to make the almspeople's clothing. Most startling of all he devised a scheme for an almshouse burial club, (although it seems unlikely that the idea was ever adopted).

Lacy was of course privileged in occupying a position of some small authority in a well-funded almshouse, so his clear relish for almshouse life cannot be taken as representative. Alternative narrative representations can only be drawn from literature, with patchy results. The pathos attached to Thomas Newcombe's occupation of a place at the Hospital of the Grey Friars, for instance, is plainly a literary device to emphasise the character's fall from grace. Little can be made of this in terms of inhabitants' perspectives. By contrast Dickens' account of Titbull's almshouse carries greater authenticity as a view of the internal politics of a house he visited, but is nonetheless 'the fiction of Dickens in his 'Uncommercial' guise'.[15] Therefore to find a more balanced picture it is necessary to cast more widely, and draw on institutional records and the comments of contemporary observers to judge the facilities on offer.

Access to almshouses supplies one criterion for judgement. It is necessary to know exactly how many almsplaces were filled. Attempts to enumerate beneficiaries can be unwitting underestimates when they rely on the number of dwellings rather than the number of intended inmates. This misreading can arise either because the charity allocated each unit to two people or because almshouses for men sometimes permitted wives and children to accompany them; for example the St Cross hospital in Winchester admitted male inmates but accommodated wives as well. The census for 1801 gives the occupancy of the hospital as 17 men and six women.[16]

Nonetheless it is vital to know that almshouse places *could* be occupied, that the house was built according to the founder's intentions and that the accommodation was habitable, because the fabric of the institutions displayed some important divergences.[17] Almshouses were often purpose built but the materials and resilience of houses could vary considerably. Stone or brick could be sturdy, as was the case with Browne's Hospital in Stamford Lincolnshire, built in the 1470s of local stone and praised by Pevsner as 'one of the best medieval hospitals in England'.[18] It was still in use as an almshouse in 2002. But even stout materials might not withstand the depredations of time or hostility. Almshouses in Flint built around 1818 of brick and thatch were condemned as hovels unfit for habitation in 1874.[19] Numerous almshouses (such as the Hospital of St John the Baptist in Chester and Wynard's almshouse in Exeter) were destroyed in the 1640s, although both cited here were eventually rebuilt.[20] In Sheffield, the men and women in the Shewsbury hospital were physically imperilled by a combination of the hospital building and its proximity to the river; four almspeople were drowned in 1768 when the River Sheaf flooded and part of the building was washed away.[21]

Not all almshouses were well-built. In West Kent a shortage of local brick-making meant that almshouses were timber framed and not very resistant to the elements.[22] Elsewhere seventeenth-century almshouses were often 'of the local mud and stud construction' with a thatched roof.[23] Furthermore, there needed to be both the will and the where-withal to supply ongoing maintenance.[24] The inmates of the Hospital of St John in Northampton were fortunate indeed, in that their stone-built quarters (dating from the early fourteenth century) were repaired in the seventeenth and eighteenth centuries and were inhabited by the almsmen until 1879.[25] Most beneficiaries of an ancient charity were not so fortunate, and even many newer hospitals were in a state of physical decay. Without adequate funds for mending, houses typically fell into disrepair and became uninhabitable.[26] In 1781, a reproachful letter to the *Gentleman's Magazine* delineated the neglect of almshouses in Twyford, Berkshire, allegedly owing to the death of all the Trustees; 'some of the windows are entirely broken, and the wall which incloses the garden is so decayed that it will probably soon become useless'. The correspondent hoped for the restoration of the poor 'to the *comfortable* enjoyment of what was certainly designed for their *comfort* as well as *use'*.[27] But human agency could do worse than to neglect an almshouse. In Manchester, a number of almshouses were demolished to make way for the laying out of a new street in 1807. When the remainder were similarly removed 12 months later (without the supply of replacement housing) the inhabitants resisted in the only way they could by staging an effectual sit-in; they

> remained in their dwellings; they kept possession at the hazard of their lives, amidst showers of rubbish, descending stones, and falling timber; they retreated from room to room as the work of destruction proceeded, dragging their beds.[28]

They were eventually persuaded to decamp with the promise of a cellar dwelling, which seems poor recompense for the loss of a house and small garden. Yet if houses became uninhabitable or were even demolished, all hope was not necessarily lost. Some communities valued their almshouses and could step into the breach. This is what happened to Brickett's Hospital in Salisbury, where the original sixteenth-century buildings were clearly not fit for purpose by the late eighteenth century. The Hospital was rebuilt by public subscription in 1780.[29]

Where the fabric of an almshouse was sound and kept in good repair, it was not always applied to its intended use. For example, when the only surviving inmate of St Mary Magdalen's hospital in Bath died in 1806, they had been the sole beneficiary for at least three years.[30] In Worcester, St Oswalds hospital technically had 28 places yet in the 1820s at least eight fell vacant when the Cathedral Dean failed to fill them.[31] Almshouses might have become appropriated to other uses including low rent or no rent accommodation for the parish poor, as was the case in many Cambridgeshire parishes.[32] Barker-Read found that in Cranbrook in Kent, almshouses were used to provide free accommodation to the master of the charity school and the parish clerk.[33] In Glentworth, Lincolnshire, one hospital building was apparently unclaimed so a local innkeeper installed two of his servants there.[34]

As this last example implies, voluntary non-residence of a habitable house was a problem for some almshouse charities, where beneficiaries chose not to make use of the accommodation afforded them.[35] Absenteeism among cathedral bedesmen in the seventeenth century apparently ran quite high, particularly in foundations closest to London. The men apparently preferred to live in the capital, and fully expected to receive the charity's associated pension there.[36] Some charities tried to monitor absentees, or at least withheld the other benefits of the charity (making them contingent on the poor person's physical presence), but such conditions could be evaded by occasional residence.

It is usually assumed that the contents of houses either had to be supplied by incoming almspeople from their own household, or were in some way 'inherited' from previous inhabitants. Some houses required beneficiaries to bring their goods into the almshouse for the charity to keep if they died as an inmate, while others allowed inhabitants to will their possessions away.[37] In either case the contents of almshouses were of necessity closely akin to the contents of people's own homes. Inventories of almspeople's possessions are rare, but references to thefts from almspeople suggest a potentially wide variety of material experiences. The goods of almswoman Sarah Portress were stolen by her own nurse in 1753, but they included numerous items of silver cutlery and two gold rings.[38] In contrast, one almsman who was a victim of burglary had a box at the foot of his bed, wherein the most valuable items were a shirt and handkerchief.[39] A box seems to have been a common possession, particularly for storage of clothing and other household textiles, as was the case for poor families in their own homes.[40] It is possible that this absorption of goods into almshouse stock was resented, and that consequently people were known to dispose of property before they took up residence; in cases of theft, one defence was to allege that 'stolen' goods had been purchased from someone about to enter an almshouse (a variation on the old chestnut of purchasing items from a stranger).[41] In Colchester, the *quid pro quo* for leaving goods to the charity was that the poor kin of deceased almsmen should have first refusal of the vacant place.[42] If almshouses were completely rebuilt, or if founders were sufficiently far-sighted, the charity might stump up for furniture and bedlinen.[43] Communal possessions might be numerous, as at Heytesbury where the kitchen and buttery were well-supplied in the seventeenth and eighteenth centuries.[44] Nonetheless, the contents of each almsroom could be quite meagre; rooms in Browne's Hospital in Stamford held only a bed, a shelf, a candlestick and extinguisher in 1731 (augmented with a second shelf and a cupboard by 1766).[45]

Management of the internal space of almshouses seems to have been left largely to inmates, so there is little or no evidence about the use of space, or other attributes such as cleanliness (although presumably a noisome house might have attracted the reproach of charity trustees, especially where cleaning was enshrined in the rules).[46] One canny set of rules required almsmen's wives to take it in turns to clean the almshouse every day.[47] Yet the internal arrangement of almshouses combined with their intended occupancy made them very different environments to institutions for the poor where people slept in dormitories (such as workhouses or infirmaries). This meant that there was much less potential in almshouses for uncontrollable disease. Workhouse fever or gaol fever (usually typhus) occasionally decimated institutional populations, whereas there were apparently few reports of an equivalent almshouse fever.[48]

Aside from accommodation, what could almshouse inmates expect? It was usual for almshouses to supply a cash pension but the value of pensions varied widely. Where pensions were sufficient to meet all normal living costs (aside from inordinate expense associated with ill-health), the result could be 'an honourable period of retirement'.[49] Yet almspeople were entirely dependent on the scale of their charity's income; if investment yields rose then benefits might be extended but the charity operated with reference to its own capacity rather than the changing shape of poverty. Milley's hospital in Lichfield was designed in the early sixteenth century to supply pensions of just 5s. or 6s. per quarter to the almswomen, and this income remained unchanged for over 200 years, by which time it was totally insufficient for the maintenance of an individual person. The value of the endowment rose sharply in the early nineteenth century, and only then were the stipends raised significantly, to 5s. per week in 1821.[50] Where almshouse property was damaged and dividends fell, the results were typically passed immediately

to the almspeople. Foundations did not scruple to reduce stipends (regardless of prevailing circumstances for the poor).[51] The Hospital of St John the Baptist in Lichfield was the subject of a visitation in 1696, arising directly from an allegation that an almsman had died 'in want of necessaries for his body' and that stipends were being paid in clipped money.[52] Conversely, rising charity incomes were *not* necessarily passed on to poor inmates, or at least not in a timely fashion; the almspeople at Woodbridge in Suffolk felt that 'their Conditions are become much worse than those who receive the Alms of the Parish' in 1718.[53] The Woodbridge charity was well-placed to mollify the almsmen, and by 1768 the annual stipend had risen to a munificent £20, but high revenues could prove a temptation to weak-willed charity managers. At the Hospital of St John the Baptist in Dunston Lincolnshire the leases of hospital property became very valuable, but successive Wardens (typically clergymen) pocketed the income while the hospital fell into disrepair and disuse. The situation was only investigated and rectified by Chancery in the mid-nineteenth century.[54] The Shrewsbury Hospital in Sheffield was very unusual in that it reduced the number of almspeople after 1768 in order to raise stipends from 2s. 6d. to 3s. 6d. per week, in response to the increasing cost of provisions. For once, a rigid endowment income was not permitted to fossilise the value of the stipend.[55]

This evidence would tend to suggest that almspeople habitually had to earn money or approach their local overseer for poor relief, but almshouses had an unpredictable relationship with both employment and parish authorities. Some founders required inmates to remain independent of relief, although few went so far as Arthur Winsley and required almsmen to give a bond with sureties for 50 pounds 'not to take Alms of the Town'.[56] Some forbade work, while others insisted on it.[57] Numerous foundations effectually compelled beneficiaries to either work or seek relief, given their meagre stipend, so time and again parishes supplemented almshouse incomes.[58] In some cases, vestries or overseers were given responsibility for managing almshouses, and so the charities were elided with parish poorhouses and workhouses. Parishes clearly saw the utility of free housing and so might try to ensure that charities were kept up to maximum capacity.[59] Therefore the line between charities and parishes might be rigidly observed, studiously ignored or entirely blurred.

Money was not the only benefit on offer, though. Clothing in the form of coats or gowns was an integral part of some benefactions. These were designed as a visual reminder of the founder's philanthropy, usually fashioned from sober shades into a long, open gown, often sporting a badge, or buttons bearing the founder's arms.[60] The widows and spinsters of Ash's almshouse in Leek in Staffordshire were perhaps more colourful than most, receiving a gown of violet cloth every two years.[61] If the supply of clothing proved at all troublesome, however, particularly in the nineteenth century, it was quietly forgotten or converted into a raised pension payment.[62] Charity garments possessed a variety of possible meanings for almspeople. They might simply represent a warm item of clothing that could be turned to account (as apparel or as an asset at the pawnshop), but they quite possibly aroused strong feelings, either as a symbol of belonging to a high-status establishment or as a shameful badge of dependence.[63] It has been assumed that the former sentiment was most prominent among almspeople, a view probably consolidated by Trollope's depiction of Hiram's Hospital in *The Warden* and its alleged life model, St Cross in Winchester; it is ironic that a 'gowned Trollopian worthy'[64] should have come to represent satisfaction and stability, when both the fictional and real-life hospitals were central to scandals about benefits not paid to inmates. Caffrey suggests a time-scale for changing sentiments towards charity clothing, by emphasising negative reactions to it by the twentieth century.[65]

Wealthy foundations might also supply extras like fuel.[66] Robert Veel's almshouse in Ilchester supplied medical aid and funeral costs in the eighteenth century, including in 1772 3s. for brandy for bathing an almsman's legs.[67] Dr White's Hospital in Bristol supplied a shilling a week to pay a nurse for the almspeople in sickness, whereas Thomas Seckford's charity employed three poor women to nurse his 13 poor men.[68] Yet even in well-funded charities money might be misapplied or simply not spent. The Master of St John's Hospital in Bath was discovered in 1734 to have reduced the quality of gowns, failed to employ a nurse, and neglected to supply heating or make repairs.[69] Poorly-funded houses that were not supposed to supply nursing had to face up to the fact that their charity was not capable of acting as a place of residential care for the physically unsound, particularly if fellow residents were not prepared to support their frail neighbours.[70] In Nottingham one woman was removed from her almsplace when she became unable to care for herself and likewise unable to afford a servant.[71] Nursing was necessarily limited even where it was supplied. At Bond's hospital in Coventry, the nurse could not care for Thomas Marriot in 1872 because he was allegedly of unsound mind and required night-time supervision; he was removed to his daughter's house and ultimately to the workhouse.[72]

A lifeline was thrown to selected almshouse inmates by the foundation of supplementary charities. This seems to confirm Jordan's 'social osmosis' theory, whereby one charity would encourage the foundation of others; almshouse pensions and other benefits might rise from the gradual accretion of endowments.[73] Extra charity could range from the munificent and formal to the token and casual. At the generous end of the scale, George Monoux's almshouse for 13 men and women in Walthamstow attracted four additional endowments between 1817 and 1842, yielding dividends of over £1585 of investment.[74] At the other end of the spectrum, in the first half of the eighteenth century, the Cordwainer's Company in Chester gave 1s. 6d. to almspeople on every 11 November.[75] Complicated payment regimes could result where almspeople of the same charity were eligible for minor variations in allowances.[76] Yet supplementary charity could also be withdrawn. In Burton on Trent during the 1770s there was clearly a desire to spread charity funds as widely as possible, so 10s. of Mrs Almond's charity that had been given to the women in Paulett's almshouse was withdrawn.[77]

In this way, the material value of an almshouse place could fluctuate very widely around an ideal template. Failures by almshouse charities to support the poor, or even treat them in line with the wishes of the founder, should not come as any surprise. 'While the system of charity and lower-class survival were deeply implicated, there was no direct or coterminous match; both had additional and different imperatives.'[78] Therefore, the comfortable and positive image of material aspects of almshouse life needs to be revised.

11.2   Autonomy and privacy

The practical aspects of life in an almshouse need to be contrasted with the potential emotional impact of admission. What was the value of a place over and above its cash equivalent? This can be assessed by examining the technical versus the practical imposition of controls, or the freedoms granted to or wrested by the inmates, the potential for privacy, and the enthusiasm evinced by almspeople for their lot.

Arguably, the autonomy of residents was always regarded as one of the inherent problems of this type of charity. What might the poor get up to, once provided with a permanent appointment to an almshouse? Founders might try to govern their almspeople by imposing behavioural clauses, specifying categories of activity that were essential or that would not be tolerated. Requirements often related to religious observance, such as the stipulation that almspeople at Dyvynog should attend Church on Sundays and be present during all prayers and sermons from the beginning to the end.[79] Inhabitants were commonly enjoined to live peaceably together. Where almshouses were built alongside schools, the almspeople might be charged with a teaching role; in one unusual case the rules included an injunction to empty and repair the privy.[80] Proscribed activities typically included swearing, gambling, overspending, petty crime, inebriation, and promiscuity. For instance, the Countess of Pembroke tried to ensure that her almswomen at Appleby were not spendthrift, by requiring 'That none of the sisters do runne on the Score in the Towne'.[81] The problem remained that policing almspeople's behaviour was fraught with difficulty. Stipends could be reduced or withheld, or fines levied, but this might only exacerbate the problem.[82] Expulsion from the almshouse, the ultimate sanction, was rarely exercised, or only after a second, third or fourth offence (and expulsion orders could even be rescinded).[83] Sexual misdemeanours such as adultery, incest or giving houseroom to women of ill fame were some of the most certain ways to court expulsion.[84]

So in practice, the control of almshouse inhabitants was typically fairly light; the provisions of the charity might include the employment of a resident master, nurse or chaplain to minister to the poor, but rarely gave anyone a disciplinary role. Similarly there might be a notional curfew, but this was only enforceable where the almshouse was built round a courtyard with a locking gate.[85] Specific indulgences could be extended to almspeople; men might be allowed to continue their trade, such as at the Trinity Hospital in Salisbury.[86] In Bristol, seamen in the Merchant's Hospital were even allowed to conduct trips abroad.[87] The only institution found to diverge dramatically from this pattern was Charterhouse in London, where the behaviour of pensioners and staff alike were subject to considerable scrutiny (and a higher than usual rate of expulsion).[88]

Indeed almshouses offered a measure of domestic privacy to a group of the poor unaccustomed to experiencing it, and combined with the usually permanent nature of the appointment residence might well constitute 'comfort and security well beyond previous or peer expectation'.[89] An almshouse place intended for single occupancy constituted an enclosed space for one person. If that person did not choose to share it, they could achieve domestic separation from all other people, including surviving children and parents. Where houses were intended for married couples or for unrelated pairs of spinsters, widows or elderly men, a two-roomed dwelling would still have offered the possibility of a room and a bed each. This amount of space dedicated to one person would have stood in sharp contrast to most poor people's domestic experiences, which constituted a series of shared spaces. In labourers' cottages, tenements, garrets and cellars, the poor shared rooms with family members. In Ardleigh in 1796, for example, no paupers lived alone.[90] Within those rooms it was quite common for different generations and different sexes to hold multiple occupancy of the family's beds.[91] The 'moral resources' offered by accommodation that contained sufficient bedrooms to separate the generations were felt acutely by philanthropists and observers towards the end of the eighteenth century, although it does not follow that the poor adopted the same sentiments.[92]

Among the prosperous there was a continuous thread of commentary that praised the efforts of the poor to remain privately independent in their own home, and cited this as one of the comforts of poverty. Families were properly accommodated within separate houses because married couples had a moral right to expect them, and a failure to achieve this constituted an aberration.[93] In 1800, Thomas Bernard (admittedly an energetic and sympathetic philanthropist) protested, 'The poor man, poor as he is, loves to cherish the idea of PROPERTY. To talk of *my* house, *my* garden, *my* furniture, is always a theme of delight and pleasure.'[94]

But socially superior observers maintained a contradictory set of discourses about the poor, and idealised images of domestic enclosure stood in dramatic contrast to, for example, perceptions of the mid-nineteenth-century urban poor. When *they* resorted to the indoors, for sleeping if nothing else, their choices exposed them to deep censure. The overflowing cellars, attics or back-to-backs of some cities, the lodging houses or overcrowded apartments in insanitary courts, were physical indictments of the domestic failings of the poor.[95] The 'public' lives of the poor, epitomised in the eighteenth century by the riotous mob and in the nineteenth century by Mayhew's people of the London streets, were seen as similarly blameworthy. Ironically the latter were badged as 'neither knowing nor caring for the enjoyments of home', even where they did maintain fierce family ties.[96] This is what Patricia Meyer Spacks meant when, considering the relation of public and private to 'privacy', she judged 'If significant public functioning, except as a problem for others, seldom belongs to the bottom classes, their lives, though "private", rarely enable physical privacy'.[97]

How should we determine the value that the poor placed on the physical independence and privacy (ultimately as individual isolation) supplied in almshouses? This must partly be read from the antipathy of the poor towards participating in communal or supervised living. This took place within any residence where there was an element of choice or self-selection for inmates, albeit notional in some cases: a workhouse, a shared lodging house, an infirmary, or a model-housing scheme would all qualify here, whereas a gaol would not (except where families chose to dwell there with prisoners). Evidence before the nineteenth century is piecemeal; in East Claydon in Buckinghamshire, four families sharing a house in 1677 operated open fires and shunned the one chimney in the building 'because every one will be private'.[98] In the nineteenth century, it is axiomatic that some aspects of *family* privacy as independence were prized very highly. Resistance to workhouses had a long history but was at its height in the middle third of the nineteenth century. When the post-1834 workhouse threatened to make all poor relief contingent on institutional dwelling, there was an outcry that extended beyond the poor. But workhouse life did not act in opposition to privacy, so much as domestic autonomy. The family was designedly broken up on admission to a workhouse, in contrast to family togetherness but lack of privacy in the independent household.

Resistance is particularly revealing in the context of model housing advocated by philanthropists and urban improvers in the late nineteenth century, which was in many ways the updated version of the almshouse.[99] Model housing of course was not free, but subject to both a rent charge and tougher moral policing, both of which were likely to render them less palatable than almshouses. Arguably, the final two-thirds of the nineteenth century was the period when the poor were most likely to refuse improvement or reform and prefer squalor to surveillance by economic superiors (and by implication, were more amenable to these forces before 1834).[100]

So, family privacy was probably highly prized. Individual privacy, though, is a more complex issue. It is clear that almspeople permitted friends and family to share their room and their bed, with or without the sanction of the charity. This might constitute assistance offered to someone else who lacked accommodation, such as where Frances Jeggot allowed Mary Smith 'to lie along with me' because Smith's husband had threatened to kill her. Alternatively, it arose from domestic help being offered to feeble almspeople; Rachel Woodthorpe shared the almshouse and bed of her uncle Joshua Crickett, who was bedridden and could not cut up his food.[101] Vertical kin were probably the most common additional lodgers in almshouse accommodation.[102] These shreds of evidence are slight but they open the prospect of poor people who, in the eighteenth century at least, sought out the physical intimacy of shared accommodation in preference to the isolation of lone occupancy. Caffrey's work on Yorkshire, though, turns up sufficient proof that close communal living also aroused tensions and conflicts between inmates (which was always inherently likely but difficult to prove). Furthermore, she contends that the use of communal areas in almshouses declined, implying that individual privacy became more highly prized by the end of the period.[103]

So to what extent was an almshouse place desirable? The munificence of the charity has usually been used as a proxy for its attractions, and this is somewhat justified; 'almshouses which were poorly maintained ... offering inadequate or no pension, were struggling to fill vacancies'.[104] Beyond material receipts, though, there lay the benefits of association with a particular charity. 'If charity is regarded as a form of circulation rather than a material thing, it tied all these groups into various relationships of application ... and it created uneven relationships of acquiescence and power.'[105] In the context of almshouses, this meant the connections between the almspeople, the founder or founding body, the trustees, and with the local community. In the case of Cathedral bedesmen this involved a tenuous connection with royalty, since bedesmen's applications had to be given royal assent.[106] Charity managers or electors could encompass powerful contemporaries including landowners, clergy, town aldermen and professionals.

It is unlikely that anyone was forced to enter an almshouse or compelled to remain there. Therefore, the fact that the poor petitioned hard to gain entry to some establishments, and that almshouse places were filled, was itself a testament to the fact that the charity was desirable at some level. The almswomen living at Jackenetts almshouse in Cambridge were chosen by rate-payers, and in the early nineteenth century the elections gave rise to some closely-fought battles; however, this might speak more reliably to the energies and interests of ratepayers than to the enthusiasm of the women.[107] More telling perhaps was the presence in a number of almshouses of waiting lists for admission. Since the number of places was fixed, would-be entrants were forced to await the death of an almsperson to secure admission, and that could entail a lengthy wait. At Christ Church in Oxford, waiting times of three years were quite usual, and some frail applicants died before they reached the top of the list.[108] Similarly, wilful resignations from charities owing to unexpected good fortune were rare, although in the late nineteenth century some charity benefits had become so overtaken by inflation that beneficiaries found it expedient to exchange their almshouse charity for a more munificent one.[109]

The high-profile presence of almspeople within a parish or town could act as confirmation of belonging (especially where admission related to local residence), and special treatment could confirm status, as well as give rise to perquisites. Men elected to St Bartholomew's almshouse in Oxford were poorly remunerated for their trouble (since none lived in the almshouse, and the stipend of 9*d.* per week was chronically low) but it is possible that admission was as much a matter of prestige as of material advancement. Public elections to the charity ensured that almsmen remained a distinct group among the otherwise undifferentiated urban poor (particularly for their electors, the town council) and the men received attention and attractive extras; for example payments to them were listed among the canvassing expenses of parliamentary candidates for Oxfordshire during the elections of 1780 and 1784.[110] These cannot have mitigated the small pension, but were possibly welcome acknowledgments of official standing. Cathedral bedesmen took part in ceremonial events and processions and yielded benefits of association, since they participated alongside senior clergymen and occasionally aristocratic families, and enjoyed an allocated seat in the Cathedral. Some events were routine, such as the arrival of assize court judges, but other one-off celebrations included royal visits, or the 1707 union with Scotland.[111] Ford's and Bond's Hospitals in Coventry were patently integral to Coventry's sense of identity, and were an acknowledged source of pride. In 1844, the King of Saxony was shown Ford's hospital when on a visit to the city, while from 1784 inhabitants of Bond's hospital were treated to an annual visit by the Corporation and 1856-1863 given ceremonial dinners for national events. The latter allegedly gave delight and gratification to residents.[112]

11.3 Conclusion

'Neat houses and neat old people, sometimes in uniform, came to form an attractive feature in many towns and villages.'[113] The propriety of this image has meant that it has dominated thinking about almshouses to date. The experience of almshouse life, however, was much less consistent. The size, location, layout and fabric of houses all contributed to the nature of the space they provided. These factors determined by founders and trustees were varied further by policies concerning admissions and behaviours. The resulting material circumstances of almshouses can be partially reconstructed to indicate the comfortable or pinched experiences of residents, and these have supplied the majority of the details in this chapter. Almshouse life *could* comprise genuinely secure retirement, with accommodation, income and extraordinary expenses all provided, within a private but not isolated setting, but this was not the standard provision. Material life was usually much less cushioned than this, with either the house or its pension being inadequate, compelling residents to maintain their acquaintance with work, begging, relief or other forms of income. When people's circumstances became acute, either through an unstable building, a starvation-level pension or through their own decay, no amount of respectable imagery could redeem almshouses for the unmitigated misery or physical exposure imposed on inhabitants.

The essential character of almshouse life though, that varied from institution to institution, lay in the traditions and relationships established among inmates, or between inmates and outsiders. Was it common for residents' status to be gauged internally not by age but by length of institutional residence, or for there to be bitter dissention about the use of outside spaces?[114] What were the constraints on sharing almsrooms with relations, a practice rarely governed by statute but nonetheless critical to the retention of almsplaces by an aging population? The evidence for tackling these sorts of questions is extremely dispersed, both geographically and chronologically, but suggests subtle differences between institutions that were notionally akin. This makes long-term shifts difficult to determine, beyond Caffrey's argument that use of communal facilities declined over time.

One plausible conclusion is that election to an almshouse could confer a measure of status substantially out of proportion to its material benefits. Indications of esteem are most clear where almspeople became embedded in community activity such as the election to charity itself, ecclesiastical celebrations or parliamentary elections. Such occasions might carry material perquisites but these were probably secondary in importance to the marks of inclusion and respect that they carried. Arguably the emotional weight accorded to intangible benefits has substantially contributed to the intellectual coherence of the neat, respectable almshouse image that has been dominant for so long.

Notes

1. W. H. Godfrey, *The English Alms-House* (Faber and Faber, 1955); P. Judson, 'A Legacy of Almshouse Building', in L. Crust, *Lincolnshire Almshouses. Nine centuries of Charitable Housing* (Sleaford: Heritage Lincolnshire, 2002), pp. 70–1.
2. *The Guardian*, 27 January 2007, 'Family', p. 4.
3. For a recent exception see H. Caffrey, *Almshouses in the West Riding of Yorkshire* (Kings Lynn: Heritage, 2006).
4. E. M. Hampson, *The Treatment of Poverty in Cambridgeshire 1597–1834* (Cambridge: Cambridge University Press, 1934), p. 69; P. Morant, *The History*

and Antiquities of ... Colchester (W. Bowyer, 1748), p. 9; Crust, *Lincolnshire Almshouses*, p. 5; *An Account of the Hospitals, Alms-Houses and Public Schools in Bristol* (Bristol, 1775), p. 14.

5. W. K. Jordan, *Philanthropy in England 1480–1660* (New York: Russell Sage Foundation, 1959), p. 260.
6. E. Prescott, *The English Medieval Hospital 1050–1640* (Seaby, 1992); Caffrey, *Almshouses in the West Riding*, p. 27.
7. W. R. Powell (ed.), *VCH: Essex* (Oxford: Oxford University Press, 1956), IV, pp. 274–5.
8. M. Barker-Read, 'The Treatment of the Aged Poor in Five Selected West Kent Parishes from Settlement to Speenhamland 1662–1775' (Unpublished Open University PhD Thesis, 1988), p. 87; E. A. Heelis, 'St Anne's Hospital at Appleby', *Transactions of the Cumberland and Westmorland Antiquarian and Archaeological Society* IX, new series, (1909), p. 193; Crust, *Lincolnshire Almshouses*, p. 25.
9. M. Dunsford, *Historical Memoirs of the Town and Parish of Tiverton* (Exeter, 1790), p. 335; Barker-Read, 'The Treatment of the Aged Poor', p. 265; R. Loder, *The Statutes and Ordinances for the Government of the Alms-Houses in Woodbridge* (Woodbridge, 1792), Rules of 1587 (unpaginated).
10. Caffrey, *Almshouses in the West Riding*, p. 31.
11. P. M. Tillott (ed.), *The Victoria History of Yorkshire: The City of York* (Oxford: Oxford University Press, 1961), pp. 421–6.
12. Loder, *Statutes and Ordinances* (unpaginated).
13. I am indebted to Eileen McGrath for the information in this paragraph and the next; see E. McGrath, 'The Bedesmen of Worcester Cathedral: Post-Reformation Cathedral Charity compared with St Oswald's Hospital Almspeople, c. 1660–1900' (Unpublished Keele University PhD, forthcoming). A later diary survives of an inmate of St Cross between 1873–96, cited in P. Hopewell, *St Cross: England's Oldest Almshouse* (Chichester: Phillimore, 1995), pp. 128–32.
14. This shopping list is reminiscent of the goods that incomers to Bond's hospital in Coventry were required to supply upon admission; [J. Cleary & M. Orton], *So Long as the World Shall Endure. The Five Hundred Year History of Ford's and Bond's Hospitals* (Coventry: Coventry Church Charities, 1991), pp. 48, 125.
15. W. M. Thackeray, *The Newcomes. Memoirs of a Most Respectable Family* (Bradbury & Evans, 1855), Chapter 75; C. Dickens, *The Uncommercial Traveller* (Chapman & Hall, 1866), Chapter 29; P. Ackroyd, *Dickens* (Minerva, 1991), p. 56.
16. *Abstract of the Answers and Returns made pursuant to 'An act for taking an account of the population of Great Britain 1801'* (1802), Enumeration Part 1: England and Wales, p. 326.
17. Some remained unbuilt; N. Yates & P. A. Welsby (eds) *Faith and Fabric: A History of Rochester Cathedral, 604–1994* (Woodbridge: Boydell, 1996), p. 107.
18. Crust, *Lincolnshire Almshouses*, p. 10.
19. Flintshire Record Office, G/B/57(c)/6, Holywell Union correspondence regarding the sale of the Flint almshouses, 1874–6.
20. B. E. Harris (ed.), *VCH: Chester* (Oxford: Oxford University Press, 1980), III, p. 182; *Remarkable Antiquities of the City of Exeter* (1723), p. 210.

21. J. Roach, *The Shrewsbury Hospital, Sheffield 1616–1975* (Borthwick Paper 104, 2003), p. 6.
22. Barker-Read, 'The Treatment of the Aged Poor', pp. 83–4.
23. Crust, *Lincolnshire Almshouses*, p. 25.
24. C. M. Carlton, *History of the Charities in the City of Durham* (Durham: George Walker, 1872), p. 33.
25. W. Page (ed.), *VCH: Northamptonshire* (1930), III, p. 59.
26. Barker-Read, 'The Treatment of the Aged Poor', p. 297.
27. *Gentleman's Magazine* 51, (1781), pp. 454–5.
28. *Manchester Observer*, 5 September 1818, quoted in G. B. Hindle, *Provision for the Relief of the Poor in Manchester, 1754–1826* (Manchester: Manchester University Press, 1975), p. 144.
29. *Caring: A Short History of Salisbury City Almshouse and Other Charities from the Fourteenth to the Twentieth Centuries* (Salisbury, 1987), p. 13.
30. J. Manco, *The Spirit of Care. The Eight-Hundred Year Story of St John's Hospital, Bath* (Bath: St John's Hospital, 1998), p. 125.
31. McGrath, 'The Bedesmen of Worcester Cathedral'.
32. Hampson, *The Treatment of Poverty*, pp. 69, 77.
33. Barker-Read, 'The Treatment of the Aged Poor', p. 289.
34. Crust, *Lincolnshire Almshouses*, p. 18.
35. Caffrey, *Almshouses in the West Riding*, p. 27.
36. I. Atherton, E. McGrath & A. Tomkins, "Pressed down by want and afflicted with poverty, wounded and mained in war or work down with age?' Cathedral Almsmen in England 1538–1914', in A. Borsay & P. Shapely (eds), *Medicine, Charity and Mutual Aid. The Consumption of Health and Welfare in Britain, c. 1550–1950* (Aldershot: Ashgate, 2007), p. 30.
37. *Orders Relating to the Almshouse &c of Dyvynog* (J. Stephens, 1731), p. 4; M. W. Greenslade (ed.), *VCH: Staffordshire* (Oxford: Oxford University Press, 1970), III, p. 281; Lich.RO, Salop Peculiar Probate Records, Will of Mary Blakemore, (1818).
38. *OBP* (21 July 2005), October 1753, Isabella Lynch (t17531024–26).
39. *OBP* (13 February 2007), December 1785, John Bateman (t17851214–9).
40. *OBP* (13 February 2007), November 1809, Esther Simpson (t18091101–33).
41. *OBP* (13 February 2007), June 1769, John Chaney (t17690628–43) and February 1747, Vincent Symonds (t17470225–3); L. MacKay, 'Why they Stole: Women in the Old Bailey, 1779–1789', *Journal of Social History* 32:3, (1999), 628.
42. Morant, *History and Antiquities of Colchester*, p. 7.
43. J. Stevens Cox, *The Almshouse and St Margaret's Leper Hospital Ilchester* (Ilchester Historical Monographs 5, 1949), p. 110.
44. Wiltshire and Swindon Record Office, 251/47, Heytesbury Hospital inventories of the almshouse 1656 and 1798.
45. Judson, 'A Legacy of Almshouse Building', p. 68.
46. Heelis, 'St Anne's Hospital at Appleby', p. 197; Crust, *Lincolnshire Almshouses*, p. 26; H. Caffrey, 'The Almshouse Experience in the Nineteenth-Century West Riding', *Yorkshire Archaeological Journal* 76, (2004), 242.
47. Stevens Cox, *The Almshouse and St Margaret's Leper* Hospital, p. 123.
48. For a solitary example see E. Hird, *The Lady Margaret Hungerford Almshouse and Free School, Corsham, Wiltshire 1668–1968* (Corsham: E. Hird, 1997), p. 80.

49. J. Broad, 'Housing the Rural Poor in Southern England, 1650–1850', *Agricultural History Review* 48:2, (2000), 155.
50. *VCH: Staffs*, III, pp. 276–7.
51. Stevens Cox, *The Almshouse and St Margaret's Leper* Hospital, p. 110; Dunsford, *Historical Memoirs*, p. 336.
52. *VCH: Staffs*, III, p. 284.
53. Loder, *Statutes and Ordinances* (unpaginated).
54. Crust, *Lincolnshire Almshouses*, p. 17.
55. Roach, *The Shrewsbury Hospital*, p. 7.
56. Morant, *History and Antiquities of Colchester*, p. 8.
57. Caffrey, 'Almshouse Experience', p. 241; Crust, *Lincolnshire Almshouses*, pp. 34, 37, 48; J. A. A. Goodall, *God's House at Ewelme. Life, Devotion and Architecture in a Fifteenth-Century Almshouse* (Aldershot: Ashgate, 2001), p. 112; Atherton, McGrath & Tomkins, "Pressed down by want", pp. 26–7.
58. A. Tomkins, *The Experience of Urban Poverty, 1723–82: Parish, Charity and Credit* (Manchester: Manchester University Press, 2006, p. 96; Crust, *Lincolnshire Almshouses*, p. 28; Caffrey, 'Almshouse Experience', p. 235–6; *Account ... Bristol*, throughout.
59. H. Peet (ed.), *Liverpool Vestry Books 1681–1834* (Liverpool: Liverpool University Press, 1912), I, p. 173.
60. P. Cunnington & C. Lucus, *Charity Costumes of Children, Scholars, Almsfolk, Pensioners* (Adam & Charles Black, 1978), p. 227 *passim*; Hird, *The Lady Margaret Hungerford Almshouse*, p. 48; Crust, *Lincolnshire Almshouses*, p. 27.
61. M. W. Greenslade (ed.), *VCH: Staffordshire* (Oxford: Oxford University Press, 1996), VII, p. 166.
62. Caffrey, 'Almshouse Experience', p. 242.
63. Tomkins, *The Experience of Urban Poverty*, pp. 224–5.
64. P. Slack, *From Reformation to Improvement: Public Welfare in Early Modern England* (Oxford: Clarendon Press, 1999), p. 25.
65. Caffrey, 'Almshouse Experience', p. 242.
66. [Cleary & Orton], *So Long as the World Shall Endure*, p. 127.
67. Stevens Cox, *The Almshouse and St Margaret Leper Hospital*, p. 121.
68. *Account ... Bristol*, p. 40; Loder, *Statutes and Ordinances*, rule 30 (unpaginated).
69. Manco, *The Spirit of Care*, pp. 110, 114.
70. Caffrey, 'Almshouse Experience', pp. 236, 240–1.
71. R. M. Smith, 'Relief of Urban Poverty outside the Poor Law, 1800–1850: A Study of Nottingham', *Midland History* 2:4, (1974), 215–49, p. 220.
72. [Cleary & Orton], *So Long as the World Shall Endure*, p. 129.
73. Jordan, *Philanthropy in England*, pp. 154, 216, 261.
74. M. C. Martin, 'Women and Philanthropy in Walthamstow and Leyton 1740–1870', *London Journal* 19:2, (1995), 136.
75. Chester City Archives, G8/6 Accounts of the Cordwainers' Company; for example see 11 November 1721, 11 November 1754.
76. *Account ... Bristol*, p. 15.
77. Lich.RO, BD13/16, BD13/17.
78. S. Lloyd "Agents in their own concerns'? Charity and the Economy of Makeshifts in Eighteenth-Century Britain', in S. King & A. Tomkins (eds), *The Poor in England 1700–1850. An Economy of Makeshifts* (Manchester: Manchester University Press, 2003), p. 118.

79. *Relating ... Dyvynog*, p. 4.
80. Caffrey, 'Almshouse Experience', p. 224; Hird, *The Lady Margaret Hungerford Almshouse*, p. 47; Crust, *Lincolnshire Almshouses*, p. 25.
81. Heelis, 'St Anne's Hospital at Appleby', p. 197.
82. Hird, *The Lady Margaret Hungerford Almshouse*, p. 49.
83. J. Stevens Cox, *The Almshouse and St Margaret's Leper Hospital*, pp. 106, 123; Heelis, 'St Anne's Hospital at Appleby', p. 197; Loder, *Statutes and Ordinances* (unpaginated, footnote under rule 6); Caffrey, *Almshouses in the West Riding*, pp. 59–62; [Cleary & Orton], *So Long as the World Shall Endure*, pp. 49–50.
84. Hird, *The Lady Margaret Hungerford Almshouse*, p. 81; Crust, *Lincolnshire Almshouses*, p. 26; Loder, *Statutes and Ordinances*, Rule 22 (unpaginated).
85. Caffrey, 'Almshouse Experience', p. 242.
86. *Caring: A Short History of Salisbury City Almshouse*, p. 8.
87. *Account ... Bristol*, p. 16.
88. S. Porter, 'Order and Disorder in the Early Modern Almshouse: The Charterhouse Example', *London Journal* 23:1, (1998).
89. Caffrey, 'Almshouse Experience', p. 224.
90. T. Sokoll, 'The Pauper Household Small and Simple', *Ethnologia Europaea* 17:1, (1987).
91. M. McKeon, *The Secret History of Domesticity* (Baltimore: Johns Hopkins, 2005), p. 260; Tomkins, *The Experience of Urban Poverty*, p. 67.
92. S. Lloyd, 'Cottage Conversations: Poverty and Manly Independence in Eighteenth-Century England', *Past and Present* 184, (2004), 69, 71.
93. Broad, 'Housing the Rural Poor', p. 158; K. Chase & M. Levenson, *The Spectacle of Intimacy: A Public Life for the Victorian Family* (Princeton: Princeton University Press, 2000), p. 147.
94. *Information for Cottagers Collected from the Reports of the Society for Bettering the Condition and Increasing the Comforts of the Poor* (W. Bulmer & Co., 1800), p. 10.
95. Chase & Levenson, *The Spectacle of Intimacy*, pp. 143, 147.
96. Mayhew on costermongers, quoted in *Ibid.*, pp. 146–7.
97. P. M. Spacks, *Privacy. Concealing the Eighteenth-Century Self* (Chicago: Chicago University Press, 2003), p. 1.
98. Broad, 'Housing the Rural Poor', p. 158.
99. S. Morris, 'Market Solutions for Social Problems: Working-Class Housing in Nineteenth-Century London', *Economic History Review* 54:3, (2001).
100. Chase & Levenson, *The Spectacle of Intimacy*, p. 149.
101. *OBP*, 3 June 1767, trial of Mary Smith (t17670603–22); 20 February 1811, trial of Rachel Woodthorpe (t18110220–28).
102. See for example Peet (ed.), *Liverpool Vestry Books*, p. 394.
103. Caffrey, *Almshouses in the West Riding*, pp. 27, 38, 61.
104. Caffrey, 'Almshouse Experience', p. 236; Caffrey, *Almshouses in the West Riding*, p. 27.
105. Lloyd, 'Agents in their own concerns', p. 117.
106. Atherton, McGrath & Tomkins, '"Pressed down by want"', p. 22.
107. J. P. C. Roach (ed.), *VCH: Cambridge and Ely* (Oxford: Oxford University Press, 1959), III, p. 147.
108. J. Curthoys, '"To Perfect the College...' – the Christ Church Almsmen 1546–1888', *Oxoniensia* 60, (1995), 381; Tomkins, *The Experience of Urban Poverty*, pp. 94–5.

109. McGrath, 'The Bedesmen of Worchester Cathedral'.
110. Bodleian Library Ms Top Oxon c. 280, fol.60, 116.
111. McGrath, 'The Bedesmen of Worchester Cathedral'.
112. [Cleary & Orton], *So Long as the World Shall Endure*, pp. 56, 130–1.
113. Crust, *Lincolnshire Almshouses*, p. 27; Caffrey, *Almshouses in the West Riding*, p. 28.
114. Dickens, *Uncommercial Traveller*, Chapter 29.

Select Bibliography

Baer, W. C., 'Housing the Poor and Mechanick Class in Seventeenth-Century London', *London Journal* 25:2, (2000), 13–39.

Bonfield, L., Smith, R. M. and Wrightson, K. (eds), *The World We Have Gained: Histories of Population and Social Structure. Essays Presented to Peter Laslett on his Seventieth Birthday* (Oxford: Blackwell, 1986).

Botelho, L. A., *Old Age and the English Poor Law, 1500–1700* (Woodbridge: Boydell, 2004).

Boulton, J., '"It is extreme necessity that makes me do this": Some "survival strategies" of Pauper Households in London's West End during the Early Eighteenth Century', *International Review of Social History, Supplement* 8, (2000), 47–70.

Boulton, J., *Neighbourhood and Society: A London Suburb in the Seventeenth Century* (Cambridge: Cambridge University Press, 1987).

Broad, J., 'Housing the Rural Poor in Southern England, 1650–1850', *Agricultural History Review* 48:2, (2000), 151–70.

Burnett, J., *A Social History of Housing 1815–1985* (first published David and Charles, Newton Abbott, 1978; Routledge, 1991).

Cavallo, S. & Warner, L. (eds), *Widowhood in Medieval and Early Modern Europe* (Longman, 1999).

Chapman, S. D. (ed.), *A History of Working Class Housing: A Symposium* (Newton Abbott: David & Charles, 1971).

Clark, A., *The Struggle for the Breeches: Gender and the Making of the British Working Class* (Rivers Oram Press, 1995).

Clark, P. & Slack, P. (eds), *Crisis and Order in English Towns, 1500–1700* (Routledge, 1972).

Clark, P. & Souden, D. (eds), *Migration and Society in Early Modern England* (Hutchinson, 1987).

Daunton, M., (ed.), *Charity, Self-interest and Welfare in the English Past* (UCL Press, 1996).

Earle, P. *A City Full of People: Men and Women of London 1650–1750* (Methuen, 1994).

Evans, T., *'Unfortunate Objects': Lone Mothers in Eighteenth-Century London* (Basingstoke: Palgrave Macmillan, 2005).

Fumerton, P., *Unsettled: The Culture of Mobility and the Working Poor in Early Modern England* (Chicago: University of Chicago Press, 2006).

George, M. D., *London Life in the Eighteenth Century* (Kegan Paul, 1925).

Green, A., 'Houses and Landscape in Early Industrial County Durham', in T. Faulkner, H. Berry & J. Gregory (eds), *Northern Landscapes: Representations and Realities* (Woodbridge: Boydell, 2008).

Griffiths, P., *Youth and Authority: Formative Experiences in England, 1560–1640* (Oxford: Clarendon, 1996).

Guillery, P., *The Small House in Eighteenth-Century London* (New Haven: Yale University Press in association with English Heritage, 2004).

Henderson, J. & Wall, R. (eds), *Poor Women and Children in the European Past* (Routledge, 1994).

Hindle, S., *On the Parish? The Micro-Politics of Poor Relief in Rural England, c. 1550–1750* (Oxford: Clarendon Press, 2004).

Hitchcock, T., *Down and Out in Eighteenth-Century London* (Hambledon, 2004).

Hitchcock, T., King, P, and Sharpe, P. (eds), *Chronicling Poverty: The Voices and Strategies of the English Poor, 1640–1840* (Basingstoke: Macmillan, 1997).

Hollen Lees, L., *The Solidarities of Strangers: The English Poor Laws and the People 1700–1948* (Cambridge: Cambridge University Press, 1998).

Horden, P. & Smith, R. (eds), *The Locus of Care: Families, Communities, Institutions and the Provision of Welfare Since Antiquity* (Routledge, 1998).

Karskens, G., *Inside the Rocks: The Archaeology of a Neighbourhood* (Alexandria: Hale & Iremonger, 1999).

King, S., Nutt, T. & Tomkins, A., *Narratives of the Poor in Eighteenth-Century Britain* (Pickering and Chatto, 2006).

King, S., '"It is impossible for our vestry to judge his case into perfection from here": Managing the Distance Dimensions of Poor Relief, 1800–40', *Rural History* 16, (2005), 161–89.

King, S. & Tomkins, A. (eds), *The Poor in England 1700–1850: An Economy of Makeshifts* (Manchester: Manchester University Press, 2003).

King, S., *Poverty and Welfare in England, 1700–1850* (Manchester: Manchester University Press, 2000).

Kussmaul, A., *Servants in Husbandry in Early Modern England* (Cambridge: Cambridge University Press, 1981).

Landers, J., *Death and the Metropolis: Studies in the Demographic History of London, 1670–1830* (Cambridge: Cambridge University Press, 1993).

Lloyd, S., 'Cottage Conversations: Poverty and Manly Independence in Eighteenth-Century England', *Past & Present* 184, (2004), 69–108.

Muldrew, C., *The Economy of Obligation: The Culture of Credit and Social Relations in Early Modern England* (Basingstoke: Macmillan, 1998).

Ottaway, S. R., *The Decline of Life: Old Age in Eighteenth-Century England* (Cambridge: Cambridge University Press, 2004).

Pelling, M. & Smith, R. (eds), *Life, Death and the Elderly: Historical Perspectives* (Routledge, 1991).

Schwarz, L. D., *London in the Age of Industrialisation: Entrepreneurs, Labour Force and Living Conditions, 1700–1850* (Cambridge: Cambridge University Press, 1992).

Sharpe, P., *Population and Society in an East Devon Parish: Reproducing Colyton, 1540–1840* (Exeter: University of Exeter Press, 2002).

Sharpe, P., 'Survival Strategies and Stories: Poor Widows and Widowers in Early Industrial England', in S. Cavallo & L. Warner, *Widowhood in Medieval and Early Modern Europe* (Harlow: Longman, 1999).

Slack, P., *From Reformation to Improvement: Public Welfare in Early Modern England* (Oxford: Clarendon Press, 1999).

Slack, P., *The English Poor Law, 1531–1782* (Basingstoke: Macmillan, 1990).

Smith, R. M. (ed.), *Land, Kinship and Life-Cycle* (Cambridge: Cambridge University Press, 1984).

Snell, K. D. M., *Parish and Belonging: Community, Identity and Welfare in England and Wales 1700–1950* (Cambridge: Cambridge University Press, 2006).

Snell, K. D. M., *Annals of the Labouring Poor: Social Change and Agrarian England, 1660–1900* (Cambridge: Cambridge University Press, 1985).

Sokoll, T. (ed.), *Essex Pauper Letters, 1731–1837* (Oxford: Oxford University Press, 2001).

Sokoll, T., *Household and Family among the Poor: The Case of Two Essex Communities in the Late Eighteenth and Early Nineteenth Centuries* (Bochum: Universitätsverlag Dr N Brockmeyer, 1993).

Spence, C., *London in the 1690s. A Social Atlas* (Centre for Metropolitan History, Institute of Historical Research, University of London, 2000).

Tadmor, N., *Family and Friends in Eighteenth-Century England: Household, Kinship and Patronage* (Cambridge: Cambridge University Press, 2001).

Thane, P., *Old Age in English History: Past Experiences; Present Issues* (Oxford: Oxford University Press, 2000).

Thirsk, J. (ed.), *The Agrarian History of England and Wales* (Cambridge: Cambridge University Press, 1967–2000), Volumes IV & V.

Tomkins, A., *The Experience of Urban Poverty 1723–82: Parish, Charity and Credit* (Manchester: Manchester University Press, 2006).

Tomkins, A., 'Almshouse versus Workhouse: Residential Welfare in 18th-century Oxford', *Family & Community History* 7:1, (2004), 45–58.

Wall, R., 'Leaving Home and the Process of Household Formation in Pre-Industrial England', *Continuity and Change* 2, (1987), 77–101.

Weatherill, L., *Consumer Behaviour and Material Culture in Britain, 1660–1760* (Routledge, 1988).

Williams, S. K., '"That the Petitioner Shall have Borne a Good Character for Virtue, Sobriety, and Honesty Previous to her Misfortune": Unmarried Mothers' Petitions to the Foundling Hospital and the Rhetoric of Need in the Long Eighteenth Century', in A. Levene, T. Nutt, & S. K. Williams (eds), *Illegitimacy in Britain 1700–1920* (Basingstoke: Palgrave Macmillan, 2005).

Wrightson, K., *Earthly Necessities: Economic Lives in Early Modern Britain* (New Haven: Yale University Press, 2000).

Wrigley, E. A. & Schofield, R. S., *The Population History of England, 1541–1871: A Reconstruction* (Edward Arnold, 1981).

Index

abandonment/desertion
  by husband   37, 152, 155, 156, 176
  by lover   7, 37, 195, 198, 202–3, 205–6
accommodation, purpose-built by employers   74–5
accoutrements/material goods of the poor   85–90, 113, 115. *See also pauper inventories*
  bedsheets   59, 80, 85, 86, 89, 258
  cooking implements   86, 87, 89
  hearth tools   82, 86
  laundry tubs   86, 90
  looking glass   59, 80, 86, 87, 89
  parish seizure of   81–2, 85–6
  plates and earthenware   86, 88, 89, 91, 115
  portable nature of   61, 116
  spinning wheel   80, 86, 88, 90
  storage in locked boxes and chests   14, 31, 61, 195, 268
  tea kettles   80, 86, 87, 89, 115
aged. See Elderly
agricultural service   170, 177–180
alehouse   7, 53, 127, 128, 129, 130, 131, 170, 172, 181–4, 197, 203
Allen, Joseph   2
almshouse   2, 5, 10, 39–40, 94, 235, 263–78
  clothing provided by   270–1
  construction of   266–8
  experience of   264–5, 277
  furnishings   265, 268
  represented in literature   266
  rules of   269–70, 272
apprenticeship   77, 138, 152–3, 255
  parish   169, 171–82
Ardleigh, Essex   13, 274
Australia   13–14, 107, 109–10, 112

Baer, William   8–9, 25
bastardy examination   131, 197

beggars   48, 126–9, 130–1, 133–5, 137, 139
  official concerns about   47
Bernwood, Buckinghamshire   250
Bevan, Charity   238
Bevan, David   238
Bigg, Maria   202, 205, 207, 208, 209
Black, John   10, 197
Blinkhorn, Feveral   237–8
Board of Agriculture   70, 102, 104
Boswell, James   8, 43
Botelho, Lynn   6, 150, 221
Boulton, Jeremy   1, 7, 10, 15, 50, 55, 204, 207
Bowman, Anne   5–6
Braintree, Essex   13, 106
breastfeeding   211–12, 213
Bridestowe, Devon   255, 260
Brill, Buckinghamshire   248, 250
Broad, John   4–5
Brown, John   138
Burn, Richard   105–6, 140

Canada   108–9
Candler, Ann, poet   106, 113
Carew, Bampfylde-Moore ('King of the Beggars')   133–5, 137
cellars   7, 14, 54, 62, 84, 95, 105, 267, 274
census   151–2, 157, 176
  1801 census   225, 266
  1831 census   254–6
  1841 census   242, 244
  'reconstructed', from workhouse registers   227–9, 235
Certificates and Returns of Divided Houses   8
charity   3, 25, 239
  attempts to evoke   38–9
  rent-free accommodation as   5, 39–40, 253–4, 259
Charity Commission Surveys   254
Charke, Charlotte   138–9

Index 289

family breakdown 15, 37, 275.
See also abandonment/desertion
footman 196
Foundling Hospital 192–3, 199, 208,
215, 217
petitions to 192–3, 201, 211, 215

garrets/attics/lofts 54, 95, 195, 274
George, Dorothy 25, 31–2, 33, 64
Green, Adrian 2, 11, 13, 106
grandchildren, care of 153–6, 205
Great Yarmouth, Norfolk 72, 91–2
gypsy 128–9, 130, 132, 133

Hambleton, Margaret 57–8
Harrower, John 136
Hartlepool, Durham 71–2
hearth 11, 72–3, 89–90, 95–6, 102,
246, 264
Hearth Tax 8, 54, 71–2
exemptions from 54, 71–2
Higginson, Jane 148–52, 156, 158–9,
162–3
Hill, Elizabeth 30
Hindle, Steve 5–6, 7, 16, 126
Hitchcock, Tim 7, 53, 210
Hollen Lees, Lynn 3, 126, 147, 223
home 11, 69–70, 95–6, 103, 112
rhetoric about 69–70, 153
homelessness 15, 35–9, 158–9
threat of 155, 159, 161
house of correction/Bridewell 125–6,
131, 134–5, 138, 171–2, 175–6,
182
household Composition
fluidity of 146–8, 152–8, 163–4
housing conditions,
standard of living 91, 94, 170,
174
overcrowding 7–9, 97, 250, 254–8,
274
housing, of poor 5, 70–1, 91.
See also cottages; lodgings.
collapse/destruction 54, 62
parish provision of 5, 77, 247–8,
253, 255–8, 259, 268
repair/rebuilding of 62, 77, 90,
91–2, 93–4
room use 83–4

sub-division 5, 9, 51, 73, 91, 95
portable 109
huts, wooden 74, 78, 103, 109–12,
115

illegitimacy 196
illegitimate pregnancy 130–1,
191–214
assistance from employer
during 196, 197–8, 199–202,
214
assistance from friends/family
during 193, 202–3, 205, 209–10,
212–14
assistance from lover 210
attitudes towards 199, 204,
211–12, 214
concealment 191, 198–9, 209–10
dismissal of pregnant
servants 191, 198–9, 201,
213–14
residential arrangements
during 192, 193, 198, 200–3,
206–210
illness, support during 154–5, 236
industrialisation, impact of 1, 73–5,
170
industry, habits of 110, 170, 174,
176, 199, 214
infants
death of 211
left in workhouse 210
sent to nurse 7, 191, 194, 198,
210–11, 213, 228

Jackson, Mary Ann 191, 193, 197,
200, 205, 209
Julian, Henry, footman 196, 197

Karskens, Grace 2, 112
Kent, Nathaniel 70, 246, 251
King, Alice 191, 193, 201–2, 211,
213
King, Gregory 70
King, Steve 4, 11, 126
King's Lynn, Norfolk 72
Kirkoswald, Cumbria 5
kitchen 73, 82–6, 90, 195, 264,
269